The Liberated Traveller Guide to Europe

How to See Europe Intelligently, Independently, Inexpensively—the Way Europeans Do

by Phyllis & Alan Kingery

D1445148

CHICAGO REVIEW PRESS • CHICAGO

First edition
First printing

Library of Congress Cataloging in Publication Data

Kingery, Phyllis.
  The liberated traveller.

  Bibliography:p.
  Includes index.
  1. Europe—Description and travel—
1971-   —Guide-books. I. Kingery, Alan.
II. Title.
D909.K56   1982   914'.0455
ISBN 0-914091-09-3

81-21747
AACR2

Published by Chicago Review Press
820 N. Franklin
Chicago, IL 60610

Perhaps it is rare to love your
mother-in-law as much as your own mother,
but we both do,
and we dedicate this book to
Margarette May
and
Helen Mummert
with affection and gratitude.

May you live in the most interesting of times.

—Ancient Chinese curse

. . . and visit the most interesting of places.

Recent Kingery addendum
(intended as a blessing)

Contents

TWENTY-TWO TYPICAL TIPS FROM THE LIBERATED TRAVELLER

HOW TO:
- deal with language and currency problems
- find inexpensive food and drink
- find the least expensive way to cross the Atlantic
- cut sleeping costs in half
- lay out budget projections for your trip
- avoid embarrassment when ordering from foreign menus
- decide whether or not to rent a car in Europe
- think in a seasoned way about the best times of year to travel
- meet and understand Europeans
- travel with little ones
- take advantage of bus, rail, boat, and air travel bargains in Europe
- stay in touch with loved ones at home
- decide about good places to visit (or avoid)
- deal with European attitudes about etiquette, travel, Americans, dining, etc.
- haggle in Europe
- pay your way with credit cards and travellers' checks
- custom-tailor your way through customs inspections
- apply for and get a passport
- discover and enjoy unusual sights and sensations around Europe
- get free travel information
- have fun that is neither fattening, immoral, nor expensive
- stay out of trouble

Preface

Today a common subject of conversation is "the high cost of Europe." Every cocktail party seems to have someone who was just over there who wants to tell horror stories about two-dollar cups of coffee or $100-a-day rooms. While it is true that Europe is no longer nearly as inexpensive for visitors as it was a few short years ago, it is clear to us that most tourists make it artificially expensive. If you insist on staying in the fanciest hotels, visiting only the largest cities, and eating in the poshest restaurants, as so many tourists do, Europe will bankrupt you in a hurry. But is that Europe's fault?

It is still possible today to visit the countries that are considered to be high-priced (e.g., Germany or Switzerland), for a total of about $20 to $25 a day per person for accommodations, meals, and entry fees to museums and other attractions. To do this requires know-how—which we hope to give you here. It asks for a little planning and a bit of forethought. It will ask you to think in terms of lesser-known places, which are generally much nicer than the large cities anyway: the costs are less, the people are friendlier, and you will not be lost so often.

We will tell you in this book how to see the best of Europe at the lowest price, as well as some secrets that the most experienced travellers know which are not often divulged by travel agents, tour group companies, or other travel books.

The first edition of this book came out in 1978. We had gotten the idea for it in 1974 when we heard friends saying how expensive Europe had become. "A month there will bankrupt you now," they said. We didn't believe it. We knew they were staying in expensive hotels and generally living it up over there. Couldn't a person still see Europe at a reasonable cost, we wondered, if he or she travelled there like a smart European would?

We did our initial research on the matter in the middle of the 1975 high season. We spent a month in Europe, did everything we wanted to do, and spent well under

$1,000 apiece, including the transatlantic flights. This convinced us that Europe was still a bargain *if* one went at it sensibly, and we began to write.

Now, many trips later and with the first edition behind us, we see a less-healthy U.S. dollar and higher inflation rates in Europe than we saw in 1975—but we know that it is still possible to see Europe on a budget. You can't do it if you frequent 4- and 5-star hotels, eat $30 meals, and ship home cases of fifteen-year-old French wine—*but you can do it.* To do so requires know-how.

This edition is once again designed to tell you not only how you can visit Europe today without going broke, but also how you can avoid embarrassing yourself everywhere you go. You don't understand their language, their currency, or their customs? That doesn't mean you have to avoid the natives, or hide behind the windows of a rented car or a tour bus. Doing so, in fact, will cost you money and cause you to miss the greatest single aspect of visiting other countries: meeting the people who live there. This book will tell you how to sidestep the problems that may be worrying you, how to have a great time, and how to have a vacation in Europe (including the air fare) for less money than you would spend having a similar outing in your own country.

We have generally avoided recommending specific hotels or restaurants. We have tried instead to tell you how a smart European would find accommodations for himself. We have avoided specific recommendations for a variety of reasons:

1. Such listings of names, addresses, and telephone numbers are boring to read, and those that pertain to cities or countries you don't visit are useless to you.

2. It would not be difficult to list the better hotels and restaurants, as some travel books do, but generally we are suggesting patronizing low cost inns, pensions, guest houses, tea rooms, snack shops, etc., and even the relevant governments can't keep track of all of those.

3. We have learned that many of the places that were recommended in other travel books doubled their prices as soon as they were listed. It doesn't work: as soon as the proprietor of one of those bargain spots learns he is named in a popular travel book, he raises his prices because he knows he will get plenty of clients from then on.

4. Recently a popular travel book writer was accused of taking money from hotels to recommend them in his books. We wouldn't wish even to get close to such possibilities, or ever to risk having such a charge thrown at us.

5. Some of the big organizations that produce competing travel books have battalions of people in Europe checking out hotels and restaurants; there are only two of us.

Instead of specific listings of hotels and pensions, we have tried to generalize about how to find such inexpensive lodgings in each country. We have dealt with restaurants in about the same way. If you have a fair understanding of what you are looking for, it usually isn't hard to find.

So basically we are going to tell you how to travel in Europe as a smart European would.

Travel should be fun, educational, and mind-stretching. It can be, and we call the technique for making it so "liberated travelling" because it is based totally on freedom and independence. Liberated travelling is the best possible way to see distant lands, and it can be the least expensive way if one wants to make it so. This book describes how it works and how to do it in western Europe.

To anyone who has twinges of uneasiness when he thinks about visiting other countries, liberated travel may sound like a dangerous thing to try. At first thought, it can create pictures in one's mind of clumsy errors and embarrassments of many kinds. We do not deny the possibility that travelling on one's own might entail small misfortunes occasionally. But we nevertheless contend that liberated travelling is the most rewarding, most stimulating, and most educational way to go. This book is designed to help you avoid or solve the small problems that are a part of visiting foreign countries and, indeed, to prove to you that such minuscule difficulties can actually be part of the enjoyment of travelling abroad.

One small warning: while we have tried to tell the exact truth about liberated travelling, resisting impulses to gloss over its disadvantages and difficulties, we are aware that many of the prices we have listed will probably be wrong by the time you read this because of the rapidity with which such figures change these days. We have consequently and purposely kept cost figures a bit vague, rounded them off, and thought of them as ballpark guesstimates. It seemed the fairest thing to do in the face of continuously fluctuating money exchange rates, seasonal price variations, and inflationary spirals.

One last caution: this is a rather opinionated book. We have made no effort to make it otherwise. Reflecting upon the quasi-French opinion that "One man's fish is another man's *poisson*," we have decided to forget any pretense of objectivity and to include our own convictions, as well as those of our friends and acquaintances from here and abroad. The first opinion we are offering, therefore, is that you have been adequately forewarned.

The second opinion we offer you is that because this book is admittedly opinionated, was written by two non-Europeans, and is composed of printed pages (which always seem to have a certain amount of sanctity), you should read it with a degree of healthy scepticism. As we wrote it, we tried to keep in mind that it is *your* interests and *your* attitudes that will establish the parameters of your trip to Europe. You should remember that fact too, and not let our opinions or anyone else's influence you too much.

Perhaps the warning is unnecessary. If you have the mind of a liberated traveller, you already know that it's going to be your trip all the way—no matter what any travel book says. And that's the proper way to think about it, in our opinionated opinion.

Bon voyage on your trip through the book.

Phyllis and Alan Kingery

Acknowledgments

Because we owe so many people on both sides of the Atlantic a deep debt of gratitude, we would like to name a few of them here. They are listed alphabetically, not in order of importance; they are all important to us. They encouraged us on this project, argued with us, gave us shelter and hospitality, criticized our prose, and offered help of every sort and magnitude as we worked. They should not be blamed for errors of fact or thinking which may have crept into the text; we hope to blame those on the publisher.

Catherine Althaus
Beat Bachler
Brent Baskfield
Jay Beauseigneur
Felix Becker
John Bertram
David Budgen
Ralph Cohen
Ted Coleman
Bill Conners
Jim Crichton
Paddy Derivan
Maurice Dunne
Ron Edison

Peter ffrench-Hodges
Andrew Glaze
Peter Green
Lisa Greenberg
Harry Harambopoulos
Elaine Heller
Mireille Henrard
Larry Hilliard
Fred Janzen
Jim Jung
Judith Karlstein
Gerhard Markus
George McGrath
Brian McGuire

Mel Montgomery
Eduardo Nery
Bedford Pace
Elisabeth Puttaert
Frederique Raeymaekers
Robert M. Ricker
Al Rogers
Rachel Semlyen
Armando Spinola
Barry Wall
Pat Walsh
Paul Weiss

All of these people deserve and have our sincerest appreciation, and we hope that they are not disappointed with this result of their help and advice.

Chapter One
What's This All About?

An adventure is only an inconvenience rightly considered. An inconvenience is only an adventure wrongly considered.

G. K. Chesterton

Europe today is no longer the bargain-hunter's paradise it used to be. Thanks to inflation, the European countries are all expensive now—some, of course, more than others. There is another problem, not by any means a new one, which faces the would-be visitor: Europe's size. Western Europe is large, encompassing well over a million square miles. This simple fact makes one realize that he has a number of basic decisions to make before leaving: where to go, when to go, and how to go. *Where* is important because it not only relates to your own personal interests, but also because some of the countries are less expensive than others. We will discuss this question in greater detail later in the book.

When is important simply because Europe is more crowded and more expensive during the high season than it is during other parts of the year. And as you will see in Chapter 2, high and low seasons vary from country to country.

How is perhaps the most important question of all. Will you drive while you're there, or take advantage of Europe's excellent public transportation systems? Will you concentrate on the biggest cities, or try to explore the countryside? Will you travel independently, or join a guided tour? We'll have a good deal more to say about all these questions from here on.

How much you enjoy Europe is pretty much up to you—and to luck. If you are in a bad humor, or are disgruntled over facing small problems, or have a lot of bad weather everywhere you go, your pleasure will be reduced or wrecked. Bad weather is a matter of bad luck; your frame of mind is something you can control.

1

Let's imagine that we can spy upon two couples who are just arriving in Europe, perhaps on the same plane. All four people have had very little sleep. The first pair, Tom and Betty, get through customs and the passport check with no difficulty. They then go to the airport's money exchange desk and change $100 worth of travellers' checks into the local currency. "I can't tell what this crazy-looking money is worth," Tom says. "I wonder if we got cheated."

Then they drag their four *big* suitcases to the tourist information desk. "We want to get a room downtown," Tom tells the young girl. "With a private bath," he adds.

"What part of town would you like to stay in?" the girl asks.

"How do we know?" Tom growls, looking unhappy.

The girl unfolds a map. She draws a circle on it, saying, "This area is popular with tourists. It has most of the museums, art galleries, nice shops, and so on."

"Yeah, yeah," Tom replies. "How much will we get stuck?"

"I beg your pardon?"

"How much will a room there cost?" Betty says.

The girl consults a little booklet. "Here's a nice place," she says. She makes an X on the map in the circle she drew earlier. "It costs about $40 American a day for a room with a bath."

"Forty bucks!" Tom says. "I thought rooms were cheap over here."

The girl smiles. "You could get a room in this same hotel for about half that if you could give up the bath."

"No, no," Tom growls. "We aren't animals. We'll take the room with the bath."

"Shall I reserve it for you?" the young girl asks. "There is a dollar and a half charge for the service."

Tom looks at his wife. "We're not even out of the airport and we're already getting ripped off," he mutters. To the girl behind the desk he says, "Yeah, we're just dumb Americans. We'll pay your fee. Call them."

A few minutes later they lug their bags out of the front door and look at all of the buses waiting there bearing names of destinations that look like Marmalade and Mayonnaise. "I can't understand what those destination signs mean," Tom grumbles. "Let's get a cab." They spend the whole trip watching the meter click up numbers. "We're going to be broke before we get to the hotel," Betty says. Tom glowers in silence.

Once they are installed in their room, Tom says, "Boy, for forty bucks you'd get more than this back home. We got a lousy view, no TV, rickety old furniture, and a bathroom that looks like it was built a hundred years ago. Why'd you want to come over here anyway? Let's get out of here and go spend some more money."

Now let's do a bit of snooping on the other couple, Jack and Barb, who have just cleared customs and the passport check without problems. There is one immediate and obvious difference between them and Tom and Betty: they are carrying only one bag apiece. This will give them a lot of freedom in the days to come—including freedom from paying cab fares, red cap charges, etc. They go over to the money exchange desk and trade $100 worth of travellers' checks for local currency. "Look at this stuff," Jack says, holding the foreign money out to Barb. "It's huge. And it's beautiful. We'll have to figure out what it's worth in our money when we get settled in a room."

They go next to the tourist information desk. "Hi," Jacks says to the young girl, sticking out his hand. Both he and Barb shake hands with the girl. "We'd like to get a map of the city," Barb says. "And some advice about rooms," Jack adds. The three of them look at the map for a time, and the girl answers some questions for them. She mentions the name of the hotel she sent Tom and Betty to.

"Forty dollars? How much without a bath?" Jack asks.

"A little over half," the girl replies.

Jack looks at Barb. "We don't care about a private bath, do we?" he asks. She shakes her head. Jack asks the girl, "Are there rooms for even less money?"

"You could stay in a pension," the girl ventures.

"What's that?" Jack asks with a grin. "Where we live, that's what you finally get after you've given thirty or forty years of your life to some company."

"Here a pension is what you might call a boardinghouse. You stay with a family in their home. A room like that would be maybe $12 to $14 a night, including breakfast."

"A chance to meet Europeans!" Jack says enthusiastically. "Want to try it, baby?"

"Sure," Barb says. "Let's save our money for something that matters."

They don't let the girl book a pension room for them. Instead they take a listing of pension addresses from her, thank her, shake hands again, and go out and board the downtown bus. After they're seated Barb asks, "What did he charge for this ride?"

"I was just thinking about that," Jack says. "I think it was only about a buck apiece. Not bad." They enjoy watching the scenery as they ride into town.

Because their luggage isn't very heavy they set off walking from the bus station to find one of the pensions on their list. They enjoy the unfamiliar sights and sounds as they walk, and they even do a bit of window shopping. The first pension they reach is full, but in the second one, which is not far off, they take a room.

They love the room. "Look at the beautiful old furniture," Barb remarks. Jack, who is already stretched out full length, says, "Wait until you feel this bed. You'll never want to go home."

"I don't want to already," Barb says. "Wasn't that nice of the man asking us to come down tonight to get acquainted and to watch TV with them? It's like being home—only more interesting."

"We're going to have a ball," Jack says. "But let's rest up before hitting the pavement. Europe's been here for awhile; it'll still be there an hour from now."

It's certainly clear which of the two couples *are* going to have a ball. Jack and Barb are fortunate in being the kind of people who know how to enjoy themselves, each other, and their circumstances, while poor Tom and Betty will find it pretty difficult to enjoy their trip. They are too cynical, too worried, and too frightened. They don't know how to appreciate the new and different; it scares them.

Here, then, are the attributes you should have to travel independently in foreign countries. You should be self-confident, curious, adventurous, and gregarious. In other words,
- you shouldn't take yourself too seriously
- you should be able to shrug off or laugh at little problems
- you should have a sense of wonder about the new and different
- you should be willing to take a few chances and to have new experiences
- you should be willing to live differently from the way you live at home
- you should hope to meet Europeans, and, as much as possible, live as they do for a short time.

And what should you do if you weren't born with all these attributes?
- Remember that most of the people you see (and who see you) in Europe will never see you again.
- Don't believe that everyone in Europe is out to take you. They aren't.
- Make an effort to expect and appreciate differences. They are what makes Europe so charming—even when they constitute small inconveniences, discomforts, or surprises.
- Try to overcome any reservations you have about talking to strangers or asking questions. Conversation is one of the best things Europe has to offer.
- Attempt to generate the courage to try strange foods, drinks, or adventures. If someone suggests climbing up to the castle rather than riding up, you may be sorry later if you don't do it. If you have an impulse to eat what the people at the next table are having, try it. It's easy; all you have to do is point.
- Keep uppermost in your mind that you're having a vacation, not facing an ordeal.

Europe is there for everyone to enjoy. Whether or not you can and will enjoy it is largely up to you.

□

Your good time on your trip certainly has a lot to do with the attitude you take with you, but obviously that is not the whole story. You may also realize that you will be surrounded, from the beginning to the end of your trip, by people who have your best interests at heart. As one example, the airline people are perfectly aware that it is in their own best interest to get you to Europe as quickly, safely, and comfortably as possible. They work hard to do just that. The tourist information people, both in this country and all across Europe, are there to help you in any way they can. The auto-rental personnel, the room renters, and the people who provide public ground travel are all basically on your side. Lastly, there are the people who have nothing to do with tourism, who will generally be sympathetic and helpful with any problem you may have—a form of kindness that may finally end by being among your best experiences and memories of your trip.

Try not to leave your sense of humor, independence, or curiosity at home. If you do, you'll soon find that you should have stayed home altogether.

□

There is one other hypothetical couple we must examine before we move on, simply because they represent such large numbers of foreign tourists in Europe: the people who take guided tours. This couple more than likely arrives on a charter flight with a group of fellow countrymen they will be with constantly during their stay in Europe.

This couple, like the others we've looked at, also have jet lag and feel dirty, but they are not confused about anything. They are with their group, their guide is there, and they have no decisions facing them. They don't have to stand in line to exchange currency, and the fact that they speak only English doesn't bother them at all. Their guide speaks six languages.

This pair, along with all those who make up their group, are herded out past the buses with the funny names to the special buses that are waiting just for them. They will be counted as they are ushered aboard, and soon they will be driven downtown to the first of the many rooms that have been booked for them. For the next few weeks they will never have to hunt for a room, they will never have to make decisions about where to go next, and they will never be allowed to decide where to eat—or, for that matter, what to eat.

The buses they will ride will be first rate, usually air-conditioned, but ordinarily without toilet facilities aboard. The quality of the tour is decidedly related to how good the guide is, but they may soon get tired of sitting on the bus for long hours listening to lengthy speeches from the guide. And some of the guides (most, perhaps) are verbose.

Some tours offer first- or second-class accommodations. The "second-class" rooms, which of course cost less, are generally palatial, and they nearly always have private bath facilities. If there is such a choice, most people on the tour will opt for the first-class rooms. Generally speaking, they are not *poor* people. Yet most of them are willing to relinquish their independence in favor of having any and all decisions made for them. Day after day they will be told to be at breakfast by X o'clock, and they will dutifully obey. They will be told when to be at the bus door, and they will always be there as specified. Most everyone is usually at the bus door early. What could happen, our couple wonders, if you were *late*?

The worst thing about tours, our couple will soon discover, is not only that they effectively prevent you from meeting any Europeans, but that they distract your attention from the countryside. You don't give full awareness to the world that is passing your window at high speed. You can't; you are too busy explaining to the people across the aisle who you are, or listening to them tell you who they are, or wondering why the two men five rows ahead of you sit together all the time and ignore their wives, or listening to the woman who feels compelled to tell you about all her evidence that the blonde woman two rows behind the driver is trying to make out with the tall bearded man on the other side of the bus, or simply wondering if the guide will soon announce a rest stop so you can visit a toilet.

They may conclude that this does not add up to an ideal vacation in Europe. You need not spend hundreds of dollars to do this sort of thing while passing through a foreign country. You could do essentially the same thing at home by joining a bridge club, a lonely-hearts group, or a computer-dating service.

Let's examine what else is in store for them a little further before we leave them to their companions, and concentrate upon the real subject of this book—the joys and tribulations of the people who are on their own. Because the independent couple can go at their own speed, make their own mistakes, and spend as much or as little as they wish, comparisons between them and the couple on the tour are difficult to make. The overall price (excluding the cost of small incidentals) has been set for the tour couple in an agreement signed long ago. They know their itinerary, which will more than likely include quite a few countries, maybe as many as ten or twelve. Although they will probably not meet or get to know any Europeans, they will eventually know their companions on the bus very well, and we would hope they like them—because they're stuck with them. The rooms they are taken to will have private baths, and they will live generally in a style that is not terribly different from the lives they lead at home. They will often be rushed—told to "be back on the bus in twenty minutes" in places that even a decathlon winner couldn't see in eight hours—and they will be hurried from place to place by people whose major interest in the trip is monetary gain. They will hear many canned spiels about why a certain roofline is unusual (when they don't even find it interesting), why they should admire a particular church door (when they really don't), and why they should be enthralled to be standing on the exact spot where Romeo serenaded Juliet (which they happen to know he didn't, and it consequently *isn't*).

Their tour of Europe will be *easy,* and perhaps that's the best thing the independent-minded person could say about it. They won't have to decide much of anything for themselves, but on the other hand, they will find themselves being told what to do time and again for the duration of the trip. They'll cover a lot of kilometers, but whether they'll see much but the horizon and a blur of scenery alongside the bus is questionable. They won't stay anywhere long enough to gain any understanding of what they do see.

*Would you like to be told
to get back on the bus
after viewing a sight like this
for about five seconds?*
The authors' photo, Spain

Now let's consider the other couple, the man and woman who are completely on their own. Let us assume that like many liberated travellers they do not have a fixed itinerary in mind. They may feel sure that they want to visit this city or that country, but generally they are prepared to be flexible, to change their minds or their route at any point for any (or no) reason. They will have no advanced reservations for rooms, but will have a hope that they can find inexpensive lodgings in pensions (boardinghouses or budget hotels) wherever they happen to be. They will presumably not go as far, overall, as the tour group couple, but because of the way they will travel, they will see and learn much more. They know that the main purpose of travel in another country is to meet the people who live there, and they will meet many Europeans during their visit. They will never be told what to do or be rushed around by anyone else, and they will stay as long as they wish at any of the places they visit. They will share everything, good or bad, with each other—not with dozens of other tourists.

Let us emphasize that when we talk about travelling independently, or "on your own," we are certainly not advocating travelling *alone.* That lonesome way of doing it is less than ideal, as bad or worse than taking a guided tour with fifty or a hundred fellow-countrymen. Best of all, it seems to us, is sharing your journey with one other person, hopefully someone who loves you and is as flexible and liberated as you are. In the hope that you will be able to make such an arrangement for your trip, we'll continue to think of you as part of a pair for the rest of the book.

As far as expenses are concerned, one would guess that the independent couple will spend a good deal less money than the tour couple. *How much* less depends entirely upon how well they did their homework and how cunning they are. But they will have given themselves a big price discount simply by deciding that they could enjoy a few weeks of a different kind of living than they have at home. Not only will they save money by not having to help pay a guide's wages, but also by foregoing the privilege of having a private bath in every room they take, and by staying in private homes rather than in fancy hotels.

Money, of course, is not the only question involved in this choice between going alone or with a group. If it were, no one would ever go to Europe at all; they'd stay home and read *National Geographic* instead. But on the matter of *how* to do it, we are convinced that the independent travellers will learn a great deal more, and have a lot more fun together than the couple on the tour. Independent travelling is a fantastic form of sharing, unparalleled in most people's lives at home. It offers the possibility of a new kind of loving for most people. It is a remarkable, 24-hours-a-day, 7-days-a-week, kind of togetherness.

Not long ago we met an American couple on a train in France who were liberated travellers in the best sense. The four of us were comparing ideas about being flexible, travelling without room reservations, and so on, when the woman began to tell a story about meeting some people on a train.

"We were travelling between Innsbruck and Salzburg about two weeks ago," she said, "watching the beautiful, snow-covered mountains as we sped along. Our compartment was shared by four large, young, Austrian males whose abilities to use English were apparently as limited as ours for speaking German. They were big, godlike, handsome types and Tom here looked as if he hated them all.''

"I felt like a midget compared to those guys," he said, and we all laughed.

"So we rode along," she continued, "unable to communicate but occasionally exchanging smiles and cookies (we had the cookies and they had wonderful smiles). We had no idea who they were until the train was coming into Kitzbühel, when they leaped up and began pulling down skiing gear from the overhead racks. Then we remembered that there was an international ski meet there that weekend, so (at my insistence) we jumped off too. It was only then that we learned we'd been sitting with part of the Austrian Ski Team. I'll never forget them!''

"Me either," Tom said. "She won't let me."

His wife elbowed him in the ribs, and went on with her story: "We had a very pleasant weekend in Kitzbühel watching the skiers, a pleasure we wouldn't have had if we hadn't been seated where we were on the train—or if we had had advance room reservations somewhere else for that night. We were really lucky."

"When we got back on the train two days later," Tom chuckled, "I told her I'd realized that not only are Austrian skiers big and hateful, but that all skiers are— and she said she had noticed that all of them did seem to have what she called 'the same stunning attributes' the Austrians did. I guess she's just never forgiven me for the fact that I was so intensely alert during that floor show we saw in Paris."

"Anyway," she said, "we have never had reservations since that incident."

"Not only for rooms," Tom said with a grin, "but also about how much the other one is likely to misbehave, given the chance."

It was a great conversation. Liberated travelling is splendid for people who love each other—and who do not take themselves or each other too seriously.

Both guided tours and liberated travelling have their disadvantages. In addition to feeling like cattle after a time, people on organized tours often complain about being fed American-style food all the time rather than local cuisine, being rousted out of bed at six a.m. so that everyone in the group will be ready to depart by nine o'clock, and hearing spiels that sound as if they've been given 10,000 times before (which they doubtlessly have).

Liberated travellers can have their own share of frustrations. They will doubtlessly be lost from time to time, they will make mistakes, and they will miss or overlook things they should have seen or done that they just didn't know about. They will occasionally be embarrassed, usually because of their own mistakes, and they will have many simple problems that an experienced guide could have prevented or have solved in seconds. And some of those problems will not seem so simple when they occur.

Unguided tours can exact a toll from those who are brave enough to try them, not only physically, but also mentally. You have to think, you have to face minor misfortunes, and you sometimes have to put up with bad luck, which perversely seems to hit more often in Europe than elsewhere. So while we think it's the greatest way to travel, there are those times . . . well, we'll try to tell you the truth about it throughout.

Although it must be clear to you already that we are not overly fond of the guided tour concept, we do feel that taking one might be a good idea for anyone who hasn't a partner to share the adventure with, or for people who are so apprehensive about the new and different that they just couldn't enjoy being on their own. We also know that some people will go on a tour on their first trip, to get an idea what Europe is all about, before embarking on independent adventures later. Nevertheless, we still maintain that, for most people, travelling in the liberated manner is the best choice, even on their first journey abroad. Europe is a very civilized place; travelling there is in no way similar to a trip down the Amazon.

But now let's talk about you. Which of the two ways of travelling sounds more pleasant to you? If you feel that your legs have not yet atrophied through disuse, that you aren't yet so set in your ways that you couldn't change your habits for a short time (*e.g.,* give up your evening martini), and that you could find sleeping in a stable in the Alps more exciting than being in your own bed, you belong in the liberated category. On the other hand, if all those ideas strike you as completely crazy, you are into the wrong book. Because that's the sort of thing we're going to discuss from here on: liberated travelling.

Travelling on your own

This book is addressed to the most first-class kind of traveller there is, the person who is independent, who is a bit adventurous, and who knows that the real purpose of visiting another country is to meet the people who live there. There is no other way to get any sort of an understanding of another country; and in our opinion it is foolish to think you know anything about, let's say, France, if you haven't met any French people—and if you've only been to Paris.

This is a book about walking, biking, hiking, and looking for transportation bargains for the longer distances. If you have a free spirit, a little courage, a modicum of stamina, a well-developed sense of humor, and best of all, a companion who has the same attributes, you can have a great European trip *sans* guide. And you don't have to be a kid to do it. We've met folks in their fifties and sixties who were travelling that way—and loving every minute of it. As we said before, you'll save money if you go this way, and you won't feel as if you're sitting through a Burton Holmes travelogue while you're doing it.

But no matter how independent you are, you may be a little concerned about having language or currency problems, about getting lost, or about not knowing what to do in some situations—and you should be. You'd be foolish if you didn't have such worries. *Everyone* who goes it alone the first time has these concerns, at least until he discovers how intelligent and resourceful he really is. Therefore, just to help you reach that wonderful realization a bit early, we are going to provide enough tips to allow you to get along nicely, to enjoy yourself, and to realize that the little challenges you will face are not obstacles to enjoyment.

Most tour buses swing around Brussels's Grand'Place square without stopping while passengers crane frantically to glimpse sights like this: the incredible Town Hall.

Belgian National Tourist Office photo. C. G. T. — Esterhazy

Most people who visit Europe on their own, particularly those on their first trip, are apt to make a number of mistakes, both big and small. The worst one is not realizing beforehand the difference between ''big'' and ''small'' mistakes. Errors in dealing with languages and strange currencies and the like are *little* mistakes. Here are *big* mistakes you can make:

- carrying too much luggage;
- trying to live as much as possible as you live at home;
- going too fast and too far;
- spending too much money (*e.g.,* for rooms in American-style hotels);
- going only to places where *everyone* goes, the places called ''musts'' in the brochures;
- seeing, but not understanding the significance of what you see;
- worrying so much about making little mistakes that you ruin your trip and miss some of the best Europe has to offer.

Any of these mistakes can do a great deal to diminish the pleasure of your trip. If you are planning a first trip to Europe, these are probably not the kinds of things that are worrying you now—which means that you are nervous about the wrong things. If you take a guided tour simply because you are worried about making a fool of yourself, and then find that you don't like being herded around all the time, you've made a *big* mistake. If you go on your own and take too much luggage and try to see too much in too short a time and get sick in the process, you've made a big mistake. But as we shall try to convince you in the coming pages, if you try to ask someone where the railway station is, and botch the language so badly he shows you a geranium, that's just a minuscule mistake, something to laugh off.

Many of the tips and recommendations we are going to give you may seem a bit obvious, particularly when you're reading them from the comfort of your chair. But you must realize that you won't be quite so comfortable when you find yourself in a town you've never seen before on a late, rainy evening, when you're tired, and when you're hoping you won't have to check into that huge expensive hotel right in front of you. You won't be so relaxed as you are now when you are standing at a bus stop in a small village in the middle of nowhere wondering why the departure sign doesn't list the next village you had hoped to visit.

While we know that many of the things we are going to tell you in the coming pages are known by the children of various European countries, we also know that in this one respect you are not as smart as they are. They know which tram to catch to the center of the city, how to buy a ticket, how much it will cost, and where to get off downtown. Will you? Of course the answer is no, so we will tell you in the ensuing pages all the tips about such matters that we can, based on our own experiences and those which have been related to us by American, Canadian, and European friends.

You may be the wisest person in your own neighborhood, but at times you are going to feel like sort of a moron in Europe. You will find yourself doing a lot of gesticulating when you talk to people, and you will hear yourself asking such idiotic questions as, "Where is the bathroom—the restroom—er, the toilet?" even when you fully understand the distinctions European attach to those words. Making such errors in Europe is really not all that embarassing because people there do not seem to be inclined to laugh at little faux pas, but no doubt you would still prefer not to make yourself feel foolish too often. So we are going to try to tell you how to read European time-tables, get on buses, cope with menus, and, yes, indeed, even how to find toilets—and what you may expect when you do find one.

Much of the advice we are going to offer will be more in the line of what *not* to do rather than what *to do*. Unlike other travel book authors, we will not try to tell you where to eat, but how to eat inexpensively, wherever you are; not where to stay, but how to find inexpensive lodgings; not where to go or what to do, but how to conserve your money and still have a good time everywhere. Later on we will give you some ideas about how to make your trip more successful by dredging up whatever sense of wonder and curiosity your education hasn't destroyed, and putting it to use to help you really appreciate what you see.

We also hope to encourage you *to ask questions* when you are lost or confused. Americans and Canadians often feel that doing so makes them seem ignorant or foolish, but they are wrong. Europeans, even those who are involved in the travel business, often make mistakes themselves and have to ask questions when they are away from familiar territory. Their view of such difficulties is this: if you don't know, *just ask* the nearest person. The typical European has had his own experiences in having to raise such questions, and he is usually only too happy to provide you with an answer to yours if he can. All that is required is to tell the other person that you have a problem and need help; nine times out of ten you'll get some sort of answer. Whether or not you'll *understand* it is another question.

We also hope to talk you into trying to blend into European settings as much as you possibly can. Most people are tempted to try to live, wherever they go, as much as possible the way they live at home. Although it seems simpler and safer to do so, it is a great mistake. We hope you will try to keep this fact in mind: you have the rest of your life to live *that way* at home. As a liberated traveller, you ought to experience, at least briefly, the way *they* live. Forget the hamburgers, TV shows, and hustle-bustle temporarily, and try to find out what *their* everyday lives are like—what they eat, how they travel, and what their pleasures are. Even though you can't *really* do it in a few days, it's rewarding to get as close as you can. It's educational, and it's fun.

Liberated travelling has little or nothing to do with one's age or gender or stamina. Generally it only has to do with one's independence of mind. We're sure that you have some sort of age and gender and stamina; as you read on in the book perhaps you will be able to decide whether you have the remaining necessary attribute—independence.

Thoughts about how, where and why people travel

There are two stories, perhaps apocryphal and perhaps not, that seem to us to illustrate perfectly how *not* to travel. The first concerns a tour bus load of passengers who were let out near the Sistine Chapel with the admonition: "Back on the bus in fifteen minutes, folks. We have a schedule to keep." Two middle-aged women rushed off the bus in this crowd, and one said to the other, "Goodness me, we won't have time to buy post cards." They hurried into the chapel, looked about for post card racks, and, seeing none, scurried back out the door.

Not far away they found a post card vendor, and proceeded to buy a number of cards, one of which showed a view of the Chapel's ceiling—under which they had been standing moments before, *and hadn't looked up to see.*

A week later the women in their office in Philadelphia were looking at this same post card. One of them said, "Wouldn't it be nice to be in the Vatican with them? You'd sure see something there!"

The other story concerns a man and woman who were driving a rented car through the Swiss Alps. They drove into one of the scenic lookoff spots, stopping their car well back from the edge. The man got out, walked up to the short protective stone wall, and took a Polaroid picture of the grandeur before him. When the picture was developed he walked back to the car and thrust it in the window to the woman. After a quick glance at it, she said, "To hell with it. It's just like all the rest. Let's go."

He got in the car and they drove away.

One hears enough stories of this sort from Europeans to begin to suspect finally that there may really be people who behave like this. Perhaps they are insecure or just frightened by the unfamiliar, but one sees them everywhere, faceless figures in rented cars or guided-tour buses. They rush from one spot to another in an endless marathon of new sights, sounds, smells and sensations, never taking the time to assimilate or understand any of these experiences. A case in point: we once met a loony couple who were attempting to drive through eight countries in ten days. "If it weren't for Luxembourg and Liechtenstein," the man chortled, "we couldn't possibly do it." They didn't talk to us for long.

A resident of Heusden, Holland (Ch. 15) expressed his view of such tourists in the following plea he made to us: "Please don't mention Heusden in your book. We don't want any more of those tours coming here. We've been restoring this whole town for years, and we're proud of it. Those buses come into town and the tourists go into the cafe and buy post cards for fifteen minutes, and then they drive away. They don't even look at this place. It makes me angry."

When we told him we were writing to people who would want to walk along the old walls, visit the windmills, and learn how a village is restored, he smiled and said, "Fine. Bring all those people you can. We'll enjoy having them."

Is there a fjord in your future?

When you meet and have such conversations with Europeans, you'll often be asked such questions as these: Why do your countrymen think they always have to stay in the largest cities? Why do so many of them think they have to go to the best hotels? Why do they always have to eat and drink the same things they eat and drink at home? Why do they ride those tour buses and try to see all of Europe within a few days?

These are hard questions to answer. But we have been amused to learn that many of the suave-appearing Europeans who ask such questions do very nearly the same things themselves when they visit countries other than their own. While they are not so inclined as Americans to ride tour buses or to stay in expensive hotels, they do seem drawn to large cities like London, Berlin, New York, Paris, Rome, and Geneva—in spite of realizing, at least when they think about *us*—that those cities are not representative, and that they are often dirty, crowded, and expensive. We also find that travelling Europeans often try to eat exactly what they have at home, and that they tend, when they can arrange it, to congregate with their own countrymen and to ignore the natives.

But they still hold us up as the all-purpose bad examples, saying, "You people don't know how to travel. You don't know what it really means." When you attempt to debate this by arguing that they make almost the same mistakes when they travel, you can nearly always expect this sort of answer: "Oh, we have our rich, superficial people people, too—but *I* don't travel that way, and neither do any of my friends." Well, we remain unconvinced: many of them are just as naive about travelling as many Americans are.

Norwegian National Tourist Office photo

It seems clear that everyone is a little afraid when he is away from the familiar, even if he is a fairly sophisticated person, but we hope that you aren't that insecure. If you do travel abroad in such a way that you make contact with some of the people who live there, you will find it an absolutely priceless experience. You will be as odd and as different and as interesting to them as they will be to you, and you will often find yourself trying to communicate with someone who *really* cares about what you say or think. You won't find that in a tour bus, nor will you find it in a foreign-based American hotel bar that specializes in very dry, very expensive martinis.

On a train ride heading east from Luxembourg several years ago, we had a chat that touched on the subject of sensible travel with a well-dressed, greying, pleasant, middle-aged European. He said, ''I don't want to insult you, but I think Americans are the most unsophisticated travellers in the world. You two are seeing something, but what about your countrymen who come over here and fly around from one big city to another?''

''What would you do if you visited America?'' we asked.

He laughed. ''I'd probably fly from one big city to another—probably New York, Chicago, and Los Angeles. But it would be a mistake, wouldn't it? It's so easy to see how silly it is when you're talking about your own country. But of course there's less choice about it in the States because your country is so much bigger than Europe, let alone any of the individual countries.''

When we replied that we didn't think he'd learn much about the United States by visiting just those three huge cities, he replied, ''That's probably true—but what does an American know about Europe after he's visited Paris, Geneva, Munich, and Amsterdam?''

We found the parallels extremely revealing. When we subsequently suggested to him that he might learn a *little* about the United States if he forgot about those three huge cities and instead visited, say, a place in New England, two or three small towns in Florida or in some other southern state, had a glimpse of the Rockies, and saw the Grand Canyon, he agreed wholeheartedly. Then he said, "So why don't most Americans do the same in Europe? Why not forget the capitals and instead visit the villages, walk in the Alps, and see the Black Forest?"

Finally all of us agreed that most tourists do not know how to see and understand the countries they visit as well as they might, and that one of the reasons is that they simply aren't given very good advice. We all concurred that most travel books are more fact-oriented than philosophical, and the literature that most tourist organizations put out is not designed to give readers any thoughts about potential problems or even offbeat travel possibilities. Then the European gentleman said, "Perhaps it's true that we often don't travel much better than you do. We shouldn't make so much fun of you Americans and your guided tours." He reflected for a moment. "We Europeans don't get any better advice than you Americans do about travelling out of country. How is the poor tourist, whoever he is, supposed to know how to travel sensibly in the countries he visits?"

"We've been thinking about that question for some time ourselves," we replied.

The other big question the Europeans are much inclined to ask (and one we think does indict Americans more than it does Europeans) has to do with going too far, too fast, attempting to visit as many countries as possible. "Why do you travel that way?" they ask. "What's the point? What would you think of one of us trying to see twelve or fifteen of your states within two weeks?"

It's hard to say what the point of such decathlon-style travel is. We certainly don't know. We suspect that even the unfortunate people who feel compelled to travel that way can't explain why they do it. It's crazy, it's tiring, it's expensive, and it's the worst way to travel. But it seems right from a distance, doesn't it? Why not see everything while you're there? You may never come back. Well, the problem is that in moving fast you don't see much of anything. You never stand still long enough to understand what you're seeing, let alone appreciate it fully. So even if rushing about seems right and, indeed, the obvious thing to do, it's still expensive, tiring, and crazy.

Although we hope that you don't embrace any notions about trying to see fifteen countries within two weeks, we are aware that the temptation to keep moving can be great, particularly when the countries are small and the distances are relatively short. But if you are going to go it on your own, please remember that each new country will bring you a new set of problems to deal with: new forms of currency, new languages, and new ways to keep you from finding the bus, train, or tourist room that you want. Every time you have to show your passport you can expect to face some new problems. And if you have to spend a couple of days just learning how to survive in each country, even visiting seven countries in two weeks will mean that you will have to spend all of your time everywhere learning what every little kid you see around you already knows.

Even people whose minds are broad and whose pocket books are thin often make the mistake of trying to go too fast and too far. We did it ourselves when we first started travelling. Now we know better. If you have no preconceived notions about what you would like to see in Europe, other than holding a desire to see, learn, understand, and enjoy as much as possible within, say, a month's time, you might consider our "two-to-three" rule—not more than two to three countries, and not more than two to three major stops in each. This theory, which is considerably less complicated than Relativity, is just based upon seeing and understanding in depth, and using bases for further exploration. From where you are sitting it may sound unreasonable (what if someone says, "You mean you didn't see Paris?"), but it is much more comfortable to know where your lodgings are, what floor your room is on, and where the toilet is, than not to have a room at all because you are on the road. It might be wise, in other words, to forget what other people expect you to do on your trip. If they care about Paris, let them go to Paris. If you care about spending a few days in Calais, that's where you should go.

Cocktail party talk about your recent trip is pointless if you know in your heart that you ran yourself to death, didn't really see anything, and ended your adventure in an exhausted condition. It is so much nicer to know, and to be able to say, "We now know a little something about France (or wherever)." It has a lot more meaning than to say, "We saw the Eiffel Tower."

Hoping that you share our view that learning something as you travel not only won't spoil your enjoyment, but will indeed add to it, we will try to tell you in the coming pages how to avoid the biggest mistake of all—seeing without understanding. We remain unconvinced that there is any truth to the proposition that just seeing (and perhaps photographing) something is all there is to travelling. Understanding, or even intuiting the meaning of what you see and what it represents, seems to us to add immeasurably to your appreciation of it, and to your pleasure in having seen it. As you will soon learn, this does not suggest that you need to be an archeologist, an ethnologist, or an expert in anything at all. It simply means that you can use your sense of curiosity and imagination to expand your mind and your pleasure, and that it is extremely enjoyable to do so. We will try to give you some clues later in the book about how to do that.

The main thesis of this book, then, is that you can save money, have more fun, and learn more if you go on your own rather than on a tour—*if* you know what to anticipate and to plan for in advance. We shall immodestly include ourselves in some of the settings we shall describe, mostly because we have made many of the mistakes you are on the verge of making, and you can learn from those errors and thus avoid making them yourself. We will also have a look at other Americans and Canadians who are today travelling in the liberated way and loving it. We will tell you *how* these people are doing it, as well as *when, where,* and *why.* And in the next chapter we'll tell you how inexpensive it can be to adopt this best of all possible ways to travel.

Chapter Two
Liberty, Frugality, and Economy

*If thou shouldst lay up even a little upon a little, and shouldst do this often,
soon would even this become great.*
—Hesiod

By definition, travelling is the most expensive way to live that has yet been invented. You have to pay to get wherever you're going, you have to pay to be there, and you have to pay to get back. Can you imagine what your everyday life would cost if it involved restaurant meals, costly trips from place to place, and hotel rooms at night? The obvious answer is that it would cost plenty.

What we hope to do in this book is to show you how to keep those expenses to what we once heard a Missouri farmer call "the littlest plenty, which can be plenty less than the biggest plenty."

The day of the outstanding two-dollar meal in Europe is long gone. Your cup of coffee (one of Europe's most expensive pleasures) may cost you that much now. Inflation rates are high all over Europe, and so, consequently, are prices. Because we suspect that most people don't want to spend staggering sums on their trip, we are going to offer a number of suggestions related to ways of saving money.

What is it going to cost? That, we shall try to argue here, will depend largely on where you go, how you live, and what sort of entertainments you look for. To keep your expenses down to a reasonable level, you will want to stay in tourist rooms or hostels. When you eat in restaurants you will want to look for those which offer "tourist menus," which are good, filling meals that carry a pre-set (usually low) price. Sandwich shops, tea rooms, and bars also often offer economical calories. Lastly, get your food occasionally from delis or grocery stores, and eat it in your room or a nearby park.

19

There are many ways to economize on a European trip. Avoid taking taxis. Ask the tourist office personnel about special discounts for city buses, trams, trolleys, and subways. Shop for discount offerings on cross-country transportation, *e.g.*, reduced rates for weekend travel. You will find that in Europe, as everywhere else, the small towns are less expensive than the big cities.

Generally speaking, although this can vary with currency fluctuations, some of the countries are more expensive than others. As of this writing (late 1981) the Scandinavian countries, England, Belgium, Switzerland, and Germany are all on the high side. At this time, Portugal and Greece are fairly low priced. The season can make a good deal of difference in prices. For those who would consider going during low season, here are the inclusive dates of those periods:

Austria 8/31-4/30*	Great Britain 10/1-3/1	Norway 9/1-5/31
Belgium 9/1-6/30	Greece 10/15-4/15	Portugal 11/1-5/31
Denmark 9/16-5/4	Italy 11/1-3/1	Spain 11/1-4/1
France 11/15-3/31	Luxembourg 11/1-3/1	Sweden 9/1-5/31
Germany 11/15-3/31	Netherlands 10/1-3/1	Switzerland 11/16-3/31

Auto rental in Europe (partly due to the high cost of fuel) is expensive— although it is considerably less expensive in some countries than in others. The train passes like Eurailpass or BritRail Pass are bargains, as are some of the rail passes the countries merchandise for use within their own borders.

We shall offer many other tips for saving money later, but here we will try simply to help you decide whether you can afford to go. On that question, here is a nice rationalization for you: you can mentally deduct something because you would have room and board expenses even if you stayed at home. If you think that it usually costs you $5 a day to eat, you can wipe out the meal line altogether. You can eat for less than that in Europe if you must scrimp. Not using electricity and fuel in your home for that month will wipe $25 to $50 off of the lodging expenses. As we know well, it's not an easy matter for a couple to decide. You can think: "Two thousand bucks is a lot of money. And we probably wouldn't get by for that. It might cost $2,500! We could buy a pretty good second car for that. We could have a great month here in the States for a lot less than two grand." And so on.

And when the two of you have been looking at the brochures from the tourist agencies and working up a real lust to go, you can think: "Two thousand isn't so much. And we'd probably get by for less anyway. It might only cost $1,500! If we don't go, we'll probably just spend the money for a dumb second car." And so on.

Many people who are not wealthy figure out for themselves how to keep their costs down. We met one such couple on a recent trip, an accountant and his wife, both in their late fifties in appearance, who were trying liberated and budget travelling for the first time. They had made a discovery. "There were a number of things we wanted to do and see in Geneva," he told us, "but we didn't stay there because I am experienced in dealing with costs, travel expense vouchers, and various way of holding budgets down."

His wife chuckled. "Herb, they're going to think you're a real penny-pincher."

---

*In Vienna the low season is considered to be 12/1 through 4/30.

"I *am*," he said. "Can't afford to be otherwise. Anyway, we couldn't find a room in Geneva for less than $19 a day. We tried a lot of places, and that was the best we found. So I said to Marge, I said, 'Let's go find out what it would cost to stay in a suburb, and what it would cost to ride back and forth on the train.' You've got to put everything in the equation, you know. If the room-cost out in the sticks, when added to the transportation costs, totalled more than $19, it wouldn't be cost-effective."

We nodded, and his wife laughed again. "You'd think we were as poor as church mice," she said.

He grinned at her, and said, "We are—as you know very well. So, to go on, we ended up in a small village a few kilometers out, as *they* would put it. The room, breakfasts included, was $8.50 a day. Only $8.50 for the both of us! The ride into Geneva was roughly 90¢ each, so our total cost per day was just over $10. We saved $9 a day, which, the way I figure things, earned us just about $27 during the three days we stayed.

"But there was yet another saving. Each morning we rode into Geneva, but we always came back before dinner. By my calculations, we were able to eat in the little village for just under half what it would have cost us to eat in the city, which saved us another $4.75 to $5 a day between us."

She giggled again, and said, "Isn't he terrible, going on like this?" But we were impressed with him. Not too many Americans figure out what he did.

"So in three days," he went on, "we saved exactly $41.70, which, if extended over our whole thirty days, would be a savings of $417. We'll really do better than *that*, now that we know how. Could you follow the calculations?"

We said we could and had, and told him that we admired him for working things out the way he had. "It's nothing," he said, "I'm used to thinking in terms of cost-benefit ratios."

His wife laughed again, and one of us said to her, "You're lucky to have a man who knows how to think this way."

"Oh, I *know*," she said, taking his hand in hers. "It just tickles me the way he talks sometimes."

He did use a little jargon, but he knew what he was doing. He was great.

It costs nothing to see sights like this.

The authors' photo, Spain

Who's going with you?

An obvious factor in the amount of money you will spend is how many people you will take along. Taking the kids, for example, would not cost so much as you might expect.

While taking children is basically not an inexpensive way to travel, the little ones do get many discounts because of their sizes and ages. Let's assume that the two of you might take two children, and that you would like to keep the overall costs to a minimum. If you cross the Atlantic on a budget, charter, or stand-by flight, you may or may not get a reduction because of the children's ages, depending on the airline, so shopping around can pay off here. If you purchase APEX tickets, your children below age twelve will be charged only two-thirds of the adult fare.

In Europe the kids will ordinarily travel for a good deal less money than you will. If you and your spouse would rent a car anyway, you can figure that the children will cost you nothing extra for ground transportation. If you would

Travelling with children adds both to the costs and the pleasure of a trip to Europe.

British Tourist Authority photo

prefer to travel by train, your children (12 and under) will get a 50% discount on most tickets. Eurailpasses are half-price for children no older than twelve, and the BritRail Pass is available in both First and Economy classes at about 50% off for youngsters of five through thirteen (those under five travel free).

The kids will get at least a 20% discount in hotels, but often only up to age ten. In pensions (small budget hotels or private home lodgings) they will frequently be let in for a good deal less—perhaps half of the adult cost. Such reductions in price, of course, are based on the assumption that the little ones will stay in *your* room—which is probably the way you'd want to have things arranged anyway.

Unless you are shrewd, the children can double your food bill. This could be true if you eat all your meals in restaurants, although many eateries offer nourishing and inexpensive children's plates. But on the other hand, you can cut food costs drastically if you get your food from grocery stores or delicatessens to eat in your room or in a nearby park. Doing so occasionally is an adventure for children, and it can keep food costs low.

Now let's look at what there is for them to see and do in Europe. There are countless museums, safariparks (zoos in which the animals run free and *you* are caged), open-air museums (which show the country's past building styles and ways of doing things), and farms, parks, and special events designed for children.

Depending on the children's ages, the parents may have to exercise their imaginations to keep the small ones interested in what the family is seeing and doing. Suggestions like these can sometimes help: "Let's see who can find the funniest sign today." "Who wants to order our meals at lunch?" and "Who has an idea for what we should do tomorrow?" Another neat trick is to give them a little money of their own, tell them what it is worth in their own currency, and let them shop for something. They usually love this idea.

Having the children along can frequently have an unforeseen benefit for parents. Most Europeans like children, and families travelling together will often be shown kindnesses that an individual or a couple wouldn't receive.

England is covered with countless museums, parks, and various sights and entertainments of interest to children. Favorite spots and sights for kids include Oxford, Cambridge, Bath, the castle and safaripark at Windsor, York's castle and Railway Museum, and, of course, London's Tower and Tower Bridge. In fact, there is so much for children to see and do in London there is a book on the market there entitled *Parent's Guide to Children's London.* It sells for about two dollars.

Germany not only has castles, safariparks, and ancient cities to dazzle children's eyes, but also a number of "children's cities"—crosses between amusement parks and fairy-tale lands brought to life. One of these, Phantasialand (at Bruhl, not far from the southern border of Belgium) is known as Europe's Disneyland. It consists of transplanted pieces of Mexico, China, Africa, Egypt, and our own old West. Just a bit east of Cologne is Fort Fun City, another big playground straight out of the American wild and woolly West.

For a small country, Holland has more than its share of attractions for young people. In addition to its canals, windmills, and flowers, it has amusement parks, safariparks, a grand open-air museum at Arnhem, children's farms, miniature cities (at The Hague and at Middelburg), and, perhaps best of all, its science museum at Eindhoven. In three or four hours here, a child will not only be greatly entertained, but will learn as much about the world around him as he might learn in a year in school. All display signs are in English. Evoluon is a unique and incredible museum to visit. It is open every day of the year except the two days of Dutch Christmas.

Babysitters in Europe, like most everything else these days, are not inexpensive. Many of them are ''professionals''—often trained nurses, and they charge stiff rates. The fees for such services will be much lower if you can just find some reliable teenager to do the job. Most tourist offices can supply babysitters' names and addresses.

Now that we've talked about a few of the types of attractions just for tykes, let's have a look at what you may expect from them when they're seeing the sorts of places *you* care about. If they are naturally enthusiastic about new sights, sounds, smells, and sensations, you'll have no problems—in fact, you'll find that you're seeing Europe through eyes younger than your own—a very pleasurable experience. If they tend to be easily bored, you can have problems. Experienced travellers who have such children try such schemes as the following:

• Be sure to let them participate in planning each day's schedule.

• Let each of them ask that the family do at least one thing each day that he or she wants to do.

• Encourage them to pick up and speak foreign language phrases.

• Let them order meals occasionally.

• Make sure that they get plenty of rest.

• Go slow. Don't turn the trip into a marathon. If you do, they will turn into monsters.

• Give them money of their own and explain what it is worth in U.S. currency.

• Take them picnicking. You will probably find that they like these little outings far more than the experience of eating in a fancy restaurant.

• Try to let them play with European children.

• Advise them that if they wish to be away from you for a time that you'll arrange it (perhaps by sending them to an English-language movie).

• Give them some exercise from time to time by letting them run or play ball in the parks.

• Encourage them to ask questions.

• Remember that they are individuals who have their own likes and dislikes which they may not be good at articulating.

• And perhaps most of all, let them know before the trip begins that you will try to respect their wishes and desires, and that they must in turn respect yours.

When you are writing to the various national tourist offices that represent the countries you will visit on your vacation, it would be wise to ask for literature about attractions for children. It would also be a good idea to ask the kids what *they* would like to know about and to ask for that literature. Then, of course, encourage them to read the material when it arrives. Most children like to plan ahead, and the brochures will help them to do so.

Travelling solo

Now let's take a look at what is possibly the least rewarding (but least expensive) travel strategy: going alone. That lonesome way of doing it is less than ideal, as bad or worse than taking a guided tour with fifty or a hundred fellow-countrymen. But people often do travel solo, and we have some experience in doing so ourselves, so let's take a look at what's entailed.

Obviously, solo travelling has its drawbacks. If you try it you will probably face periods of loneliness unless you are very self-sufficient. You will have no one with whom you can share your fun and excitement, or your worries and fears, for that matter. But the go-it-alone approach can have its good points. For one thing, you will have more opportunities to meet Europeans when you are alone. They tend to be quite helpful when they see a person struggling down the street with a suitcase, or standing at a crossroad looking at a map with a perplexed expression. And lastly, if you are a truly liberated person, travelling alone will certainly allow you to go where you wish and do what you want without being constrained by anyone else's ideas or desires.

However, if you are a woman travelling alone, you would be wise to think carefully about your own safety. In Europe, as elsewhere, the cities are generally more dangerous than the villages, and port areas are worse than shopping or theatre districts. Nighttime, of course, is more risky than daytime. If there is any doubt about such matters, inquire of the hotel personnel or the tourist office people whether it's safe to walk around this or that area, whether it's safe to ride the buses at night, and so on. And follow their advice.

While you might reasonably expect most of your encounters with Europeans to be pleasant, you could run into problems here and there. A woman by herself is considered fair game for whistling, vulgar comments, and pinches on the derrière in parts of Spain and Italy, for example. You may also find it difficult to gauge intentions in Europe when a man tries to buy you a drink. Such offers are frequent, even when you are with someone. Perhaps all you can do in this situation is to insist on buying the "next round."

If you wish to avoid unwanted attentions, wear conservative clothes—no shorts or low-cut blouses, and avoid dallying around streetcorners, small bars, and "nightclubs." If someone does annoy you by his remarks or exaggerated attention, you can ignore him, simply say "No!", or put him down by some such remark as "Is this an example of European culture?" If things come to the worst, remember that the police in Europe are excellent and will come to your aid if necessary.

Travelling alone for a man is not much different than it is for a solo woman. The advantages include cutting travel expenses in half, the increased possibilities of meeting other people, and having absolute freedom to decide what to do and where to go. The disadvantages include feeling lonely (which can be unrelenting for all but the extremely gregarious), not having someone to share the triumphs and frustrations with, and letting loneliness put you into situations that probably wouldn't have occurred if your partner had been along.

The latter possibility brings pictures to one's imagination of an American man standing in the middle of a dark, wharfside bar looking about innocently, hoping someone in the assemblage of B-girls, hoodlums, prostitutes, pimps, and con-artists might befriend him for a while. There really isn't much doubt about whether or not they will, nor much doubt about whether he will get out with his watch, money, and/or good health. There are many places in Europe that look like stage sets for Bogart movies, and they can be tempting to a man who has temporarily lost his good sense because of a lack of companionship.

There are also many nice places where unaccompanied men can meet women: on the trains, in ordinary bars or restaurants (*e.g.*, England's pubs), swimming areas, hotel lobbies, and in the tourist information offices. If he were to engage in this sport, however, a man would be well off to obtain some understanding of the various national characteristics regarding dating. In Scandinavian countries, it is said, a man can state his intentions pretty clearly to the object of his attention, who will simply say yes or no. (We know of no one directly who has put this theory to the test.) In other places, one hears that more subtlety is required. In France, for example, it is said that respectable couples are chaperoned carefully during early courtship, a thought that contradicts the average outsider's idea of the average Frenchman.

By its very nature, independent travelling seems to work best for two people together, each of them being able to expand the other's horizons and understandings and share their griefs and triumphs. But a man or woman alone will have a better chance of being invited into the family circle in pensions, or of meeting and talking with people on the trains and buses (if you rent a car, you will have committed yourself to an absolute aloneness unless you pick up hitchhikers). If you walk or bicycle, you will find yourself in many areas the recipient of much attention and kindness from those you meet on the trails. For a naturally solitary sort of man or woman, travelling alone in Europe has many points in its favor.

One great disadvantage to solo travelling is the "single supplement," a charge that is often levied by hotels whose rates are geared to putting two people in a room. It can be expensive, and worse yet, some hotels aren't interested at all in renting a room to a single person, presumably because they feel they might later have to turn away a couple who would between them have paid more for the room.

All in all, then, unless you are a truly outgoing, uninhibited sort of person who can meet and talk easily with strangers, we would recommend finding someone to go with you. To make such an arrangement is to reduce the possibility of robbery, rip-off, venereal disease, or simply being bored silly.

Cutting the costs of the capitals

When visiting Europe, most Americans are tempted to experience the capitals and other large cities in the countries they visit, even when they know that these metropolitan areas are expensive, crowded, and occasionally dangerous in some sections. Sometimes tourists even realize that these cities, like Washington and New York, are not especially representative of their countries—but who can resist the lures of Rome, Paris, Copenhagen, Amsterdam, or London?

All such European cities, again like Washington and New York (and Chicago, Denver, Los Angeles, etc.), are more expensive to visitors in accommodations, food, and transportation costs than are the smaller towns and villages in the surrounding countryside. With the high taxes and inflation rates in most European countries at the present time, and the U.S. dollar's sponginess, the costs of most of the big cities are enough to break a tourist's heart—and his budget—into bits.

There is a way to beat these costs, to reduce them drastically. It involves nothing more than seeing these big expensive cities without ever actually sleeping in them. We shall use London as an example of how it works for two reasons: London, if not the *most*, is one of the most expensive cities in Europe now; and it is the biggest European city in area, an important matter because commuting is basic to this idea. In other words, if the scheme works for London, it can work for most other large European cities.

The basic idea is simple; its details can be a bit more complex. London, like all other large cities everywhere, offers its visitors countless day-trips to various interesting spots outside the city. These trips can be made by car, bus, train, or commercial tours, and some of them require as much as two hours plus from central London. The simple part of our idea is this: if one can make these day-trips *from* London, he can just as easily make them *to* London from any place that is not too far out. Why stay on the most expensive end of such round-trip jaunts?

Let us say right now that anyone who has money to burn can find great comfort and pleasure in London, or in any of the rest of Europe's large cities. Since most of us are not that fortunate, we shall continue here to discuss our strategy to save money. It is said that it is still possible to find a room in London (presumably what the British call a "B and B," a bed and breakfast arrangement) for fifteen dollars a night per person; if so, they are very scarce and hard to find. The average person will be forced to pay from $30 to more than $50 a night to sleep in Britain's capital.

Meals are extremely expensive in London. Rides on the subway (the tube) and on the doubledeck buses are surprisingly high-priced. When you add to all this the costs of getting into museums, movies, special events, and the theatres, you will find that life near Big Ben, the Tower, and Westminster Abbey is shockingly expensive.

Now let's suppose that instead of staying in London you go to one of those places the London day-tours visit, a town that is two hours or less from London. In such a place your daily expenses will run about half what they will in London, you will not be lost all the time, and you might even meet some British people. One qualification to following this idea is that you should have a BritRail Pass, which of course you can also use for travelling around the United Kingdom. If you had to buy tickets for your commuting back and forth to London, you'd be better off just to stay there. It should be possible to do the same thing by bus or by car, but the buses are not as fast as the trains, and auto rentals in England are not cheap.

There are smaller towns and cities all around London that offer such possibilities. All travel times given here are by train. Bath is 70 minutes west of London, and other towns in that direction which are worth considering are Salisbury (one hour plus) and Swindon (sixty minutes). To the southeast is Sevenoaks (thirty-two minutes), Tunbridge Wells (forty-nine minutes), Canterbury (one hour and thirty-one minutes), and Rye and Hastings. One hour directly south is Brighton. To the northwest is Ely (one hour and twenty-three minutes), Cambridge (one hour), Norwich (about two hours), and Chelmsford (about 30 minutes). To the north lies Lincoln (two hours), Peterborough (fifty minutes), Northhampton (one hour and fifteen minutes), and St. Albans (30 minutes). To the southwest is Winchester (one hour), and Farnham (one hour).

We have picked locations here somewhat at random, but with the idea of going no further from London than two hours. We will include York because it is such a tourist target and because it is only slightly more than two hours from London, being on a main rail line that carries the new high-speed trains. It would be an ideal place to use as a base camp, not too far from London or Edinburgh.

There are many advantages in having a spot like this you can return to every night. The most obvious is that you do not have to live out of a suitcase; you can unpack and for a few days have a home away from home. B and B's are easy to find in the small towns. You will probably get to know the people who operate the facility. And you will often find that you can get a pretty good discount off the regular daily rate if you will stay for several days.

The general idea may be complicated by your own plans. If you fly into London from the States, you may want to have a room booked ahead, stay there the first night, and move out to a smaller town the next day. If you wished to move on to a smaller place on the day of your arrival, it would be simple enough: a combination of the good ground transportation from Gatwick or Heathrow Airports to London, and possibly the use of the tube system, would quickly put you into the correct London rail station for your departure. Any good travel agent, British Tourist Authority official, or BritRail office in the U.S. could advise you on details.

If you instead arrange to land in Ireland, Northern Ireland, or Scotland with the intention of seeing any of those countries before visiting England, you should consider purchasing an ''open jaw'' air ticket that would allow you to fly into one place and eventually depart for home from another. Such tickets can only be arranged with certain fares, but they can often be split between airlines, with one flying you from the States and another flying you home. This can often be set up in connection with inexpensive APEX or Super APEX fares, but the rules and restrictions on it change frequently, so you should get help in arranging it from a good travel agent. And you would probably be wise to doublecheck the plan with the airline(s) involved or another travel agent before buying the tickets.

Such an ''open-jaw'' arrangement could work as well for starting your trip at Edinburgh, for example, eventually moving south to a place from which you could make day-trips to London, then crossing the Channel, and finally flying home from some place on the Continent. This would save you time, energy, and money in not having to backtrack at the end of your trip to the same airport you flew into.

You might investigate buying two one-way transatlantic tickets, one into Edinburgh, say, and the return flight home from someplace further south. This need not involve any real cost penalty if you can get the best fare. Stand-by tickets are a possibility here.

Watch for special offers from organized tour groups or airlines that might fit your plans. One possibility here is to have a room booked for your first night over, a limited program that some tour operators are now offering. Doing this would allow you to get over jet-lag before moving off into the countryside.

Don't overlook special offers from organizations like BritRail International. In late 1980 and early 1981, for example, this company was retailing special train passes and inexpensive hotel accommodations for four or six days at extremely low prices. Because they are innovative, you can expect other such interesting offerings from them in the future.

If you can't make non-stop flights from home directly to your chosen destination, consider ''add-on'' fares, which can often carry you to exactly the point you wish to reach for very little additional money.

Ask your travel agent whether you can have free ''stopovers'' at any point that might solve your itinerary problems. Some fares will allow you to stop over at one or more points before reaching your final destination.

If commuting in and out will work for London, huge as it is, we are convinced that it will work in most of the rest of Europe's large cities—none of which are big enough in area to make you commute as far as London does to stay off the high-priced land. However, it would offer little benefit in some of Europe's major cities, either because they are not terribly expensive, or because their country's ground transportation systems are not efficient. Some of these would be Lisbon, Madrid, and Athens.

Large cities that would seem to us to invite living out and commuting in would include Amsterdam, Brussels, Paris, Geneva, Vienna, Berlin, Frankfurt, Munich,

Copenhagen, Oslo, Stockholm, Rotterdam, and The Hague. Unless you were in very close to any of these cities, you should have a Eurailpass to make the idea work on the Continent. Living outside of, as opposed to inside of, the big cities will save you a good deal of money on your vacation. If you don't believe it, consider this: the people who live in the various European countries like to visit their big cities occasionally to shop, see the sights, or visit the museums. Most of them make such visits as day-trips. They don't want to pay what it costs to spend a night there. Why should you?

Tips on tipping

Tipping in Europe, as elsewhere, is simply a matter of judgment. We are solidly against overtipping anywhere, as are most of our European acquaintances, but it does seem to us that if one causes any unusual problems (perhaps because of his inability to read or speak the local language), it is appropriate to leave something. But not much, particularly if the service is included.* If the bill doesn't answer that question, ask the waiter. If his answer is "yes" there is a 15-20% tip included in the bill. In such circumstances, and when the service was outstanding, some of our European friends leave two or three small coins, while others leave nothing on the table.

One has to wonder: if they haven't done anything special for you, why should you tip hotel porters, chambermaids, or concierges? Shouldn't the hotel or restaurant—especially when there is a sizeable tip built into the bill—pay the wages of the chambermaid or the waiter, rather than you? Should you pay the bartender for doing his job, especially when he's charging you extremely high prices for your drinks? Remember that when the service is included you are not obligated to leave anything more, which will help you to avoid overtipping. And that can be avoided without any embarrassment across Europe, with the exception of most of France and taxi drivers nearly everywhere.

We will not include information here about the costs and tips for porters outside of hotels (e.g., in railway stations) for several reasons: they are almost impossible to find in Europe; if you are a truly independent traveller you won't be carrying enough luggage to need their help; and if you should find one and use his services, you will find that most of their fees are standard (per bag) and posted, with additional gratuities gratefully accepted. Perhaps because porters are rare, they are not cheap. Self-push carts are usually in evidence in railway stations and air terminals, but it is often hard to find an empty one.

---

*"Service included" translates as "service compris," "einschliesslich Bedienung," "servizio compreso," "servicio incluido," or "bediening inbegrepen."

GENERAL TIPS ON TIPPING

Country	Wide-Spread	Restau-rants	Taxis	Barbers, Hair-Dressers	Cafes, Bars	Cham-ber-Maid (per day)	Cloak-Room Attend-ants, (per item)	Theatre Ushers	Hotels
Austria	yes	1,2	10%	10%	small coins	35-70¢	35¢	none	porter or bellboy, 35¢ per item; concierge $1.50 per service
Belgium	yes	1,2	20%*	10%	if not incl., 15%	none	35-70¢	15-30¢	porter, bellboy, 50-70¢ per bag; concierge $1 per service
Denmark	no	1	none	none	none	none	25-50¢	none	porter, bellboy 40¢ per bag
Finland	no	1	none	25-50¢	none	none	25-30¢	25¢	porter up to 50¢ a bag
France	YES	1,2,3	10-15% (min. 1F)	15%	small coins	75¢	50¢	25-50¢	porter 50¢ per bag; room service 25¢; 50¢ a day for concierge if he provides service
Germany	no	1,2	10%	10%	0 to 25¢	none	25¢	none	50¢ a bag for porters
Gr. Britain	no	3	10-15%	10%	none	$1.00	10-20¢	none	20-30¢ per bag; $1.00 for service from concierge
Greece	no	1,2	0-10%	10-20%	small coins	none	15-30¢	25¢	30¢ per bag for porters
Iceland	NO	none	none	none	none	none	none	none	none
Ireland	yes	1,2,3	10%	20%	small coins	40¢	20¢	none	porters 30¢ per bag
Italy	yes	1,2,3	10%	up to 10%	small coins	35-60¢	50¢	15¢	35 to 50¢ a bag for porters
Luxembourg	yes	1	10-15%	15-20%	small coins	none	none	none	10% to hotel staff
Netherlands	no	1,2	15%**	none	none	0-50¢	25¢	15¢	10-20¢ a bag; 50¢ a day for hotel porter
Norway	no	1,2	0-5%	40¢	none	none	30¢	none	30¢ a bag; $1.00 for porter
Portugal	yes	1	15%	10-15%	if not incl., 10%	$1.00	6-12¢	10-15¢	15¢ per bag; $1.00 per service from concierge
Spain	no	1,2	5-10%	10-15%	small coins	$1.00	50¢	15¢	30¢ per bag carried
Sweden	no	1	10-15%	10-15%	small coins	none	40¢	none	60¢ per bag
Switzerland	yes	1	15%***	15%	small coins	$1-$1.50	60¢	none	60¢ per bag; $1.00 for service by concierge

1. Usually included in the bill; if not leave 15%.
2. Additional small coins, usually about 5%.
3. May or may not be included; if bill doesn't say, ask.

* None in Brussels.
** None if taxi has meter.
*** None in Basle or Zurich.

Lastly, we must add that our figures are just averages. You will no doubt feel compelled to leave more than is indicated here if you stay in big cities, fancy hotels, or resort areas—another reason to avoid such places. You have to give a little thought to the whole thing: if you stay in a hotel for just one night, you do not need to strew coins around to everyone when you leave; but if you stay for several days (and particularly if the concierge or head porter has provided you with special services), you will feel obligated to tip.

A last tip for you: if you don't know what an appropriate tip for a service you have received should be, ask the person: "What is a fair tip for you?" Nine times out of ten you'll get a reasonable answer.

Now that we've talked about ways of saving money, let's look at something that's going to cost you: the infamous European Value-Added Tax (called VAT for short, vat of what we leave to you to decide). It is also sometimes called TVA, or BTW, or by other alphabet-soup abbreviations. The VAT, which is only charged on some items, begins at eight percent of the purchase price, and goes as high as thirty percent on "luxury items." This tax can be rebated, at least on purchased items above a price established by law in each country, to any tourist who is going to use the purchase outside of the country of origin. But many stores won't give the rebates at all, and many that do will ask for a fee for doing the necessary paperwork. The personnel of large department stores who are used to dealing with tourists will often just deduct the VAT percentage from the purchased item's price, but small shopkeepers who want to keep the tourists coming will more often just fill out the required forms and remind you to show the forms, your receipt, and the purchased items to the customs people when you leave the country. When this happens, you will later on get a check for the amount of the tax you had to pay. It will be mailed to your home address.

Many people feel that it is just as well to forget it (except, perhaps, for "luxury items") because of the hassles involved. In any case, you will see many "Tax Free" signs, which should not give you the impression that you will necessarily save any money in the stores that so advertise. It is truly a matter to be cynical about, perhaps to the point of figuring that the so-called tax-free shops have doubtlessly marked everything up to cover this "generosity," or feeling that if they won't give you the rebate you're entitled to (without extra fees), you'll buy somewhere else. If you buy a fairly high-priced item to bring home, you should ask the shop proprietor if the cost is high enough to entitle you to a refund. If it is, ask him to fill out the required forms. In the U.K., for example, shopkeepers are not required to fill out these forms for purchases of less than about seventy dollars, but many of them will do so for smaller amounts if asked.

Although we've not tested this theory for ourselves, some people say that the shops which charge value-added taxes can and will wrap, insure, and mail your smaller purchases back to the States for about what your refund should amount to. It might be worthy of exploration.

Basic recommendations for saving money

Like almost everything about liberated travelling, staying within a limited budget requires nothing more than a little good sense. Not only can you not stay in top class hotels in Paris, Monaco, and Palma if you are restricted in the amount of money you can spend, you shouldn't even visit such cities unless you can force yourself to avoid fancy hotels, casinos, and five-star restaurants. If your travel budget is limited, you should plan to try to live in a quieter style than you might adopt when travelling in the United States. You might, for example, consider getting by on one large meal a day (you'll usually get a good "free" breakfast with your room), and think about travelling occasionally at night on the trains in order to avoid room costs. There are many ways to save money when travelling in Europe, and we will offer a few of the basic rules for doing so here.

You'll have to travel light. If you are burdened with heavy bags, or anything that you can't carry comfortably for long distances, it won't work. Taxis in Europe are expensive.

Your plans should be flexible, meaning that it won't ordinarily work to have advance hotel reservations. In Europe you usually have to pay for reservations you don't keep.

You should be willing to ask questions, even naive ones. Doing so, especially about transportation possibilities, can save you money.

You'll need to give up some of your usual ideas of comfort and convenience. American-style comfort in Europe is only available in American-style hotels, which have American-style prices.

Remember that you're there to learn and to have fun, not to participate in a track meet or a road race. The rule of thumb is: the faster and further you go, the more you'll spend.

Don't automatically assume that you have to stay in the biggest city or cities shown on the country's maps. Visits, perhaps; living there, at the high prices that prevail in the metropolitan areas, no.

Don't waste money tipping unless someone has really gone out of his way for you —and then leave only two or three of the smallest coins. Movie ushers expect to be tipped (but not much), and when you see a sign that reads, "Don't forget the guide," you're being told that a tip of approximately twenty to fifty cents is expected. Not *required,* but expected.

Where you go can affect your budget; the next chapter will provide some further thoughts on this.

If you really face budget strictures, don't think about renting cars over there. See Chapter Seven for an analysis of the related costs involved in doing so.

Look for travel bargains such as books of discount bus and tram tickets, museum passes, and round-trip or return-fare discounts.

Try to find out where the natives eat, and have your meals in such places. Doing so can save you as much as fifty percent in food costs.

Keep in mind that your body will be happier while you're putting all those strange foods in it if you get some exercise from walking or biking. Getting sick will cost you time and money.

Learn to deal with Europe's currency and coins. Chapter Six will tell you how—and why.

Start your room-hunting activities before sundown. If you don't, you may end up sleeping in a high-priced hotel.

Find rooms in boardinghouses or pensions whenever and wherever you can.

Know what you're doing if and when you telephone home. See Chapter Twelve for pertinent details.

And lastly, to really enjoy liberated travelling, you should be ready and willing to initiate and encourage conversations with people everywhere. Not only will the tips you'll get increase your knowledge of the country you're visiting, but they'll often save you money.

Later in the book we will be discussing a variety of other ways to save money as you travel, but here we will illustrate one of our fundamentals—that asking questions can save you money—with a small tale about a small train station in a small town in Denmark.

We had tickets for an express train from Copenhagen to Amsterdam, a route that crosses the water via Rødby, Denmark, and Puttgarden, Germany, and then goes across northern Germany toward Holland. Well, in our usual rather careless way of travelling, we had instead meandered west and south of Copenhagen into southern Denmark, stopping in small villages as we went. Finally we found ourselves faced with a crazy problem: to use the tickets we had purchased, we would have to go clear back to Copenhagen, which seemed ridiculous.

Although we knew that our problem was of our own making, and that we'd probably have to buy tickets from where we were down to Hamburg to meet the express train, as well as losing what we'd already paid for from Copenhagen to Hamburg, we went into the train station in this little Danish village and explained our problem. The people there were kind, sympathetic, and helpful. "How nice of you to want to see more of Denmark than your return tickets allowed," they said as they set to work to right things for us. They issued new tickets at no charge from where we were clear to Hamburg, and said when they gave them to us, "Even though there is no charge for these tickets you will have paid a little more by coming here than you would have if you had used your tickets from Copenhagen. If you can wait for some phone calls to be made, maybe we can get that small difference refunded to you."

When we said to forget it, they smiled and said, "Perhaps it was worth a little more to see a little more of Denmark." At that point we certainly thought so ourselves. It was also worth a good bit to ask that first question.

Some friends have related to us another little story which also shows that using your wits and asking questions can be profitable. When they were on their first trip to Europe they landed in Amsterdam. They decided to visit the long dam between the old Zuyder Zee and the North Sea before they had their Eurailpasses validated —so the trip, as they put it, "was to be out of pocket." Early research showed that there were day-long guided bus tours up there for 35 guilders each (about $15 at that time). Not wanting to spend $30 on this jaunt if they could help it, they began to ask some questions of people in the train station. Someone finally told them that they could buy a ticket for one day's unlimited bus travel for 11 guilders each (about $4.70). The buses which provide this particular bargain leave from in front of the central train station, although they subsequently learned that these "Day Rover" tickets are available everywhere in Holland. They took the latter deal, of course, saving more than $20 and giving up the opportunity of having someone face them during the whole trip telling them such things as "there is a Dutch cow" and "that's a windmill." All in all, they were quite pleased with themselves, having saved over twenty bucks—the price of two double rooms and four breakfasts.

We will discuss many other ideas for saving money throughout the rest of the book. For now, if this way of travelling interests you, read on. After providing a few thoughts about where to go and what to expect of Europe, we will delve into such mysteries as those related to language problems, finding rooms, how to eat inexpensively, and how to deal with Europe's mass transit systems. At the end of the book we will offer some suggestions about what to wear and to take with you, as well as money-saving tips for crossing the Atlantic.

For now then, *if* you go, *where* will you go?

Some trips can end up being more expensive than one might have anticipated.

Air France photo

Chapter Three
Whither, Oh Liberated Traveller?

. . . a man must carry knowledge with him if he would
bring home knowledge.
—Spanish proverb

We have already made a strong argument against trying to go too far in Europe, and we hope it made sense to you. Assuming that it did, let's look at some of the facts related to deciding where you will go. The question obviously depends upon your basic interests, the amount of time you will have, and what you feel that you simply can't miss seeing. There are even more basic factors, one of which has to do with which countries are best for people who are travelling independently.

It seems clear that some European countries are less enthusiastic about hosting independent tourists than attracting large organized tour groups. We would name Spain as one example of this. She does get a lot of tour group business, especially from France, England, and Canada, and to some extent from the States, and a person travelling there on his own sees many small indications of a lack of interest in independent travellers. The buses and trains are a bit difficult to use, not many people speak English (even, often, including the tourist information office personnel), and pamphlets and brochures are often printed only in Spanish. It is doubtlessly a wonderful day for a hotel operator anywhere to have fifty or a hundred foreigners taking rooms, as opposed to just one or two of us, and we have the idea that that pretty much composes Spain's way of thinking yet about tourism. We're sure that it is something that will change, perhaps soon, but today it is a bit tough there for anyone who hasn't a fair command of the Spanish language.

Obviously a country's attitude toward tourism is an important factor to anyone like you who does not wish to be dragged about by a multilingual guide. In the places where some thought seems to have been given to making life easy for you, whether you're alone or just with your spouse, it can be very pleasant. Countries that we think have tried to make their tourist information offices really effective, their rail systems easy to use, etc., include England, Denmark, Holland, Switzerland, Austria, Belgium, and Germany.

So it might be wise, particularly if you are a first-time traveller, to begin your adventures in one of the countries where such things can be worked fairly effectively, and save the places that are a little harder for the end of the trip—or for another visit to Europe. You can get over the idea of feeling like a boob pretty quickly where the problems aren't too difficult, and you can even learn how to surmount or circumvent your problems in such places, but it can be a real bother if you go first to an area where you lose every little battle. What you are planning to do is going to be a challenge to you wherever you go, but it is harder in some countries than in others.

Now we must discuss the personal factors that may be important to you. Do you want to bicycle? That's possible over much of Europe, and it is easy and inexpensive to rent bikes. But unless you like wheeling up and down mountains, Belgium, Holland, Denmark, and the northern parts of Germany and France are most ideal for two-wheeled adventures. Do you want to hike? That's good anywhere. Do you wish to camp out? Camping is popular in every Western European country. Do you enjoy music or art? If so, you will probably want to visit some of the large cities, although you will find great works of art and fine concerts even in the hamlets. Do you wish to see what Europe was like centuries ago? That's possible in many places (a high percentage of cities and towns have old-town areas), and castles and fortresses are everywhere, but especially along the Rhine in Germany. Two of the most beautiful are near Fussen, Germany. One of these in particular, Neuschwanstein, looks like Walt Disney with taste. In fact, it is; it served as the model for the structure at Disneyland. Good food? Every place except England, and for people with limited budgets, Spain. France deservedly holds the honors here. We suspect that the worst food the French eat is better than *our* best.

If you are interested in bright lights and nightclubbing, you are going to be drawn to the large cities—and you will find that such entertainments, as here, are not cheap. If you prefer a quieter sort of night life, you may well be attracted, as we are, to the smaller villages. While we have to confess that some of these little places can be awfully quiet in the evenings, they often have a certain magic about them, especially after the sun goes down. It's hard to describe, and we don't find it in the large cities at all. Perhaps it is sort of what the world you saw as a child was like— clean, pleasant, enjoyable, and fascinating. Do you remember? What ever happened to that world we saw then? Have we just become busier, more cynical, hardened, or older, or has it disappeared from America? We still find it on our evening walks in the small towns and villages of Europe. But indeed, as native-born, middle-class, middle-Americans, we had no dreams ages ago of canals, huge mountains, cobblestoned streets, windmills, walled towns, or castles; what we did see, like you, was a world that had a certain amount of mystery, that was populated by strange people who said incomprehensible things (adults), and that sometimes had a fine magic about it. If you are lucky, you can again sense and enjoy that strange world in Europe. The aura of strangeness, of being just slightly out of focus, is very much like what most of us experienced as children. Their big cities seem very much like *our* big cities to us, but the little towns often have that long-forgotten mysteriousness about them. It can be a joy if you can find that again. And that may be the best argument of all for visiting and staying in the smaller towns of Europe.

Europe's small towns can have a certain magic, especially at night.   York, England, Dept. of Tourism photo

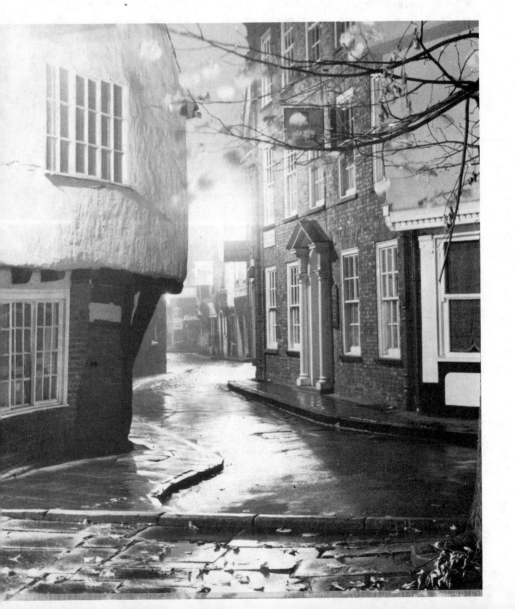

There are numerous cities in Europe that are considerably larger than villages which we have visited and enjoyed immensely, places like Berne, Innsbruck, Salzburg, and Venice. But you will find, as we have, that it is easy to get lost in cities as large as Paris, Rome, or London, that they are often dirty and industrialized, and that prices for everything (except clothes) are usually higher than one finds in the small places. As we suggested earlier, you have an option: you can stay in the small towns outside of the cities and take the trains in to visit the museums, go to concerts, or whatever. What we are opposed to is the idea that one has to *live* in the cities, even temporarily, or, worse yet, to visit *only* the cities. We are convinced that to meet the people and to get an idea of what life is really like in any given country, you have to visit the countryside.

But we have a suspicion that even American tourists who aren't all that crazy about art (*i.e.,* people who haven't been to an art museum in the States for years) automatically assume that they must visit the country's largest metropolis to tour its art museums. If one really loves fine art, then he *should* visit cities like Amsterdam, Paris, and Madrid—but if he doesn't, it can be a mistake. In the same way, some tourists feel it essential to see Amsterdam's canals, almost as if they didn't know that all of Holland is covered by canals, most of which are cleaner than Amsterdam's.

One sometimes hears Europeans discussing their own views of their cities in this way: "I won't go into Amsterdam (Paris, Rome, etc.) if I can help it, and I know the language, and what goes on there, and how to stay out of trouble." They will inform you that they do have drug problems in their cities, and, consequently, people who prey on innocents in order to feed their habits. They exaggerate, we think, but who wants to do a survey to find out whether or not it's true?

There is one other point to consider on this big-versus-small-town question. If you happen to want to see small, out-of-the-way places, you have no choice but to travel on your own. The guided tours generally take you only to the larger cities, *i.e.,* no smaller than Innsbruck or Venice.

There is one other matter you might wish to give careful consideration, and that is the question of *when* to go. We have been in Europe during various times of the year (a couple for all seasons?) and would generalize about the matter in this way. Summer is the worst time to go, because that's when everyone goes, and that's when prices are consequently the highest. During winter Europe is pretty much American-tourist-free, which is great, but the flowers are mostly gone, many things one would like to see are closed, and the weather can be unpleasant—although in most places not as unpleasant as you might imagine. But the days are short, and usually sort of grey, which is bad both for sightseeing and for taking pictures. The best times, we think, are what the airlines used to call the shoulder seasons, April-May and September-October. During these periods the weather is usually nice enough for walking and bicycling, most of the "sights" are open (although some of them do close as early as October 1 and do not re-open until May 1 or May 15), and you are not continuously crowded off the walks by other camera-carrying gawkers. May or September would be ideal if you can arrange it. If you are not going on a charter flight and wish to go in the spring, you should consider buying a ticket for a departure of no later than the last day of the low season. If you are going in the fall, plan to go no earlier than the day after the high season is over. We will explain this in more detail in Chapter Eighteen.

Winter (the off-season in Europe, excepting the skiing areas of Italy, France, Germany, Switzerland, and Austria) is somewhat surprising in that there are still a lot of tourists—they just aren't Americans or Canadians, generally speaking. But it is clear that thanks to the absence of North American visitors, there are usually far fewer people bumping into you wherever you go. Prices, for example for rooms, are sometimes less—but not always. It is surprising to learn that some hotel owners do not reduce room prices during off-season periods. Apparently the reason is that winters are fairly nice, and the natives (including the many who must stay home and mind the store, or pension, or whatever, in the summer) are on the move. Having tried it both ways, we conclude that an off-season visitor will certainly find smaller crowds and prices than a high-season tourist will—but perhaps not so much smaller as one might guess. Late spring or early fall are ideal, everything considered.

Here is a stunning argument for off-season travel.

Austrian National Tourist Office photo

For people who just can't get away except in the summer months, June is by far the best choice. June is not considered the real high season in much of Europe, simply because the school children there do not begin their summer vacations until the end of June or even the middle of July, which means that Europeans can't travel until mid or late summer. So July and August are the months with the highest prices, the most tourists, and the hottest weather.

Next to the lower air fares, perhaps the greatest advantage of off-season travel is that Europeans who like tourists (and there are many who do, believe it or not), are pleasantly surprised to see you if it is not July or August. "Why are you here now?" they ask. Any answer you give will interest them because they seem to believe that one of the peculiarities of hot weather is that it brings out hordes of Homo Americanus, a genus that is pretty much unknown in the cooler parts of the year. It is clear that many of the best people-to-people things happen when they recognize that you are not just an ordinary American or Canadian tourist or businessperson.

People who dislike large crowds would be wise to consider avoiding places that are having big special events. In 1977, for example, so many tourists went to Antwerp for the "Rubens Year" it took hours to gain entrance to the Royal Art Gallery. Even after the high season was over, people had to wait in three lines, the first two just getting them into the main line to get into the building. The gallery and P.P. Rubens works of art will still be there in other years, and will be a lot easier to get in to see. If you have no choice about visiting during such crowded occasions, try to get there early—and take your patience with you.

If you aren't absolutely fixed on every point of your itinerary, it is a fine thing to have the independence of mind to switch directions occasionally. Sometimes such alterations in planned routes happen accidentally, and when they do, it's great if you can laugh it off—as two young American girls we met in Freiburg, Germany, were able to do. They told us that they had just come from Fribourg, Switzerland. "Someone told us that Freiburg was great," they said. "So we bought our train tickets and ended up in Fribourg, Switzerland." We all laughed. "It was a stupid mistake," they said, still giggling. "But the Swiss town was great too, and we spent several days there. Anyway, we've made a pact: whenever either of us ever talks to anyone who's going to Europe, we are going to say, 'Be sure to visit Freiburg' just like our friend told us. We think it's good advice; you can't miss no matter which one you go to."

And you can't miss if you are flexible enough to change your mind here and there, whatever the reason is for doing so.

If you are free of compulsions to travel as far and as fast as possible, and would like to settle down here and there and, rather than living out of a suitcase every night, see an area in some detail, Europe has a new sort of program to offer you. Liechtenstein's version, which is one of the best ones, is described in Chapter 16. Like most good ideas, the concept is simple: you make arrangements to spend three to ten days in a given location, in return for which you get high discounts on accommodations, meals, sports activities, visits to museums and art galleries, and so on. These programs differ from place to place and season to season, but generally they provide the possibility of making day trips into the countryside from a given spot, and then returning that evening to ''home'' (a room that has your dirty clothes scattered about).

There are many such programs, and we have examined only a few of them in detail, but generally they seem to us to be a good, economical way to enjoy and to learn something about Europe. If the idea interests you, ask the national tourist office(s) that represent the country or countries you want to visit for more information. We will discuss a few other examples of these programs in Chapter 16.

Generalizations about a few countries

Here are some brief impressions of some of the countries you might wish to visit. We will expand upon them in later chapters. Here and in other places throughout the book we will also be trying to characterize various cities for one reason or another. We will not, however, describe or even mention most of the towns we have visited, nor do we intend to try to tell you where *you* should go. We leave that to your own imagination. Because our main intention is to tell you how to get around, enjoy yourself while doing it, and survive once you get somewhere, we will discuss particular places primarily from the standpoint of liberated travelling.

Before we discuss specific countries, however, let's have a quick look at how some of them have close relationships with each other—which, if nothing else, will avoid misunderstandings when the names of these combinations are used later.

One of the best known is the United Kingdom, which includes England, Wales, Scotland, and Northern Ireland. The Republic of Ireland is a separate country.

Luxembourg and Belgium are close, sharing (to an extent) languages, currencies, and trade benefits.

Liechtenstein and Switzerland are friendly, both using the Swiss franc, the German language, and the Swiss Holiday train pass.

Scandinavia consists of five countries that have close relationships: Denmark, Finland, Iceland, Norway, and Sweden.

The Benelux countries—Holland, Belgium and Luxembourg—form a kind of loose-knit federation, but the countries are rather different from each other. Although architectural styles and geographical features don't differ much from one to the other, languages, clothing, and attitudes toward life do.

Holland has a pleasant rural and seagoing character. Amsterdam is fairly cosmopolitan, at least in outward appearances and in both good and bad senses of the term, but Rotterdam and The Hague are less so, and the smaller towns and villages are ordinarily downright provincial. The whole country is pretty much that way, which is part of its charm to outsiders. One feels he has really seen a rustic after he's encountered a Dutch farmer, fisherman, or housewife in their traditional garb—including wooden shoes. The Dutch virtues, cleanliness, frugality, and the results of these attitudes, make Holland a little different from any other country.

Belgium, by contrast, is more cosmopolitan, more French, one might say, than its neighbor. This is particularly apparent in Brussels, where French cooking, manners, and speech are common. But indeed the Belgians are generally friendlier than the French, and more able to deal with the queer behavior of foreigners than the Dutch. This tiny country serves as the headquarters of NATO and the European Common Market, and the people there—at least the Brusselites—are pretty worldly as a consequence.

Luxembourg is neither worldly nor rustic—it is tourist country. Luxembourg City, which is about all that most tourists see of the place, is a menage of hotels, souvenir shops, and travel offices. The Luxembourgers are basically friendly enough, but the impression that most tourists get of them is that their strong suit is selling postcards and overnight accommodations.

It is not easy to tell when you cross the border from one of these three countries to another (indeed, it isn't even necessary to show your passport for one of these crossings), but if your senses are at all attuned to differences, you'll see some when you deal with the people who live in these three small countries.

France is beautiful. It offers everything to the tourist: mountains, beaches, little hamlets, and big cities—including Paris, a huge, fascinating metropolis that pretty well lives up to its reputation as the most elegant place on earth. But as incredible as it is, Paris is certainly a very large and not especially friendly city, and it (and France generally) can be horrendously expensive unless you are very careful with your money.

Here it must also be said that France is not a good place for the first-time independent traveller to begin his explorations. At the *end* of a visit to Europe, after he had gotten some problem-solving experience, the visitor might be able to enjoy France, but we think he'd be better off to get the initital experience elsewhere.

Like France, Italy is an extremely attractive country that gives the visitor a spectrum of sights and sensations ranging from mountains to some of the world's most exciting art and architecture. Italy has endured a great deal over the past (and is still facing terrible political and economic problems), but today it is a favorite country for sightseers everywhere. And it should be. All roads do lead to Rome, and its other world-famous cities, such as Florence and Venice, are magnets to travellers who have a sense of history and a love for great art and music.

In the recent past the country has been strike-ridden, and it has faced other sorts of upheavals as well. But from the visitor's standpoint, the tourist offices are effective, and the country is not comparatively expensive yet. But be wary; there is a terrible inflation problem, and prices may not remain particularly appealing much longer.

Britain, of course, is one of the top targets for American tourists, partly because of the close ties between the two countries and partly because the American will face no real language barriers there. Like Italy, England is beset by problems these days, but some of these difficulties are to the traveller's advantage, *e.g.,* the favorable exchange rate that exists at this writing between American dollars and English pounds.

One of the best arguments for visiting the British Isles on a European exploration has to do with going there *first*. We have already discussed the degree of culture shock involved in arriving out of the blue (so to speak) into a country where you can't understand what anyone says, can't read any sign you see, and can't understand the coin of the realm. If visited first, the countries of the United Kingdom reduce this sort of culture shock by fifty per cent or more. There you can speak to the nationals (although some of their responses will be difficult to understand), you can read the signs (although some of them will have words which are spelled in amusing ways), and you can understand the coins and currency (Britain has finally adopted a decimal currency, like other European countries, that is similar to American or Canadian money).

England is very different from the United States, but it certainly doesn't strike the person who is visiting Europe for the first time as completely alien. Not only is it simple and easy to read menus there, as well as signs at bus stops, but you can also ask dumb questions of anyone you meet and have a seventy-five-percent chance of understanding their answers. If you can arrange to visit England before you go to the Continent, you will find that you've reduced your ice-cold-shower culture shock to more of a toe-in-the-water-before-leaping-in sort of change in life-style.

Austria is the *Sound of Music* brought to life. It is covered by mountains that equal or exceed the beauty of Switzerland's, not to mention lovely little villages that are frequently found nestling in the deep valleys looking like calendar scenes rather than the homes of hard-working farmers. Generally Austria doesn't seem to be as expensive as many of the European countries, and it is certainly an enjoyable place to visit.

Switzerland is probably almost as fine as the Swiss think it is. It is almost four countries, Swiss, German, Italian, and French, and the variations in language, dress, and food that reflect these nationalities are apparent in different parts of the country. There are picturesque villages everywhere, not to mention such fine sights as snow fields, waterfalls, and glaciers.

But Switzerland is an expensive country, and tourists there often feel that they are appreciated more for their money than for themselves. But is is certainly full of marvelous sights, and it seems to be high season there all year around for visitors and for the Swiss who make their living merchandising food, drinks, rooms, watches, and winter sports.

Germany is a land of many contrasts. You can take a boat down the Rhine, visit or sleep in a castle, go back in time hundreds of years, see incredible cathedrals, visit great centers of industry, or camp up in the mountains. Many of the larger cities like Hamburg and Munich are pretty heavily industrialized and consequently crowded with mobs of people and automobiles. But the small villages are often idyllic, and the really ancient towns, for example the ones that lie along the famous Romantic Road, will show you exactly what the dim past looked like. Prices in Germany are pretty high, but it is still possible for a traveller on a budget to have a good time there.

Sunny Spain has a lot to recommend it. For one thing, it's relatively inexpensive. It offers visitors a great variety, not only in providing beaches on both the Atlantic and the Mediterranean, but also mountains, forests, and winding rivers. Its architecture encompasses nearly every kind known to man, including Arabic, Moorish, and early Roman. It also has some beautiful towns near the southern French border, such as the Monacoesque resort of San Sebastián. It is a country of white buildings, red roofs, tiles and glazed bricks, stone walls, courtyards, and weirdly decorated spires and towers. By European standards it is a very large country, so visitors who travel on the ground have to budget quite a lot of time to get from place to place. This is also true because many of the country's trains are slow, and they often miss their scheduled arrival times—occasionally by quite a lot. And summer is not a good time to visit; it gets so hot there that even government officials close their offices in late summer and move their business to the northern seacoast. As stated earlier, it is not an ideal country in which to learn how to travel independently for a first-time visitor to Europe.

It seems clear that the way to go into the French-Italian Riviera—Monaco, Monte Carlo, Nice, Cannes, and San Remo—would be aboard a great white ocean-going yacht. It is indeed one of the playgrounds of the world's rich, but it is possible to do the area in a more modest style. Not everyone there is a millionaire, and you needn't be either. You can swim for free in the Mediterranean, and you can live very nicely for a few dollars a day. You can also sit in the sidewalk cafes and rub elbows with people who are not pinching francs.

Belgium, as small as it is, is a very important European country, being the headquarters of the European Common Market. Although it has less than ten million inhabitants, it has more than eight hundred people per square mile, making it one of the most densely populated areas of the world. Popular towns with American visitors are Bruges and Ghent, both of which are near Brussels and are marvelous ancient cities to be explored on foot or by bicycle. It is a fairly easy and pleasant country for liberated travellers, partly, no doubt, because the Belgians like tourists and are used to foreigners of every description.

During 1979 Brussels celebrated her 1000th birthday, and during 1980 Belgium commemorated its 150th year as an independent country.

The land of great explorers, Portugal today is enduring hard times. This is apparent to visitors when they see the down-and-outers and gypsy con-artists (especially in Lisbon), the occasional disintegrating buildings, the political slogans painted everywhere, and the many Portuguese sitting around who are simply people who cannot find anything productive to do. The gypsies are often trying to sell fake wristwatches and ''gold'' rings, and they can be annoying if they aren't turned off quickly and authoritatively.

But lush, green, tropical Portugal offers the visitor a number of counterbalancing factors. There one finds fine weather year around, miles of splendid beaches, wonderfully friendly people, and proportionately low prices. The latter factor provides the tourist with the possibility of inexpensive rooms, meals and ground transportation.

One of Portugal's most interesting sights is the bullfight. Here they do not murder the animal. Instead they treat you to a panorama of sights, sounds, and colors: brave cape-work; beautiful dancing horses; and the spectacle of barehanded men wrestling with the enraged bull. For more on this sport, see Chapter 14.

We have found Denmark (and the rest of Scandinavia, for that matter) to be very expensive. In addition, these areas are quite far from what one might think of as the center of Europe. On the other hand, a novice liberated traveller couldn't find a better place than Denmark to learn how to travel without professional help. The country is splendid, the people are great, and everything having to do with getting from here to there has been made understandable and simple. The tourist offices, marked by green and white signs showing a lower case ''i'', are excellent, their personnel being quite friendly and helpful.

Copenhagen is large, brightly lighted, and, again, expensive. The city has about one million people, one-third of whom own bicycles. It is a city of open sex, open-faced sandwiches, and interesting old buildings—many of which are open for visits. It has a large port area watched over by ''the most photographed lady in the world,'' the Little Mermaid. Pension accommodations are available, but, generally speaking, only during the high season. And any traveller who has the least interest in how he spends his money and his time has to reckon with Copenhagen's location. It is more than twelve hours from Amsterdam by the fastest express train.

Southern Denmark is charming. The area is covered by small villages, many of which have a fairy-tale look about them. Tourists who are short in time or money could get a good impression of Denmark in this general area, just above Germany, without going so far from the center of Europe as Copenhagen.

Like Denmark, Sweden is expensive, and as you can see on any map, it is a lot larger. Extending up through the Arctic Circle, it is populated in its northernmost parts by reindeer and Laplanders. It is a long, long way from the middle of Europe, a fact that anyone contemplating visiting there must consider. But it is just a short jump across the water from Denmark. People usually cross from Copenhagen to Malmo, or from a half-hour's train ride north of Copenhagen, from Helsingør (called Elsinor, its castle is popularly but inaccurately referred to as Hamlet's) to Helsingbord. Generally we have been pleased with the tourist offices we've visited there. The Swedes claim that they like tourists, and their tourist offices are sufficiently pleasant to make you believe the statement. But off-season travellers should note that these information offices in smaller towns and villages are open only from the 15th of May to September 1st.

No one has ever set foot on all the Greek islands, as an old saying goes, and it's no doubt true. One suspects that all of Greece's islands haven't even been counted, let alone trod upon. Greece is a surprising country to visitors in many ways. It may indeed have been the home of civilization, but it's also a modern country. It is not so "foreign" as you might expect. For example, English is officially the second language in Greece. And monies of other countries are accepted without a blink nearly everywhere.

Here are a few other surprises having to do with travelling in Greece. Rather than tourist offices, you usually find "Tourist Police," who can be recognized by having those words on their uniform and little flags which tell what languages they understand and speak. You ordinarily have to pay about $1.50 extra (beyond entrance fees) to take pictures in museums. It is either expensive (flying) or time-consuming (sailing) to reach the outermost places, *e.g.*, Rhodes, Crete or Corfu. Motor vehicles seem to have the absolute right-of-way everywhere and at all times in Greece. Watch yourself; you could be run down. *Look both right and left* before crossing streets. And lastly, walking shorts on men or women are accepted in Greece, but not in monasteries, churches, or cathedrals.

And here are some surprises you can observe everywhere. Many place names, even when spelled with Roman letters rather than Greek letters, are spelled in slightly different ways on different signs or in different pieces of literature. You can buy beer and booze in the pastry shops, and pastries in the tavernas (not to mention excellent sandwiches!) You can use the telephone for local calls at many businesses (and particularly at sidewalk kiosks) just by handing over two drachmas (around 5c). "Supermarket" is a word commonly seen on signs on stores in Greece. They are *not* supermarkets in our sense of the term, and many of them are not even grocery stores. Can you imagine a hardware "supermarket" that is about 10 by 20 feet? This lovely country is HOT and packed with tourists during July, August, and September.

Scotland may be the most undersold of all of Europe's countries. If this is so we do not know why. Perhaps the British Tourist Authority, which bears the responsibility for telling the world about Northern Ireland, Scotland, Wales, and England, has not given Scotland the attention or publicity that it deserves.

Edinburgh is so attractive that we have made an exception to our rule of not talking about Europe's capitals (see Chapter 16). Its cities whose names are known around the world, Inverness, Dundee, Perth, and so on, are all well worth visiting. Its many incredible lochs (lakes, if you wish) are incomparable sights, and its countless seaside towns and island villages are magnetic attractions for visitors and shutterbugs.

Scotland's prices are reasonable, distances are short, the scenery is magnificent, and the inhabitants are wonderful. As this book makes clear, we have a tendency to say exactly what we think, but in this case we will quote what other people think: we have never met anyone who has visited Scotland who hasn't fallen in love with the country and the people who live there.

No wonder Ireland's color is green. The whole country is adorned in multi-hued shades of green like a fine garden. And in a land that has produced such giants as Yeats, Joyce, Behan, Swift, Burke, Goldsmith, Shaw, and Wilde, it's small wonder that every Irishman seems to consider himself a man of letters, a wit, and a raconteur—not to mention a man who can hold his liquor, sing, and tell jokes even about himself. Everyone, nearly everyone has a ready smile on his face.

The country is not expensive for visitors, partly because it is covered by B and B's, guest houses, and farm houses that offer reasonably priced lodgings. It is also covered with sights: pleasant little farms, castles, fishing villages, old ruins, delightfully old-fashioned pubs, hills and mountains, and pretty homes sporting the most colorful doors one could imagine.

Dublin, the capital, while not the most exciting city we've ever visited, has its share of charms. First and foremost of these is that nearly everyone you meet will give you a friendly smile and, if you encourage it, friendly conversation as well. Listen to this typical toast, for example: "May you be in Heaven half an hour before the Devil knows you are dead." There are some nice and fairly inexpensive day-trips to interesting spots outside Dublin, and perhaps the best bargain of all is to take doubledeck bus #33 from the city center to Enniskerry. This little village is often called Ireland's fairest, and it deserves the title.

Dublin also has fine theatre to offer, with the Abbey being the national play-house. The annual theatre festival, offering many premieres, is held in late September and early October.

And until you've heard the singing that often prevails in Irish pubs, you ain't heard nuthin!

Iceland is one of Europe's great surprises. Many visitors love the place—and we number ourselves among them. It is a misnamed country; it really doesn't get that cold there. In fact, with all its steaming geysers and active volcanoes it's pretty warm, at least underground. The Icelanders use that warmth to heat their homes and offices. Any traveller who is attracted by the unusual would be wise to consider a stop in Iceland, and anyone who passes through the place (*e.g.*, with Icelandic Airlines) should give thought to buying one of the available stopover packages. We'll describe how it works in Chapter Eighteen.

As everyone knows, Holland is a land of flowers, canals, and windmills. It is also about fifty percent larger now than it was originally, thanks to its industrious inhabitants. But it is still tiny, encompassing only about sixteen thousand square miles. It is a diverse country, much of it very old, while other parts are quite new, the land having been stolen from the sea in recent years. It is an excellent country for the first-time traveller to learn how to go it alone because its generally excellent tourist offices are everywhere, its train system is easy to use, and it is relatively inexpensive (at least outside Rotterdam, The Hague, and Amsterdam). It is one of Europe's great surprises, partly because it offers some sights that cannot be seen anywhere else in the world. We will still explain this a bit further in Chapter Fifteen.

Now we will make a suggestion having to do with some countries we've never been in—although we hope to visit them in the future. But logic, if nothing else, suggests that if you can't afford the countries with the popular names—those situated across central western Europe that we have just mentioned—you might consider the eastern European countries: Bulgaria, Czechoslovakia, Rumania, Hungary, Albania, Poland, Yugoslavia, and the U.S.S.R. Although they are all obviously different from one another in many ways, they have one thing in common from our viewpoint. They are, generally speaking, considerably less expensive than the central western countries. Russia, which is said to be very expensive these days, is an exception.

We hear tales about beautiful rooms and all three meals for ten dollars a day or less in these eastern countries, about their inflation rates over the last few years being very small, about fantastic government-subsidized travel arrangements, and about the possibilities of seeing beautiful and memorable sights for very, very low expenditures. And it is said that pretty much everything seems to be open in all of the eastern countries except for Russia, where a bureaucracy named Intourist makes your decisions for you. Judging from what people who have been there have told us, we haven't been able to generate much enthusiasm for travelling in the U.S.S.R. One hears too many tales about high prices, not being able to go where you wish, and bureaucratic lassitude (even in Intourist) to feel very excited about the possibility.

While all of the other Eastern European countries are comparatively inexpensive, we have the impression from the tales of our friends that Hungary, Czechoslovakia, Poland, and Rumania are "best buys" these days for American tourists. At any rate, if any of them interest you, you can investigate further by writing to their respective national tourist offices. And the American Automobile Association has a booklet, "Travel Guide—Eastern Europe" that provides excellent information about them. It certainly catches one's attention to read a boast by Yugoslavia that a visitor can spend fifteen days on the Adriatic Coast for what it would cost to spend only *nine* days in western Europe, especially when you also hear that other countries of eastern Europe are even easier on your pocketbook.

The eastern European countries do require visas, but these documents are simple and inexpensive to obtain through the respective countries' embassies or consulates in the United States.

Other sources of information

One thing you can do to help with your planning is to write to the various national tourist agencies in the U.S. They will send you a wealth of free information, especially if you ask the right questions. Be explicit. If you plan to do some hiking, tell them, and they will send you information about hiking trails (which, for example, blanket even the mountainous areas of Switzerland). If bicycling is your thing (God bless you!), they can tell you where to rent the machines and the best places to ride. Ask for city maps of any of the towns that interest you. You'll get them, at least if the towns you mention are of any size at all. Ask for information on the prices and accommodations in hotels, pensions, and private homes. Ask for available discount coupons that can be used for eating, shopping, and sightseeing. Ask anything and everything; the chances are that you'll get some kinds of answers. These are professionals you're dealing with, and their business is to answer your questions.

Here is an alphabetical listing of the national tourist offices in Canada and the United States.

AUSTRIA

Austrian National Tourist Office
200 E. Randolph Dr., Suite 7023
Chicago, Illinois 60601

3440 Wilshire Blvd.
Los Angeles, California 90010

1010 Ouest Rue Sherbrooke
Montreal, Quebec, Canada H3A 2R7

545 Fifth Avenue
New York, New York 10017

1007 N.W. 24th Avenue
Portland, Oregon 97210

2 Bloor Street East
Toronto, Ontario, Canada M4W 1A8

736 Granville Street
Vancouver, British Columbia,
Canada V 62 1J2

BELGIUM

Belgian National Tourist Office
745 Fifth Avenue
New York, New York 10022

DENMARK

Danish National Tourist Office
75 Rockefeller Plaza
New York, New York 10019

3600 Wilshire Blvd.
Los Angeles, California 90010

151 Bloor Street West
Toronto, Ontario, Canada M5S 1S4

FINLAND

Finland National Tourist Office
75 Rockefeller Plaza
New York, New York 10019

3600 Wilshire Blvd.
Los Angeles, California 90010

FRANCE

French Government Tourist Office
9401 Wilshire Blvd., Suite 314
Beverly Hills, California 90212

645 N. Michigan Avenue
Chicago, Illinois 60611

1940 W. Sherbrooke
Montreal, Quebec, Canada H3A 2R7

610 Fifth Avenue
New York, New York 10020

323 Geary Street
San Francisco, California 94102

372 Bay Street, Suite 610
Toronto, Canada M5H 2W9

GERMANY

German National Tourist Office
104 S. Michigan Avenue
Chicago, Illinois 60603

700 S. Flower Street
Los Angeles, California 90017

2 Fundy, P.O. Box 417
Place Bonaventure
Montreal, Canada H5A 1B8

630 Fifth Avenue
New York, New York 10020

GREAT BRITAIN

British Tourist Authority
John Hancock Center, Suite 3320
875 North Michigan Avenue
Chicago, Illinois 60611

Suite 2115, Empire Life Building
1712 Commerce Street
Dallas, Texas 75201

612 South Flower Street
Los Angeles, California 90017

680 Fifth Avenue
New York, New York 10019

151 Bloor Street West
Toronto, Ontario, Canada M4W 1A8

GREECE

Greek National Tourist Organization
168 N. Michigan Avenue
Chicago, Illinois 60601

627 West 6th Street
Los Angeles, California 90017

2 Place Ville Marie
Montreal, Quebec, Canada H3B 2C9

645 Fifth Avenue
New York, New York 10022

2211 Massachusetts Avenue, N.W.
Washington, D.C. 20008

ICELAND

Icelandic National Tourist Office
75 Rockefeller Plaza
New York, New York 10019

3600 Wilshire Boulevard
Los Angeles, California 90010

IRELAND

Irish Tourist Board
230 N. Michigan Avenue
Chicago, Illinois 60601

510 W. 6th Street, Suite 317
Los Angeles, California 90014

590 Fifth Avenue
New York, New York 10036

681 Market Street
San Francisco, California 94105

69 Yonge Street
Toronto, Canada M5E 1K3

ITALY

Italian Government Travel Office
500 N. Michigan Avenue
Chicago, Illinois 60611

3 Place Ville Marie
Montreal, Quebec, Canada

630 Fifth Avenue
New York, New York 10020

360 Post Street
San Francisco, California 94119

LIECHTENSTEIN

All Swiss National Tourist Offices
provide information on their small
neighbor.

LUXEMBOURG

Luxembourg Tourist Information Office
One Dag Hammarskjold Plaza
New York, New York 10017

MONACO

Monaco Government Tourist Office
New York, New York 10017

NETHERLANDS

Netherlands Information Service
City Hall
Holland, Michigan 49423

Netherlands National Tourist Office
576 Fifth Avenue
New York, New York 10036

681 Market Street
San Francisco, California

Toronto Dominion Center
P.O. Box 311
Royal Trust Tower, Ste. 3114
Toronto, Ontario, Canada M5K 1Ks

NORWAY

Norwegian National Tourist Office
75 Rockefeller Plaza
New York, New York 10019

3600 Wilshire Blvd.
Los Angeles, California 90010

PORTUGAL

Portuguese National Tourist Office
The Palmer House
17 East Monroe Street, Room 500
Chicago, Illinois 60603

1 Park Plaza, Suite 1305
3250 Wilshire Blvd.
Los Angeles, California 90010

1801 McGill College Avenue
Montreal, Canada

548 Fifth Avenue
New York, New York 10036

390 Bay Street, Suite 1718
Toronto, Canada M5H 2Y2

SCANDINAVIA

Scandinavian National
Tourist Office
(Denmark/Finland/Iceland/
Norway/Sweden)
3600 Wilshire Blvd.
Los Angeles, California 90010

75 Rockefeller Plaza
New York, New York 10019

SPAIN

Spanish National Tourist Office
Suite 915 East
845 North Michigan Avenue
Chicago, Illinois 60611

665 Fifth Avenue
New York, New York 10022

Hypolita and St. George Streets
St. Augustine, Florida 32084

3160 Lyon Street
San Francisco, California 94123

60 Bloor Street, West
Toronto, Ontario, Canada M4W 1A8

SWEDEN

Swedish National Tourist Office
75 Rockefeller Plaza
New York, New York 10019

3600 Wilshire Blvd.
Los Angeles, California 90010

SWITZERLAND

Swiss National Tourist Office
104 South Michigan Avenue
Chicago, Illinois 60603

4 Frontenac, Place Bonaventure
P.O. Box 1162
Montreal, Quebec, Canada H5A 1G5

608 Fifth Avenue
New York, New York 10020

250 Stockton Street
San Francisco, California 94105

Commerce Court West
Toronto, Ontario, Canada M5L 1E8

*Modern Iceland
is still prehistoric
in appearance.*

Another possibility you might consider is to talk to other people who have been there. People usually like to tell about their experiences and to give advice, so encourage them to do so. People who have been G.I.s in Europe are good candidates for this; you can be sure they didn't travel like royalty.

It is almost too obvious to say that a good travel agent can give you immeasurable help. Certainly some are better than others, but most of them work hard to keep up on the latest travel information and they can give you good advice. You should realize, however, that they make their income from commissions paid by airlines and tour-group companies; they are not in business just to give advice. But you can certainly feel free to ask them for further help if you order Eurailpasses or your transatlantic flight tickets through them. And if you wish to check on their standing in their profession, look to see if they display evidence of belonging to A.S.T.A. (American Society of Travel Agents). If they do, they at least have some experience in the travel business. If you wish to check them out a bit more, call the nearest Better Business Bureau.

If you make your plans as you go along, in every country you visit you can go to the national tourist office of the *next* country on your schedule and get maps, brochures, listings of pensions and hotels, etc. As in the U.S., this will get you the literature free of charge, and allow you to do a little advance scheming on the train going to wherever is next.

You should also read other travel books. There are many good ones, but certainly the Michelin Guides have to be high on anyone's list. They are accurate, comprehensive, and invariably up-to-date. By contrast, we do not feel so constrained to give top marks to the book that many travellers consider to be their bible, Frommer's *Europe on 15 Dollars a Day.* We have checked on some of the budget hotels and pensions he recommends, and we've found many of them to be closed, or to have higher prices than he quoted (reflecting a recent price hike made possible, no doubt, by the mention in Frommer). But our main beef against "15 Dollars a Day" has to do with the implication that one can live for anything like that in Europe these days. We have travelled as frugally as anyone this side of a Bulgarian gypsy could, and we couldn't do it—and we don't think anyone else, unless he is carrying a back pack and a sleeping bag, can do it either. Nevertheless, Mr. Frommer does publish well-written, interesting books, and his tips on what to see and how to conserve funds are often excellent. Perhaps he, like all the rest of us, is just a victim of inflation.

One such book that we do like is *Let's Go; Europe,* a sprightly, informative publication that is written by Harvard students and brought up to date each year. It is clearly addressed primarily to young people and, perhaps for that reason, it suggests flexibility and frugality, and it provides many good tips for saving money.

The other well-known travel books all have their vices and their virtues. We are generally impressed with the travel guides written by Eugene Fodor, Temple Fielding, and Myra Waldo. All of them are well written, and they provide information about nearly everything you need to know to visit the countries they discuss. They are especially comprehensive in their discussion of the larger cities. Fielding often seems to display considerable bias on a number of subjects, but we give him credit for including warnings about the possibility of being robbed or cheated in various places.

Neither Mr. Fodor nor Mr. Fielding recognize liberated travelling as either sensible or practical. Ms. Waldo, on the other hand, calls it "the ideal way to do it" with three provisos: if you have someone for a travelling companion, if you can avoid the worst of the high season, and if you "have that wonderful sort of nature that can bear up gracefully under all sorts of petty annoyances." We couldn't agree more.

Lawrence and Sylvia Martin's guides are good, partly because they are so readable, and partly because the Martins occasionally include themselves in the portraits they present. Sydney Clark's "All the Best in _____" books are also well done. We like Mr. Clark's word-pictures, and we again appreciate his having the courage to include himself in his descriptions, and to admit occasionally to his own uncertainties and healthy scepticisms.

For anyone who is planning to visit Holland, KLM Airlines has published a series of little pocketbooks. The series includes such titles as *Surprising Amsterdam, Happy Holland,* and *Guide to Holland's Museums.* There is another one that covers all of Europe entitled *KLM's Motoring Guide to Europe.* They are available from KLM Royal Dutch Airlines, 437 Madison Ave., New York, New York 10036.

One last book that we consider to be excellent for liberated travellers is George Oakes's *Turn Right at the Fountain.* It details walking tours through London, Oxford, Cambridge, Edinburgh, Copenhagen, Amsterdam, Bruges, Paris, Rome, Florence, Venice (a remarkable achievement, considering how confusing and illogical Venice is), Vienna, Munich, and Geneva. It is an excellent and timeless book. He has another minor classic as well: *Turn Left at the Pub,* a description of walking tours in the English countryside.

It would also be a good idea to brush up on your knowledge of European history if you have the time before you go. This seems especially important to us for people who will visit Britain. You can't begin to understand a place like Westminster Abbey if you can't recall who did what to whom, and why, and when, and how.

We have to confess that we do disagree with a good deal of what appears in other current travel books. Generally they emphasize seeing the large cities, visiting the most tourist-infested places, and patronizing the fancy hotels. The ones that give specific recommendations about what clothes to carry with you invariably advocate taking entirely too much, and most of them attempt to convince you that to have real freedom you must rent a car over there—and they don't explain the associated problems (which we will in Chapter Seven). We've read in them that one should have a travel agent book all of his sleeping accommodations in advance; that, even though they aren't required, he should get certain shots before going; and, of course, that he would be wise to consider taking either a guided tour for his whole trip, or a series of shorter tours while over there— all suggestions that we find misleading or nonsensical.

We hope that you won't let these other travel guides—with their "you can't miss this" and "this is a must" phrases—confuse you too much. In our view there are no "musts" but one: every traveller should do exactly what his own personal desires and sense of curiosity dictate. We feel relatively sanguine about the whole thing. We are convinced that if you have the chemistry of a liberated traveller you'll exercise a considerable degree of caution about all of the suggestions you read in any of the travel books—including this one. We hope you do.

Chapter Four
Great Expectations

*It's a complex fate, being an American, and one of the
responsibilities it entails is fighting against a superstitious
valuation of Europe.*
—Henry James

Much of Europe looks as if it were created for calendar photos.

It is very difficult for the person who is about to visit Europe for the first time to know what to expect. What pictures do you have in mind? Small cars, and lots of them? Mountains, small villages, castles and fortresses? A slower pace of living than we enjoy(?)? More and better trains than in the States? Cobblestoned streets? Open-air flower and fruit markets? Parks and fountains? Museums? Old buildings? Well, you are correct. You are seeing in your head what you will see in Europe.

What you don't see, if you haven't been to Europe before, are the countless small and sometimes not so small differences between the way the people there live and the way we live. You have yet to experience the extreme difficulty one can have in simply finding a toilet. You are about to learn that you have never before really seen traffic problems, not of the type they live with where streets are narrow, parking is often impossible, and cars often have to drive or park on the sidewalks. You'll be shocked the first time you have to back into a doorway to let a car get by. You are going to live among people who can't imagine how anyone could ever drink tap water. You will find some of these differences to be annoying, and you may begin to wonder early in your visit, "Why can't they do things *right*? Why do they put up with all of these inconveniences?"

The answer to that, of course, is that the Europeans are not at all put out by these "inconveniences." To them, these little surprises that bother you are simply the way things are—and always have been. And by inconveniences we are not referring to anything so broad as language problems; we're talking about the possibility that when and if you get to use a shower, it probably won't pulsate, it won't massage you, it may not be especially warm, and it may just be a teeny tiny trickle of water. We're saying that if and when you rent a car, its gearshift will seem to work backwards, the headlight switch will be seemingly nonexistent, and that the instructions in the glove box which explain all these things may be written in hieroglyphics. We're saying that when you finally get sick of that good European food and decide to order something that is described in the menu as an American-style hamburger, you probably won't recognize what will finally arrive at your table. What will you do? You'll do nothing, because you can't—and you shouldn't have expected anything else.

In most respects, Europeans seem to be less taken by creature comforts than we Americans. They don't expect to be given a big bag for their purchases at the grocery check-out counter—unless they pay for one. Many of them consider central heating as wasteful and decadent, and most of them do not share our belief that a person needs to bathe every day, that every hotel room should have a private bath or toilet, or that there should be a filling station on every corner. It's different, yes, but don't be misled by it; try to remember that most of our great art, music, and literature has come from Europe. European culture is very old, and it works in all of its aspects for the people who live there.

We hope that you won't finally reach a point where you begin to think that Europeans are less civilized than we Americans are. Nothing could be further from the truth. They just think differently about a few things than we do, and when you encounter these differences, all you can do is be good-natured about them. You can live in Europe in the American style if you wish to—and if you are willing to pay for it—but why do so? You can do that at home.

Expect to encounter differences—both large and small—between their way of living and yours. And be prepared to accept those differences, or to laugh them off. You'll be the foreigner on this trip, and you'd better take whatever sense of humor and tolerance you have with you.

One of the difficult things for Americans in Europe to understand or to accept is the way public toilets are often operated. In the first place, they are often not easy to find. Secondly, although this isn't true everywhere, many of them have a feature that is surprising to Americans: a middle-aged attendant who watches everyone, unlocks cubicle doors (for a fee), and expects to be paid something for whatever (or no) reason. Men often get away without paying them anything, but women will ordinarily be trapped into making a little donation. We can only suggest the following to avoid this situation if you are poor, frugal, or easily embarrassed: use toilets in public buildings (museums, government office buildings, etc.), on the trains, and in small cafes and snack bars, all of which will be free of money-grubbing attendants. This is also true, at least generally, of toilets in banks and department stores. But whatever facilities you use, don't expect towels or tissue; you won't be disappointed so often. Phyllis was told in London that she would have to pay "an extra charge" if she looked in the mirror, which was apparently kept safely behind locked doors. But don't get too unhappy about these overseers and their Trinkgeld dishes; they really don't have very nice jobs, keeping those places clean.

It can sometimes be a problem to find a toilet at all. We have just mentioned a few places where they can be located, and they are also always available in bus and train stations (often *with* attendants). But the easiest place to find them is in the bars, which are everywhere. We have often observed that Europeans will walk into such places just to use that facility, and will walk right back out the front door afterwards. If you are too embarrassed to do that and feel that you should drink something before you leave, you may find it a stratagem that is pretty much self-defeating.

At any rate, European toilets and their attendant problems constitute a pretty fair example of the type of thing that surprises the first-time visitor. Another one is the difference between European etiquette and our own. All in all, we think that most Europeans can be extremely generous, even with strangers. If they like you, they will buy you drinks, furnish you meals, and even put you up at night. We have the strong impression that in most places it is considered extremely gauche not to know how to respond to such kindnesses. Perhaps the only definite rule that can be stated is one that would apply equally in the United States: you cannot repay a kindness with money. If someone has you in for a meal, it is okay to take flowers, a plant, or some other small gift—but, like here, you can never offer to pay money for such hospitality. It also appears that they like to receive little notes expressing gratitude afterwards.

If someone treats you to a drink, you can buy the next round, but if you've got to go, you can't leave the price of a drink on the bar so he can have another one when he's ready. Were you to pull that, some Europeans would tell you something like this: "I bought you a drink so I could enjoy the pleasure of your company. It is not the same gesture when you want to buy me one but won't stay here. You are trying to pay me, and you are insulting me." And most of the ones who didn't tell you that would be thinking it.

Generally speaking, we think that most Americans have better manners than most Europeans. We notice, for example, that they often forget to say "thank you" when you do something for them or give them a gift. It is also true that they will often move ahead of other people in lines (except for the British, who seem to love to stand in queues for hours), or interrupt when you are talking to, say, a ticket seller. It's strange: they seem to have a more rigid code of interpersonal conduct than we do (*e.g.*, they don't start using first names as early in a relationship as we do), but we are better with the nearly unconscious little gestures of politeness. But anyway, if you are as courteous as we've just given you credit for being, you may want to watch for all these little nuances and try to fit in as well as you can.

Getting along with the natives

There is another, less-pleasant side of this question of interpersonal relationships you may find yourself involved in with Europeans. It is not likely that you will ever be subjected to anything derived from anti-American attitudes in Europe. We think that most Europeans like Americans pretty well, seeing us as a people who are generally gracious and generous. The French and the Spanish are not overly fond of us, but most other people on the Continent are—even when they laugh at the way many of us travel. You could, however, find yourself the victim of anti-tourist biases.

The anti-tourist sentiment is hard to define, but anyone who has travelled anywhere has a suspicion that nearly anyone who makes his living off of tourists can, at best, be very impatient with them, and, at worst, really hate them. We think we saw an example of this on one of our trips in the last two years. We were sitting on a bench in a train station looking at a timetable. A man sitting next to us reached over and pointed to the name of the town we were talking about. "Going there?" he asked.

We said we were.

"Nice town," he said pleasantly, just as a train pulled in. "That's your train," he said, and grabbed our one small bag and rushed to the train. We followed, and he quickly ushered us onto one of the cars and handed us the bag with a smile. It was the *kind* of smile he gave us that aroused our suspicions, plus the fact that we were rushed aboard so fast that we hadn't been able to do what we always do, look at the destination sign on the side of the car. So as the train pulled out we asked the man nearest us if it was going to the city we intended to visit. He shook his head.

Two stops later we got off at a large station and waited for the right train, which showed up a few minutes later. We couldn't be sure, of course, whether our "benefactor" on the bench had simply been mistaken, or whether he was a tourist-hater. When we thought about his show of teeth, we concluded that he was probably the latter.

There's nothing you can do about this sort of thing, of course, but to grin and bear it if it happens to you. After all, when you think about it, if you run into one person who causes you trouble out of the millions you'll be around, that's not bad. You probably will witness some various kinds of discourtesy, people shoving through doorways, or crowding into a line ahead of you, but all you can do there is ignore it or shake your head and waggle your finger at them. That sometimes—not always—will embarrass them into backing off. But try not to let such little matters bother you, because if you do, it can eventually spoil your vacation. Try to keep in mind that Europe is crowded, like New York or Chicago, and that people in those places sometimes forget their manners too.

Some tourists deserve every bit of dislike they earn, but the problem with that is that all of us who are innocent of wrong-doing receive the same spite. Common complaints against American tourists in Europe include rude behavior, being loud, speaking to Europeans in English without having the courtesy to ask first whether the other person speaks the language, and asking such dumb questions as, "Why don't you put your prices in American dollars?" Such boorishness hurts us all by creating people who hate Americans—or at least those Americans whom they see every day.

Although it isn't nearly as likely now as it was during our Vietnam years, you might even see or hear evidences of outright anti-Americanism somewhere in your travels. There are people in Europe who will be sure that as an American you are both a boob and a warmonger. They will hold the belief that you are surely richer than anyone should be, that you're superficial, and that you are doubtlessly in favor of seeing the rest of the world encouraged to adopt your way of life. If nothing else, this should show anyone how foolish his own stereotypes of other people are.

As far as real anti-American sentiments are concerned, one could run into them in several countries. Many Spaniards do not care much for Americans, primarily because of our country's relationship with the former Generalissimo Franco and his regime. As stated elsewhere, the French waste little affection on us, partly because they find it difficult to think about what American troops did for them in World War II. We have heard from them that they find it difficult to feel gratitude for any sort of help from "outsiders." The Germans are reputed not to be fond of us, primarily because they lack affection for the thousands of American troops stationed in that country. But none of these generalities are totally true. It is not difficult, for example, to find Germans who are very fond of Americans, often because of the days of the Berlin airlift. It's odd, isn't it? The French would apparently never have forgiven us if there had been a Paris airlift.

Elsewhere, as far as we can ascertain, Americans are generally accepted as being no different from anyone else—a concept that might, but shouldn't, shock some of our countrymen. But let's be fair about it: since we are about to endeavor to stereotype the various Europeans on the basis of our own opinions and those of European friends—let's first have a look at *the American* as he is seen through European eyes. It creates a figure you may or may not recognize—but it is who you are generally expected to be by Europeans, at least until you prove otherwise.

Europeans think we are all well-to-do people who put our own comfort higher than it should be on a human being's scale of values. They are not surprised when we find occasion to be rude or unthinking, and they do not hold us in the highest esteem as tourists. They are not ordinarily surprised when any tourist behaves badly, for that matter, but many of them tend to expect to receive small discourtesies from any of us—and are, of course, pleased when they do not. At any rate, they are often inclined to hold Americans at arms-length at first. Asked to explain, they say, usually with some embarrassment: "We see you as the world's best businessmen—and we often want to be sure about what you are after before we open up to you."

On the more positive side, they often stereotype us as generous, gregarious, and extremely friendly (and indeed some of them think we are overly friendly at times). But while they are inclined to think and talk about tour-bus Americans and "fifteen countries in ten days" gags, many of them recognize that many of us travel that way because we usually have little or no background in dealing with other currencies, customs, or languages, and are often afraid of making fools of ourselves. But they are nonetheless surprised by our lack of sophistication. "You are the most capable people on earth," they say. "But you don't seem to be able to deal with *little* problems. It's hard to understand."

So it is consequently easy for most Europeans to think, based upon the majority of Americans they see, that many of us are rich, naive, and occasionally somewhat discourteous. Ironically enough, this is to the advantage of any American who is otherwise; when you contradict the stereotype, Europeans are likely to open their arms to you. If you are pleasant to the Europeans, they'll be pleasant to you in return.

It is extremely unlikely that anyone will say anything even remotely anti-American to your face. If you do have the good fortune to get into conversations with Europeans, what you *will* often hear is the low esteem they sometimes have for each other. You will hear that the Danes and the Norwegians often feel emotions about the Swedes that fall far short of genuine love, and that the Swedes can reciprocate those feelings. You will learn that the Belgians and the Dutch like to make jokes about each other, usually good-natured ones. Any Frenchman you meet may take verbal shots at any of his neighbors, and any non-Teutonic European you encounter may have an unkind word to say about the Germans.

As stated elsewhere, we have observed ourselves that the Germans can occasionally be a bit boorish. We were once on a Europabus travelling through Germany when the driver was listening to a radio program that was broadcasting some anti-American gags. He turned the volume up to an annoying level, and we politely asked if it could be turned down a little. He refused, saying, "The German people on this bus want to hear this program." Perhaps he was right. The German passengers were obviously enjoying the broadcast, but we felt that they and the driver had very poor manners. *That* is the sort of dumb thing you might encounter. But generally we have felt that most of the Europeans really hold Americans in high regard. Many of them remember our help in World War II, our assistance in rebuilding afterwards, and our help in such tragedies as the recent flooding in Florence. The odds are high that you will find that they generally hold Americans in high regard, and that you will consequently be the recipient of the greatest sort of kindness from the people you meet.

And we want to reiterate here that the whole purpose of travel to another place is to meet the people who live there. We don't think it's possible to over-emphasize this idea. If you're anything like us, you'll find that such relationships are the most important aspects of your trip—if they happen—and it is likely that whether or not they occur will depend entirely on how outgoing you can be, or at least pretend to be. We are so fond of Holland and Denmark because it is so easy and pleasant to meet people there. But we have been to a number of beautiful spots in Europe where this didn't happen, and those visits really didn't quite make it for us. We don't think that just looking at and photographing old cathedrals and churches or visiting museums is the name of the game.

But even in a country where the people are especially friendly to outsiders, like Austria or Denmark or Holland, you have to be a little sensitive to local or regional customs. The best illustration we can think of to prove this point has to do with two small towns in east central Holland. The towns are named Urk and Staphorst, and they and their conservative, deeply religious inhabitants seem to have been transplanted here from another planet, or at least from another century. Like our Amish, these folks have their own ideas of what is right or wrong, and most of those ideas have to do with how one should behave on the Sabbath.

A Dutch friend told us that some people were stoned for riding bicycles in Urk on a Sunday not long ago, and you can read signs there yet today suggesting that in the inhabitants' minds, feet are entirely satisfactory for Sabbath locomotion. The Staphorstians dislike having their pictures taken, especially on Sundays, which tourists try to do frequently because of the odd clothes the villagers wear to church. These good people have been known to show their resentment over this by breaking photographers' car windows, their noses, and their cameras. A Netherlands National Tourist Office warns readers about this in the gentlest sort of way, reminding that "you are not in a zoo" when you are there. It seems to us if you left in an ambulance just because you had taken a photo, you might well wonder if you hadn't been in a zoo.

We were told that the people in these tiny villages are so distrustful of the evil outside world that they never travel or mingle with people from nearby towns. That would suggest that there has been a good deal of inbreeding in both places over the years, which might account for some of the strange behavior of these good folks.

Urk and Staphorst are interesting places to visit, and you would be perfectly safe there as long as you showed some understanding of their lives and customs. They might not be especially friendly to you, but as long as you behave yourself and let it be known by your actions that you realize that they have a right to live as they wish, you'll be all right. In fact, if you have that sort of sensitivity, you'll get along pretty well anywhere in Europe.

Part of that sensitivity has to do with taking pictures *anywhere* you go. You will find areas where people dress in regional or historical costumes and *want* tourists to take their pictures (usually for tips, which makes the whole business a bit unappealing to us). On the other hand, you will also visit places like Urk and Staphorst where people are not much interested in becoming an entry in your photo album, especially *if you don't ask their permission first.* Even one of the Beefeater guards at the Tower of London told us how much he resents having visitors snap pictures of him without asking—although he was perfectly willing to pose, smile, and so on, for shutterbugs who requested him to do so. It's not really difficult to understand when you consider the fact that if foreigners came into your hometown every day of the year and took pictures of you because they thought your manner of dress or your behavior was odd, you'd probably get annoyed too. So picture-taking in Europe, like other aspects of a visitor's general demeanor, is just a matter of common sense and courtesy.

And as far as common sense is concerned, there is a good deal to be said for exercising all you have in adverse circumstances in Europe. A person would be wise to keep a tight rein on his temper and avoid yelling or making a fuss over what could just be a misunderstanding. Unless you know the Europeans well and are conversant in the language being spoken, you are liable to misunderstand anything in almost any situation—and you'll really look like a boob if you lose your temper over some small matter that may not even be what you thought it was, or that didn't mean what you initially thought.

Generally then, finding friends, people to talk to, and someone who will make your temporary home-away-from-home a real home has a fantastic importance. It can be the greatest single experience of your trip. You'll know that the first time it happens to you, or when you get into a private home and find yourself temporarily accepted into peoples' lives in their own living rooms. Whatever the circumstances, you will find most Europeans pretty tolerant of you, because you're American—and you'll find that they can like you a great deal if they see that you are genuinely interested in them.

Who the Europeans are

Although we will subsequently have more to say about the character of the people you will meet in the various countries, let us offer here a few preliminary observations about them. These generalities, which reflect our own biases and those of our European friends, should not be taken too literally. People vary a great deal from person to person, and you will often meet someone in one of the countries who seems to be a living disproof of such stereotypes as we are about to give you. Nevertheless, these characterizations seem reasonably true to us, and we hope that they will give you some idea of what to expect of your soon-to-be hosts.

The British appear to us to be holding onto their collective belief in themselves and their society in the face of their current difficulties with the same tenacity that brought them through the horrors of World War II. If a visitor to England were not up on current events, he would find little reason to surmise from their behavior that the British are facing any problems at all. They seem to us to be as happy, as busy, and as occasionally odd (by American and Canadian standards) as they ever were.

If the British ever really had any of the "reserve" they've been credited with, it seems to have disappeared. Today they are very friendly and outgoing, and if you start a conversation with any of them, they seem quite inclined to talk. And everyone talks to everyone in that great English institution, the pub. In fact, an old adage goes: "The British go to pubs to talk and drink. The Welsh go to pubs to drink and sing. The Scots go to pubs to drink."

The French, of course, are the world's gourmets, and they still spend a lot of time and energy in preparing, eating, and drinking the best foods and wines to be found anywhere. They build beautiful automobiles these days, and they have considerable traffic problems as well. We have the impression that many of them are not overly fond of Americans, but that may just be a narrow view in

The British call these "magpie houses."

The authors' photo, England

the sense that they don't waste much love on *anyone* who isn't French. This chauvinist attitude is reflected in their love for their language. Most Europeans seem to feel flattered when you make even pathetic efforts to speak their tongue, but not these people. Your high school French will get you nowhere with them. If they condescend to answer you at all (which they often won't), it will ordinarily be in English—which, of course, isn't usually all that good either—but why should they care? They consider it an inferior language, which is mighty interesting in view of the fact that French is not one of the world's ten most-spoken languages. But we do have to confess that this is more of a problem in Paris than elsewhere in la belle France; the natives in the small towns and villages are a lot more tolerant than the Parisians are. Perhaps the whole thing is similar to what a foreigner might think if he only met New Yorkers while here, as opposed to all of us more pleasant hicks in the rest of the country.

The Spanish are pretty disorganized right now. They have just come out of forty years of living under a totalitarian government, and they have some difficulties in knowing what to do with their newly emerging freedoms. They do not seem to be very cultured when compared to other people in Europe, not having the same command of languages or general savoir-faire that many of their neighbors possess. They are usually regarded as being a friendly people, but perhaps because of language difficulties we have not found them so.

Some people who visit Spain are bothered by the rubbish they see strewn around, mostly not in the cities, but along the roads and railbeds. Unlike other Europeans, the Spanish are inclined to toss things anywhere. And some visitors are annoyed by the constant din of automobile horns, motorcycle engines, and clanging pots and pans. Spain must be the noisiest country in the world (although some travellers think that Italy holds that questionable honor).

One of the Spaniard's best-known characteristics is his strange sense of time. His idea of business hours is 10 a.m. to 1 or 2 p.m., and 4 or 5 p.m. to 8 p.m. Contrary to long-standing rumors, he is less likely to spend his afternoons in bed than in a bar or cafe, where he will engage in lengthy debates on any and all subjects with his cronies. But visitors are well advised to remember that almost everything (including tourist information offices) will be closed for some hours in the afternoons.

If you speak good Spanish, you'll get along all right in Spain. If you are unilingual, like most Americans, you won't find Spain easy to conquer. In either case, in our opinion, it is not the easiest country for the liberated traveller to begin his or her journey. It might be a nice place to end it, when money is running short, but you might find it, like Scandinavia, a bit far off from what you and most geographers think of as the center of Europe.

Generally the Dutch are friendly and kind, many of them speak good English, and they can be extremely pleasant and hospitable to people who visit them. Like the Belgians, they are pretty closely packed together, but their general good natures seem to us to offer some disproof of the theories about what overcrowding can do to humans and other animals. The Dutch seem very good at accepting and institutionalizing almost any viewpoint, no matter how odd it might be. One political dissident there has complained that ''it is no fun to beat your head on a rubber wall forever.'' In view of their recent problems with their Indonesian immigrants, it might be said that they are *too* tolerant.

The Dutch are unquestionably the world's best hydraulic engineers, and they really like anyone who wants to learn something about how they control water. They have also been credited with being the kindest people in Europe, and we see no reason to argue with that assessment.

Let us add a footnote here about Holland, simply because many Americans have forgotten about the past close ties between the Dutch and ourselves.

Our forefathers, the Puritans, came from there. To be historically correct, we should say that they came *via* the Netherlands, but even their relatively brief stop in Leiden had a great bearing on what the United States came to be. It was there that they learned of a number of ideas that were not practiced in the England of the early 1600's. Among these ideas were such foundations of democracy as freedom of religion, the need for free education, the importance of the written ballot, and so on.

In 1782, Holland loaned two million dollars to our struggling new country, a favor that was eventually expanded to a total of 30 million badly needed bucks— a sum that would amount to at least ten times that much today. You can see the house from which the first loan was made, if you are interested, at Singel 280 in Amsterdam.

Holland was the first country to recognize the United States as an independent, sovereign country.

Many Dutch people still have an enormous fondness for Americans because of our part in the country's liberation from the Germans in World War II, and for the help we gave them through the Marshall Plan in the late forties— when they faced starvation, devastation, and flooding resulting from the war.

The Belgians are suave, hard-working, fond of pleasure, and they all seem (at least when compared to us) to be gourmets. They are big eaters, and they love good food and the products of the grape. They are also great walkers, thinking nothing of ''strolls'' that would cripple the average American. And they have one other rather well-known characteristic: they are inveterate hand-shakers. They will shake hands with you every time they see you. It's a nice custom.

Luxembourgers are generally jolly folks, if slightly reserved with strangers, but always ready for a good time. As one native put it to us: one Luxembourger, a souvenir-shop employee; two Luxembourgers, a beer-drinking bash; three Luxembourgers, a band. Nearly all of them seem to be able to handle some English. This may be a reflection of their country's tourist industry, because most of them speak to each other in Letzeburgesch, a strange tongue that is the broadly used language. To give you an idea how impossible this dialect is, their national motto, ''We wish to remain what we are'' translates into this, *Mir woelle bleiwe wat mir sin.* French is the *official* language here, but school-kids begin to learn German first (presumably because it is easier for them, being close to Letzeburgesch). Then they learn French, and finally English.

The Icelanders are beautiful people. Asked if he could explain why the women there are so attractive, a tour guide in Reykjavik said (with obvious pride): "They eat good food, they get a lot of exercise, and their complexions are usually excellent —perhaps partly because we don't burn fossil fuels here, and therefore have the cleanest air possible." Both the men and the women of Island (as they spell Iceland) are robust in appearance, and they seem given to jokes and laughter. Most of them speak good English, and they seem to enjoy conversation, whether it is on a light level or of a more serious nature.

The Portuguese are also wonderful, friendly people. In spite of generally low wages and a high unemployment rate (16%), the Portuguese are extremely generous with others, and they seem to like foreigners. They will rush to your side if you are lost, sick, confused, or starting to make some sort of faux pas. They are friendly, big-hearted, sometimes shy, usually temperamental, and invariably helpful. Many speak English and those who don't often speak French or Spanish. These charming people constitute Portugal's greatest asset for tourists.

The Germans today, as in the past, are quite industrious. In a few short years they have transformed their country from devastation into one of the richest nations in the world. They still appear to be as methodical and as inclined to admire (or assent) to authority as ever, but today they are also prosperous, all of which may contribute to the fact that many of their neighbors view them with dislike. The Germans of the northern areas of the country can be especially officious, humorless, and sometimes downright unpleasant, although we haven't seen too much of this sort of behavior in the Bavarian regions of the south. We once asked a railroad official a question and got this response: "You notice that *I* speak perfect Oxford English? I notice that I can't understand one damned thing that *you* say—*in your own language.*" Many Germans do speak good English, and if they like you and are on their best behavior they can be excellent hosts—which often involves the drinking of large quantities of good German beer.

The Swiss, the world's bankers and watch makers, usually speak not only English but several other languages as well. They are used to dealing with everyone from everywhere, and they consequently seem cosmopolitan to Americans. They are somewhat aloof, usually, and not especially friendly to outsiders. Their reputation for straightforwardness, honesty, personal frugality, and cleanliness seems well deserved. The final cost for all of these attributes shows up in their prices, which are very high. Switzerland is an expensive country for the tourist, but nevertheless one that many of us can't resist visiting.

The Swiss are hard-working folks who tend to worry that other people have more fun than they do. "The French work to live," they say mournfully, "while the Swiss live to work." They hope to change this in the future, but it sounds a bit like an alcoholic's dream of taking over a temperance union. One can imagine them saying, "Now here is a rigid educational and social program designed to make all of us more fun-loving. We will follow it precisely." And everyone would.

It is really difficult to characterize the Austrians, even in a superficial way. They are lively, fun-loving, and they like tourists—as well they should, as important as their tourist business is to them. Many of them are rotund, a consequence of the excellent Austrian beer, ice cream, and pastries they love so much. They are enjoyable people to know, generally, and being as tourist-oriented as they are, many of them speak good English. They are more inclined to take life easy than their Swiss and German neighbors. They like to complain about their high taxes which result from the country's extensive social programs. While many of them think these programs have gone entirely too far, most of them seem to be politically apathetic. They love their coffee, pastries (which are very rich) and wine—and they like to sit and talk, or walk and talk.

The Irish, who may just outclass the Australians as beer-drinkers, are extremely friendly to outsiders. They are generally carefree, enjoying long conversations or singing sessions in the pubs. They are always ready with a smile, an extended hand, and a cheery comment, even to strangers. They are charmers.

As we have said elsewhere in the book, the image of the Scot as dour and stingy is 100% wrong. Instead, he is friendly, generous, and fond of life and people. He is not adverse to an occasional pint, and, in spite of the old joke, likes to drink *and* talk in the pubs. A small warning: he may not be overcome with gratitude if you refer to him as "Scotch," or if you tell him how much you enjoyed England. He is a Scot, and he would be interested to hear your impressions of Scotland.

The Greek people are charming. We would rate them along with the Portuguese and the Danes as the nicest people in Europe. A Greek will laugh with you, and even offer you instruction in learning to be as carefree, devil-may-care, and fun-loving as he is. They often do see themselves that way, and they find no shame in it —nor should they. But you can count on them getting serious instantly if you get into any trouble—getting lost, let's say, when they will rush to your side. Generally they are emotional, kind, friendly, a little sly at times, and almost always ready for a laugh, for music, and for a good time. And yet they work hard, long hours at their jobs.

It's a mixture that's hard to fault. They will frequently make you wish you were Greek, at least in attitude. They do keep the same hours as their brethren in the other southerly European countries. Shops are open from 8:30 to 14:30 on Mondays, Wednesdays, and Saturdays; and from 8:30 to 13:30 and from 17:30 to 20:30 on Tuesdays, Thursdays, and Fridays. It will be something like that when you visit, although the specific hours may have been changed. They do from time to time.

The Italians claim that they like fast cars, fast driving, and fast women, not necessarily in that order. They also, we notice, like beer, wine, fish, and a tremendous variety of strange calorie-laden starchy foods. They build the world's fastest and most beautiful automobiles, and their country is constantly embroiled in political squabbles and labor strikes. Disorder and disorganization constitute the Italian way of life, and we would be surprised to learn that any of them would want to have it any other way. The country is not as clean as many others on the Continent, and, as we will find occasion to warn you later, has serious crime problems in the large cities and on the trains.

But most Italians are friendly, and they seem to like to talk to people who visit their country. They are certainly more friendly in nature than the French or the Spanish. They love to spend their afternoons in cafes and wineshops arguing loudly with their friends, waving their arms, and laughing.

There is a world of difference between the northern Italian and the southern Italian. The southerners (including the inhabitants of Rome) are much like the Spaniards. They close their offices and shops in the afternoon, and later stay open during much of the evening. The northerner, on the other hand, keeps about the same hours as most of the rest of Europe, and is not enthusiastic about the late meal hours of his brethren to the south.

As far as the Scandinavian countries are concerned, the Danes are as friendly as any people could be, the Swedes are a bit dour, and the Norwegians are a little reserved. It appears to us that more Danes speak English than not, and that most of them are always ready for a joke or a laugh. They are fantastically friendly to outsiders. By contrast, the Swedes, who seem to be able to do and make anything and everything, almost seem to have a national inferiority complex—and if so, no one knows why. Like Denmark, their country is highly socialized, a society that looks pretty good to most visitors, but they don't seem to be too happy with it themselves. Lastly, Norway is a sparsely populated garden spot that looks like a beautiful international park, and the Norwegians want to keep it that way. They are "offish." A Norwegian friend told us that when one of his countrymen looks out the window of his mountaintop cabin and sees another house two hundred miles away, he thinks, "They're getting too damned close."

Well, at any rate one can say that it is possible to see a number of differences between the people of the various countries in Europe, and that all of them are different from us in surprising ways. And we believe strongly that observing and exploring these little differences is one of the most fascinating aspects of a trip to Europe.

If you didn't find the foregoing generalizations satisfying, and if you would really like to increase your appreciation of the people and countries you are going to visit, you should read some of the well-known books about the various Europeans. Probably the best conceived and best written of all of them is James Michener's *Iberia,* a marvelous book that should be read by anyone who plans to visit Spain. Not only does it tell who the Spaniards are, and how they got that way, but it provides a fascinating explanation of Spain's "differences" from the rest of Europe. At one stage in his discussion, Michener makes this interesting observation: " . . . I had known Japan, and it, like Spain, was feudal, ritualistic, devoted to honor and committed to maintaining a closed society. In fact, I found Spain to be the Japan of Europe . . . . '' We were struck by the comparison, since one of us has lived for several years in Japan, and was able to concur with the analogy.

Other similar books, not always so interesting as *Iberia,* are *The Italians* by Luigi Barzini, *The French* by Sanche de Gramont, *The Germans* by Adolph Schalk, *The English* by David Frost and Anthony Jay, and *The Scandinavians* by Donald S. Connery. There are many others, of course, but any of them will give you a perception of the people you will be living among that you just can't get on your own during a brief visit.

Tourist offices

One of the most pleasant surprises for the outsider visiting Europe is to learn of the existence of the tourist information offices in every town of any size at all. We have nothing like these offices in the United States. In Europe you will find them everywhere, and you will often put them to use, especially to help you find sleeping accommodations. These offices will make you realize that Europeans are much more interested in dealing with travelling people than we Americans are. But in the high season when the office is packed with travellers asking dumb questions like, ''Where are the department stores?'' or ''Can you tell me the things you people like to eat?'' the tempers of the people behind the counters can be a bit short. Well, don't go during the high season if you can avoid it, and in the spring or fall you'll find people in these offices who are willing to try to respond to the dumbest question you can think up, *e.g.,* ''Where could I get a real American cheese omelet—or hamburger—or martini?'' In the fall or spring, they might tell you. In the summer, they'll say, ''In Philadelphia.'' Who can blame them, when they are going to hear five hundred such questions that day?

Even a tourist information office can have a surprising appearance.

The authors' photo, Spain

But ordinarily, if you're pleasant, they'll be pleasant. They'll tell you how to walk up to the castle, how to find a room, how to work the telephone, or how to say "mushroom" in Schwitzerdütsch. In fact, if they were always open, day and night, Sundays and holidays, we wouldn't have written this book.

You might as well know before you start your odyssey that not all of the services these offices provide you are free. Most of them, for example, charge a small fee to make reservations for you by telephone for sleeping accommodations, and many of them charge small sums for maps and brochures. This is not really surprising when you learn how expensive this whole system must be for a small country like Holland, or even the larger countries like England or Germany. In Holland, for example, there are more than seventy big VVVs and over five hundred smaller ones throughout the country, and to pay all of the people involved, these offices are forced to charge fees calculated to recover the cost of the printing of some of the publications they provide. It's a fantastic bargain, at least in the sense that we know that *we* would have a difficult time getting about without the help these offices provide, and it would be almost impossible for the first-time traveller to exist without the services they offer.

Occasionally, though, the tourist office personnel can give you problems, particularly when they only seem willing to talk about ritzy hotels, when you are asking about pensions. Sometimes they will only help you reluctantly on such problems, if at all. You have to insist upon what you want when that happens. Presumably part of the problem on this is that they really do believe that we're all rich. It's impossible for them to imagine that any of us really could run low on funds.

But we suspect that the whole problem is deeper than that. We know that in many places the big hotels do "contribute" to the finances of the tourist offices, and that some of the people in those offices will freely admit that they "always try to fill the hotels first." We have never been taken by collusion or conspiracy theories, but one does begin to wonder just how close the hotel people and tourist bureau personnel are in some of these places. Many times we have asked for addresses of pensions or boardinghouses in tourist bureaus only to be told "I don't know where any are." Well, perhaps they don't know, even if they had lived there all their lives, but we would find several ourselves within a short time.

Nevertheless, we will give Europe's tourist offices high marks. They are usually well organized, and the people in them are ordinarily pleasant and helpful. They can't solve every problem that their clients bring them, but, in our view, they usually try hard to do so. They are the people to see if you get into any trouble from which you can't extricate yourself.

How to pace yourself, to see, and to be cool
No matter how much you bone up beforehand you will face some surprises when you get to Europe, some pleasant, and some not. Even if you have

visited Europe before, and are returning to a place you visited in the past, you might be wise to be prepared for disappointment—at least a degree of it. Even if by some miracle the place hasn't changed, it still won't be what you remember—and the great likelihood is that it *will* have changed. It will probably be bigger. There will be more high-rises than you recollect. The nice little restaurant you remember will be gone, perhaps replaced by a Wimpy establishment. Prices will be higher, and people may be less friendly than they were before. At any rate, they will be changed: at the very least they will be older. There will be more cars, more filled parking spaces, more noise, and more pollution than evidenced by the pictures in your head.

Thomas Wolfe was correct. Everything does change, and not always for the better. We mention this sad truism because we have fallen victim to our own memories before, and felt afterwards that it would have been better not to have expected so much. It would have been smarter to have realized that things would be different from before.

It is a world of change, and Europe is no exception to that rule.

People on their first trip over often make the mistake of trying to go too fast and too far. Let us consequently offer you a thought about *pace.* Here we are not talking about how many countries you visit, as we did in Chapter One, but instead about the pace you will adopt in a given country, or even in a given city.

At times, time flies in Europe. Especially early in your trip, when everything is new and different, and when you're still thinking, "Wow, look at that! Nothing like that at home," you *can't* get bored. But you can and may get tired of it later on, and if you still have the typical American compulsion to run on to something new, you may find that the something new is boring you too. If so, we suspect that you are overloading your circuits; you are taking in more than you can digest through your eyes and ears. The best thing at that point might be for you not to go *faster,* to see something else, but to *slow down* for a short time.

It can be a very nice, relaxing thing to sit down in a park or sidewalk cafe and just watch the people stroll by (most of whom, you'll probably notice, are strolling at a lot slower gait than your usual road-runner style). It can be a nice change of pace to say "We don't have to see this museum in one hour. We'll probably never be here again." It can do wonders for your feet, your back, and your psyche (probably in that order) just to slow down occasionally and look in the shop windows, gawk at the crowds, or, indeed, just sit on the balcony of your room and look at what's to be seen.

Such moments are, and should be, a part of Europe. It's a slower place than the United States, and the American compulsion to run is a great disadvantage. You will not physically or mentally be able to run like that all the time you are in Europe. Initially you will probably try, in spite of this warning, because nearly everyone does, but sooner or later you'll pay a price for doing so. Most of us were not built to be marathon runners, and in spite of all the thoughts you'll have about how limited your time is, you'll wear out your body and your patience if you keep moving at high speed. The occasional slowing down doesn't really cost you time in the near future. It will gain you a better impression and understanding of what you yet have to see.

As one example of how an intelligent traveller might pace himself, we will mention the 350-mile trip between Sweden's Gothenburg and Stockholm by boat on the Göta Canal and the many lakes and rivers it connects. The trip takes three days and two nights, and it is very leisurely. Shorter trips are possible, and you can return to your starting point by rail if you wish. But it is a scenic trip. You will pass through many locks, see castles and old forts, enjoy part of the Baltic Sea coast, and have many opportunities to get off for short walking tours.

These trips are popular and often booked well ahead by travellers who do have patience, and they are only run between early April and the end of August. It might seem terribly slow to many tourists, but in actuality it is probably about the right pace for anyone who really wants to see what he passes.

Another pleasant possibility for travellers who have conquered the "fifteen countries in ten days" mania is a canoe trip down Belgium's Lesse River. To make this trip, one can catch an early train from Brussels on *"un beau jour à Dinant"* ticket, which would take him to the town of Anseremme. There he would change trains and proceed to Houyet, arriving there at around 10 a.m. There, right outside the train station, are the boats. A two-person canoe will cost about thirteen dollars. With it, one goes down the beautiful Lesse River, stopping where he wishes to see caves, eat the lunch he's brought along, and arriving finally back in Anseremme about five hours later. From there he can get a direct ride back to Brussels.

If is a dry summer, call 082/222325 to ask if there is enough water to go down the river. At best, the river is never deep enough to drown anyone. And it is not a tiring trip because it is with the current of the river.

The season for these trips is May 1 through the end of September. It is necessary to book ahead for the last weekend of June, because many people make this little trip then.

One could also start this adventure from the villages of Dinant or Han-sur-Lesse (described in Chapter Fourteen). But it is a simple little trip to arrange, and if you like small boats and nice scenery, it could give you one of the most charming and unusual days of your visit to Europe.

Because so many travellers visit only the "name" places like Bruges, Ghent, or Brussels, we are going to suggest here another possibility for going at things a bit differently if and when you visit Belgium. Similar out-of-the-way sights and entertainments can be found in every country, and they usually offer the advantage of being less tourist-infested and less expensive than the "must" places described in all the brochures.

Belgium has forty miles of sand beaches on her north coast that offer the tourist some unusual vacation possibilities, attractions that are available to visitors who are on their way to or from England on the ferry boats. Many travellers who are using Ostende as their arrival or departure point for cross-Channel trips also use this pleasant little town as a base to explore the northern coastline by rented bicycle or on the little trams that run all the way along the coast.

The area south is somewhat less expensive than that to the north of Ostende. It brings the traveller through many small villages and varying sights, all of which he can visit if he wishes. If he is using Ostende as a base for this seaside exploration, he will find lodgings there from about nine to thirteen dollars for a bathless double, with pension accommodations a bit less. One particularly attractive place just south of Ostende is the "Zon en Zee" (say it slowly and you'll hear its meaning in English). It's quite inexpensive, and its price includes the use of its swimming pool—and optional full board at a reasonable rate is available. This is not a hotel, but a "Social Holiday Home," a Belgian invention worthy of investigation when and if you find one in your travels.

In the other direction, northeast of Ostende, one can leave the tram or his bicycle to see fishing villages like Zeebrugge, little places like Blankenberge (reputed to be the least expensive town on the Belgian coast, with bathless double rooms running as low as $8.00 a night), and a really remarkable sight, the bird sanctuary of Le Zoute. Called "The Zwin," it is a 300-acre paradise for birds of every description. Most of them are wild, living in their natural habitat, but there is a small area where some of them are caged so that people who do not wish to walk all day can see the different types in a short time. In total there are more than 100 species of birds in residence here. The park costs only about $1.00 to enter, and visitors are encouraged to bring picnic lunches with them (there is a restaurant on the ground for those who do not). Binoculars are useful to have here, as are boots, at least on damp days (and the boots can be rented on the grounds). On Thursday and Sunday mornings at 10 a.m. you can join the curator for a fairly long stroll through the ordinarily-off-limits nesting areas. It's a big and lovely place, and because part of it extends into Holland, it provides the opportunity to bicycle or walk into another country.

The nearest town to the park, Le Zoute, is an expensive place, but one can come there from elsewhere on the train, rent a bicycle, and bike out to and through the park. Although The Zwin is open year around, buses run from downtown Le Zoute to the park only during July and August.

A ride along this scenic coastline, whether by bicycle on the good bike paths or on the little tram, could be a wonderful, lazy, carefree change of pace for many American tourists. Bike rental rates run about $3.00 a day, and it costs about the same amount to ride the little tram down the whole coast, a run of 2½ hours.

And let us add one rather strange suggestion for seeing *better* what you will see. We have discovered that if you want to *see* and remember that castle or beautiful view you are looking at, you should close your eyes for a moment and visualize something that is familiar—say, your kitchen or living room at home. After a few moments of this, open your eyes again—and for some reason we can't explain, you'll see what you're looking at with a new kind of clarity. It's like taking a photograph with your eyes and your mind. Try it; maybe it will work for you too. We'll have a bit more to say about seeing and appreciating in Chapter Fifteen.

Europe is a charming place, and all of the countries have much to offer to anyone who visits. Your trip there can be less than pleasant, though, if you go with the wrong expectations. On the other hand, if you have a good idea of what to expect, and you can maintain your sense of humor, your natural curiosity, and your tolerance for things that are new and different, you'll have the time of your life. And you'll find that if you can laugh it off when things don't go exactly right, some of the worst times and the least pleasant experiences will eventually stay with you among your best memories of your trip.

An American acquaintance who has travelled everywhere and has a good command of Spanish provides a case in point. One night he found himself in Cádiz, on Spain's southern coast, and he couldn't find a room. He visited many hotels and pensions, without success, and then tried to get back out—but the buses and trains had stopped running by that time. He then attempted to get a seat in the train station for the night, but found it locked up. So he finally ended up sitting up all night in a cafe frequented by Cádiz taxi drivers, and left town on the first train next morning.

"You must have been exhausted and disgusted, weren't you?" one of us asked.

He laughed. "I was, all right, but I got over that. Now the whole thing is one of my best memories. Boy, those taxi drivers told some of the wildest stories I've ever heard. I've been travelling in Spain for years, but that night I learned what the country is all about. It's now my best memory of Spain."

So if you're lucky enough to be able to take yourself and events without too much seriousness, you'll one day find yourself saying to your wife or husband, "Wasn't that interesting (amusing, wonderful, horrible) when we got lost in the Alps and missed a meal and had such a time getting back to that little town?"

It's true: an interesting bad experience makes a better memory than a dull good experience—if you have the heart and soul of a liberated traveller.

Chapter Five
What Did He Say?

They spell it Vinci and pronounce it Vinchy; foreigners
always spell better than they pronounce.
The Innocents Abroad, Mark Twain

Please take me to a brain surgeon.

Do you have fried tapir on your menu?

Where can I find an extraordinary building?

Please bring me a pail of dry dead wine.

So it goes in the world of the phrase book. It is not a rare sight in Europe to see a poor tourist, his forehead bathed with perspiration, fingers twitching over his little phrase book, and eyes flicking about in search of a phrase that is at least close to what he needs, which is, let's say, "Where is the train station?" He finally finds one part of his question in the French section and the balance in the German part, so he says *"Wo ist la gare?"* His pronunciation is so poor that the European in front of him, who knows both French and German, can't understand what he's trying to say. So after a moment the European answers in flawless English: "I didn't follow you on that. What is it you want to know?"

One meets many Europeans who speak not only good English, but two, three, or four other languages as well. No amount of rationalization about their *needing* to be multilingual because of having nearby foreign-speaking neighbors will ease your embarrassment if, like most Americans, you can't ask where the toilet (or cathedral, or whatever) is—or, if you can *ask*, you can't understand the answer.

Just imagine that you are sitting in a first-class compartment on a train watching the scenery flash by as you speed down the smooth tracks at nearly one hundred miles per hour. You are in a compartment which has fantastically comfortable seats, and over your head in a luggage rack is the wine and lunch that you and your travelling companion will share later. In addition to the two of you, there are three other people in the compartment: a young Italian man, a German woman, and a Frenchman.

The other three were there when the two of you entered the compartment a couple of minutes ago, and they were involved in a conversation in German and French. They greeted you and asked the inevitable question, which you somehow understood, and you replied: "Americans." Immediately all three of them began to speak English, asking you where you've been, where you're going, and so on. Now you are in the midst of a fascinating conversation which tells you a great deal about Europe and Europeans, not to mention the excellent tips you're picking up about things to do and places to stay where you're going.

Only later does it occur to you that they all spoke *your* language rather than their own, which makes you feel grateful to them and mentally accuse yourself of being a clod. Well, as two clods to another we'll have to agree with your self-analysis, having often felt that way ourselves. But it is clear that riding the trains in Europe is not only enjoyable, but educational as well. You learn to know the natives, and you get tips that will never appear in any brochure or book. ("Would you like to hear about a fine cave near my home that all the kids play in—that no tourist has ever seen?")

It is hard to understand why such conversations are so easy, pleasant, and frequent on European trains, while people on American trains or airplanes so often sit in stony silence, engrossed in their magazines or their own thoughts. Certainly the configuration of the European railroad car has something to do with it, with most seats facing each other. But it goes beyond that. One suspects that Europeans are just better conversationalists than we Americans are, perhaps because they are more interested in other people. That wouldn't be surprising. Whereas our country is large and homogeneous, and everyone generally has the same language, background, and customs, the Europeans face a great diversity of tongues, currencies, political ideologies, and traditions. It may be that they just have to try harder than we do. At any rate, we have always found it pleasant to sit with them in the railroad compartments.

Neither of us is conversant in French, German, or Italian, and we have had moments in Europe where we felt like morons because of it. Worse yet, we were sure that we sounded like morons to the other person involved. Imagine this hypothetical conversation as it might hit the ears of a ticket seller in a European railway station: "We want go Sore-broken on train. Can we for a moment dismount in between of? Must we attempt in owning—er, leasing—renting—take reservation for this journey? Is it cost money to reserve? How many money? The train is when? What vegetable—which place—er, where this train track is at?''

You must confess that if someone came up and talked like that to you, you might feel that he wasn't terribly bright. In such a situation, this listener really can't help wondering why someone couldn't deal with a few simple words and ideas, at least. A moron could do that, he might think, and we agree. If you are capable of speaking one of the European languages, it will probably influence your decisions about where to go. If you do not have such an ability, like most Americans, you need to have some idea what you will be facing, and perhaps a few tips about how to get by.

First of all, you do not have to speak any foreign language like a native (except French, in France) to get by in Europe. Indeed, you will frequently have the pleasure of talking to people who speak excellent English, sometimes better than your own. But when you can use English with people there, speak slowly and distinctly, and keep it simple. Say ''for two'' rather than ''a double''; ask for whiskey, not a ''shot of red-eye.'' Remember that English is their second or third language. As an example of the fact that they have problems with our language too, we quote this from a Dutch policeman's handbook designed to help in dealing with English-speaking accident victims: ''How many hands, legs, feet, etc. do you have?'' and ''What's wrong with the lady's toes?'' Or this, from a train lavatory sign: ''To get water turn handle indifferently to the right or to the left.''

You can often read much of what is written in other languages if you don't panic. We saw the following on a theatre marquee in The Hague:

Walt Disney's Beste Tekenfilm
Sneeuwitze en de 7 Dwergen
De Film voor jonge en oude

And in Spain: *Jesuchristo Superstar.*

Another tip: watch the numbers that come up on cash registers. They'll tell you (in good Arabic numerals) what you owe, if you can't understand otherwise. (And if you know Arabic, why don't you know French or German?) At any rate, this is easier than trying to read their handwritten bills. Generally they write numbers much in the same way we do, with three exceptions: 1's are often written like little pyramids; 7's usually have the vertical leg crossed; and 9's are ordinarily written like small g's above the line. Thus their written numerals are:

1 2 3 4 5 6 7 8 9.

If you *do* have confidence, or cheek, you will find that slurring what you say in another language or speaking a bit gutterally (especially in German) will help immensely. One of the reasons for this is that many words in the most-spoken European languages are similar to English words meaning the same thing. In German, for example, the phonetic rendition of ''hotel'' is Hoh-tell; ''restaurant'' is Rehs-tow-rahng; ''roast beef'' is Roast Bif; ''steak'' is Beefsteak; ''Lamb'' is Lahm; and ''Whiskey'' is Vhisky. So we recommend that when you are speaking German, no matter how badly, you change all the w's to v's, the v's to f's, and speak gutterally. After all, they do!

In French, we find such close similarities as these: "Excuse me" is Ek-skeu-zeh-mwah. Now think about it. That *is* close. Don't let it throw you if you haven't had any French; if you can roll words a bit, spread syllables a little, and give a slow "a" sound to the endings of some words, you can pass in most places, even if not in France itself. "Pardon me" will become par-don-eh mwah; "hotel" is oh-tel; "have you" is a-veh voo; "coffee" is ka-feh; and "omelet" is om-leht. Now you won't starve, wherever you're at.

In Spanish, "h" is always silent; "j" is pronounced like our "h"; and "r" or "rr" is trilled, if you can manage it. While many Spaniards speak only Spanish, or Spanish and French, they do not seem to be overly sensitive about how poorly a foreigner speaks their language. We have observed that they are often amused by Mexican or South American accents, however. But unlike the French, they seem to like to hear one try to speak their language, and they are not given to laughing or even sneering if you make mistakes.

The Italians, the Austrians, and the Dutch are similarly untroubled by hearing someone mangle their languages, and they seem to like you for trying. It is a good idea to learn at least a few words and phrases of the language of any country you visit, even those like Holland or Denmark where everyone seems to speak some English, mostly because of the reason just stated: the people who live there will like you for it. And as we will argue here and there throughout the book, having them like you is several thousand times better than having them ignore you. Being able to say "hello" to someone in their language will get you a long way in Europe, believe it or not. The following little tale illustrates that fact.

We were bicycling through a small village in Holland on a mild winter day when we saw a man walking along with a little girl. When we said *"Goeden morgen,"* he said "Good morning" back in English without a trace of accent. As so often happens, he somehow saw that we were Americans at first glance. We stopped by the curb, and asked, "Say, could you tell us where we might find a cafe open in town?"

"You're Americans biking through here just before Christmas?" he asked.

"Yes," we said, "just seeing the sights."

He smiled broadly. "That's *great,*" he said. "For you, the cafe is at my house. Come on, this way."

When we tried to object that we really didn't want to take advantage of his kindness, he said, "Nonsense. I want my wife to meet you anyway. She'll love it. She speaks good English."

We had a wonderful lunch with these wonderful people, and made friends we'll never forget. Before we left we asked them why they had shown two strangers such kindness. The woman, who spoke perfect English, replied, "We just like people."

"That's true," her husband answered, "but it's more than that. You looked different from most tourists, being here at this time of year—and on bicycles at that. And it seemed friendly of you to speak to me in Dutch. I couldn't understand what you said," he went on, grinning slyly, "but I could tell that it was friendly, whatever it was."

Swiss National Tourist Office photo

"Parlez-vous anglais?"
"Oui."
"Which way to Berne?"

Minimum survival vocabulary

In our opinion there is an absolutely minimum vocabulary you should have to survive in a foreign country. And when we say "to survive," we do not mean to raise questions of life and death; we are talking about survival in terms of maximum enjoyment in any given country. You may disagree with our choices, but then you're probably wrong about a lot of things. This, then, is our list of words and phrases that will allow you to fit in, wherever you go:

railroad station	*hello* or *good day*	*inexpensive* or *cheap*
thank you	*yes*	*hotel*
please	*no*	*room*
I don't understand	*toilet*	*breakfast*
where is . . . ?	*men*	*good-bye*
how much is . . . ?	*women*	*entrance*
do you speak English?	*I'm sorry*	*exit*
	pardon or *excuse me*	
	too much	

For this little vocabulary we have eliminated numbers for now. We'll list a few later. You can always hold up the right number of fingers. It sounds dumb, but you'll find yourself doing it. As you may have noticed, much of our word list is budget-oriented ("how much," "too much," and "inexpensive"). Indeed, "breakfast" fits in the same category, because it is important to be sure that breakfast is included in your room price. So all of these words and phrases have been included here because they seem basic to survival, to blending into the scenery, or to saving money.

Beyond the use of this little vocabulary, which we will translate into several other languages shortly, the tricks for communicating with people are fairly simple. You do a lot of pointing for ''where'' questions, and hope that your victim does the same. Produce your map and let your informant point to places you inquire about. Write down the names of places you ask about, because they often hear something in our way of talking that confuses them (and what it is, doubtlessly, is mispronunciation). Written or printed out, place names are not confusing—unless you don't use *their* spelling, which in many cases is different (*e.g.*, Köln for Cologne.)

It appears to us that a little proficiency in French and German, along with your English, will get you through almost anything in any back corner of Europe. For this reason we are first translating our basic survival vocabulary into these languages. We will indicate the English pronunciation where it isn't apparent from the appearance of the word or phrase.

English	French	German
railroad station	*la gare*	*der Bahnhof*
thank you	*merci* (meyr-see)	*danke schön* (dahn-keh shuhn)
please	*s'il vous plaît* (seel voo play)	*bitte* (bit-teh)
I don't understand	*je ne comprend pas* (zhuh neh kohm-prahn pah)	*ich verstehe nicht* (ick fehr-shteh-heh nihkt)
Do you speak English?	*Parlez-vous anglais?*	*Sprechen Sie Englisch?*
where?	*ou?* (oo?)	*wo?* (voh?)
how much?	*combien?* (kom-b'yehn?)	*wievel?* (vee-feel?)
hello *or* good day	*bonjour* (bohn-zhoor)	*guten Tag* (gooten-tahk)
yes	*oui* (wee)	*ja* (ya)
no	*non* (noh)	*nien* (nine)
toilet	*lavabo* or *cabinet*	*Toilette* (twah-lettuh) or *Klosett*
men	*messieurs*	*Herren* or *Männer*
women	*dames* (dahms)	*Frauen* or *Damen*
excuse me	*excusez-moi* (ex-ku-zeh mwah) or *pardon*	*Verzeihung* (Fehr-sigh-hoonk)
too much	*trop cher* (tro share)	*zu teuer* (tsoo toy'r)
inexpensive *or* cheap	*bon marché* (bohn mar-sheh)	*billig* (bill-likh)
hotel	*hotel* (oh-tel)	*Hotel*
room	*chambre* (sham-breh)	*Zimmer*
breakfast	*le petit déjeuner* (luh peh-tee day-zhuh-nay)	*Frühstück* (frew-shtewk)
good-bye	*au revoir* (oh rev-wahr)	*Auf Wiedersehen* (ow vee-der-zehn)
entrance	*entree* (ahn-tray)	*Eingang*
exit	*sortie*	*Ausgang*

That tiny vocabulary will keep you more or less alive anywhere in Europe, although there are many situations you won't be able to cope with. It always throws you a bit, for instance, when a uniformed official opens your compartment door on the train and says, "Gersneezle?" You don't knew whether to give him your ticket, your passport, or just say, "Yes, indeed. And how's yours?" Equally confusing is the cash-register end of the line in grocery stores, where the checkout woman always says something, and you don't know whether it is "What a nice day!" or "You're gonna hate those apples."

For our early trips years ago, Alan took the trouble to learn quite a repertory of French and German words and phrases, which was great. However, among the phrases he learned was: "Do you speak French?" (or German or Italian or whatever). For some time he kept asking people this question, and then listening to an unintelligible response. Finally one day he said, "Why do I ask people that? It doesn't do any good." The message is: don't learn phrases that won't help you, because you'll use them in Europe and make things even worse.

Well, you may go someplace where even English, French, and German won't pull you through, so let's translate the same words into Italian and Spanish.

English	Italian	Spanish
railroad station	*stazione*	*estación*
thank you	*grazie*	*gracias*
please	*per piacere*	*por favor*
I don't understand	*non capisco*	*no comprendo*
Do you speak English?	*Parla inglese?*	*¿Habla usted ingles?*
where?	*dove?*	*¿dónde?*
how much?	*quanto?*	*¿cuánto es?*
hello *or* good day	*buon giorno* (bwohn djyor-no)	*buenos días* (bweh-ness dee-ahs) or ¡*Hola!*
yes	*sí*	*sí*
no	*no*	*no*
toilet	*ritirata or gabinetto*	*excusado* or *retrete*
men	*signori*	*señores* or *caballeros*
women	*signore*	*señores* or *damas*
excuse me	*scusi*	*dispénseme* or *lo siento*
too much	*troppo caro*	*demasiado*
inexpensive *or* cheap	*buon mercato*	*barato*
hotel	*albergo*	*hotel*
room	*sala or camera*	*sala* or *habitación*
breakfast	*colazione* (koh-lah-tzyoh-neh)	*desayuno* (day-sah-yoo-no)
good-bye	*arrivederci*	*adios*
entrance	*entrata*	*entrada*
exit	*uscita*	*salida*

Although we have decided against including translations into Eskimo and Swahili, we are going to include two more—Dutch and Danish.

English	Dutch	Danish*
railroad station	station	Jernbanestationen
thank you	dank U	tak
please	als't U blieft (ahst u bleeft)	vaer saa venlig
I don't understand	Ik begrijp het niet	Jeg forstar ikke
Do you speak English?	Spreekt U Engels?	Taler De Engelsk?
where?	waar?	Hvor? (vohr?)
how much?	hoeveel? (hov-fayl?) or wat kosthet?	hvor meget? (vohr ma-yud?)
hello or good day	hallo or goeden morgen	god morgen
yes	ja	ja
no	neen	nej (nai)
toilet	toilet or W.C.	Toilette (twah-let-tud)
men	heren	Herrer
women	dames or vrouwen	Damer
excuse me	exscuseer	undskyld (own-skeal)
too much	te veel	for dyrt
inexpensive or cheap	goedkoop	billig
hotel	hotel	Hotel
room	kamer	Vaerelse (vay-rul-suh)
breakfast	ontbijt	Morgenmad or Morgenkaffe
good-bye	vaarwel** or goedendag	farvel
entrance	ingang	Adgang or Indgang
exit	uitgang	Udgang

*The pronunciation of many of these words is about the same in Norwegian and Swedish, even though the spelling is often a little bit different.

**This is correct, but many of the Dutch say "Da!" when parting, and they seem to consider it a bit of an insult or slight if you take leave without saying this little musical note. Listen for it; it's rather nice.

And, finally, just to remind you that you may have language problems wherever you go in Europe, we give you this sentence: The man stared through his windscreen out over the bonnet of his motorcar at the metalled road as he listened to his wireless and wondered who the lad was who had just sold him the tin of petrol he had in his boot.

It is difficult indeed to know what to say about a people who give towns such names as Knockin, Snodland, Airshow, Wormit, Up Holland, and Hutton-le-Hole. Is it all really serious? Is Hutton really a hole? Is the name before that a town, or a slur on the Netherlands? Given the British sense of humor, it's hard to know for sure, but one indeed suspects that such names are in no way intended to amuse in- or outsiders. But they do, nevertheless.

English signs can also occasionally be entertaining to visitors from foreign lands. Examples are traffic signs which read, "Give Way"; notices in buses and trains that warn, "Mind Your Head When Rising from Seat"; and the rather immodest words on London post boxes which refer to the two slots by these words: "London" and "All Other Places."

English pronunciation is the most fun and the most confusing of all to Americans and Canadians. "Grosvenor" is pronounced "Grovnor"; Harwich is "Harich"; and Glouchester is "Glouster."

To bring this subject to a close, we will point out that streets are gates, gates are bars, and bars are pubs. Perhaps you already know that you can't speak French, German, or Swedish. Now you must realize that you can't speak English either, not the way *they* speak it. But you must understand that they had the language first, and that the rest of us are interlopers of sorts. It's not really a problem most of the time, and you'll doubtlessly find yourself charmed to hear how they deal with the mother tongue.

You may even learn how to speak English before you come home.

A postgraduate course

And now, just for handy reference, here are a few postgraduate words and phrases. Phonetically speaking, the word "pharmacy" or "apothecary" in most any country will get you to what we call a drug store. "Free" or "libre" will work almost anywhere to indicate "open" or "available." "Hotel" seems to be pretty much of an international word, as we have seen. In most places "dentist" slurred into "dawn-teest" or "dehn-teestah" will get you to one of those chaps, and "medicin" or "medico" or "dottore" will be understood as "doctor" or "M.D."

Here are a few numbers in the languages we've already looked at. We only give them phonetically, and you will hear some interesting similarities here and there:

	French	German	Italian	Spanish	Dutch	Danish
1.	uhn	eins	oo-noh	oo-no	ayn	ayn
2.	duh	tsvigh	doo-eh	dohs	tway	toh
3.	trwah	dry	treh	trays	dree	treh
4.	kahtre	fear	kwah-troh	kwah-tra	fear	fear
5.	sank	fewnf	chink-weh	theen-koh	fife	fem
6.	seess	zeks	say	sehss	zess	sex
7.	set	zee-ben	set-tay	see-ay-tay	ze-ven	seev
8.	weet	ahkt	otto	oh-choh	ockt	oh-deh
9.	nuff	noyn	noh-vay	nway-veh	neh-khen	nee
10.	dees	tsehn	dee-yeh-chee	dyeth	teen	tee

A few other words and phrases that might be useful for anyone who wants to get past the first-grade level are:

English	French	German
Is it far?	*Est-ce que c'est loin?*	*Ist es weit?*
telephone office	*téléphone bureau*	*Telefonbüro*
post office	*poste* or *bureau de poste*	*Postamt*
the check, please	*l'additión, s'il vous plait*	*Meine Rechnung, bitte*
small	*petit*	*klein*
large	*grand*	*gross*
with bath	*avec bain*	*mit Bad*
without bath	*sans bain*	*ohne Bad*
ice	*glace*	*Eis*
a ticket to ...	*un billet pour...*	*eine Fahrkarte nach ...*
Is the tip included?	*Est-ce que le service est compris?*	*Ist das Trinkgeld einbegriffen?*
please speak slowly	*parlez lentement, s'il vous plait*	*bitte langsamer*
Air mail stamp	*par avion timbre-poste*	*Luftpostmarken*
a timetable, please	*un horaire, s'il vous plait*	*einen Fahrplan, bitte*
I am sick	*Je suis malade*	*ich bin krank*

And now let's briefly discuss the words or symbols you will see on toilet doors, which may or may not indicate "male" or "female." Many of them just say "toilet" in one language or another, and you will ordinarily find two more doors inside, one for women, the other for men. Over much of Europe, such doors as these are frequently adorned with black figures, one with a skirt, the other with trousers. Those are the easy ones. Then there these symbols: a circle (for women); a triangle (for men); and two circles (men and women). W.C. (water closet) is also seen frequently in various countries.

Authors' photo. Spain

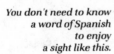
You don't need to know a word of Spanish to enjoy a sight like this.

In Italy, the men's rooms are marked *"signori,"* the women's *"signore"*—and they are perhaps the most difficult ones to remember correctly. Common names elsewhere on men's toilets are: *Herren, Männer, Caballeros, Messieurs;* on women's: *Damen, Frauen, Dames, Señoras.* Never confuse the French word *"Privé"* with "privy"—it simply means "private," and it has nothing to do with toilets.

One last word of advice on this subject: when you are asking a European how and where to find a toilet, don't ask for a bathroom or a restroom. To most Europeans, a bathroom is a place where one takes a bath, and a restroom is a facility found in bus and train stations where one may sit and wait for his departure. When you want to find a toilet, ask for a toilet.

And for the moment we'll stop there. We'll have a few more suggestions on words and phrases in Chapter Eleven, where we deal with the most potentially embarrassing, humiliating, and fearsome invention of modern man: the European menu. For now let us just remind you that seeming to have confidence when you have none is perhaps the most important single factor in dealing with languages. Throat-clearing, muttering, pretending to have a natural speech defect, etc., are all helpful, too, but the best thing of all is to have a few words and phrases at your lips (so to speak), ready to confuse the person you're "talking" to as much as he's confusing you.

Buy and take phrase books in French or German, or take both with you. If you will visit a number of countries, the *Berlitz World-Wide Phrase Book* is useful. It contains translations into sixteen languages and even some oddities like Swahili, but it doesn't, strangely enough, include Danish. It is published by Grosset and Dunlap.

And the following may be the most important tip we will give you in this book. If you really like the people, and if you really want to know what they are all about, you can talk with Europeans everywhere if you smile and are a bit outgoing. Europeans are usually a bit shy or reserved themselves, but if you say something first, most of them will start talking (almost always in English), and you will find that they are really interested in you. Generally they are curious about North America and Canadians and Americans, just as you are curious about them, and these little conversations in the trains or cafes are, at worst, interesting, and, at best, fascinating. Try it; you'll be astonished to learn how charming you are!

We would say that the best bets for having such chitchats in trains or buses are Holland, Denmark, Italy, Austria, Luxembourg, Southern Germany, Portugal, and Belgium. Possible, but not so likely: Sweden, France, Norway, and Switzerland. Surprisingly, you may not find it too easy in England either—at least not on the trains. The British do their talking in the pubs.

Having such conversations is a matter that clearly depends upon luck, timing, and the individuals involved. But indeed, if you can speak a given language like a native, you'll enjoy yourself in any country where it is used. If you can't, like most unilingual Americans, we still think that your best chances for really getting to know people lie in the small pensions anywhere, and, more generally, in places where English is commonly used, *e.g.,* England, Wales, Scotland, Holland, Denmark, Belgium, Austria, and Switzerland.

It can nevertheless happen anywhere. Some years ago we spent several hours in a second-class train compartment with a Yugoslavian mother and daughter. The four of us were unable to communicate with each other except through the use of a German phrase book we were carrying, but we did share lunch all around— and somehow we all became friends. Our "conversation" lasted for almost three hours, and it was fascinating.

It was obvious from their clothes that they were not well-to-do. The mother especially appeared to be a weatherbeaten peasant woman, but they both looked as if they had worked hard for what they had, and that didn't seem to be much. The mother became interested in our little German camera, and through the daughter and the phrase book asked us a number of questions about it—the last of which was "What did it cost?"

After perhaps twenty minutes we got the price converted from American to German to Yugoslavian money, and gave them our answer.

The old lady mused for a time over what must have sounded like a fortune to her, looking at the camera from one side and then the other. She then spoke rapidly to her daughter for a time, who turned again to the phrase book and began to try to tell us what her mother had said. After an interminable length of time we got the message, which was (we think): "She says that you have a beautiful camera. She says she has no camera, but six children instead. She thinks she is the luckiest."

We all laughed together, and we tried to tell her that we agreed. At the end of the ride we exchanged American and Yugoslavian coins (we think they came out ahead by six cents), and parted with smiles and more words that communicated nothing more precise than the closeness we had all achieved in such a relatively short time. We hope that they still remember us today, because we will never forget them.

So, once again, what we're suggesting is simply that learning to say "eat" in another language is better than not learning to say anything, and it is also better than learning something complex that is not quite right: "Would you be so kind as to direct me to a nearby and highly regarded coal mine?" So keep it simple, learn what you learn well, and—*have confidence.* You might as well; it doesn't do you a bit of good not to have it.

Chapter Six
Large Bills with Small Values

Q. How will I learn the current value of a franc?
A. When you try to buy a cup of coffee with one.

Generally, Europeans seem to be pretty honest, but when a tourist holds out a handful of coins to a shopkeeper with the words, "I don't understand this funny money. Take what you need," he's asking to be cheated. When he doesn't count his change for a purchase, he deserves to be shortchanged. When he gives travellers' checks to a money changer and doesn't even count what he gets back, he's stupid.

Some years ago, in Belgium, we found a wonderful pension quite near the train station for six dollars (double room and breakfasts). We liked the room, the location, and the service—and we stayed for several days. During that time we came to know all the members of this beautiful family, all of whom did what they could to make our stay pleasant. It was idyllic. When we checked out we were given a bill which we started to pay, and then, for some reason, decided to figure for ourselves. We had no reason to distrust these people; we had just gotten into the habit of scrutinizing bills that were presented to us. Lo and behold, it was correct on a daily basis, but it totaled one more day than we had been there. It was doubtlessly an honest mistake, and the lady of the house appeared to be chagrined. Whatever happened, we did not spend six bucks for something we didn't get.

We had a similar situation in a little town in Austria on one of our more recent expeditions, but in this case the error was not an honest one. When we checked out, the proprietor attempted to overcharge us by one hundred schillings, which at

89

that time was worth about four U.S. dollars. Because we had already figured what the bill should be, we were able to tell the man immediately that he'd made a "mistake." Well, he looked surprised, apologized profusely, and cut his demand in half. We realized later that he'd been so startled by being caught that he had finally cheated himself.

When you arrive in a country, one of your first tasks will be to visit the currency exchange in the railroad station, or, if the lines are too long there, in a nearby bank. These operations have little signs up that tell you what *their* currency is in relationship to yours, and the clerks behind the counter sometimes tend to sort of throw it at you. They usually don't count it out to you as our bank tellers do. Well, lines notwithstanding, we still think it is a good idea to give the stuff a quick count. Why should you assume that that little man is honest? He won't assume that about you. He will usually demand your passport and will compare your photo to your face, and he'll look carefully at your checks to be sure they are good—so you should be as cautious as he is. Don't trust him either. Count your money. At least be sure that it totals the same as the printout figure he will give you for a receipt.

A unit of currency from a given European country may be worth more than a U.S. dollar (e.g., the British pound) or worth a tiny fraction of a dollar (Italy's lira, for example). The paper money may be a good deal larger than a dollar in size, or considerably smaller, but one cannot make the mistake of thinking of it as Monopoly money. It is the coin of the realm, and should be treated with care and respect. The most important thing of all is to learn and to remember what it is worth in relation to your own money. If you can make quick and reasonably close conversions to dollars in your head of any price you see, you won't make mistakes such as paying more for something than you thought you did.

We will not deal here with specific conversions, simply because the exchange rates change so frequently. Instead we will show how to make quick mental conversions no matter what the exchange rate is wherever you find yourself.

Let's assume that in the first country you visit you learn that the current exchange rate is $.095. Each unit of the foreign currency is worth about a dime, which means that you can get a rough conversion by dividing any price you see by ten.

In the next country you visit, you learn that the exchange rate is $.19. Here you divide prices by five to get a rough conversion.

If the exchange rate is $.03, multiply prices by .03 (or by 3, remembering to move the decimal point two places left in the result). This will give you an exact conversion.

If the rate is near $.50 (.47 to .53), divide prices by two.

All of this is easier than it sounds, and a little practice will make perfect. It is important to get a rough formula worked out, remember it, and use it when making purchases or paying bills.

If you have a pocket calculator with you, simply multiply the prices you see by the current conversion rate, wherever you are. If you don't have a calculator along, fill in the current conversion rate in any country you visit in the grid below, and devise your own rough conversion to U.S. dollars. You might wish to check your logic and arithmetic by filling in the "Examples" column with two entries: put down an arbitrary price in the foreign currency and multiply it by the current conversion rate to get an exact translation; then put down the same price and apply the rough conversion you have worked out to see if the result is close to the exact conversion. If so, you're in business. If not, you'll need to figure out a better rough conversion formula.

Country	Current exchange rate	Rough conversion to dollars from European prices	Examples

It would be a good idea to make *exact* calculations if you are going to buy anything of major cost; the rough conversions, however well done, can be off a long ways on large numbers. And it is wise to be sure when you cross a border to get the appropriate conversion values in mind as well and as soon as you can; it is not a paying proposition to be spending one currency on the basis of another currency's conversion value.

So it is important to learn the conversion rates and to count your change—always. It can be a bit difficult in a new currency, but you can at least do it roughly —and you can learn how counting it out as you pay for things. This is a far better way than paying for everything with bills and not counting returning change, and finally (when the change gets heavy), holding out a handful of it to allow some entrepreneur to take as much of it as his conscience will permit. This is putting an unfair temptation in front of people.

When you learn a country's coins, try to become familiar with their size differences. There are many tales about small rip-offs in England that are made possible by visitors' lack of understanding of the values of English coins. The Dutch have one- and two-and-a-half-guilder coins that aren't terribly different in size, and we have heard tales about unscrupulous people picking the slightly larger coin out of the innocent's hands when they should have taken a guilder. We haven't had this happen ourselves, but we have had the experience of pulling out change and starting to pick through it, only to have the entrepreneur try to stick *his* fingers into it. Apparently tourists *do* let people do this sort of thing. We hope that you won't.

Some airlines and banks can provide you with little currency converters, which are useful to have in Europe. Here are a few generalities about some of the currencies, with all "sub-units" worth one one-hundredth of a "unit":

Country	Currency Units	Subunits	Country	Currency Units	Subunits
Austria	schillings	groschen	*Iceland*	kronur	aurar
Belgium	francs	centimes	*Italy*	lire	---
Britain	pounds	pence	*Monaco*	French francs	centimes
Denmark	kronor	øre	*Norway*	krone	öre
Finland	markka	penni	*Portugal**	escudos	centavos
France	francs	centimes	*Spain*	pesetas	centimos
Germany	marks	pfennigs	*Sweden*	kronor	öre
Holland	guilders (florin)	cents	*Switzerland*	francs	centimes

*In Portugal, the dollar sign is used to divide escudos from centavos. In other words, 30$50 means 30 escudos, 50 centavos; $50 means 50 centavos. They don't seem to have it right, do they?

There is a strange situation in Luxembourg, where Luxembourg and Belgian francs compete as legal tender. The real problem is that the Luxembourg currency is not accepted anywhere outside the country, so it must be exchanged before leaving the little Duchy's borders. If your stay there is to be a short one, you can just bring in or trade there for Belgian money. But don't take Luxembourg money *out* with you. You'll own it forever. The same thing holds true for Ireland and Britian. British or Irish money works in Ireland, but the Irish gelt isn't accepted in England.

Finally, you do lose a little every time you trade currencies, so it is ordinarily best to be a bit conservative each time on how much you trade for. As American Express puts it, and we quote: "There are three instances when you can incur a currency exchange cost: A. When originally converting your money from U.S. dollars to a foreign currency. B. When you convert one foreign currency into yet another foreign currency. And C. If you convert unused foreign currency back into U.S. dollars." That means that they get you at least twice in each country. Ordinarily you can trade for the next country's currency before you get there, or you can wait until you arrive, but do get rid of everything (but the few coins you might want for souvenirs) before you leave Europe. You can trade such currency back through U.S. banks, and you say you will, but will you? Do it there—and remember that foreign coins are usually not convertible in this country.

Negotiable instruments
Most European visitors carry travellers' checks with them, and many bring credit cards of one sort or another. Travellers' checks work very well, but they should be cashed in banks or other official money-changing agencies. Shops and hotels have to pay something extra to cash them, and this additional amount is always passed on to you. And in our experience, it costs something extra to convert with the man who will sometimes approach you on the train as you near a national boundary, in spite of his assurance that he represents a bank. He probably does, but it costs something to have him there—and you have to pay it.

If you turn too many travellers' checks into the currency of a given country and then have to reconvert some of that money to another currency when you leave, you will have lost twice on the transaction. But some countries, for example Belgium, charge a flat fee for converting any amount up to a fairly high level, which means that you will pay the same fee for cashing one check or a number of them. Really frugal people will want to examine how the cashing fee is charged—whether it is a simple percentage or a flat fee—and then make their decision about how many checks to cash at a time.

It is possible to purchase your travellers' checks in any foreign denomination you wish, which is especially advantageous if you are planning to stay in a particular country for a fair length of time. As you would guess, these checks are just like the currency specified, which has some advantages, *and* the disadvantage that any left over have to be converted back to American dollars at some loss. But in Britain, for example, it is expensive to cash dollar travellers' checks, so anyone who planned to spend some time and money there should consider buying checks in pounds. If this idea interests you, you should investigate the possibility with your bank.

Inexpensive and unusual entertainments are easy to find in Europe.

Swiss National Tourist Office photo

If you do look into this matter, you will probably discover that:

- you may get a better rate of exchange here than you can get in Europe (and here you can shop for the best rate; in Europe you usually can't);

- you will be able to buy travellers' checks in foreign denominations at a better rate than you can buy the comparable currency;

- you can do this even through small banks, often at the same rates the big ones offer;

- you should finally trade any foreign denomination checks you have left for dollars before leaving Europe.

Another tip: some travellers' checks cost one percent of the amount you purchase as a fee, but you can obtain them without charge from some banks, savings and loan organizations, and Thomas Cook travel agencies. In order not to get into fusses with people who cash them, it is probably wise to have checks from a well-known company like American Express (which does charge the one percent) or Cook's, which is well known all over Europe. If you purchase "off brands," you may find it quite difficult and time-consuming to get a refund in case of loss or theft. At the other extreme, you can get refunds on American Express checks in Europe even on holidays, Saturdays, or Sundays. If it *is* such a time when the AE offices are closed, you can go to any Holiday Inn or Avis Rent-A-Car agency to get an emergency refund (of up to one hundred dollars) to hold you until you can get the balance on a regular business day.

You would be wise to keep a record of your travellers' check numbers in several different places, just in case you lose them or get robbed and have to have them replaced. You would also be well advised to carry the receipt given to you when you purchased the checks for your trip. It is possible that you could be refused replacement if you lost some checks and couldn't even prove that you ever owned them in the first place. In such cases, what is most likely is that the refunding office will call or telex the U.S., which at the very least will mean some delay. Another thought: if you are travelling with your wife or husband, it is a good idea to have some of the checks signed by each of you. On one of our early trips we didn't think about this, at least not until we were in Europe, when we realized that one of us owned all the funds, while the other was destitute. Fortunately for the destitute one, we didn't ever get separated.

American Express has devised a way to help you if you want to get checks for someone who can't be present to sign them when they are purchased. They will let you fill out a "In Blank Purchaser's Application Form," which will permit you to take some unsigned checks to your travelling companion. He or she can then sign them and a form that is sent back to AE for their records. It is also possible to order AE checks by mail or by telephone. This can be done through their offices or banks that handle their checks.

One last tip: some places will not accept travellers' checks which have been countersigned with a felt-tipped pen.

Credit cards are useful to have in Europe. One sees many shop windows, cafes, hotels, and restaurants bearing the decal "welcome" for American Express and Diners cards, and often for MasterCard and Bank Americard. The cards can relieve you of having to hold so much currency in each country, and they can be used to pay bills if you run out of funds altogether. It would be a good idea, though, to have hidden somewhere in your luggage the name, address, telephone number and cable address of the office to contact in case of loss or theft.

We have investigated to find out whether a tourist who ran out of money in Europe could go to a bank, as he could in the States, and borrow money against his MasterCard or Americard. As it turns out, you can't—not even from an American bank over there. You can go to a bank when you first arrive, deposit money, and get special Eurocheques you can use anywhere, but the whole thing strikes us as being complicated. If you do get into real money troubles, you can have cash wired to you from the United States—or you can go to an American Consulate (where you're going to have one hell of a time getting any money, no matter what your reason). So the best thing is to make a good guess at how much you're going to need, and to take at least twenty-five percent more than that amount in travellers' checks. They are good forever. You can always spend or redeposit whatever you have left when you return home.

We have also had a look at the possibility that one might carry cashiers' or certified checks to Europe, or even a letter of credit and a separate letter of identification issued by his bank, but it appears that he might never get any bank anywhere over there to exchange currency for them. He *could* cable his bank at home and ask that funds from his account be transferred to a bank in Europe, but this would take four or five working days and cost a bit in fees, cable costs, etc. Bank officials generally advise that the best insurance against running out of funds is to have extra travellers' checks tucked away, or to have an American Express card with you—which you can use to obtain cash.

In some shops you can cash personal checks for purchases, and if you have an American Express card you can cash one in any of their many offices for up to one thousand dollars (one or possibly two hundred dollars in cash and the balance in travellers' checks). This should carry you through any sort of emergency, because you can exercise this privilege every twenty-one days.

At the risk of sounding like propagandists for American Express by mentioning their services once again, we will mention a nice form of insurance they will provide you against running entirely out of funds in Europe. You can ask your bank for an AE preferred customer card, which will allow you to cash one personal check, one time only, at any AE office anywhere for up to $500 in travellers' checks. There is no charge for the card, you do not have to be a regular AE cardholder to get it, and you won't get it at all if your banker doesn't have a high regard for your credit rating. These cards are good for only six months, but it is possible to apply for and get one time and again. Note: if you are going to try to obtain one of these little pieces of insurance against possible destitution, give your banker a bit of lead time. The idea is so new that not all banking officials know about its existence yet.

Lastly, you might carry at least a little cash with you, especially if you have a fairly safe way to hide it. U.S. dollars are useful in Europe. Not only can they be spent just like local currency in a number of places, but often they can be converted into any country's money at a better discount than will be charged for travellers' checks.

Ways to spend your money

Now after all the foregoing about money values, how to convert it, and so on, let's take a look at some ways to spend it—or avoid spending more of it than necessary. Haggling is a perfectly acceptable way of conserving money in Europe. It is a skill that, by and large, most Americans don't possess. We all think that we do a good job of haggling over car prices, but any car dealer will tell you that he gets his way ninety-nine percent of the time. So if you are an automobile salesman, you need not waste your time on this advice. If you're anyone else, you'd better read on.

In Europe you can haggle over room prices or over merchandise in places like flea markets. It's accepted and expected. You cannot get away with it, of course, in most ordinary stores or businesses. The process, done properly, is a simple one; it requires no yelling, wrestling, or unpleasantness. These rules should be kept in mind:

1. The haggler (you) never insults the seller (and this is easy to do when the seller is merchandising items he made himself).

2. If the seller insults you (''You're cheap!''), walk off. Don't turn back.

3. You are playing his game, and he knows the rules, as well as what the bottom figure is. In other words, you'll never really win; but if you're persistent, you may get a healthy discount. The lowest figure you can get the seller to agree to is fair to both of you. He'll make some profit, and you'll get a ''deal.''

Frankly, we don't think that the way to go about it is to say ''too much!'' whether you're dickering for a room or for a piece of merchandise. That cheapens the whole thing. If it's a room, all you have to say is, ''That's a bit more than we can afford. Have you a room for less?'' If your opponent doesn't speak English, and you don't speak his tongue, you are stuck with the ''too much'' phrase we gave you in Chapter Five. Or, better yet, ''Sorry, too much.'' Unless it's a rainy night and he knows that he has the last room in town for rent he'll often then offer you a better price (probably for a different room, but not necessarily one that is any less desirable than the one you just looked at). If it's a piece of merchandise, all you have to do is to smile, and shake your head. If at that point he doesn't suggest a better price, say ''thank you'' and start to walk away. Nine times out of ten he'll try to stop you by offering you a better price. As a rule of thumb, we'd suggest that if you do make the seller an offer (when you have no idea what the item is really worth), that your offer always be half or less of what he asked. A much better strategy, obviously, is to have done a little research and to know that what he is asking thirty rubles for could be purchased for ten or twelve or fifteen. If you know *that,* you know how to haggle with him. Then you smile and say, "How about eight rubles?"

The seller never thinks badly of you (in this case, or, indeed, in the American car-selling game) for trying to get a better deal. He will consider you an idiot if you pay his price. It is a game in which almost anything goes but trading insults. Shopping (research) helps; beyond that, the whole thing is an art rather than a science. Phyllis once made a very good deal in a small shop in Spain without saying one word (and she does speak good Spanish—when she wishes). She was looking at an item she wanted that was marked 280 pesetas. She looked at it, picked it up, put it down, and dug into her purse and pulled out a 100-peseta bill. She dug around some more in her purse but seemed to find no more money. She picked up the thing again. She put it down. She looked in her purse again (she was still holding the 100-peseta note). She looked at the thing again. She finally shook her head and started for the door. The proprietor got there before she did, and he was holding the item in his hand. He held it out to her and reached for the bill she was holding.

It was probably only worth 50 pesetas, but she was pleased with her purchase, and it was obvious that he was too.

You don't have to be nasty to haggle. You only have to be a little bit cunning. And you really are foolish if you don't do it. It will work and is expected in any flea market, and in many, perhaps most, bazaars and shops of less character than big department stores. Any of these places may have marked prices that are two or three times what is really expected, and in Italy, even in the best stores, discounts are given on almost any pretext. There a shopper can get a price cut for paying with travellers' checks, for referring to himself as a "professional" who is purchasing something for his work, by claiming to be a "regular customer" of the place, and so on. It would always be worthwhile to ask, and will almost invariably be worth something in the smaller shops, particularly some of those which sell souvenirs.

Lastly, let's talk about the so-called duty-free shops which are located in various airports—on the aircraft side of customs. They are simply little stores that do not have to charge local taxes. You may or may not find lower prices there on many items, but you will find it possible to get big breaks on such health-related products as cigarettes, candy, and booze. All we can suggest on this is again to try to make comparisons: if you are interested in a specific item like a certain model wristwatch, it would be wise to compare its U.S. price, country-of-origin price, and duty-free airport shop price. One should not assume, in other words, that a duty-free shop will provide him a lower price on a given item than anyone else will. As one example of this, we have noticed that the woolen clothing items in the duty-free store at Keflavik, Iceland, are much higher priced than comparable items in downtown Reykjavik (many transit passenger only stop here for an hour, which means that they can't get downtown). So it isn't wise to assume that any of these places are necessarily providing great bargains. We are not convinced that one can get good deals on wristwatches or cameras in any of them. It is generally true that their biggest bargains are the items that are ordinarily highly taxed, *e.g.*, tobacco and liquor products or perfumes.

You can get an idea of the airport duty-free shop prices before you go if you wish. You can write for a catalog of their wares. For the Amsterdam Airport Shopping Centre, which boasts of the lowest prices in tax-free shopping, you can write to:

P.O. Box 7501
Schiphol Airport
Holland

or, easier yet, to:
KLM Royal Dutch Airlines
437 Madison Ave.
New York, NY 10022

If you are flying with Icelandic, you will be making a stop at Keflavik International Airport (which also advertises the lowest prices in tax-free airport shopping). As far as we know, this is the only European one you can get into *before* travelling around the Continent (unless you are going to Dublin and your flight makes a stop at Shannon). The others will not allow you in unless you are on a departing flight. So if you want to buy something to use *over there,* Keflavic and Icelandic is your only chance. For that catalog, write to:

Duty-Free Store
Keflavik International Airport
Keflavik, Iceland

Getting such catalogs will help you to make the price comparisons suggested above. On most flights you can buy cigarettes or liquor at duty-free prices on the aircraft or in the international terminal from which you depart. Note: you will not get as good a selection of brands on the aircraft as you will in the store in the terminal.

Here, then, is a summary of ideas that will help to make your money go further:

1. Check the addition on all bills you receive, whether for rooms or for meals.

2. When exchanging currencies, always count the money you are given and check the total against your receipt.

3. Get a rough conversion figure in your head for each country.

4. Don't tempt others by holding out money for them to pick through.

5. Count the change you are given when you buy something.

6. Examine each country's coins and get an idea of how they differ from each other.

7. Be conservative about amounts whenever you convert monies unless there is a flat conversion charge.

8. Keep a record of your travellers' check numbers in a safe place.

9. Be prepared to haggle over prices.

10. Shop and compare prices on everything you spend money for.

11. Check menus (*e.g.,* in restaurant windows) to find out whether value-added taxes and service charges are included in the prices listed.

12. Perhaps most important of all, resist the notion that foreign currency is "play money"; if you can't take it seriously, try to remember that you traded good American or Canadian cash for it.

Try to bring back some of that money you take over there; you'll need it to develop your film.

Chapter Seven
Why Not Leave the Driving to Them?

They broke a window and stole everything out of my rented car, including a bag of garbage. They did leave the seats. . . .
—unidentified American tourist in Italy

To anyone who is interested in automobiles at all, the divergent characteristics of the various European makes is a matter of fascination. Auto buffs make such remarks as, "No one but a German could build a Mercedes or a Porsche, and no one but a Britisher would build a Morris Minor." The statement has some truth: European automobiles do mirror their builder's stereotypes. The excellent finish, engineering, and rigid quality control of the Mercedes, BMW, or Porsche cars do reflect the Teutonic virtues of preciseness, concern with detail, and desire for perfection. The Swedish cars, the Volvos and the Saabs, show the strength, durability, and safety-consciousness that is generally associated with the Swedish character. The Ferrari, the Maserati, and the Lamborghini all display the Italian's "joie de vivre," the desire to live for the here and now, to enjoy, and to be carefree. French cars are generally built for comfort, beauty, and an occasional desire to be unique. The case is probably the hardest to make in relation to the British, who build everything from Rolls-Royces to sports cars to miniature economy sedans, ranging over the quality spectrum from mechanical perfection to rather careless production techniques.

But mostly because of their high taxes and gasoline prices, Europeans do build some of the world's most interesting and efficient economy cars. They are all available to the visitor for purchase or rental, and most European guide books say that "having a car in Europe is ideal for the freedom-loving American." We will offer our opinion on that idea after giving you some information about how you can buy or rent a car over there if you wish to do so.

101

Would you like to drive through streets like this one?

The authors' photo, Germany

First of all, if you are going to rent, lease, or purchase a car, visit an American Automobile Association office before you go. Even though you might decide not to rent (from Avis, Hertz, or Auto-Europe) through them, they can give you valuable advice. And if you're going to purchase a car, you are going to need their help. You do not have to be an AAA member to use this service.

Since car rental is a simpler subject than outright purchase, let's examine it first. But everything we say here about licenses, insurance, and so on will also apply to buying a car. Rentals in Europe are generally under one of three plans: 1) unlimited mileage with single pickup and dropoff point, under which you can drive as far as you wish with no added charges; 2) time and distance, which costs less than the other plan basically, but for which you also pay for each kilometer you drive; and 3) unlimited mileage one-way arrangements, where there are no added mileage charges, but the car is to be dropped at a point different from the pick-up location.

In most cases the unlimited mileage plans decline in cost after a period of a week or two. As of this writing such a plan would get you a car in the smallest class for between fourteen to twenty dollars a day, depending upon where you pick it up, how long you keep it, and so on. A car in the largest class would run from thirty-five to sixty-five dollars a day.

There are other costs to be reckoned with, such as insurance, gasoline, and taxes. Insurance requirements and costs are complex and often vary from country to country, so we will not discuss them here. Gasoline costs run as high as $3.50 per U.S. gallon across Europe. Rental tax rates differ from country to country, so it is wise to find out which country would be best for starting your trip. Since this is not an insignificant matter, we will list them here, showing the percentage of tax that is added to rental fees (1981 rates);

Austria 31.3%	Ireland 10%
Belgium 16%	Italy 18%
Denmark 22%	Luxembourg 10%
Finland 16.28%	Norway 20%
France 17.6%	Portugal 7%
Germany 13%	Spain 3%
Greece 18%	Sweden 23.45%
Holland 18%	Switzerland none
	United Kingdom 15%

There are many kinds of rental plans. Some require that the car be returned in the country in which it was rented, others specify that it must be returned to a different country, and some require that it be returned to the same *office* from which it was rented. There are unlimited mileage budget plans, which, as you would imagine, involve pretty tiny little cars. At the other end of things, you can even rent camping equipment, up through six-bed motor homes. In addition to all of these options on models, plans, taxes, and so on, there are also "off" and "on" season rates which will affect the rental rates, in some cases by substantial amounts.

Since there are so many possibilities that all of this is difficult to understand (as well as boring), we have decided to lay out a hypothetical renting situation for you. You are going to rent a medium-sized car, a Peugeot sedan, for twenty-one days. You are picking it up in France, and you will return it in France to one of the firm's designated cities. You make a fairly long tour around the Continent, but averaging only one hundred miles a day, and when you return the two of you will have spent for transportation well over twice what two train passes would have cost. This is one reason why we advocate travelling by train in Europe. It's a lot less expensive than going by car.

It is possible, of course, to rent a car for just a day or two almost anywhere you go, and this idea is worth considering for areas where there are not good bus or train connections. But let us pass on a thought that has been proposed to us by European friends: it is not wise just to deal with the first rental agency you see. It would be more economical to get a list of all the local rental agencies, perhaps from a tourist office, and to compare their rates because often there are small but reputable agencies that charge a good deal less than the better-known outfits. The tourist office personnel will tell you where they are, and will often be able to tell you their rates.

You should bear in mind that rented cars are usually easy to spot, and to someone with larceny in his heart that means "tourists," which in turn means cameras, luggage, and other sorts of potential valuables. Never leave anything showing in the car, and you would even be wise to leave nothing of value locked in the trunk. Leave the glove box empty and standing open to show that it contains nothing of value. When parking you may be asked by someone if you wouldn't like them to watch your car, and if you say "no" your likelihood of having it robbed then goes way, way up.

Your rented car itself could be stolen. Car theft is growing crazily in Europe. To single out Italy as an example, over 42,000 cars were stolen there in 1975 alone, with only one-third of them recovered. This problem is worst, of course, in large cities. Several hundred cars were stolen in Amsterdam alone last Easter (of all days!), a nice example of this potential danger that could certainly wreck one's vacation. How would you like to show up at the rental agency saying, "Well, I don't suppose you're going to be happy about this, but . . . "?

There are other potential problems to think about in relation to rented cars. Did you scratch it up, or was it that way when you got it? If you have an accident, do you have to pay the daily rental fee while the machine is being fixed? Do you have to pay for the repairs, or do they? (Call the rental agency if it breaks while you have it; if *you* have it fixed, you'll be stuck with the repair bill.) It would be wise to think of all such possible occurrences when you lease the machine and to have an agreement about them, in writing if possible. If it succumbs to old age or mal-treatment while you've got it, do they pay for its return, or do you? Some of these matters seem to be well understood in the States, but can you be so sure that your feelings on such problems will be the accepted opinion in Europe?

Leasing appears to be a less-expensive scheme, running perhaps three-fourths of the total cost of renting an automobile. Under this plan, you are in effect buying the car with a guaranteed repurchase, which means that your cost will consist of a pre-calculated depreciation figure, gas and insurance costs, and fees for driving papers.

Lastly, if you rent or lease a car you may be charged a refundable security deposit or made to prove that you have an internationally recognized credit card. Your U.S. driving license will now be accepted in every Western European country, but it might be wise to invest a few dollars in an International Driving Permit, which, among other things, is printed in a variety of languages. They can be obtained from the AAA. It would also be wise, of course, to think hard about the kinds of in-surance you might buy over there to cover yourself adequately against accidents or liability.

There is one rental possibility worth considering for groups of four to six travellers, and/or people who want to get off the beaten track, and/or people who are economy-minded. Renting a camper (motorhome, caravan, recreational vehicle) can be a good deal for tourists who are independent. These homes-away-from-home provide all linens and eating utensils, a kitchen, beds to sleep four to six people, and some of them have a full bath. In 1980, a deluxe model (a GMO Open Motorhome) rented for $60 a day during low season, and $100 during high season (June through August).

An intermediate size (a GMO Opel Europacamper), which is equipped like the vehicle just mentioned except that it has no bath facilities, rented in 1980 for $50 a day during low season, and $80 during high season (does this help you to understand why we keep arguing that you shouldn't go over during high season?)

A small motorhome (such as a VW camper) can be rented for as low as about $50 a day (particularly in the U.K., where campers carry low rental fees).

All in all, for people who like to camp and cook, and to get off the main roads, the camper-vacation offers a good way to hold down expenses and to see what the countries are really all about. There are many good organizations in the U.S. that offer such arrangements, and several of the best-known are Europacer Tours, Auto-Europe, and The Kemwel Group.

Buying a car

The possibilities for the outright purchase of a car, if not quite endless, are at least mind-boggling. You can order the car before you go, or just buy it there. It can be new or used. You can buy with the intention of bringing it home, or you can take a guaranteed repurchase agreement. You can even buy it duty-free. Again, you need AAA or someone like them to get you through the required morass of paperwork, and to help you make choices between the variety of possibilities.

One tax-free purchase possibility comes to you through the courtesy of the Netherlands government and an organization named ShipSide. This company

In Europe cars are small, and parking places are smaller— or nonexistent.

The authors' photo, Holland

will sell you any model of two dozen makes of European or Japanese automobiles, not to mention a variety of bicycles, motorcycles, and scooters. Sales are tax-free, and delivery (at Amsterdam airport) is immediate. Vehicles can have either European or American specifications (not at the same price, however), and all arrangements can be made beforehand, or in Amsterdam. Your purchase will also include gasoline for 100 miles, registration and plates, a European road atlas, a motoring guide, and a spare fuel can.

ShipSide also ships automobiles back to the U.S. Excluding marine insurance, surcharges, and handling charges, rates from Amsterdam to the East coast range from $200 to $400, depending upon the car model and size. The firm's American address is ShipSide, Inc., 609 Fifth Ave., New York, New York 10017.

A similar organization that AAA works through is Auto-Europe Inc., which offers many different cars for sale in many different countries. This firm will re-purchase cars on the basis of calculated depreciation during the time you've used it, or provide help in shipping it home. There are numerous other companies in the States or in Europe that handle such transactions, some of which are directly associated with the auto-producing companies of Europe (*e.g.,* the U.S. retail dealers).

What the auto factories may do is another matter. Under the so-called "overseas delivery plans," American imported car agencies are authorized to sell you one of their cars for delivery in Europe, with the finer points of the transaction being set by the parent company in Europe. But don't overlook the fact that the American dealership gets paid for such transactions, that car dealers are not noted for their expertise in such matters, or that you are basically in a "buyer beware" situation when you make such a deal. You don't have to worry about being overcharged, as far as we know: the costs and fees are set by the factory. But it would be well to read all the fine print, to understand everything about shipping costs, etc. You are not so likely to run into dishonesty as incompetence on one of these "overseas delivery plan" deals.

At the present time it appears to us that one cannot save money by purchasing a small car in Europe rather than in the States. Auto-Europe admits this in their literature. It looks as if savings are possible on large, expensive cars (the rich get richer. . . .). Advocates of European car purchase and pick-up argue, however, that such an arrangement will take care of your transportation expenses while you are there, and it will—but we still can't see that it is economical.

Part of the dollars and cents problem is associated with the high cost of shipping the machine home. You then face further cash outlays: the requirement to pay a federal excise tax at the point of entry, followed by the time and expense in getting it to your town, and then the necessity of registering and licensing the car with the state. For a time such manufacturers as Volkswagen, Volvo, Porsche, and Mercedes-Benz were shipping cars they sold overseas to the States for very low costs on their own ships. Anyone who wants a specific make should check with the factory or an authorized dealer to learn whether the manufacturer has such arrangements.

There is one other possibility to examine: purchasing a used car in Europe. If this interests you, you should look at an article entitled ''Buying a Used Car in Europe'' by John Wilkes in the May 1975 *Road and Track* magazine. As Mr. Wilkes points out, and we have seen ourselves, good buys on older European cars are available everywhere in Europe. The article will tell you how to find such bargains, how to buy them, and how to go through the required red tape. It occurs to us that if you have a hankering for an elderly economy car, this just might be a good way to get it —and to get a cheap ride through Europe at the same time. Tax rates and currency conversions could affect *where* you might do this. You obviously need to know a good deal about cars to avoid getting stuck with a lemon.

It also seems to us that the *Road and Track* article we mention would be good reading for anyone who is thinking about driving in Europe, no matter on what basis. It is full of information about insurance requirements, registration, camping, and so on. For that matter, anyone thinking of renting *or* buying an auto would be well-advised to go through back issues of *Road and Track* and learn something about the models that interest him. The magazine has a well-deserved reputation for producing fair and informative articles about cars of foreign manufacture.

Some visitors, particularly those who plan to stay in Europe for two or three months, will buy a used camper vehicle and use it both for their transportation and sleeping at night. It is possible to buy such vehicles reasonably in northern Europe, and to sell them later *at a profit* in southern Europe. It is not possible to sell vehicles like this in some countries (*e.g.*, Greece), but it can be done in most places. It's an idea for anyone who knows a bit about cars and prices, and who likes camping out.

Driving in Europe

Let's see if we can touch on a few matters of importance to anyone who is considering driving in Europe. Other than in the United Kingdom, driving everywhere in Europe is on the right. Traffic signals all over the Continent are in international symbols, none of which should give anyone of average intelligence any problems. Posted speeds are fairly low, except for some of the really modern superhighways, for example the German autobahns, and for Denmark, where there are no speed limits. Many roads are patrolled carefully, sometimes by police aircraft. Police are often authorized to collect fines right on the spot—and these can run as much as eighty dollars per violation.

Fairly rough tabs are charged for going through many mountain tunnels, ranging as high as twenty dollars. Unless you have a Ferrari (and possibly not then), it is not feasible to make five or six hundred miles a day in Europe. Indeed, it is not easy to make three hundred, and for that matter, who wants to? Emergency road service is excellent nearly everywhere, with special telephone boxes available for calling for help, and, in some areas, special patrols on major roads by members of the automobile clubs to provide help in case of problems. Most major European auto clubs will provide their services to AAA members.

Gasoline prices in Europe are rather unpleasant. The rates over there average about three times higher than in the U.S. at this writing, with costs in some countries even higher than that.

As far as driving at night is concerned, you will find that motels have been springing up everywhere along the roads of Europe. And unlike the United States, European countries encourage drivers who are tired to pull off the road and sleep in the car for a while. The railroads will haul your car on many major routes on night trains, but they want a pretty pfennig for doing so. If this interests you, you might wish to ask the German Federal Railroad office for their booklet *European Car Carrying Trains,* which lists all the trains of Europe that carry automobiles. It is free of charge. Their address is 11 W. 42nd Street, New York 10036.

There are safety regulations that you will have to familiarize yourself with if you are going to drive over there. In some countries young children are not allowed to ride in the front seats of cars, and seat belt use is compulsory nearly everywhere. Drivers caught on the road without the belts on can be fined on the spot, and in some places your insurance will be invalid if you have an accident while you are not wearing belts. In some countries you are supposed to sound your horn in certain situations, while in others you can be arrested for doing so. In Spain, for example, passing is only legal if it can be accomplished within a prescribed distance or amount of time, and you must sound your horn or flash your lights before overtaking. Drinking and driving are frowned upon, to put it mildly, especially in England and Scandinavia, where such an offense can get you prison time no matter how important you are (or think you are). Nearly everywhere, unless you are on a "priority road," the driver to your right has the right-of-way; he can (and will) pull out in front of you, even if you are on a paved road and he is on what looks like a cattle trail. Lastly, if you have to stop your car by a highway, you are required in most places to put up a little triangular warning sign behind the spot.

There are many other rules, regulations, and traditions in Europe that vary from country to country. Generally speaking, bicyclists have more right-of-way rights than in the U.S., and in many places you will be in really big trouble if you hit one, even if you didn't break any laws in the process. In many areas, you will have to obtain blue discs (usually from the police station or the tourist office) to put in your windshield when you park. Elsewhere you will find either those little horrors, parking meters, or, more likely, every parking spot you can find filled with a car, a motorcycle, or an outdoor fruit or flower stand. Driving in much of Europe is neither much fun nor particularly easy, and parking is worse.

Incidentally, for approximate conversions from kilometers to miles, multiply by six and drop the last digit of the result.

One thing you should be aware of when trying to decide whether or not to drive in Europe has to do with people's attitudes toward automobiles over there. In many parts of Europe a car is a man's proudest possession, and anyone who bumps, dents, or scratches it is in for trouble. Such minor accidents can cause screaming and even fist fights between the drivers, and onlookers often join in these frays, taking sides and keeping the fracas going until the police arrive to break it up. This possibility is yet another reason why we think one would be wise to think carefully before deciding to drive through Europe. Even hitting the bumper of the car behind when you are parking is liable to involve you in a yelling contest with someone—or worse.

Finally, it might be pointed out that you could be at a disadvantage in being on the road with drivers who have lived in Europe all their lives. If you are in mountainous country, they will certainly know how to drive the blind curves better than you do. They are used to better-handling cars than ours, and they generally know more about driving in adverse conditions, on slippery roads, for example, than we do. And not only are we inexperienced at driving in narrow streets, we are totally unfamiliar with how they move out of the way (which sometimes involves getting their vehicles up on the sidewalk) when a bus or truck approaches. Lastly, they drive harder than most Americans do. When you are on one of their super-highways and see headlights flashing in your rearview mirror, *get over* and stay over. You've been signalled that something is overtaking you at probably over 100 miles per hour, and possibly as fast as 150. There aren't many "Sunday drivers" in Europe. Statistically, your chances of being killed on European roads are several hundred times greater than they are in the U.S.

Whatever the driving conditions, Europeans certainly drive differently than Americans or Canadians do. They often pass on curves and on rises they can't see over, and they speed through the narrow streets of towns and villages at incredible velocities. There is some method in this madness: they are used to such race-driver techniques, all of them, and the vehicles on both sides move to the edge in these situations so three cars can use the road abreast. Nevertheless, us outlanders aren't used to such maneuvers, and we tend to drive like beginners in the eyes of the natives. Doing so can elicit many hard looks and screamed imprecations, none of which will help to loosen the already-frayed nerves of the foreign driver.

Most travel book authors say that having a car to use on your European vacation is the best idea since the invention of banana splits. It will give you freedom, they tell you. You can go where you want, when you want, unhampered by train schedules or fixed plans. It saves you having to pack and unpack all the time because you can just throw things in the car. And lastly, they say, it is an economical way to travel.

We disagree. We both drive, we like foreign cars (having owned quite a number of them), and we are all for freedom, doing our own thing, and being frugal. But we disagree because we are unenthusiastic about having to watch the road, decipher traffic signs, and make highway decisions (Should we pass him? Are we going the right way? Is that a cop?). We tend to worry about the fantastically heavy traffic in some parts of Europe, particularly in the bigger cities. We have seen the severity of their parking problems. We have fears that using the car as a suitcase is asking to be robbed, especially at night. We would not like to get into an accident and a yelling match with a driver who didn't speak English. We wouldn't be enthusiastic about trading the fun of meeting people on the trains and buses for spending the whole time just talking to each other, as charming as we both are. Many of the roads over there are terrible. And lastly, as we think we've shown, it's not an economical way to travel, especially if you are alone or with only one other person.

In the United States for many years and in many areas one has had to drive whether he wished to or not. In Europe there are marvelous mass-transportation systems, and to us *they* give you the freedom from headaches and problems, as well as the luxury of a relaxing vacation.

If, after all that, you still want to drive in Europe, let us suggest keeping the following thoughts in mind:

• Shop for the best rental deal.

• Always wear the safety belts when you are driving.

• Remember that the vehicle on the right ordinarily has the right of way.

• Study the basic traffic and road signs before you set out.

• Try to understand the rules for rental, insurance, and dropoffs before you sign a rental agreement.

• Attempt to get an understanding of the rules of the road, wherever you find yourself, so you can deal with any emergency that may crop up.

• Don't drink if you are going to go on the road.

• Expect to run into parking problems.

• Plan to remove all your possessions from the car when you leave it for overnight stays, and even leave the glove-box door open to show passers-by that you have left nothing of value in the vehicle.

• Get good advice and maps before you set out, especially if you are heading for a destination that is not a large city.

• Watch your rear-view mirror constantly.

• If you belong to an automobile club at home, carry some identification with you that proves the fact.

• Be careful.

AUTOMOBILE-RELATED WORDS AND PHRASES

FILL IT UP

faites le plein	French
Ich möchte tanken	German
fate il pieno	Italian
llénelo el tanqué	Spanish

CHECK THE OIL

vérifier l'huile	French
den Oelstand prüfen	German
controlare il livello dell'olio	Italian
comprobar el aceite	Spanish

CHECK THE BATTERY

vérifier les accumulateurs	French
die Batterie prüfen	German
controllare la batteria	Italian
comprobar la bateria	Spanish

CHECK THE TIRE PRESSURE

vérifier le gonflage	French
den Reifendruck prüfen	German
controllare la pressione delle gomme	Italian
ver la presion de las ruedas	Spanish

CLEAN THE WINDSHIELD

essuyer le pare-brise	French
die Windschutzscheibe putzen	German
pulire il parabrezza	Italian
limpiar el parabrisas	Spanish

I WANT _____ LITERS.

Je voudrais _____ litres	French
Ich möchte _____ Liter	German
Lo desidero _____ litri	Italian
Desearia _____ litros	Spanish

PLEASE FIX THIS . . .

S'il vous plait, voulez-vous reparer . . .	French
Können Sie bitte diesen . . . . reparieren	German
Per favore mi ripari questa . . .	Italian
Haga el favor de arreglar esta . . .	Spanish

WHEN WILL IT BE READY?

Quand est-ce que ça sera prêt?	French
Wann wird's fertig sein?	German
Quando sarà pronto?	Italian
¿Cuando estara listo?	Spanish

A MAP

une carte	French
eine Strassenkarte	German
un carta	Italian
un mapa	Spanish

(Cont. next page.)

IS THIS THE ROAD TO . . . ?

Est-ce bien la route de . . . ?	French
Ist das die Strasse nach . . . ?	German
È questa la strada per . . . ?	Italian
¿Es este el camino de . . . ?	Spanish

Chapter 8
You're Going a Long Way, Baby

Do you know what day this is? Thursday?
So we're in Germany? No, Germany was yesterday.
Is this Austria? Maybe it's Friday.
— Two little old ladies on a tour bus

Everyone knows that most European countries are pretty small. Compared to the United States or Canada, in fact, all of them are quite small. Here is an approximation of their areas. It will give you an idea of what sorts of distances travel over there involves. And, for purposes of comparison, let us add that Connecticut has about 5,000 square miles, Illinois has 56,000, and California has 159,000.

Country	square miles		Country	square miles
Austria	32,000		*Monaco*	11
Belgium	12,000		*Norway*	125,000
Denmark	17,000		*Portugal*	35,000
France	213,000		*Spain*	196,000
Greece	51,000		*Sweden*	173,000
Holland	16,000 (and still growing)		*Switzerland*	16,000
Italy	116,000		*United Kingdom*	94,000
Luxembourg	1,000		*West Germany*	96,000

These figures should not give anyone the idea that seeing fifteen countries within two weeks is workable or even sensible. The total is well over a million square miles, which is a lot of area for anyone's itinerary. We once embarked on a trip around Holland with the intention of learning how long it would take to see the

113

high spots of such a small country. It took more than five weeks, and we didn't by any means see all of it. That experiment did a great deal to convince us that it is foolish to try to see all of Europe in one trip. It seems to us to substantiate our contention that a tourist would be wise to think small when making his travel plans—small, at least, in terms of the countries he would try to visit.

The following is the sort of table that misleads many Americans when they are making their travel plans. It shows how quickly a person can get from one major metropolitan area to another.

Between ...	Rough number of hours by fast train	Between ...	Rough number of hours by fast train
Barcelona – Geneva	9	Paris – Nice	9
Paris – Brussels	2½ – 3	Amsterdam – Copenhagen	12 – 13
Frankfurt – Amsterdam	5	Zurich – Brussels	6
Munich – Amsterdam	9	Rome – Munich	14 – 14½

As the first item on the table indicates, you could certainly go from one country, through another one, and arrive in the third in a short period of time. You should not, however, conclude from this that you'll see anything of France except a blur on that trip. You'd spend most of the trip in France, and most of it at eighty to ninety miles an hour. It is possible to go through a lot of countries in a short time, but it isn't possible to *see* them in such a time span.

It is extremely difficult for many people to decide how to travel through Europe. They often think about how small the countries are and how quickly a person can get from one to the other, and they plan a back-breaking itinerary for themselves. But they still worry: Am I going to be travelling too fast and too far? It has always been a difficult "how to" question, and it still is, but there is one certainty: right or wrong, it is a decision that has to be made in the early stages of planning.

Britain's new Inter-City 125 trains are fast and ultra-modern.

BritRail Travel International, Inc., photo

Train passes

If you are not going to rent, lease, or buy a car in Europe, you are still going to have to decide *before you leave the United States* how you will travel around once you're there. The reason you have to decide this at such an early stage is that if you are going to get a Eurailpass or a BritRail Pass, you will have to buy it *here*. Neither of them can be purchased in Europe.

Just as there is much to be said for European rail travel, there is a lot to be said for the Eurailpass, the best-known of the rail passes and the one we shall discuss first. The Eurailpass is relatively inexpensive, and it can save you a lot of problems. With it you won't have to buy train tickets, which means that you can avoid long lines, language problems at ticket windows, and having to have so much currency in each country. It is a pass, as its name suggests: all you have to do is hop on any train you wish and flash it when a ticket-taker comes through.

Eurailpasses are available in two forms, first or second class, but the latter type is only available to people under twenty-six years of age: in 1981, they cost $260 for one month, and $330 for two months. First-class passes cost $230 for 15 days, $290 for 21 days, $360 for a month, $490 for two months, and $600 for three months. Children up through twelve years of age were half-fare.

So in addition to unlimited train travel for the time specified, what do they offer? They give you reduced fares (ranging all the way to no charge at all) on some bus, steamer, and ferry trips, and discounts on some private railways, bus systems, and mountain lifts. In addition, reservations, which are sometimes required for express trains, are often overlooked for Eurailpass holders, especially for short-distance trips. However, it is always wise to get reservations on TransEurop Express (TEE) trains, and on any train in Spain, for reasons we shall explain shortly. With a Eurailpass, you do not have to pay the supplementary fees that are charged for using the TEEs, which is a real break because these supplements are fairly sizeable.

Although no Eurailpass brochure would admit this, the pass will provide you with a free night's sleep any night you want it, or haven't been able to find a room at an acceptable price. No room available? Hop on a train and go somewhere. You can come back the next morning after a free night's sleep.

We went to Vienna one night just in order to get a bit of sleep. We had been unable to find a room at an acceptable price in Innsbruck, so we decided to go to Venice on a 1:30 a.m. train and we boarded it. Because it was summer, the train looked like a mob scene from a DeMille movie. Every car was packed with people, in the compartments, aisles, toilets, everywhere. We leaped back off and jumped on another nearby train—which was not crowded, and which happened to be going to Vienna. After a good night's sleep we had breakfast in Vienna, saw a few sights, headed back west again. The scenery on the way back to Innsbruck was just magnificent.

This sort of sleeping arrangement can be made with more forethought than just hopping aboard the train at the last minute. It can be done that way, though, and if you're fortunate enough to get a compartment to yourselves, you can slide the seats out into beds and have a great night. And when you get a crowded train you sleep sitting up—which isn't too bad either. The seats are usually very comfortable. But you can get a bed, if you wish, either a sleeping compartment (expensive), or a couchette, a little bunk you sleep in without undressing—because in first class there are four to a compartment, and in second class there are six—men and/or women. A second-class couchette will cost six to eight dollars a night and it will require a reservation. You can occasionally get them from an official on the train, but it is safer to reserve them beforehand through a train station —especially in the high season.

We learned recently that travel writer Arlene Becker had just concluded a thirty-day Eurailpass tour of Europe in which she spent eleven nights on the trains to save time and money. As we have, she found it entirely satisfactory, although she wouldn't do it more than three consecutive nights—and we would agree with that. Even under the very best of circumstances, you won't get as good a rest as you would in a nice, quiet bed. Incidentally, she agrees with our views about how pleasant it is to meet the Europeans on the trains. She said that she was "the recipient of the greatest warmth and hospitality that I had ever encountered from strangers. These experiences were the real highlights of my trip."

Even if you have a Eurailpass, which can only be first-class (unless you are a young student), it is often a mistake to sit in the first-class cars. Indeed, if the second-class cars are jammed (which they sometimes are, because not many Europeans will pay fifty percent more to sit on a seat with a little more padding), you may not have much choice. But you will find that if you sit in second-class, the train official who takes tickets and checks passes will occasionally comment, "You should be up there, in first class." Well, you don't have to go, and in our experience, the people you are sitting with will like you for being where you are. They seem more willing to talk to you and offer advice than will the people in first class, who are often engrossed in their particular versions of the *Wall Street Journal*.

Perhaps it's a toss-up: in first class you will often meet other tourists who will give you good tips about places to see and to stay; in second-class you will meet the natives, who will tell you about themselves and their country. Either conversation can be fun and interesting, but we perhaps prefer the latter—because it seems to happen more frequently, and is quite often more useful. But wherever you sit on the train, you will usually find that you have to start the conversation. Europeans often have a thing about seeming to push themselves on other people. They like conversation, but they won't often start it.

One last remark in relation to planning and Eurailpasses: having such a pass can have a surprising effect on your itinerary when you think about it. On one early jaunt when we used Eurailpasses, we had a roughly clockwise route planned, thinking that going from A to B to C was a logical, sensible way to arrange things—and it was, and is, but it's not necessary with a Eurailpass. You could find, as we did, occasional compelling reasons to deviate from such a logical plan and go from B to F and then back to C. Why not? The pass entitles you to unlimited travel.

And one other remark about the Eurailpass itself: when you have it validated in Europe (*i.e.*, have a railroad official fill in the beginning and ending dates) it must be filled in *correctly*. If he makes an error, you may end up living with it. Any alteration to the filled-in dates on the Eurailpass invalidates it. So you might be wise to figure the start and finish dates yourself, write them down, and show them to the official before he begins to write on that expensive little card. If he agrees, fine; if he doesn't make him explain before he puts in the dates. And remember that Europeans write dates differently from our way: they write the day first, and then the month. To them, in other words, September 1 is not 9/1; it's 1/9.

If you want one, you can buy it from the Austrian, Italian, French, German or Swiss national railway offices or through your own travel agent. It will be given its beginning and ending dates in Europe when you first use it, and you will then have the right to over 100,000 miles of travel in sixteen countries: Austria, Belgium, Denmark, Finland, France, Germany, Greece, Holland, Ireland, Italy, Luxembourg, Norway, Portugal, Spain, Sweden, and Switzerland.

England offers the BritRail Pass, which is available in a variety of forms. In 1981 these were the rates in American dollars:

	Economy class			First class	
	Adult	Youth	Child	Adult	Child
7 days	$ 99	$ 86	$ 50	$140	$ 70
14 days	$150	$133	$ 75	$210	$105
21 days	$190	$169	$ 95	$260	$130
One month	$225	$199	$113	$299	$150

Children up to age five travel free. The Children's Passes are for ages five through thirteen. The Youth Passes are for ages fourteen through twenty-five, and are available only in economy class. BritRail Passes must be purchased in the United States; they cannot be obtained in Britain.

The BritRail Pass has some advantages over its counterpart on the Continent, the Eurailpass. As indicated, it can be obtained in the less-expensive second-class form if one wishes. But even the first-class version is less expensive on a daily basis than is the Eurailpass. While the Eurailpass becomes invalid at midnight of the last day, the BritRail Pass will allow you a last trip that extends into the day after the pass expires if you leave before that final midnight and make a single trip without any stopovers. In other words, you could leave Glasgow or Edinburgh at, let's say, 11 p.m. on the last day of the pass and spend most of your trip to London during the day after your pass had officially expired.

Other advantages of BritRail include ship crossings to the Isle of Wight and steamer passages on Lake Windermere. For night trips, you will be able to get inexpensive sleeping accommodations on the trains. Lastly, you can buy Seapass tickets in conjunction with the BritRail Pass. They are valid for a number of ferry routes to the Continent: the northernmost one is between Harwich and the Hook of Holland; the most southerly route is between Newhaven and Dieppe; and there are others in between. There is also a Seapass to Ireland for $60 round trip, economy class.

The BritRail Pass itself is not valid for travel in Ireland, nor for crossings to the Continent, the Channel Islands, or to Ireland. Further information and current prices on BritRail plans are available from BritRail Travel International, 630 Third Avenue, New York, NY 10017; 510 W. Sixth Street, Los Angeles CA 90014; 333 N. Michigan Avenue, Suite 1212, Chicago IL 60601; 55 Eglinton Avenue East, Toronto M4P 1G8, Ontario; and 409 Granville Street, Vancouver, B.C. V6C 1T2.

Every country on the Continent offers rail passes that are valid for travel within its own borders. All of them but the Swiss, French, and British passes can be purchased in Europe. Here are a few comments on the unusual ones. The Swiss Holiday Card covers rides on the trains, boats, and postal buses, which not only go to the villages the trains can't reach, but to just about everyplace that doesn't happen to be served by rail lines. It works only inside of Switzerland's boundaries, with one exception: you can use it to ride into and back out of Liechtenstein on a postal bus.

Ireland offers a "Rambler Ticket" for eight or fifteen days of rail travel. There are also passes that allow travel on both trains and buses, which are worthwhile because the buses go to many places that the trains do not. Portugal has several rail discount plans that may be purchased there with passport.

Another special train pass (which can be purchased only in Europe) is the Benelux Tourrail ticket, which allows travel through Holland, Belgium, and Luxembourg for ten consecutive days. It cannot be used on TEE trains without payment of a supplementary fee, but can be used just like a Eurailpass on all others.

The Scandinavian Rail Pass allows you to travel more than 15,000 miles through Denmark, Finland, Norway, and Sweden. It is good for twenty-one days. It will allow free or half-price ferry crossings from one country to the other. It is available only at Scandinavian railway stations or at Scandinavian Railroad offices in major European cities.

Italy's pass for visitors can be purchased in Italy (with passport), and it is valid for various periods ranging up to one month. The Austria Ticket, as it is called, is available in first- or second-class forms for eight to fifteen days, and it can be purchased in the U.S. or in Austria.

If you decide against buying a rail pass, there is a fantastic array of discount travel schemes available in the various countries. (Oddly enough, the railroads of Europe seem to want to carry human beings as well as freight.) We will describe some of these bargains shortly. But for now, let's have a look at the reasons for *not* buying any railroad pass:

1. *You are going to buy or rent a car.*
2. *You are going to walk, bicycle, or hitchhike on your trip.*
3. *You are going to travel a sufficiently short distance* overall that you can get by for less by buying second-class tickets than you could by using the first-class Eurailpass. If you only want to visit a few places in two or three countries, you could save money by not investing in Eurailpasses. But we have figured relatively short itineraries both ways, and it appears that one has to be considering a *really* short trip overall to make the second-class tickets total less than the cost of the pass. One can compromise: if you are going to spend some time in or near your point of arrival or departure you might wish to buy a pass to cover just the mid-part of your trip. It is a matter that deserves a bit of mileage checking and calculation.
4. *You have no self-restraint.* Many people who have a Eurailpass or BritRail Pass in their pockets have found it difficult to settle down for two or three days in some idyllic spot they've found because of thoughts like, "I could be seeing something different now" and "Every day it stays in my pocket, I lose money." The pass can be like cash in a spendthrift's jeans. It is easy to feel that you aren't getting your money's worth if you don't travel constantly. But if one gave in to that feeling, he would find himself in motion for his whole vacation, which sounds like a form of punishment Danté might have dreamed up.

During our first trip to Europe, one of us gave in to such feelings during the first few days ("My God, it's *costing* us to sit here!"). The other one, who, like many women, has a good deal of restraint about a lot of things, would then utter soothing remarks such as, "A rest every day keeps the conductor away" and "Don't be such a rush-about!" Mr. Rushabout finally pretty much got over the problem and subsequently behaved like a reformed smoker seeing someone with a cigarette in his mouth, giving contemptuous looks to people scurrying through train stations, sure that they were Americans moving day and night because they had Eurailpasses. While most of these people were probably just Europeans heading home from work, he was doubtlessly right occasionally. There are people who move about Europe with glazed, unseeing eyes, firmly gripping their Eurailpasses and shuffling along wondering how they can possibly get through three more countries before the following sundown. If you detect any signs of this malady within yourself, do not buy a Eurailpass! Buy a treadmill instead and stay home.

Indeed, the basic disadvantage of the BritRail Pass or the Eurailpass is that they will encourage even the most liberated traveller to keep moving. Even when you find a nice place where you would like to settle in for a few days, you'll find yourself inclined to think that you're wasting money each day that pass is dormant in your pocket. You'll never really see anything if you do keep moving, and, of course, it's much nicer anyway to stop travelling for a day or two from time to time. There are only three solutions to this problem for the person who doesn't wish to be moving continually:
1. Buy a long-term pass with the conviction that you won't let it force you to keep going when you'd rather settle down for a time;

2. Buy two seven-day passes for your three- or four- or six-week vacation, and thereby leave yourself a number of days for stopping over;

3. Don't buy a rail pass at all.

If you let the possession of a little card control what you do in Europe and when you do it, you will have imposed upon yourself a regimen as deadly as any tour operator might have thought up.

Riding Europe's trains

European trains, which by our standards are marvelous, are with few exceptions clean and on time. Believe it or not, they leave on time, and they arrive on time! Fantastic. Most of them are electric, and the ones that aren't are diesel-powered, which means that all of them are clean and free of noise. There are two classes, first and second, the differences being that first costs about fifty percent more than second, and the latter compartments are always more crowded. These trains come in a variety of forms: the fast, luxurious TransEurop Expresses, the regular express inter-city trains of each country, and the local trains. Some of the associated jargon in French and German is:

English	French	German
first class	*première classe*	*erster Klasse*
second class	*deuxième classe*	*zweiter Klasse*
TransEurop Express	*TEE*	*TEE*
ticket	*billet*	*Fahrkarte*
express train	*le rapide* or *l'express*	*der Schnellzug*
local train	*omnibus*	*Eisenbahn* or *Zug*
sleeping car	*wagon lits* or *voiture-lits*	*Schlafwagen*
dining car	*voiture-restaurant*	*Speiswagen*
one way	*aller seulement*	*einfach*
round trip	*aller et retour*	*hin-und zurück*
timetable	*horaire*	*Fahrplan*
arrival	*arrivée*	*ankunft*
departure	*départ*	*abfahrt*

European trains are fast. You can go from Innsbruck to Salzburg in a little over two hours, and on to Vienna in another three hours. It is a good idea to get seat reservations on the really popular trains—*e.g.*, the express trains—although in most of the traveling we've done we've not bothered with it. But it is necessary to get such reservations for the international TEE trains. In any train there will be a small sign on each compartment indicating which seats (if any) are reserved (*reserviert*). Always look at that sign. Even if no one is in a seat that is reserved, it does belong to someone else. He might not claim it, but it is likely that he will get on somewhere and take his seat.

There is railroad-associated jargon in Italy that might fool you: "*acceleratto*"

You can set your watch by the comings and goings of Europe's trains.

Swiss National Tourist Office photo

refers to the slowest, local trains, while "*direttisimo*" refers to the expresses, and "*rapido*" means the fastest, extra-fare trains. And in Spain, "*expresso*" trains are not express trains; they are slow locals. In fact, Spanish trains are something else. The Talgo trains are up to anyone's best. They are fast, clean, and they require reservations. The others, the "workers' trains," *expressos,* and so on, are generally rather slow (because they stop everywhere), and the equipment is outdated and often not terribly comfortable. Furthermore, some of the rail beds seem a bit less stable than one expects to find in other parts of Europe, giving a ride that fits one's imagination of what a stage coach with a square wheel probably felt like. But we have been on good ones which would certainly top most American trains.

But the schedules, purchase of tickets, finding the right train, and so on in Spain is no big deal if you don't mind occasionally indulging in a bit of sign language. We cannot say that the trains are well marked (or marked at all), so as we state elsewhere, ask questions to be sure. Another oddity is that the Spaniards require Eurailpass holders to get seat reservations in advance. You can't avoid this: if you get on a Spanish train that has open seats everywhere, you'll be put off at the next stop if you don't have a seat reservation. Perhaps the biggest surprise is this: Spain levels a penalty for foresightedness, in that it costs you *double* if you purchase a train ticket more than twenty-four hours ahead of its departure. They seem to want you to buy it thirty to sixty minutes before the train leaves, no matter what kind of waiting line that may entail. Ah well . . . .

Lastly, an interesting note: because Spanish tracks have a wider gauge than the rest of Europe's, passengers coming from France have to change trains or wait while the train is lifted up so the wheels can be set to fit Spain's tracks! This is not true of the Talgo expresses that run between Geneva and Barcelona. These modern trains carry a system invented by a Spanish engineer that allows the gauge to be changed almost instantly.

Some of the English trains are about like some of the Spanish ones: slow, dirty, and noisy. But most of the long-distance trains there are fine, and the new Inter-City 125's are tops. (The "125" stands for miles per hour, a speed that can't be obtained on existing railbeds.) They are smooth, luxurious, and extremely quiet.

Incidentally, it is well to avoid train travel in the U.K. on Sundays if possible. Many of the better trains don't run on the Sabbath.

A note about French trains: as with many of the trams in European cities, you must "validate" SNCF tickets by sticking them into a yellow- or orange-colored machine before you board the train. If you don't, you may be fined.

Like other European countries, Greece has a good ground-transportation system. Unlike most of them, her rail system is not so super. Train arrivals and departure boards in the station are printed in Greek, which tells most of us almost nothing. The people who man the windows are capable of understanding sign language and destinations written in English, and try to be helpful, but the whole business is complicated. In addition, the trains are slow. Rail travel in Greece has one great advantage: it is the cheapest form of transportation there.

Greek buses are nice (some of them offer television!) they are relatively cheap, and they are faster, generally, from A to B than a train—but because of Greece's traffic, the buses aren't all that terribly quick either. But there are express buses which do not make stops, except for "rest" or food stops, and they are fine. All tickets carry a seat reservation, although this is usually ignored on short local runs. A caution: the seat numbers are on the back of the upright part of the seats. If you have seat no. 8, for example, it would be logical to sit in the seat behind that number. Logical perhaps, but wrong; if you did that, you would be in seat no. 12. Sitting in seat no. 8, you will see no. 4 ahead of you. It's confusing, but the Greeks understand it, so you should too.

The last form of Grecian transportation, which is naturally an important one there, is boat travel. This ranges from hydrofoil to small charter boats to large ferries. The larger boats are generally comfortable, clean, and crowded. But food and drink is readily available, and there are always interesting people to chat with. Landlubbers will find this an absolutely exhilarating way to go.

The European railroads offer another nice service in shipping your bags (or, in some countries, your bicycles) ahead for you at a small charge. If you don't pick them up the same day, the baggage personnel will charge you a minuscule fee for storage, which they levy for holding something beyond twenty-four hours. But a warning on this: some countries in Europe will no longer ship your bags to a destination different from where you are going—inside the country. You can do so if you are shipping to another country. It is something you have to check wherever you happen to be.

Not everything is perfect about rail travel on the Continent. There are so many public servants engaged in such absurd tasks as checking passports and changing money from one currency to another that it is easy to think how much better off everyone would be if they could devise ways to unify on monies and languages, and to relax their border regulations a bit. There are also many thousands of people, thanks to the vastness of the public transportation networks and tourism programs, who provide information, sell train and bus tickets, etc. It is surprising and yet unpleasant to find that many of these people can be extremely short of patience, although you will often have to have plenty yourself to wait out the long lines during the high season. Some couples have found that the men in these jobs will be nicer and more helpful to the woman than her escort, while the man will usually do better with the females at the windows than his wife could. They've also discovered that the same phenomenon occurs even when they go to the wrong person—*e.g.,* to the railway ticket seller just to get information: if it is a man, he ordinarily won't tell the male customer a thing, but if *she* goes to the window he'll straighten up his tie, brush back his hair, and be very helpful. It works more times than not, so you might want to try it too.

Incidentally, we might mention here that travelling across Europe by railroad is going to require you to become conversant with the twenty-four hour clock system. If you've been in a branch of the military service, you will recall how it works; if not, it's not difficult to learn. In fact, like the metric system, it makes a great deal of sense. After you become familiar with it you may wish we'd use it instead of the silly AM/PM system. This is the schedule:

Our Way	Their Way	Our Way	Their Way	Our Way	Their Way
1 a.m.	100 or 0100	9 a.m.	900 or 0900	5 p.m.	1700
2 a.m.	200 or 0200	10 a.m.	1000	6 p.m.	1800
3 a.m.	300 or 0300	11 a.m.	1100	7 p.m.	1900
4 a.m.	400 or 0400	12 a.m.	1200	8 p.m.	2000
5 a.m.	500 or 0500	1 p.m.	1300	9 p.m.	2100
6 a.m.	600 or 0600	2 p.m.	1400	10 p.m.	2200
7 a.m.	700 or 0700	3 p.m.	1500	11 p.m.	2300
8 a.m.	800 or 0800	4 p.m.	1600	12 p.m.	2400

Note: 0015 is fifteen minutes past midnight. To convert times past 12 noon to what you're used to, just subtract 1200—*i.e.*, 1900 less 1200 gives you 7 p.m.

For those of you who, like us, are always a bit mixed up over 12 a.m. and 12 p.m., it's a wonderful system. But like it or not, it is what you will deal with in Europe.

Once you know 1 a.m. from 1 p.m., about the only problem you have left with train travel is finding out what track (or ''bin'') your train is scheduled to depart from. This is relatively easy. You simply look for the ''Arrivals'' and ''Departures'' boards in the station and look across from your scheduled departure time, where you will find the track number. In most places the stairs to the various tracks are clearly marked with track numbers, and the tracks themselves are designated by overhead signs.

Keep in mind that just because a train is going your way is no sure indication that the *car* you happen to leap on will end up there. The Europeans switch cars off here and there, so always look at the sign *on the car* (when there is one) that gives its destination. In addition, it does no harm to ask a train man or your fellow passengers unless you're absolutely certainly that you're okay. It is also a good idea for long trips to check on the departure times of TEE and other fast trains. While they don't run as frequently as the slower trains, you could find that a short wait for one could get you to your destination much sooner than a local train would.

There is one serious disadvantage to the Eurailpass. When you show it to the ticket collector, it gives him no indication of where you are going (or think you are going). So he will just assume that you know what you're doing, which, indeed, you may not. If you had a regular ticket from Amsterdam to Paris and showed it to the conductor on a train headed for, say, Berlin, he would be able to tell you then and there that you were on the wrong train. With the Eurailpass you might get clear to Berlin before you realized that you'd made a mistake, although you probably wouldn't get further than Hamburg if you were awake and alert. So it's not a bad idea to say the name of your destination when you have to show your pass to a conductor. If he can understand you, and if you are on the wrong train, he will say so—and you probably won't understand him anyway. But you might . . . .

It's *always* a good idea to check and double-check if you have any question at all. Admittedly anyone you ask such a question as ''Is this car going to Berlin?'' will probably think you're stupid, but it would be even more stupid to go somewhere that you didn't want to go. And while this sounds like good advice, you can't always believe the answers you get. We've had quite a bit of misinformation, even from train officials. In one case we asked three trainmen who were standing talking to each other where to catch the train for Paris. They gave us three different answers, and were standing looking at each other with surprise when we walked away. And if you do have a ticket, don't discard it after it is punched; you will probably need to show it (or a pass) to get out of the station at your destination. If you can't, you'll be forced to buy a new ticket then and there.

Most railway stations have railway information offices or windows that should *not* be confused with tourist information services. The ones that give rail information are usually labeled ''*Renseignements des Trains*'' and/or ''*Zugs-informationen*.'' The people in these areas do not usually display pleasure when a tourist walks up and starts asking about hotels.

Dining on European trains is quite an experience. It usually works like this: a man comes through the cars taking reservations for first or second serving. When you make this choice he gives you a little ticket. You then simply show up at the dining car at the appointed time. The meals are ordinarily delicious, beautifully served, and multi-course, but not exactly inexpensive. Some of the trains have snack bar cars, and others have people pushing food carts through the train, selling coffee, beer, and snacks. You can also often buy such goodies from the train windows in the stations where the train stops. But this never happens when you really want something, and what those guys sell isn't very good anyway.

It is not a great idea to jump off of the train to buy food or drink in the stations. Many train stops are just for two or three minutes, and you could find yourself standing there watching the train (and your companion) accelerating away down the track. Perhaps the best idea of all is to bring your own lunch on the train.

Incidentally, there is no drinking water on European trains, at least on ninety-five percent of them. As we will suggest in the chapter on packing, it would be wise to take a small unbreakable bottle with you so you can carry some water on the trains for drinking or brushing your teeth. And you will see a little decal on many train windows showing a bottle with an X drawn through it. This does not mean no drinking; you can drink anything you wish on the trains. What it does signify is that you should not throw bottles out of the window.

A small note about an unusual feature of train travel that might surprise you has to do with four-footed passengers. Many Europeans, particularly the Germans, love dogs, and you see the animals everywhere, usually on leashes, often muzzled. You may also find one on the floor near you on a train. Its owner will have paid for it (at a reduced seat rate), and it will behave itself. But tourists are often shocked when the compartment door opens and a dog strolls in. Now you won't be.

And now we will mention a couple of important things about the train stations themselves. No matter how you travel through Europe, railroad stations will be important buildings in your life. They provide you with just about everything: toilets, telephones, transportation (including city transportation, because buses, taxis, and sight-seeing buses stop near them), luggage lockers, tourist information, and money changing. Sometimes they even have showers you can rent, various kinds of shops, and their restaurants and cafes are ordinarily excellent.

The train station can have another important function in your life: your landmark, so to speak. Once you have settled into a room you will presumably know about where it is in relation to the train station (if you are travelling by rail). You'd better be sure you do, because you're going to have to go back there, so try to note how you go when you first find your room. Then when you go out walking, perhaps window shopping in the evening, you will always be able to get back to your lodging even if you become lost—which you doubtlessly will. Wherever you are in Europe, people you question may not know where your pension or your street is, but they'll understand ''train station'' however you say it. And even if you can't understand what they say, they have a habit of pointing directions—so that once they get you back to the train depot, you can get back to your room from there.

Most of the big stations have luggage lockers, while smaller ones often don't. In the latter, you can check your luggage (in the ''left luggage'') to be held for you while you go eat, explore the town, or find a room. It's not expensive, and, as far as we know, it's absolutely safe.

Most of the larger cities such as London, Brussels, and Paris, and indeed, many of the smaller ones like Seville and Basel have more than one railway station. A bit of research and forethought is necessary for deciding which one is best for you to come into in terms of hotel locations or your eventual departure. Trains going to certain destinations will leave from a specific station, so this is certainly worth checking out when you are making your departure plans.

London has many railroad stations which serve lines that radiate out into England in various directions like a sunburst pattern. You must find the correct station for your departure from London. You cannot get on many runs even from Victoria or King's Cross, which are extremely large stations.

If you do plan to travel by train, you would be wise to order a copy of *Cook's Continental Timetable* through a Thomas Cook travel agency, or ask one of the national tourist offices for a current copy of *Time-Table of the best trains in Europe.* The Cook timetable costs a few dollars, while the latter one is free. Either will save you from having to stand in line to ask questions in the train stations about departure times, the towns a given train will pass through, or whatever.

Flying

It could be possible that someplace along the way in your journey *time* could be a more important consideration to you than *money.* For that reason we will offer a bit of advice here about intraEuropean flights.

It will probably come as no surprise to you to learn that such flights are expensive, not only when compared to travelling on the ground, but even as compared to flying similar distances in the United States. Secondly, they are usually crowded, which means that reservations well in advance of flying dates are important (the Europeans never have ten different lines all leaving from the same point to go to the same destination as we often do.) Thirdly, by American standards, they are not especially comfortable. All of the foregoing may relate to the fact that distances are generally pretty short by our way of thinking, and also that ground transportation is good, fast, and relatively inexpensive.

European airlines, like our own, generally require you to check in about an hour before the aircraft departs (which is often somewhat late). Nevertheless, give it at least an hour by the schedule. The person at the check-in desk will take your ticket and give you a boarding pass, more than likely. He may not allow you to carry on your carry-on-size baggage, because some of the aircraft are small and closely packed, *e.g.*, Fokker 27's, although longer flights will use American aircraft such as DC-9's. You may or may not run into a security check, but if you do, you can expect a rather superficial pawing through your things and over your body. Then you will be walked or bused to your aircraft (many airports there do not have the extendable walks right to the aircraft). On board, the chances are likely that you'll be cramped into a seat half as big as you are, and that you'll be offered nothing more than a bad imitation of orange juice and a newspaper you can't read.

Incidentally, while you are waiting for your flight in the terminal, do not be confused by the information boards, which often list first and tourist classes separately. The boards may call for tourist-class passengers to load on as much as an hour before the first-class folks board, and when *they* get on, the plane flies. However, this is not even a potential problem on relatively short flights, which are often one-hundred-percent tourist class.

Buses, boats, and bargains

European buses are super. Many of them are equipped with radios, extra drivers, and multilingual hostesses who will explain the passing sights, and perhaps serve sandwiches and cold drinks. Many of the cross-country European runs are more like tours than bus runs, where the fare includes the cost of meals and nightly lodgings. These buses do not, in other words, run at night. It is usually necessary to reserve seats on them, even for short runs. Most of the Europabus fares are discounted to Eurailpass holders, and some of them are free. Two of the nicest that are free to the Eurailpasser are run #241 from Paris south across France to the Riviera, and the route through Germany on the Romantische Strasse from Weisbaden or Frankfurt down through Rothenburg to Fussen or Munich. Europabus fares, incidentally, are often more expensive for an equivalent distance than second-class rail tickets—but they are still a nice change of pace from the trains, and they provide alternatives to the trains' departure times and routes.

Yet another pleasant way to travel in various places in Europe is by boat. Many of these trips are free to holders of the Eurailpass, including steamers on the Rhine; boats from Passau or Linz to Vienna on the Danube; lake steamers plying such bodies of water as Lake Constance, Lake Wolfgang, Lake Geneva, etc.; and ferry crossings to Denmark and Sweden. Obviously this is not a fast method of travel, but it's romantic, and it's worth doing if time permits.

The day boats from the Continent to England (which are not included on the Eurailpass or the BritRail Pass) offer pleasant, fairly inexpensive rides, while the night boats leave something to be desired. Everyone tries to find a place to stretch out, and many of the boats (particularly the British ones) seem to be designed to make this impossible. Anyone taking a night boat would be well off to try to book a cabin (available for both first and second class), or at least a reclining chair. Such reservations should be made well ahead, but it is usually possible to get one from the boat's purser at the last minute if you are willing to wait in line. This happens because many people book but don't show up.

Incidentally, it is often necessary to exchange your ticket for a landing card with the boat's purser. Waiting until the last minute to do so can cause you many problems, not the least of which is that you can't get off the boat. Bargain hunters should be prepared to find on these boats little duty-free stores that sell candy, perfume, cigarettes, and liquors at reasonable prices. The Danes run an extremely inexpensive ferry (the Olau Line) from Sheerness, England, to Vlissingen, Holland or to Dunkerque, France. The Danish fares are almost as economical as the Seapass ticket you can get in conjunction with the BritRail Pass, and the Danish ships are reputed to be very nice.

For a little more money, you can cross the Channel between the U.K. and the Continent in less than an hour aboard a hovercraft.

Lastly, we will tackle the slightly complicated subject of special travel deals available in some of the various countries. It is complicated because there are so many different kinds of possibilities. The Europeans really believe in mass transit, and the people who operate these systems are forever thinking up new ways to lure people onto trains and buses. We'll describe some of the ones we know about, occasionally giving prices that are correct at this writing but which probably won't be when you use them.

In addition to the Swiss Holiday Pass we mentioned earlier, the Swiss offer a wide array of travel bargains. They sell a half-fare pass for about twenty dollars a month, which enables the holder to buy tickets on trains, boats, and buses for one-half the market price. Like other European countries, they have a pass for senior citizens (men over sixty-five, women over sixty-two) that costs about twenty-five dollars a year. They have reduced fares for groups of at least ten people, half-fare rates for children (and dogs!), and they sell rides on their Alpine Postal Buses, which travel the high, narrow routes the trains can't get to. The Swiss try hard in this business.

The Germans are also enthusiastic about trying to separate you from your devalued dollars—but as gently as possible. They offer railroad discounts ranging from three to twenty-eight percent for round-trip tickets. Children are carried free or at half-fare, depending upon their age. Students and visitors to trade fairs and exhibitions get twenty-five to thirty percent discounts, and reduced-fare tickets for long distances are available.

The French provide reductions of twenty percent on round-trip railroad tickets covering at least fifteen hundred kilometers, family tickets that give seventy-five percent reductions from the third person on (including servants!), and tickets that give good discounts for groups of ten people or more.

The Dutch have also thought up a few great travel ideas which might interest you. They have special eight-day discount train tickets in both first and second class, allowing unlimited travel for the period for a little over thirty dollars and a little over twenty dollars, respectively. They offer a "Day Rover" ticket for about $9.50, with extensions of up to four days at approximately two dollars a day. The "Day Multirover" ticket entitles two people to unlimited travel for a day for about fifteen dollars. As indicated elsewhere, their Day Rover bus tickets are even less—considerably less.

Those not holding Eurailpasses might be interested in the Amsterdam-based bus lines (with such strange names as Magic Bus and Sunshine Bus) that travel across Europe at very low rates. We priced one from Amsterdam to Copenhagen that was a great deal less than a second-class rail fare for the same trip.

The Belgians have special rail "Runabout" tickets for five, ten, or fifteen consecutive days in either first or second class, or a similar ticket for five days which the holder can choose from within a period of fifteen days. For about twelve dollars it is possible to purchase a card which will permit fifty percent reductions

Postal buses carry people and mail into the high altitudes.

Swiss National Tourist Office photo

on all fares for a full month. Their *un beau jour à* _____ tickets include not only discounts on the train fare, but also entry fees to places visited and tickets on buses and boats where applicable. There are other cut-rate excursions of two, three, or four days to various scenic places within or even outside of Belgium. These discounted fares include all transportation costs, accommodations, entry fees, and breakfasts (and in some cases, all meals). Information about these offerings can be obtained from any railway information office.

In Luxembourg you can buy a rail ticket with no destination specified for a whole day of travel for about three dollars. For approximately nine dollars you can get a pass that will allow you to travel in Luxembourg for any five days within a period of fifteen days.

Almost anywhere you can buy special tickets for weekends and holidays with a half-fare return.

Italy's B.T.L.C. tickets provide large discounts for second-class travel on the trains for eight, fifteen, twenty-one, and thirty-one days. There are also tickets at thirty percent reductions for distances of three thousand kilometers within a month's time. Larger reductions are available for larger groups, and there are many other bargain rates which you should be able to obtain from your travel agent.

Young people can often get special transportation discounts in Europe if they bother to ask about them. As one example, Belgium's Acotra organization, a non-profit group that is not a travel agency but simply a group of people who care about young folks, offers real deals on short- or long-distance travel to people in their early years. If you are under twenty-six, they can help you to get a forty percent discount on train travel in Europe, or sizeable cuts on air travel to elsewhere. If you do not fit that tender age-bracket, they will still help you to find budget accommodations in the Brussels area if you wish (see Chapter Ten).

A similar organization in Holland is the NBBS, which has been helping young people with travel or accommodations problems for many years. This organization also sometimes helps people over twenty-six (but usually not over thirty-five) to book rooms outside of Holland, in arranging discount flights, and so on.

Such helpful groups as those listed above require that their clients belong to the Student Air Travel Association or the International Student Travel Conference. They have offices in all the major (and some minor) cities of Europe.

Every country has such discount arrangements, and if you do not plan to drive or to buy a Eurailpass, you should ask the national tourist offices that represent the countries you will visit to give you current information about these possibilities. The multiplicity of mass transportation systems in Europe presents the visitor with the opportunity to design himself a custom-made vacation, depending upon the amount of time he has and where he wishes to go. It is probably fair to say that transportation is Europe's biggest bargain for the tourist, and that anyone who thinks hard about how he will travel there can save himself a good deal of money by taking advantage of the various possibilities.

Chapter Nine
All Around the Town

The soul of a journey is liberty, perfect liberty,
to think, feel, do just as one pleases.
—William Hazlitt

To anyone who has ever travelled on the ground across the United States, there are no really long distances in Europe. It's a long way from Amsterdam to Lisbon or to Moscow, admittedly, but who does that? What people usually do is travel from, say, Brussels to Luxembourg, and that's a two and a half-hour train trip. But even that is the "long-distance travel" we discussed in the last chapter. Here we are going to talk about *really* short distances—a few city blocks to a few kilometers—between nearby towns, for example, or just around the towns themselves.

Assuming that you are not burdened with a car, and that your legs are of approximately the same length, how will you get around the cities you visit? Or from city to city, if they are not too far apart? You might walk or bicycle—and, really, you know, unless you like to see everything in a blur, those are nice slow ways to go. Some areas of various European cities are closed off to cars, and some towns allow no cars at all.

It may be a good idea when you only have a short time in a large city to take a sight-seeing bus tour. It would at least show you the high spots, and will help you to get your bearings by showing you the city's top sights in air-conditioned comfort. If you ever do take such a mini-tour, do a bit of cost comparing first. Some of them are cheaper than others. But if you don't have some sort of guide, you're at least going to have to get a map. And you may have to ask some questions. If you haven't got a great deal of time, you just can't afford to sail around on your intuition.

There are, however, possibilities other than bus tours, biking, or walking all over in order to see the big towns. European cities generally have excellent transportation systems involving such vehicles as trams, subway trains, buses, double-deckers, and double-length buses with a big hinge in the middle. All of them are relatively inexpensive, they will take you anywhere (if you can figure out their routes), and they run with great frequency. They are a little bit esoteric in some respects, and we will provide some tips on using them a few pages from here.

If you are going to do much of this sort of thing, ask the tourist bureau folks where you can buy a book of tickets, which will give you, say, ten rides at a highly discounted price. Such discount tickets are available in every large city. If you are going to visit London, for example, you can purchase a "Go As You Please" ticket for 3, 4, or 7 days of travel on the city's buses and subways. All of them include a free ride on a half-day London sight-seeing tour. You can also get a one-month "Open To View" ticket which will get you into more than 400 tourist attractions. These tickets must be purchased from BritRail before you leave home.

You can also rent a bicycle, which is a wonderful and inexpensive way to see a town. But whatever you do, if you care about your money and blood pressure, try to avoid taxis. They are expensive, the drivers can be unpleasant, tipping is often required (!), and their meters and charge systems are beyond human understanding. In addition, baggage may be charged at ridiculously high rates, and you may be told that you are under "night rates," which are even more outrageous than the often-fictitious day rates. After all this, the chances are high that you will be called unpleasant names because the driver didn't find your tip agreeable (except for Finland, Copenhagen, Brussels, and a few isolated small areas elsewhere, drivers do expect tips, usually ten to fifteen percent). If you can't avoid taking a cab and the driver tries to do one on you, keep your seat and tell him to take you to a police station. In our experience, this always brings a whole new attitude into the discussion.

While it is a good idea to avoid taxis anyplace in Europe, especially if you have to worry about your budget, taking them in Belgium is a real no-no. Belgian taxis cost the most incredible amounts. They are reputed to be the highest in the world. If you do have to take one here, you do not have to tip the driver. This is official in Belgium, so you should not be cowed into parting with coins beyond the fare unless you want to give them.

A number of years ago in a foreign capital we had a taxi ride that was obviously about five times longer than it needed to be. We had studied a map of the area and knew that our ride should have covered no more than ten blocks, but it went on and on and on before we finally neared the destination we'd asked for. Seeing a policeman standing on the next corner, Alan suddenly said, "Let us out here." By the time the driver got the car stopped its front bumper was practically touching the cop's leg. The driver turned and asked us for a fare that was at least a half-dozen times higher than it should have been. When we began to argue about it the cabbie got very angry, so Alan jumped out and motioned for the policeman to come over.

After telling him where we'd started from, Alan told him what fare the cabbie was demanding, whereupon the cop started yelling at the driver. With his help, we soon settled on a reasonable fare, although the cabbie clearly wasn't convinced of that when he drove off with his tires shrieking. It is best just to stay out of taxis altogether if you possibly can. You can probably use the exercise anyway.

Walking

We once stayed overnight in a small town in Belgium called Louvain, the home of a sizeable university. It is an elderly, charming place, and its inhabitants are characterized by the way we were treated when we first arrived. We went into a little bar, ordered a beer apiece, and asked the bartender if he knew where we could find an inexpensive room.

In a loud voice directed to the other dozen people in the place, he said, "Hey, couple Americans here want a low-cost room. Anyone got ideas?"

We were soon surrounded by these friendly folks who asked us a few questions and, in fact, bought us several more beers. They eventually made some phone calls but had no luck in locating a room for us. Finally one of them said, "I know where there's a little inn a ways out. I'll take you there in my car." He did, and on the way he drove us around a bit to show us his town. He also took us to a local "night club" that looked to us like a cross between a bar, a bowling alley, and a billiard parlor, bought us a couple of drinks, and introduced us to some of his cronies. It was a very pleasant evening for us, and when he dropped us at the small inn, he asked, "When will you be coming downtown in the morning?"

"Probably around eight o'clock," we said.

When we came out of the inn the next morning, he was sitting there in his car. "Hi," he said. "I wanted to save you a long walk downtown. Hop in."

We were certainly grateful to him but we couldn't ignore the irony involved in how sympathetic some people are because you don't have a car. In our case, it's crazy; we like to walk. By its very nature, liberated travelling requires quite a bit of walking. Anyone who plans to travel this way and isn't used to walking would be wise to get in shape for it before leaving home. It won't add to your vacation to have sore legs for the first half of your trip. Remember that five miles in Europe is the same as five miles at home, even if they do call such a distance eight kilometers (which makes it sound even worse).

When you arrive somewhere and find a room, you will probably want to dump off your belongings in your room and go out on a preliminary exploration. If you're staying in a small hotel, first pick up a map at the desk and have a quick look through the posts cards that will be for sale there. They will give you some idea of the names of the top spots in the vicinity, which will allow you to find those spots on your map—or to ask the concierge, porter, clerk, or whoever, how to get to any of them that interest you. Even if you got all the literature in the United States and have read it carefully, you will probably have forgotten everything by this point.

The authors' photos, Holland

*There are fascinating sights everywhere —
if you just travel slowly enough to see them.*

At any rate, the post cards will show you what the natives believe (or believe that the *tourists* believe) are the best places to go. They can be helpful.

Once you have a map, all you have to worry about is whether or not you can read it. Every country, province, and town of any size in Europe will supply you with maps, many of which are readable, and some of which are printed so small that they're not. Some of them do not have the orientation we are used to, *i.e.,* north at the top of the map. And may of them have those strange names that make you wonder why *they* can't learn to spell: Köln, København, Bruxelles, Lisboa, etc. Nevertheless such maps are invaluable, especially when you are in a place where any question you ask of anyone is answered in a language you don't understand.

When you get a map in a city in which you have just arrived, mark the location of your lodgings on it (with the help of the hotel personnel or pension owner, if necessary), and also, if possible, the location of the train station in which you arrived. If it is a town of any size, mark the route of your first little exploration on the map, watching street signs as you go. That in itself may be a good trick, because most European street markers, where they exist at all, are little postcard-size signs on the corners of buildings. And they are usually across the street from you, which means that you can't read them anyway.

If you do get lost and want to get back to your hotel or pension, note the nearest street sign, see where it is on your map, and walk one block in any direction and find another sign. Locate *that* street on your map and you'll know which way you're going. If you luck is like ours, you will always have gone in the opposite direction from your room location, or at least at right angles to it—but of course that's the odds: you had only one chance in four of guessing right. Now at least you have a rough idea of which way to go, and a continual checking of street signs against the street names on your map will soon bring you back to your home away from home.

It probably sounds pretty simple and obvious to you, but you'll learn when you get there that just as some streets have no signs showing at some corners, some of the streets on the map aren't named either. It sometimes can strike one as a vicious plot to make the poor dumb tourist look even dumber than he or she really is.

When all else fails, stop in a bar, or sit down at a table in a sidewalk cafe, or stop at an outdoor ice cream stand, and when you are drinking or munching upon whatever refreshment you ordered, spread your map and stare at it for a time. The odds are eighty percent in your favor that the proprietor or a nearby client of the establishment will offer you advice. If that doesn't happen—as painful as it is to ask "Where am I?"—ask. Someone will help out. And in that situation it is nice to have a map so you can point to the place you want to go.

Hint: If all you want to know is *which direction*, generally, to go to see that castle you've heard about, *keep asking*. The European, naturally, thinks he can tell you how *far* to go *this way, where* to turn, which way, and so on, because he is inclined to believe that you can understand simple phrases in whatever language he is familiar with—but if you *don't*, ask "Is it this way?" and point with your hands. He'll usually get the idea and give you directions that are rather general.

And don't ignore the advice; as you'll soon learn, it's terribly helpful to know that you should be heading *this way* rather than *that way* to reach that point you want to get to, especially when you are walking. Europeans can and will be helpful to visitors if given half a chance. And anyway a fantastically high percentage of them speak English better than you speak German, French, Flemish, or whatever. And sometimes better than you speak English.

They are all well aware that we're not overly bright anyway. After all, how could *anyone*—even an American—be standing on the Gran Via, or in Saint Mark's Square, or in front of Buckingham Palace, or on the bank of the Grand Canal, and not know where he is?

But let us add this: even when you do get what sounds like good advice from one of the natives (pointing off in some direction and saying "Go this way,") continue to check street signs against your map. Some of the Europeans aren't too bright either.

Once you've explored the area around your hotel and gotten a little experience at finding your way about, you will probably want to visit the nearby museum, cathedral, art gallery, or whatever, that every guidebook calls a MUST. To do so, you should first talk to the personnel in your hotel or pension, or to the friendly people in a nearby tourist information office. Whoever it is, ask them how to get there: Is it within walking distance? If not, which bus should we take? Which side of the street should we catch it on to go the right way? What will the trip cost?

Don't be afraid of it. You've already explored the immediate vicinity of your hotel; now you're just going out a bit further (you've graduated from the sixth grade, and are now doing the eighth-grade thing.) If and when you get there, you'll find it easy to get back. After this experience, you'll be prepared to explore the rest of the city, and, indeed, the rest of the country.

A warning: when you are out for a stroll anywhere in England, you are going to get maimed or killed in a hurry if you can't learn to look to your *right* before you cross streets. If you can't remember that, always look both ways. But it is true: motorcars drive on the "wrong" side in that country—and it's useless to look to the left before stepping off the curb because nothing ever comes at you from that direction.

Another caution: when you are walking in places that are dangerous, for example, in the Alps, try to get a little advice from the people who live there (perhaps the personnel in the local tourist office) before you proceed. Don't be fooled by how nice the weather is where you are in the valley; a few thousand feet up that grey you see may be a blizzard. We were in Switzerland one warm July, and the mountain hike we *really* wanted to take, which had been recommended to us by another tourist who had done it, was not possible because an avalanche had ripped the path away from the side of the mountain a few days earlier. These slides can apparently hit at any time, even in the summer, and it is wise to check with people who know what has happened and what could happen before you go up to play Hillary-Tenzing on the slopes.

Hiking is big in Europe. As we mentioned earlier, even rugged Switzerland is covered with hiking trails. The paths are well marked, and the Swiss National Tourist Office will happily provide you with routes ranging from very short to full-day trips. As an aside, we recall that when we were marveling to one Swiss national about the helicopters that patrol the mountain paths, apparently watching for accident victims, he said, "Don't you know how money-hungry we Swiss are? If you fell up there in the hills, they'd pick you up all right—but you'd pay! Probably right on the spot, even before they'd let you in the machine."

"You Swiss are all heart," we said.

"That's us, okay," he replied. "We'll help anyone in any way—as long as it pays."

And we read in the country's promotional literature about helicopter service costing "some $9.50 a minute." Watch your step. Don't fall very far from a hospital.

You might wish to consider trying the least-expensive travel technique of all, in spite of your age and state of health, and travel like the young people do, with your possessions, a small tent, and your sleeping bag on your back. It would be a marvelous thing to do. It would take a bit of planning, courage, and self-confidence, but you would be absolutely free if you could do it. The people you'd encounter would think you were the greatest, and we'd agree. But you'll have to turn to other instructions if you want to do that, because we don't know how.

But we sure like the idea. You would certainly have to have quite a bit of time (maybe a whole summer) to do it, good legs, and first-class hiking boots or shoes. For short distances it would be a fine way to travel. Some of the hiking groups there maintain trails and clubs you could use, including hostels and overnight shelters. The German Hiking and Climbing Association, D7 Stuttgart 1, Hospitalstrasse 21B, operates six hundred such overnight shelters!

The castles of Europe are usually situated in high spots, for reasons that are apparent when you think about it, and they often have cog railways or cable cars running to them for lazy tourists. They also offer good opportunities to get some exercise. We have walked up to many of them in many countries, feeling like the new barbarians coming with cameras rather than weapons. To us it seems to add to the visit, particularly if you want to try to imagine what life was like in those places when they were *really* in operation.

On a day not far in the past when we were at Fussen, Germany, it was raining. We decided nonetheless to walk up to both of the nearby beautiful castles of King Ludwig. It was a steep but enjoyable walk among the trees and flowers, and in spite of the rain we enjoyed it. Even with the downpour we felt that it added to the whole mini-adventure to walk up. It wasn't a matter of saving money; we just wanted to do it that way. It seemed right. Maybe it will to you, too.

Local town-to-town buses

Although we mentioned buses in the last chapter, discussing their use to cover long distances, we are going to say something more about them here, not in the city-bus sense, but more in terms of short hauls between towns. It is often necessary to use these buses, because as good as Europe's train system is, the trains don't go everywhere. The short-haul buses often serve the points that the railroads can't reach.

While you will find postal buses elsewhere, Switzerland's and Austria's are the most well known. You will often see them in those countries, climbing the mountain roads to haul the mail from one place to another. They also carry passengers on these regularly scheduled runs, and since they go where the trains *don't,* they often provide the only way to get to some of the high spots. They are equipped with three sets of brakes, piloted by excellent drivers, and, by law, are always given the right of way.

There are some areas of Holland that are not served by trains. Examples are some parts of the polder regions in the east, and some of the island areas of the country's extreme southwest. In such areas you have to take buses, which is not as easy to do as riding the trains.

There are numerous Dutch bus companies, and, perhaps because of competition, ticket prices are very low. The Eurailpass will not be accepted on these lines, which are private endeavors, but "Day Rover tickets" are available, which, depending upon where you are and where you are going, range from about $3.00 per person per day to $5.00 per day. They are usually purchased from the bus drivers (not all of whom speak good English, but who will try like mad to help you), and the ticket is good only until midnight of the day of its validity.

The Dutch bus system is low-cost, efficient, and kind of crazy. Except for very large cities, you will find no bus stations. You do find bus stops everywhere with printed signs that give destinations and departure times—which is fine if you know where you want to go. If you don't know for sure, or need to transfer someplace, or have some other question, just ask a driver and hope his English is equal to the task of answering you. Most buses have reduced schedules on holidays, but these are plainly indicated and understandable to a careful reader of signs. Some runs are dropped during the winter, a fact that may not be known by some of the drivers, although many of them carry schedule books for all of the lines. On one of our 1975 trips, we intended to visit Flevelhof to see the demonstrations of cheese-making, the children's farms, etc., which the brochures claim to be "Open every day throughout the year." Perhaps so, but after four drivers told us that we could get there by bus, and three said we couldn't, we gave up. We later learned how we could have gotten there, and that our problem was that the drivers on one line often don't know another line's schedules.

If you can read maps, brochures, signs, and expressions of bewilderment on the drivers' faces, you can go far (but not too far without leaving Holland) on the Dutch bus lines. Actually what you should do, if you plan to go into areas not served by the railroads, is to go to a V.V.V. (tourist office) and ask the people there to write out an itinerary for you, listing, from point to point, the name of the bus company, the line or number of the bus, and even departure or arrival times if you wish (although you can always get these times from the signs at the bus stops). Anyway, this should make it fairly easy to you, at least if one of the bus companies in question hasn't just revised its schedules a few days earlier without notifying the V.V.V.s of the fact. The V.V.V. personnel all say they would be happy to provide such a service, and they concur that you would be smart to get such advance information before riding the buses.

It probably wasn't fair to say that Holland's manner of getting buses from one small town to another is crazy. It's more correct to say that such systems in every country over there are strange to Americans. For example, in Spain you get on buses at the front or at the back; you buy your ticket on the bus or in a bus station; and if you do have to get it in a station, you can count on the fact that the bus will depart from the station—or from somewhere else. "I have a little trouble with that myself," one Spaniard admitted to us. The trick on the buy-the-ticket-in-one-place-and-catch-the-bus-somewhere-else confusion is to look at the bus number on the ticket, and then find a bus (or bus departure sign) with the number on it. It also helps (sometimes) to point this way and that to the ticket-seller and ask some multi-lingual question such as "Donde esta la autobuss—to depart—uh—Ausgang—from?" If you're lucky, you may get some sort of vague compass heading in return. And the best trick of all there, of course, is to be able to speak Spanish.

Sometimes the ticket (if there is a ticket involved, as in dealing through a bus station) will list the date, price, departure time, bus number, and perhaps seat number. If you can tell one from another, perhaps by a process of elimination, you've nearly got it made. Read the ticket carefully. Figure out what it says. Then all you have to do is to find the bus. By our experience, you probably never will.

If you have a Eurailpass, always show it when buying tickets on short-haul buses or even funiculars (cable railways). Sometimes you will get a discount or even a free ride. When we caught the bus from Fussen, Germany, to the nearby Ludwig castles we were let aboard free because of our rail passes. You never know.

City transportation
Outside of a finger in the eye, one of the least-fun things in the world is standing at a bus or train stop for lengthy periods of time wondering how much it costs, which one you should take, whether you get on at the front or the back, whether or not you have to stamp the ticket when (and if) you get one, and so on, while tiny tots with all the savoir-faire that you lack leap aboard and ride away, probably right to the place you wanted to go. Well, here is a tip: after you've read the bus stop sign (which in most places tells quite a bit if you can decipher it) and have figured out which one seems like it might get you close to where you want to go, just watch those smart little (fill in your own word here)—or their elders—and do what they do. Ordinarily you will get on the front of the vehicle and pay the driver, but not always; sometimes you will see people getting on at the back and paying a man there,

which should tell you quickly what you need to do. Whichever is the case, watch which coins the people ahead of you put down, and just give the man the same ones (or something slightly larger). Say the name of the place you want to go (or better still, have it written down on a piece of paper you can show), and if you've leaped on the wrong bus or tram, the driver or ticket seller will shake his head and say something incomprehensible. Then you hop back off and prepare yourself mentally to try again with the next bus or tram. If it's the correct one (*i.e.,* your money is accepted and you get a ticket), sit down and start watching either street names or the signs at the stops you pass, many of which list the various stops with an arrow pointing at the one the sign occupies. If you do somehow get to the place you had hoped to reach, and you plan to return to your starting point at some time in the future, look at the bus number and name again when you dismount. If you don't forget them (which you probably will), you will later be able to take it going the other way right back to where you began the whole adventure.

Incidentally, most buses seem to bear the same numbers, names, or destination signs no matter which way they're going on their routes, which means that you can be standing at the right stop for the bus you want, only to learn finally that it was making its return run from your destination. And if that happens, you'll probably be forced to buy another ticket at the end of the line, before it starts back. So read the signs carefully, and say your destination to the ticket seller. If he shakes his head and points across the street to a stop on the other side, now you'll know why.

One can indeed feel like such a dunce, and rightfully so, trying to perform this simple act that any town drunk or imbecile over there could manage easily with his eyes closed. It may give you a bit of agony the first time or two, but you've got to do it. After you've ridden the buses or trams once or twice, you'll suddenly realize you're an expert at it.

Or you'll be lost.

If that happens, hail a taxi and learn how expensive it is to be less capable than all those little _____s you saw earlier.

And let us add that it is invariably much easier to catch a bus to a place like Paris than to get one to a place with a name like Artichoke or Cauliflower or whatever—which perhaps constitutes another argument for staying in the small towns. Once you take the bus from Sauerkraut to Munich you'll know what number it is and where it stops—which means that you'll know how to take it back. But if you stay in Munich and want to take a quick run out to see Sauerkraut, you're going to have one hell of a time figuring out how to do it.

Incidentally, many trams and some buses in Europe do not carry ticket-takers and -sellers. For these you usually buy your ticket from a machine at the tram stop and insert it in a machine in the vehicle to have it stamped. There are usually signs in several languages (including English) explaining that you can be fined for riding without a ticket. And the officials do spot-check occasionally.

British city buses are easy to use. The stops are well marked with signs, maps, and understandable information about which bus goes where. On most of them you

you get on and take a seat (smoking on the upper deck only, please), and eventually someone in uniform will come to sell you a ticket. All you need to say is where you got on, and where you want off, and you will be given a ticket and told the price. They run frequently, and fares are not too high.

All in all, walking through the cities of Europe is doubtlessly the best, most healthful, and safest way to get about, but sometimes it just isn't possible because of the distances involved. For long distances across-town buses are possible, but we've already discussed them; let's talk about subways or ''metros'' here.

First of all, these undercity railroads need not bring unpleasant pictures of rape and robberty to your mind, as they might in some American cities. They are safe, as far as we can deduce (maybe it's just that no one thinks we're worth robbing or raping). Secondly, they are not difficult to use *if you know the line number or name, and the final destination point.* They are fast, incredibly inexpensive, and perfectly acceptable to use if you have a little bit of advance information—which you can usually get from a tourist information office, or, better yet, from the people who operate your hotel, hostel, camp, or pension. All you have to do is to tell them where you want to go, and they will tell you how to identify the proper line(s), and the proper direction (usually the last stop on a line), and, if required, the stations at which you transfer to other lines.

We would give very high marks to the metros of London, Madrid, Paris, and Brussels. They are clean, quiet, fast, and inexpensive. Not only that, but the personnel who sell tickets seem more than happy to give advice and solace to weary, lost, confused tourists. A New Yorker would be astonished by these twenty-first-century subways, and also by the pleasant ticket sellers.

It's really pretty easy. We've done it everywhere with nary a hitch—and you can do it too. But if your destination isn't far off, we'd guess that you, like us, would prefer to walk. The scenery is so much nicer above ground.

Biking it

It would be the understatement of all time to say that bicycling is popular in Europe. There are five hundred thousand bicycles in Amsterdam alone, and three hundred thousand in Copenhagen! (and perhaps four in Madrid; it is not by any means a big thing in Spain. You can pretty much forget bicycling there.) Elsewhere everyone seems to have a bicycle, and there are special bike lanes, turn lights, trails, and so on, almost everywhere. For the budget traveller this provides a magnificent opportunity: they can be rented inexpensively, hauled on many of the trains for very little, and even in some areas picked up at one railway station and returned to another. At many train stations you will find bikes being rented in the back of the station (often near the baggage area), while private entrepreneurs are renting them outside the station. We have been told it is always better to deal with the official renter in the station. Incidentally, Europeans usually say ''lease'' rather than ''rent.''

Since rental rates vary from country to country, and indeed even within a city (because the railways and private entrepreneurs are competing), we will only describe how the whole thing works in Holland. There you can rent brand new bikes, male or female, ordinarily single-speed (surprising, at least until you think about how flat Holland is), with built-on locks and lights for about $3.00 each for the day. Wherever you go, excluding Spain, you will see rusty old clunks in numerous places being rented by private individuals, and in areas that aren't so flat as the Netherlands, you will find multi-speed machines available. The German railroad system advertises bikes for rent for DM5.00 per day (about $2.50 U.S.) if you have a railroad ticket or a Eurailpass; otherwise they cost twice as much. You can buy a "cycle ticket" to take the bike on the train for about a dollar. The Germans also suggest a few scenic bike tours in their literature ranging from four hundred to eight hundred miles. We kid you not, those folks bicycle!

The Swiss are less optimistic about your legs and your stamina, apparently. They suggest bike routes in their literature ranging from eight to thirty-five miles. Perhaps we might quote several of these to give you an idea of what they have in mind.

Discovering Castles in Canton Aargau: Birrfled (four miles away from Brugg) is the starting point for this discovery trip of medieval castles. It leads you via Möriken to the castle of Brunegg (in private hands), the castles of Wildegg and Lenzburg (both museums), Veltheim, Oberflachs, Schinznach Bad (well-known

Netherlands National Tourist Office photo

It is an understatement to say that bicycling is popular in Europe.

spa) and the castle of Habsburg (museum) and back to Birr. Duration: two and one-half hours, twelve miles.

On the Romantic Katzensee near Zurich: If you're looking for an idyllic bathing spot whilst in Zurich on a hot summer day, then try cycling from Seebach station through the shaded woods to Katzenrüti (picnicking spot) and further to the Katzensee (with beach and Waldhaus restaurant). Return via Affoltern. Duration: one to one and one-half hours, eight miles.

Along the Shores of Lake Lucerne: This excursion can last a whole day as there are so many spots worth looking at along the way. Set off from Lucerne station and head for St. Niklausen and Kastanienbaum in the direction of Tribschen (Richard Wagner Museum). The most beautiful stretch is along the lake till Winkel-Horw beach. Return to Lucerne. Duration: one to one and one-half hours, eight miles.

The Dutch tourist people put out a nice folder called *Holland: Cycle Land,* which contains a map showing routes all over the Netherlands, as well as information about buying or renting bicycles, and descriptions of "cycle trips." These little tours run from two to seven days, and the tab includes the route description, the bike, insurance, and room and full board. Depending upon the tour, they figure on twenty to twenty-eight miles per day, and you can arrange to have luggage sent on ahead of you from point to point. The brochure is available from the Netherlands National Tourist Office.

This would be a very fine way to see part of Holland, but indeed we have found that the routes (*fietsroutes* or *fietspads*) are usually so well marked that free-lance trips work very well too.

Bike rentals are fairly inexpensive in the Scandinavian countries. At this writing, it is possible to get one in Copenhagen, for example, for $3.00 a day from Kobenhavns Cyclebørs, along with a refundable deposit, which is common in these countries. In addition, various tourist associations provide bike tours at reasonable prices. They include the bike, all lodgings, maps, all meals, and range from twelve to twenty-four dollars a day.

Denmark's Fyntour organization, which arranges all sorts of tours, stays in the country, and summerhouse accommodations, also offers long bicycle tours. For the bicycle, all meals, and overnight lodgings, they charge from twenty-two to twenty-six dollars per day per person. The tours are six to seven days long, and they even offer one at a much cheaper price (about eleven dollars a day per person) where you furnish the bike, cooking utensils, and sleeping accessories. These particular tours are all on Funen, which is the large island in the center of the country.

We had one little problem in renting bicycles on one of our trips that is possibly worth mentioning. We may have misunderstood, but we got the idea the bike man wanted to hold our passports while we had his bikes. A policeman became involved in the ensuing debate. He told the bicycle guy in no uncertain terms we did not have to let him hold our passports. "Where would you be," he asked us (we think), "if you had an accident and didn't have the passports?" Finally the rental man was satisfied to take the numbers down from the passports (in lieu of deposits) and let us take the bikes. But in some places, deposits as well as passport identification procedures are required.

Bicycling is a fine way to travel in Europe. Nothing could be less expensive or nicer, in our opinion. May we give just a handful of impressions of what it is like? First of all, you are free—no schedules to stay within—not even your own. You may have your lunch with you. You ride along at a reasonable pace, looking at the scenery, the churches and castles, the gardens, and the quiet little houses. There is a small element of danger: suppose you have a flat tire or a car knocks you over? What if you get lost? Will you be able to find anyone with whom you can communicate well enough to get you going where you want to go? You notice how nicely you are treated by people in restaurants and parks; you've become one of *them,* and they accept you as such. You get somewhere, finally, *anywhere*—and you can think, perhaps foolishly—what American has ever been here before? And you know that you're *European* to the tourists who go screaming by on the bus or train; you're a part of the local color. It's a nice feeling.

And Europeans are ordinarily quite interested in you when you bicycle up to them. Often they will invite you in for a beer or a coffee and a little chat. They seem to sense that you are more genuinely interested in them and their country than the folks who peer out of windows of cars or tour buses, and of course they like you for that.

To us such little bike tours are the opposite of the guided tour. They are unguided non-tours. They're yours, not someone else's. There's nothing between that front wheel and the horizon but your mind, scenery, and, perhaps, chance. You are really on your own on a bicycle in Europe.

The first day we were ever in Delft, Holland, we were out exploring that lovely town on bicycles we had rented at the railroad station. With its stately old buildings and tree-lined canals, its ducks, and its flowers, Delft hit both of us as a kind of remembrance of how we had felt years ago when reading *Hans Brinker and the Silver Skates.* We eventually passed by the Delft factory where the world-famous blue pottery is made, and went in to look around. It was very interesting, and we saw not only many examples of Delftware, but also learned how it is created. We were particularly fascinated by watching the young girls hand-painting on the intricate designs, and we stayed for quite a while.

When we left, there was a tour bus from Amsterdam standing by the front door that had not been there when we went in. It was packed with American tourists who had already been through the Delftworks and been herded back on the bus. "How many did you count?" we heard the driver ask the hostess. "Thirty-eight," she replied. "But I'd better get on and count them again. We don't want to leave anyone behind." We mounted our bikes and rode away to see the rest of Delft as the bus pulled out to return to Amsterdam.

Perhaps this little tale will allow you to decide whether you would rather have been one of us or one of the thirty-eight on the bus who really didn't see Delft at all.

Chapter Ten
Inside Information about Inns

. . . until we have limbered up our imagination we continue
to think as though we had stayed home.

—John Erskine

One often hears people saying, ''I won't travel in Europe until I can go first-class.''
It is a mistake to do that even if you can afford it. If you do, you will get the same
unfriendly, supposedly respectful treatment you get in any luxury hotel anywhere.
Going first-class will shield you from ever meeting and enjoying Europeans,
prevent you from reaching any understanding of any country, and generally make
you feel that you never left home.

If you travel more modestly you will stay with private families, which will show
you something of their everyday lives. These places are invariably clean,
and the hosts are friendly and charming nine times out of ten. They will show you
kindnesses that no amount of money would buy you in a big hotel. And you ordinarily don't have to book them ahead, which gives you the flexibility to change
plans or directions at any time.

There's little point in saving for years until you can afford to do Europe
in first-class style. It's comfortable, but boring; it's posh, but unfriendly; it's
American, not European.

We think ''first-class'' is tenth-rate. It's safe, much like staying on the beach
rather than going into the water.

The room in a private home or "pension" has many advantages beyond its price, which can be as low as half what a comparable room in a hotel would cost. The rooms are usually large, ordinarily nicely furnished, and, in our experience, invariably clean. The people who operate these little businesses are usually quite pleasant to their guests, often asking you to join them in the evening for a beer, to watch television, or to play with their children. At their best they can almost provide you with a home away from home—but such accommodations are sometimes difficult to find, even when you ask people to help you locate one. Sometimes they just shrug and tell you they don't know where any are. Perhaps they don't. They often respond to such questions by trying to send you to some fancy hotel they know about.

It is often not easy to understand the differences between accommodations in hotels, pensions, and private homes. Most tourists, and, indeed, many Europeans consider a pension room and a room in a private home to be one and the same. Strictly speaking, they are not. A pension is more accurately defined as a small hotel of sorts which may offer two or three meals a day. Some of them, on the other hand, will offer only breakfasts to their clients. And yet you will see many "pensions" that are not hotels, but simply private homes. The *Gasthaus,* found mostly in Austria and Germany, is most commonly an inn licensed to serve meals and drinks and which lets rooms as well. These establishments usually offer full-board accommodations. And lastly, the tourist room in a private home is just that, a spare room that is rented out. Since so many people refer to pension rooms and tourist rooms as being the same thing, we will not draw many distinctions between them from here on—but we do recommend the tourist room in a private home pension as usually being the least expensive and the most enjoyable accommodation.

The advantages of pensions

Most of the national agencies will give you literature on accommodations in their respective countries, but these listings usually appear to stop short of describing all of the pensions or tourist rooms in private homes. Perhaps this is understandable, and indeed their seeming reticence to tell you about such places when you are there may simply suggest that they do not have the time or manpower to keep up all of the listings, especially for lower-priced rooms.

But Europe is covered with homeowners who would like to pick up a few dollars this way. Sometimes such people will approach you in the station when you get off a train, asking if you'd like a room for the night. You will also often hear about good deals on rooms from other tourists who have already been where you are headed. But you will sometimes find that the proprietors of such rooms will only rent to you if you'll agree to stay more than one night. They claim they can't afford to wash the linens every day.

When you arrive in a town to look for such inexpensive accommodations, you should have already marked the names and addresses of the places that intrigued you in your hotel/pension listing you obtained from that country's national tourist office in the United States. The best way to proceed is to get to a telephone in the train station and call as many of them as necessary. When you hit one that is not too far away and is priced right, walk over and look at it. Perhaps you will want to check your bags in a locker before you go. If you can't get to a phone and you are going out on a hunting expedition, definitely leave your baggage at the station. But often you will find that you can do everything by phone but examining the room and saying a final ''yes'' or ''no.''

When you can find a room in a pension or a private home it can, at least at its best, be *your* home for a short time too. We have had such places all over Europe, but we have never yet had one which included a private bathroom. Would this bother you? Many Americans can't conceive of taking a room that does not have a private bath and toilet. To get a room ''with'' anywhere in Europe is an expensive business, and once one experiences doing without such facilities he will realize that it's really not all that important. If the toilet isn't too far away from your room or on another floor altogether, you won't really be inconvenienced. You will usually have a wash basin in your room which you can use for cleaning up or for washing out small items of clothing, and you'll find that even when the hotel or pension is filled you won't often have difficulties in getting the use of one of the toilets.

It's a matter of economics, really. Having private facilities with your room can double its cost as compared to a room without; in our opinion it is a pretty poor investment. One would be better off to save that extra cost for something that really matters. You'll have a private bath when you get back home.

But many Americans even find it hard to imagine staying in a room in a private home regardless of the bath situation, perhaps because they fear they will be uncomfortable, or the rooms won't be clean, or the proprietors will somehow gyp them. It's possible, but we've never had such problems in private home pensions, although we have in a few small budget hotels. We believe what someone once told us: ''Most pensions are operated on a lot of love and a very small profit.''

We once heard an interesting story related to the subject from the Director of the tourist information office of Maastricht, Holland's oldest and southernmost town. Maastricht was the first Dutch town to be liberated from the Germans, back in 1944. About 280 members of the 20th Division of the U.S. Army and members of their families met in Maastricht in 1974 for the thirtieth anniversary of their entry into the city, and it was a joyful occasion for them and the city's inhabitants. There were already many tourists in Maastricht when this huge group of people arrived, and the V.V.V. Director had booked every available room in town for the former GIs and their families in hotels, pensions, and private homes. When the group arrived he told them about these arrangements, and to his surprise he heard from some of the people who had been booked into pensions and private homes that they were not happy. ''If some people get rooms with private showers in the hotels, why can't we?'' they asked.

The V.V.V. Director finally asked them all to stay where they were booked, and told them he would try to move everyone into hotels the next day.

The following morning they all came back to the V.V.V., and the ones who had stayed in pensions and private homes were full of tales about their hosts' generosity, friendliness, and charm. "We no longer want to move to hotels," they said. "No way!" At that point, having heard how great their friends had been treated, the people who had been in hotel rooms the night before insisted on being moved to pensions and private homes!

The story proves a contention we have had for some time: if an American stays in a pension or tourist room one time, he'll never resist the idea again afterwards.

Why stay in a hotel when you can stay in a 600-year-old home like this — for a third the price?

The authors' photo. Germany

Pension problems, camps, and hostels

We have talked about what is ordinarily good about staying in pensions or private homes in Europe; now let's look at what is sometimes bad about such accommodations. Some of them, unsurprisingly, are not located in the central part of town. Some of the listings of hotels and pensions tell how many meters (a meter is just over a yard) each establishment is from the town's train station. If you don't have this information when you call one of them, ask how many minutes' walk it is from the station, or which bus or tram you should take—as well as where to tell the driver to let you off. Occasionally they will volunteer to pick you up in their car.

Some European houses have stairways that are so steep they would frighten a mountain goat. There is nothing you can do about these except be sure you have one hand free for the railing.

Occasionally pension proprietors have little or no command of English. This is bad because you will be staying in such places partly to get to talk to and to learn from them, and also because such people can always give you good tips about what to see and do in their locality—if, of course, they can talk to you.

You should always ask if breakfast is included (which it usually is); if it isn't, the room price should be very low.

As in most European hotels, many pension rooms have two single beds, sometimes side by side, sometimes not. We leave it to you to think about the ramifications of that, and whether or not it is something you want to have among your considerations.

There is one other cost factor in the hotel-versus-private home question. Many hotels have to charge a "sojourn tax," but we have never stayed with a private family that asked us to pay anything beyond the room rate.

Many European homes do not have refrigerators. One result of this lack of refrigeration is that you will often be served hot milk for your coffee, or a thick yellow cream-substitute that does not have to be kept cold. Either of them works perfectly well, and you'd get exactly the same thing in most of the fancy hotels.

The ramifications of what to our country would be a dearth of washing facilities often become apparent when you stay with a family that rents out several rooms. You may be allowed free showers, or asked to pay a small sum, perhaps twenty-five or fifty cents, for the hot water and towels. You may be told that the hot water will only be available at a certain time, or indeed you may get into places where you just can't arrange for a shower at all. If this is a matter of interest to you, you should ask about it before checking in at pensions or small hotels. You might also wish to ask where the toilet is in relation to the room you are considereing.

Most such rooms have a sink and running water, but occasionally you will get one that only has cold water. If this matters to you (*e.g.*, you want to wash out things in the room), it is something you should check before you commit yourself.

Before we get to the subject of "real" hotels, let's have a quick look at other inexpensive ways of getting a night's sleep. Camping out is one possibility. There are many, many campgrounds in Europe (there are more than 1,350 in Germany alone, 350 of which are kept open during the winters). Many of them have lodges for guests who do not have tents or camper vehicles. The fees for camping range from fifty cents to two dollars per night per adult, depending upon where you are and what facilities a given camp offers. An international camping carnet will get you a price reduction at most camps.

Another possibility is provided by the hostel. These quasi-hotels are ordinarily for young people (they are often called youth hostels, in fact), but sometimes they provide rooms for older tourists. There are often stringent requirements about check-in times, when one has to be inside at night, and so on, but they offer extremely inexpensive sleeping spaces for as low as about a dollar per person. There are many of these in Denmark, Finland, Norway, Sweden, and Belgium, as well as dormitories and "sleep-ins," any of which are worth investigating if you can't do better, and they are often open to people of all ages. But many of them are open only in the summer. One caution: it might be well to avoid such accommodations that only furnish dormitory space because one hears many tales of thievery in such situations. We know an American couple who got robbed in one of these dorms by another American. They lost clothes, luggage, everything.

Anyone who is interested in using hostel accommodations in Europe should write to the International Youth Hostel Federation, Delaplane, Virginia 22025. If you are a student, send proof of your college status, a small photo of yourself with your name on the back, and your nationality and date of birth to USSTS, 866 Second Avenue, New York 10017 in order to get an International Student Identity Card.

Budget hotels

There are all sorts of hotels all over Europe: refurbished castles, luxury hotels, (*e.g*, the Imperial or Sacher in Vienna, or the Bayerischerhof in Munich, or the Hotel de Paris in Monaco), and first class, ordinary, and budget hotels—not to mention American establishments like the Hiltons, or the motels that are appearing at an increasing rate, often some distance from the central city areas. We will not discuss the expensive American-style establishments here, assuming that you can stay in them in the United States when you are travelling on your expense account. Many of the small, budget hotels (many of which are called "pensions") are very nice. They aren't fancy, and they aren't expensive. Occasionally they are less expensive than the tourist rooms in the same area.

A tourist travelling in Europe on a budget will soon learn that appearances do not mean much. Sometimes a small hotel's lobby area looks rather dismal, while the rooms above are quite nice—and the reverse can prove true. Sometimes "hotels" in the larger cities are one floor of a large building that contains offices, restaurants, etc., on other floors. The private homes that offer pension rooms usually look exactly like what they are: private homes. Generally the best idea is to ignore the neighborhood and even the outside appearance of the building. Ask to see the room, and make your decision on the basis of its appearance. And remember that you aren't going to be living there very long in any case.

Some of these hotels and their prices deserve a bit of explanation. A double room in many parts of Europe will be fifty to one hundred percent higher priced than a single, and most doubles contain two single beds. With a double room, you pay more—to sleep apart. This is not a consideration with pensions, which usually provide rooms with two or three beds, and we were once in one that could have slept six or eight people. At any rate, we have frequently asked for and gotten a single room with a single room price. This can be arranged surprisingly often in small hotels, especially when it is fairly late in the day.

If you are thinking it might be embarrassing for two people to ask for a single room, you are correct—it is when you first try it. But if your experience is similar to ours, you would find that generally it doesn't seem to bother *them*. Their single beds are usually quite adequate for two people (if they like each other, and are not too large) and the request seems to cause most of the European hoteliers no chagrin at all. We confess that we have tried it in a few places where we got a simple ''No,'' and we understand that it is against the law to rent a single to two people in Austria, Belgium, Switzerland, and Luxembourg, but often the desk clerk or proprietor will just smile and say ''Okay.'' And we have seen evidence that whether the law of the country agrees to this practice or not, it is often considered to be a matter no one needs to know about but the travellers and the hotelier. But it can't be done in Belgium, and there it wouldn't be worth much anyway— often a double room isn't a lot higher than a single. But taking a single hotel room, where you can, is one way to beat the high tariffs.

There are a few more tricks in finding and getting inexpensive rooms. Always ask to look at the room before signing up—a European would. Haggle—a European would. Say, ''Well, it's nice, but it's a bit too much for us.'' Unless you've just seen the last available room in the place, and it's still early in the day, you may be given a new price at that point—a price that is substantially lower than what you were initially quoted. They don't want the room standing empty all night, you know. But there is a point beyond which this kind of thing won't help, apparently because innkeepers have to pay certain taxes and fees to the government for your stay, and if the price gets too low it's just not worth it to them to let you in. But there are those times when God smiles upon you, when a little old lady or old man approaches you in the train station to ask if you'd like a nice room, or, indeed, when you discover a ''hotel finder'' in the station. You tell him what you want, as best you can describe it, and your price or price range, and he will make arrangements for you by telephone. The last time we used one of these chaps, several years ago, we gave him twenty-five or thirty cents for his help.

Try to get a room price that includes breakfast. Usually in Europe they do, but not always. The breakfast can be a real savings if you can stuff away a big one, because it may allow you to skip lunch—or just get by on a bag of pommes frites or some ice cream. You can also try to get on a demi- or semi-pension or full-pension arrangement, where you will be furnished two or three meals a day at a small cost—a matter we will explore further in the next chapter.

Lastly, always begin your room-hunting escapades before the sun goes down. Perhaps a small anecdote will illustrate why.

We got into a small town in Austria late one night in the midst of a heavy downpour. Even in the rain the town was as charming as we had been told it was by people we had met on the train, and we really wanted to spend a few days there. We decided that there was no point in both of us getting soaked, so Phyllis waited in the small train station while Alan went out to find a room. He was gone for nearly two hours.

When he returned he was damp and dispirited. By that time Phyllis wasn't in the best humor either. "I don't find any pensions," Alan reported. "The hotels are full, with one exception, and it's pretty expensive."

"Let's take it," Phyllis said, and so we did. It was a nice room with a shower, the only private bath we had on that trip, but bed and breakfast for two was about seventeen dollars U.S., the highest price we had paid for a room in several visits to Europe. The next day we moved, having found a number of homes marked with little signs reading "Zimmer Frei" (free room). The one we took was seven dollars for bed and breakfast for two.

When we left a couple of days later we took a train early enough in the day to get us to our next stop before dark. We had been reminded of something we had known for a long time: it's not easy to see those friendly welcoming signs in the dark, and it's impossible in a rain storm.

Accommodations in various countries

The only countries where we have had no difficulties of one sort or another in finding rooms in pensions or private homes are Germany, Austria, Holland, and England. And even there we are exaggerating a little, in the sense that you can have trouble with this anywhere in Europe, if you arrive so late that you can't get addresses from the tourist office—or if the village is so small that there is no tourist office at all (or perhaps any private rooms available either)—or if you arrive somewhere on a holiday or a Sunday. That can be grim.

But in these countries the whole business usually works as it should. You can go into a tourist office and explain what you want—and they'll help you find it. To be fair, we have to say that this is *usually* the case anywhere in Europe. You may get a little talk about nearby expensive hotels—but it's easy to deal with that. But there are those horrible times when the tourist office isn't open, or when the only pensions you can find out about are full, or sound as if they are fifty miles away. Then you have a problem.

We have not been able to find out why it is often so difficult to find pension accommodations. We have studied the question from one end of Europe to the other. In Switzerland we were told that at least in some places private individuals are not allowed to display signs advertising rooms for tourists. This is not true in Germany or Austria, where signs reading *ZIMMER FREI* or showing a white bed on a green background are often displayed in windows.

It is consequently ideal to have a list of the country's lodgings with you wherever you go, a document the appropriate national tourist office in the United States should be able to furnish you before you leave. For individual cities you visit, you can usually get such listings from the local tourist information office—if it is open. Now we will give you some vague ideas about what you may face in the various countries.

Austria

In some countries you will find that you can stay on a farm for a time, if you wish. Austria's tourist literature, for example, provides these thoughts on the subject. "Generally, a minimum stay of a week is required and advance reservation through a local tourist office or a regional tourist board is necessary."

It is ordinarily not difficult to find reasonably priced lodgings of any sort anywhere in Austria, although, as you would imagine, doing so is not all that easy during the high season in Innsbruck, Salzburg, and Vienna.

Belgium

As elsewhere in Europe, it makes sense in Belgium to stay outside of Brussels and visit the attractions there by the fast, modern trains. The natives believe that doing so will cut a visitor's costs by perhaps one-third. It is possible to do this from Ghent or Bruges, favorite cities with Americans, but it is just as possible from Antwerp (which is only thirty minutes away by train) or from Liege, Louvain, Namur, Charleroi, Ypres, or Kortrijk. These are all charming cities, and both food and sleeping accommodations will be cheaper than in cosmopolitan Brussels.

If you do stay in Brussels itself, you will find that unlike many other European cities, it sometimes presents the visitor with problems in finding rooms in May, June, and September. It is a business city, rather than a tourist haven, and since the influx of businessmen falls off during July and August, it is often possible to find rooms during those months—the times when other cities are packed.

For those who would be interested in a really small town to locate in temporarily, a top choice would be Rochefort, which is southeast of Brussels. It is an elderly little place with a nice castle overlooking it (now a girls' boarding school), hotels ranging up from about twelve dollars a night for two (or around twenty-three dollars for a pair who will take two meals a day at the hotel), and some pleasant walking tours in the vicinity that the local information office can tell you about.

Lastly we shall briefly mention the accommodation possibilities in those two lovely, ancient, and popular cities, Bruges and Ghent. Budget hotels in Bruges range from about fourteen dollars to nineteen dollars for a bathless double. It is possible here, however, to find double rooms in private homes for six dollars to thirteen dollars. There is a hostel in Bruges, but it only serves students.

In Ghent, bathless double rooms range from twelve to twenty dollars, but it is possible here to find cheaper lodgings. There is a youth hostel that offers extremely low prices and has some private rooms for people past their more tender years.

In Brussels, young travellers should contact C.H.A.B., Traversiere St. 6 (by the North Station), telephone 219 47 50, for help in finding inexpensive accommodations. Another possibility is Acotra (again named with an acronym, although they don't admit it to the extent of using periods), a non-profit association for welcoming, accommodations, and travel services in Belgium, and they charge nothing for their services, nor do they seem to take much note of receding hairlines.

Denmark

You can stay on a farm in Denmark, usually for not less than a week, where you will live and, if you wish, even work with the family. This does cost some money, though not much, and the whole thing can be set up by the tourist office people. The high season here, incidentally, is from June 12 through August 28. The tourist offices have booklets that show pictures of the farmhouses, and give a complete description of the facilities and the price rates. For more information, ask the Danish National Tourist Office for the latest *FYNTOUR* booklet.

Excluding the winter season (when the hotels have special low prices), it is extremely difficult to find inexpensive accommodations in Copenhagen, but it can be done across the southern part of the country—at least if you know what you are doing. All across Denmark, you will find these possibilities: small inns, in small places, that are usually old, comfortable, and quiet, and that often serve delicious and fairly low-priced meals. As one example, there is one of these in Dragor, a short bus ride out of Copenhagen, that runs ten dollars to eleven dollars for a bathless single in the high season—not cheap, exactly, but considerably less than any room you're likely to find in the big city, and Dragor is a beautiful, ancient, fishing/ferry dock village. This inn is called the Faergegård. Another possibility is the rental of summer homes. The rental fee, depending upon the house, of course, would run from seventy-five to one hundred twenty-five dollars a week during the summer, and somewhat less in the spring or fall. When you think about it, a couple could get a place to live and a place to sleep, at least in the spring or the fall, for about four dollars to six dollars per person per day.

If you do find yourself in Copenhagen, you might want to visit "Use It" on Magstraede 14, a few minutes walk from the central railway station. The people there will provide you with information about cheap rooms, inexpensive places to eat, and good places to visit.

For a couple on their own, it appears that the best possibilities for tourist rooms or pensions are in southern Denmark, not too far above the German border. People here seem a bit more interested in tourists than the Danes further north are, and we think there are consequently more rooms available proportionately than in much of the rest of Denmark. Kolding, a little village directly north of Hamburg, has a few fairly expensive hotels and two budget hotels, a Mission

Hotellet and the Hotel Denmark, both of which let rooms in the range of $5.50 to $7.00 for a bathless single, double that for a double. The people we talked to in the hotels seemed to have no reservations about renting a single room to a couple if they want it (fits one's picture of Denmark, doesn't it?). In another nearby village, Rodekro, we found only two hotels, the Jernbane (Rail Station) Hotellet and the Rodekro Hotel, which is actually an inn known for its meals. The first is fairly sizeable for such a small town, but the latter has only four rooms. Both hotels rent rooms for about $7.00 per person, including breakfast. If there were tourist rooms available here, we couldn't find them.

England

In England it is possible to obtain listings of pensions and budget hotels from the British Tourist Authority offices, but finding a place to sleep in England is usually not a difficult matter anyway. "Bed and breakfast" establishments are everywhere, and many of the little pubs have rooms "to let" upstairs. The tourist information offices will book you a room for a small fee, and occasionally (as in London's Victoria Station) you will find a free booking service. Prices are ordinarily set on a per-person basis, which means that a double room will usually, but not always, run twice the price of a single. The British are not adverse to renting a single room to two people, but this will save you nothing if they charge by the body. Many of them, however, will give you a discount on such an arrangement of twenty-five to thirty-five percent of the cost of a room for two, and sometimes more.

The British tourist offices provide a "Book-a-Bed Ahead" program. For about two dollars they will reserve a room for you by telephone for your next stop.

France

The *Syndicats d'Initiative* (tourist offices) are generally quite helpful in finding whatever kind of accommodations you desire. It is possible in Paris to find fairly inexpensive rooms, but you will have to be more careful than usual here about whether or not they are clean. It is not uncommon anywhere in France to have hoteliers insist upon pension meal arrangements, so it is wise to check this out before signing up. If you are interested in low-budget accommodations, you will find student hotels and hostels, dormitory rooms, and camps everywhere.

Germany

Inexpensive sleeping rooms are usually not hard to locate in Germany, in spite of the generally high prices there. Many private homeowners rent out rooms, and they are invariably clean and usually budget-priced. *Zimmer Frei* accommodations may or may not include breakfasts.

Greece

Greek hotels of class A, B, and C are expensive, partly because they always furnish "private facilities" with their rooms. Class D and E hotels are worth looking at.

This area inside Rothenburg's walls is always packed with day-trippers' buses — at least in the summer.

Pension rooms (often indicated by signs reading "Room to let") are usually pleasant and inexpensive, although the proprietors often do not speak English. The tourist police can provide the names and addresses of these places. A bathless double room in a pension will cost between $9 and $12.

Like Portugal and Spain, Greece has state-owned hotels, often called "mansions" or "guest houses." These are generally restored period homes, left as they were originally except for the inclusion of modern plumbing. We have visited some of them and liked them a great deal, but often found them difficult to locate or get to. They are not exactly inexpensive either, ranging from $21 to $30 a night for a double room. But you can be assured that you will never confuse one with a Ramada Inn.

Holland
Perhaps because the Dutch like to have people into their homes, many of them rent out spare rooms at reasonable prices. And it should surprise no one to learn that the rooms are super-clean, and that the breakfasts are generally large, more varied, and better than in other European countries.

Italy
The way to avoid high expenses for sleeping in Italy is to look for third- or fourth-class hotels, many of which are quite agreeable, or to stay in a *pensionne,* which translates literally as "boardinghouse." You will find rooms in such places for five to six dollars a night per person.

Luxembourg

The central railway station area of Luxembourg City, the more-or-less first impression of the city that visitors get who arrive by train or by bus from the airport, is touristville. The area is crowded by hotels, restaurants, airline offices, and tour buses. And tourist-haven-Luxembourg is not an inexpensive place to visit, although it is generally less costly than Belgium or Germany. Budget hotels range from about nine to twenty dollars a day for bathless singles, and twelve to twenty-seven dollars a day for bathless doubles. Some of them include breakfasts in their price, while others do not. The tourist information offices (and there is one right outside the train station) will furnish literature about these places, and call any of them for you without charge to check space availability or to ask any other questions for you.

Portugal

Here you will find hotels of every class: estalgems (privately-owned top-class inns), pousadas (state-owned revamped palaces and monasteries), motels and pensaos (boardinghouses) of every description. The estalagems and pousadas are popular and should be booked well ahead. Pousadas, which have three classes, range from $14 for a double to $19 during high season, and about 20% less during the low. At the other end of the price scale, the pensaos offer double rooms for $7 to $14 a night.

Most rooms include private bath/toilet facilities. Full-board arrangements are possible, at least if you stay for a minimum of two days. Breakfasts are ordinarily included in room prices. Children under eight will get a 50% discount on meals. All establishments have complaint books guests can use if they are dissatisfied. Accommodations run about 15% less during the low season, November to February.

For tourists who wish to do their own cooking, apartments and villas for two to eight people are available at reasonable rates (which vary over four seasons). Basically one has to take an apartment for at least three days, and a villa for at least seven.

Spain

Spain offers every sort of sleeping accommodation from beaches and parks (free), *pensionnes* (''pen-see-o-nays''), hostels, *alberques* (more or less comparable to our motels), and small hotels (all inexpensive, some more than others), *paradores* (comparatively cheap), to large, ritzy, first-rate hotels (sky-high prices, at least for Spain, but many of them would not look very expensive in relation to many American counterparts). The hotels are rated one- to five-star, and all of them charge you for breakfast whether you eat it or not.

It is illegal for a Spanish hotelier to demand full-board rates, although it can be done in a pensionne. In fact, cheaper hotels, hostels, and pensionnes can legally add twenty percent extra on your bill if you refuse to take at least one of their two main meals each day of your stay.

Like Portugal's pousadas, the paradores are established and operated by the government. They are intended to provide travellers with pleasant but inexpensive lodgings. Except for those along the Mediterranean coastline, which are new buildings, they are renovated castles or palaces. And while they are high-class places, they are cheaper than privately operated lodgings of the same category. They are so popular that it is very difficult to get into one without reservations far in advance. A query about them to the Spanish National Tourist Office will bring you Circular 19, which will tell you where they are located and what each of them offers.

The tourist information offices will provide you with a listing of hotels and pensions that lists names, ratings (by stars), addresses, and telephone numbers. These lists also include a rough guide to what the various habitations in the various categories cost, but in our judgment it is *rough*. On our last visit to this sunny country, one hotel had a different judgment about its category than the tourist office did, and its and their prices were consequently different. But it is possible to find lodgings everywhere, and they are pretty inexpensive, all in all. Double room prices there are not twice as much as single-room prices, as elsewhere, but they are not terribly far from it.

Sweden

You would be wise to contact the Swedish National Tourist Office, from wherever you are, to get a listing of sleeping accommodations before you visit this large country. Perhaps the Swedes don't consider themselves as rich as the Danes think themselves, but we sensed that it is just as difficult there to find rooms in private homes. The reason, we suspect, is the same as in Denmark: the government grabs such a big bite of the take that people either won't rent rooms or they do so *sub rosa*—and as someone said to us, "If the government can't find them, how can you expect to?"

Helsingborg is a fairly small and very interesting old Swedish town with many sleeping accommodations, but if you should find nothing there that suits you, you might bus out to Rää, a pretty little village on the North Sea. There you will find an old and pleasant inn, the Rää Wardshus, which costs about eight dollars year around for a bathless single. That's not exactly inexpensive by central European standards, but then nothing is in Sweden. Each room at the inn has hot and cold water, and a free bath facility available to you nearby, and the place is charming in a marine/anchors-aweigh sense all around.

The tourist information offices in Sweden are very helpful, and their cheerful staffs will call around and get you any sort of room for a fee of less than a dollar. Rooms in private homes go for about five dollars a night for one person, possibly with, but more likely without bath facilities. The least expensive of the budget hotels will run at least twice that figure. The tourist information offices can supply you with all the maps, help, and advice you might want. In the smaller villages these offices are open only from the fifteenth of May to the first of September. A single room in a budget hotel, hotellet, or inn will run about eight to fifteen dollars, with doubles costing seventeen to twenty-two dollars. The two-people-in-a-single-room trick is possible in this country.

General tips

It is always advisable to look at a room before taking it, not only to make sure that it is clean, but also because in some countries there are laws requiring that prices be posted inside hotel doors, while no rules exist about what you may be quoted at the desk downstairs. You will often find that the government bureaucracy, doubtlessly because of interests in tourism, is on your side. As an example, if you feel you've been ripped off in a Spanish or Portuguese hotel, ask for the complaint book. Because your complaint, if written down, will get to the government, the innkeepers will often stop arguing with you at that point. Wherever you are, if you have a legitimate complaint and the hotel proprietor doesn't have a complaint book, pay a visit to the nearest tourist office.

Most of your accommodations in Europe will be super clean, but at least in Spain and Italy we'd advise you to look at the sheets on the bed before agreeing to anything.

Italian tourist offices are generally places where you can get help you need. In fact, the personnel in these offices will call around and make room reservations for you at no charge, a nice service that you won't get in many other countries.

A few other tips related to European accommodations: when looking at rooms check to see whether the free-standing ''closet'' that ordinarily inhabits hotels or tourist rooms has a key and will lock. Often the keys have been carried off by previous guests. For this eventuality, you might want to take a ''travel lock'' with you to provide your own security. These locks will secure either your room door at night while you are inside, or, if you get one that works with a key, will lock the wardrobe while you are out of the room.

There is probably not much danger to your possessions in a pension or tourist room, but in hotels the room keys are often available to anyone who wants to pick them up, either at the desk or when they are hung on a hook outside your door (and they usually aren't convenient to carry with you, as many of them are attached to small wooden bowling pins). It is only slightly comforting to know that your valuable possessions are locked in a little wardrobe that anyone with a hairpin or pocketknife could get into in about three seconds (but the travel lock suggested above would certainly give you more security than those dinky little wardrobe locks). But anything is better than leaving that Nikon on the bed. We would certainly not advocate leaving cash or passports in these cabinets. We have been in too many hotels and pensions where every room had such a wardrobe, and every one of them could be opened by the same key. Another thought: more times than not these little closets have two doors, one of which locks with a key, while the other has a sliding mechanism inside to secure it. If you slide this device, the key lock will hold both doors. If you don't it may be possible to pull both doors open even after you've locked the one with the keylock. If you are in a hotel and have anything with you that is valuable, consider using the hotel safe.

You should take a look at how your room is located in relation to stairs and to know which way to go from your door if a fire were to break out (or in).

We have frequently found that hotels have rooms available in the ''attic,'' up two or three flights of stairs, that will rent for far less than the rooms on lower floors. These rooms are often very nice, and they are money-saving accommodations that have a better view of your surroundings than the higher-priced rooms at lower elevations. You can also often get a discount by agreeing to stay for two or three days, wherever your room is located.

A source of potential embarrassment in hotel rooms is a small button in the wall that looks to American eyes like a light control. It may be a light switch, but more frequently it will summon the maid or someone who provides room service. It is difficult to know what these buttons are for when they are unmarked, but sometimes they will have the figure of a person or of a light engraved on them.

If you find that you don't have any hot water at the sink in your room, look under it before you yell at the proprietor. You may find a tiny little water heater there that has an off-on switch that simply needs to be turned on.

Depending upon what your departure plans are, you may want to ask what the check-out time is. You will find that pension proprietors are usually more flexible about this than the hotel people are.

Sometimes you will find that if you ask in a pension if it is okay to wash out some things in the sink in your room, the lady of the house will suggest that she will just throw your things in with her washing. They will also usually be willing to loan you irons, needles and thread, and so forth.

Ordinarily a *garni* is simply a hotel or pension that offers its clients no meals other than breakfasts.

Many travellers leave their passports with hotel personnel overnight to allow them to copy down the information required by the police. We certainly do not think this is a good idea. If asked to do so, they will either copy what they need from it then and there or get it back to you immediately, or, at most, within an hour. We'll explain our reasons for *not* leaving it there overnight in Chapter Thirteen.

If you stay in the sorts of places we have been recommending, you will probably never have a television or radio available. So if you can find a few cubic inches of space in your luggage, it might be nice to take along a pocket radio. Not only will it let you listen to music, but also to hear the news of fresh disasters from home from time to time on Armed Forces Radio or Radio Free Europe.

You will discover that European lights, especially in hallways or over stairs, are often wired to turn themselves out not long after you've turned them on. This is okay if you expect it and move right along so you won't get caught in the dark in unfamiliar territory. If that worries you, take along a small flashlight.

The VAT tax (described in Chapter Two) can be charged on anything and everything, including sleeping accommodations (how does a room have value added just because you slept in it?). Unless they do a large business, budget hotels and small pensions do not have to pay the VAT to the government, but occasionally they will add on such charges anyway (in which case they will keep the added revenue and neglect to report it to the government). If the place is small and you suspect that you are consequently being ripped off, ask the proprietor for his VAT number. If you wish to press the matter, you can call the local VAT office and find out whether you should have been charged the value-added tax. If not, your lodgings proprietor will be in big trouble, and you should get your money back. But we have an idea that if you ask your host this question directly, he's going to change his mind about asking you to pay the tax if he's not paying it himself.

It is always wise to book seaside accommodations in advance, and of course this is particularly true during July and August.

Lastly, we think it is a good idea to note down the place's name, address, and telephone number when you take a room. It is embarrassing to go out and then not to be able to find your pension again, and worse not to know where it is so that you can ask directions. In addition, if you should leave something behind it is useful to be able to get in touch with the people where you stayed. They won't be able to reach *you*.

So like most everything else about Europe, room finding can be a sort of esoteric business. Whether or not it works for you can be a matter of luck, good or bad, rather than something to do with your lack of skills, languages, or shysterism. We have had numerous unpleasant experiences involving a great deal of time and walking trying to find rooms (usually in the larger cities, which may be some sort of an argument for our small-town compulsions), and we have occasionally been lucky enough to find the right place at the right price with little or no effort. If you can't find a room without using up a lot of your time, it may be wise to let the tourist office people do it for you, even if they do charge you a small fee.

Sometimes people do write ahead to a hotel to book a room for their first night or two in Europe. We have some friends who tried to arrange for a room in this way. In their letter they asked for ''a room with a bath, a double bed, and, if possible, a nice view.'' They received this answer:

My dearest Sir and Wife:

My heart is so happy with your plan to stay in our hotel! You may be emphatic that our every room (all) has a view of stupendous nature! Disfortunately, all of them do not have a bath, of which we have one on each floor at the end. Also double beds we are not having. My wife and I are great in beds, not baths. But we can take care of you! I will lash two of our one-body beds together with rope—will that be nice for your interesting purposes and sleeping?

We have towels (clean) and very fine food you can partake! You will so enjoy! We will meet you together with ceremony and festival on the 24th. Please look forward as we do! Don't worry, we will take good care of you on the bed! We are most expectant to see you happily.

Your servants, etc.,

When there is no room . . .

If you ever do have the misfortune of being unable to find a room in a town where you've arrived, and there is no tourist office open to help you, you will have exactly three choices available to you: to go on to another town; to check into a hotel (regardless of price), at least for one night; or to pay a visit to the police. Even if you should have to go into a more expensive hotel for the first night of your stay, you can always look for a less-costly room the next morning. If you can't find a hotel with a reasonable price when you arrive in town, go to the local police station. (Although you might want to think twice before trying this in Spain. It might not work there.) Generally European police are quite nice, and they often keep lists of pension and hotel rooms at the station. In fact, we have heard many tales about the police making arrangements by phone for weary travellers, and then taking them in a squad car to the establishment's front door. We have also heard of them letting people sleep in one of their cells when even they couldn't help find a room! It wouldn't be ideal, but one can think of worse possibilities.

Well, we said three choices, but there's also always the long ride on the train (if you have a Eurailpass) when all else fails. And in case you ever do this, we will add this tip: it is best to find a night train that is making a long run within one country, which is not easy because many of the countries are so small. But you could do it in France, Germany, Austria, Italy, or Spain. The reason for trying to do this, of course, is to avoid being awakened for passport checks at borders. And this is why one might, as we mentioned early in the book, veer occasionally from his itinerary and take side-trips. With a Eurailpass, you can do such things without incurring extra costs. It would also be possible, of course, to catch a TEE train and go to another country. The TEE's do not stop at national borders; they carry officials on the trains who check passports, and in these trains you can have a porter go through the redtape for you so you won't be awakened. But if you do this, *be sure to get your passport back* in the morning!

There is one time in Europe when you should make advance reservations for rooms, and that is over holidays, particularly off-season ones like Christmas and New Years.

We learned this before one Christmas holiday when we were travelling through Europe, learning what we could about off-season travel. The weather was quite pleasant for wintertime, ranging from thirty-five to forty-five degrees Fahrenheit. We had seen that there were far fewer tourists than in the high season, and we had learned that Europeans are ordinarily quite interested in and friendly toward off-season travellers.

We had planned to find a small, quiet town where we could just take things easy over the two days of Christmas. It was a good idea, but it didn't work. Europeans do like to travel at Christmastime, which means that some pensions and small hotels are closed, while the ones that are open are often filled up. That is the disaster we ran into. We visited one small town after another on Christmas Eve, and we had no luck at all in locating a room. It was horrible. It got darker and darker, and none of the tourist offices were open. We telephoned addresses we had in our literature in one village after another, and in most cases no one answered. Both of us began to think "What are we going to do? Will we spend Christmas Eve in a police station?'' Each new village was a fresh input to our despair. ''Why did we leave that town we stayed in last night?'' we both wondered. ''If we went back there, would our room still be available? Would the pension still be open?'' It was bad. Really bad. It was not the best Christmas Eve we've ever had, to put it mildly.

In the fourth village we visited, we talked to the young man behind the only open ticket window in the train station. He was very sympathetic with our problem, so much so, in fact, that he said, ''I would be happy to take you in, but I have only a one-person room. You would be uncomfortable.'' He then called a number of nearby pensions and hotels, without success, and then he seemed to feel as despondent as we were. After a time, he said, ''I don't know how to call it by telephone, but I've just thought of a small hotel north of here that will be open. I'll tell you how to get there.''

Within an hour we were sitting in a charming room in the old hotel he had named. It was almost midnight. ''Where did we go wrong?'' one of us asked. ''We're supposed to be expert at this sort of travelling.'' Well, to be candid about it, we still felt like experts right then. We were, after all, in a room. That's one of the odd things about this sort of travelling. Things can go wrong, from time to time, but they always get resolved—and when they do, you can feel good, even heroic, because *you* solved the problem (even when, as in this case, you didn't).

All we can suggest, in conclusion, is to get all of the hotel/pension literature you can before you leave; to be prepared to insist on the kind of accommodations you want with the tourist bureau people; to have a bit of patience; and to haggle with the people who rent the rooms. It's not a trivial matter; as we pointed out at the beginning of the chapter, doing it right can mean hundreds of dollars in your pocket over a month's time. And it isn't just the money that's at stake. If you believe, as we do, that a tourist should try to meet the natives, you'll soon find that getting a sleeping room in a private home is one of the best ways to do it. The director of the big hotel will never seek you out to get chummy with you, nor will he invite you up to share coffee with him. The pension- or home-owners will; if they didn't like people, they wouldn't be renting rooms. And believe us, once you try what they have to offer, you'll never go back to the fancy hotels if you can possibly avoid it.

Chapter Eleven
A Loaf of Bread, a Jug of Wine, and an Anti-Diarrhetic

Better beans and bacon in peace than cakes and ale in fear.

—Aesop

If you visit Europe on a limited budget, an average day might go about like the following. You'll get up fairly early in the morning, wash up, and have the breakfast that was included in your room charge. Most likely it will at least include croissants or hard rolls, butter, jelly, and coffee or tea, a breakfast many Americans don't much like at first, and enjoy even less later. In the low countries and Britain it will usually also include fruit juice, a hard- or soft-boiled egg, tomatoes, cold meats, and cheese. You can have other things if you wish, but they will cost you extra. So you eat heartily, filling yourself up because you have become accustomed to eating lightly at lunch.

At lunch you restrain yourself just a bit, having only a pastry and coffee, or an ice cream, or something of that sort. It is pleasant to have such a little snack at a sidewalk cafe, watching the people stroll by as you eat.

For dinner, if your budget permits, you will go to a small restaurant (preferably to one which has its menu posted in the window in order to avoid unpleasant surprises at check time), probably to order the meal of the day (*prix fixe* or tourist menu). It will be good and wholesome, and it will cost only two to three dollars. "Couldn't eat that inexpensively at home," you'll think to yourself.

Dinner time could have a slightly different scenario, especially if your budget didn't seem all that healthy. In that case you would probably visit a grocery store or a delicatessen in the late afternoon to get some food to eat later in your room or in a nearby park.

165

This is not a bad way to eat, actually. You might even find that you'll be eating less and feeling better than usual. But one can hope that your budget won't be so limited that you will be forced to live that way each and every day. One of the great treats Europe has to offer an American is its cuisine, and it would be unfortunate for any visitor not to be able to experience some of the various styles of dining that are popular there.

Different meals in different countries

The French are, of course, the world's gourmets. Tourists who have been in France have fond memories of *escargot* (cooked snails), pressed duck, and such common meats as chicken, veal, lamb, and beef that have been fixed in ways that make them enormously surprising to the American palate. It is almost impossible to single out any food as being representative of this country, because everything there is excellent. Even a plate of eggs in a French drugstore can send an American to the nearest telegraph office to tell the folks at home what a lunch he just had.

Austria is famous for its pastries, its best-known being *Sachertorte,* a wonderful kind of chocolate cake. *Apfelstrudel* is another favorite that is not alien to Americans, and yet another common and fattening dessert is ice cream served in an endless variety of ways. The country is famous for its *schnitzels* (veal), the most familiar to Americans being the breaded one, *weiner schnitzel.*

Scottish and Irish food is generally excellent, in spite of the fact that too many dishes are served with french fries. Favorite main courses are fish (always good), chicken, beef, and eggs in various forms. Such small sea-dwellers as prawns and scampi are always available. The top-selling drinks in both countries are beers and ales, most of which are quite unlike and far better than ours.

You can eat very well in Greece. As elsewhere, if you can find places where the natives eat, both you and your wallet will do well. The tavernas often serve excellent sandwiches, and the little "tea room" cafes provide good eating at good

"A table with a view, please."

Austrian National Tourist Office photo

prices. Fish dishes come in many varieties and are almost invariably fine.

German food is generally excellent. The best food, at least to most visitors, includes *weiner schnitzel* and the many kinds of sausages (*wursts*) such as *bratwurst* or *weisswurst*. Dumplings are also popular here. If one has a desire to fit in with local customs, he will usually have beer with his meals. Like Austria, Germany is covered with *konditorei,* pastry shops that sell an infinite assortment of fattening goodies.

Compared to Belgian or French cuisine, British food doesn't get high marks. But we will disagree with other travel writers who are so highly critical of what our English friends eat. Generally (but we confess not always) their food strikes us as pretty good. In fact, you can get excellent meals in London if you will pay the price. And you can also have good sandwiches, if you like, for very low prices. It is easy to find tea shops, snack bars, and delicatessens everywhere you go, and most of them serve good, if not outstanding, food. The national dish is fish and chips (*i.e.,* french fries) and puddings and custards are big favorites. Another popular repast that is worth trying is steak-and-kidney pie. Real gourmets may not find Britain their favorite country in Europe, but most of us can find the food quite satisfactory there.

Most visitors to Belgium eat very well, and as in France, expensively, if they can afford it. But it is not necessary to spend a lot to eat in this little country. Indeed it is possible to get a filling meal for less than two dollars in many of the small bistros, and one could get by on three dollars a meal forever if he had to. Ham, steak, goose, cheeses, and fish of many types are favorite dishes here. The cooking is not dissimilar from France's, at least in the sense that there is much emphasis on using spices and wines, as well as in making the plate look appetizing. Many travellers, in fact, consider the food in Belgium as good or even better than France's. Favorite repasts include omelettes of many kinds, trout, beef, chicken, mussels, eels, and fantastic pastries and cakes. And here, as in Holland, the potatoes we have misnamed french fries (which they call *pommes frites*) seem to be more of a national pastime than a type of food.

One excellent Belgian appetizer is *tomatoes aux crevettes*, which consists of a tomato stuffed with tiny shrimps. It's delicious. Also excellent is their *jambon d'Ardennes,* surely the best ham served anywhere on the planet. Because Belgian servings are very large, it is considered acceptable to order just one or two à la carte dishes rather than an entire dinner—especially at lunch time.

Holland's cuisine is generally a bit more ''home-cooked'' than Belgium's or France's. It can be very good, but the Dutch don't appear to be all that interested in strange recipes or cooking techniques. They do love fish, of course, and one sees fresh fish stands everywhere (and, occasionally, can observe the locals sliding uncooked fish down their throats). It should surprise no one to learn that they are also devoted to cheeses and cheese dishes.

A favorite pastime here (and in Belgium) is to walk along nibbling on a little bag of french fried potatoes (*pommes frites*) covered with a delicious *frite* sauce that is a form of mayonnaise. These crisp potatoes are completely unlike our greasy version of french fries. Lastly, any visitor who tires of Dutch food should try one of the countless Indonesian cafes or restaurants. These places serve many smaller repasts, but the all-out, many-course rice dinner (*rijsttafel*) is a feast that should be experienced at least once. If you try one, you won't need to eat again soon.

Scandinavia is justly famous for open-faced sandwiches and the smorgasbord. Fish and pastries are excellent in these countries, and while the food is generally good everywhere, it is also generally expensive. A visitor can cut costs by avoiding alcoholic drinks (if you must have something along this line, ask for the house wine instead), by eating his big meal at noon, and by trying the menu of the day.

A budgeteer can survive pretty nicely in Luxembourg, as far as eating and drinking goes, if he is willing to look around a bit. Reflecting the generally high prices for everything in this small country, meals—including ''tourist menus''— are fairly costly, but they are well prepared, and you will get larger portions of everything than you will in France. In an average small restaurant, a half-chicken with french fries will cost in the range of $4.25, no bargain by American standards. But it will be filling, including perhaps a couple of pounds of potatoes.

Portugal's food and drink is ordinarily excellent, and if obtained from small restaurants, snack bars, or tea rooms is not expensive. Fish (*peixe*) is served in countless ways (sole and turbot seem to be invariably delicious). To avoid unpleasant surprises, skip *lulas* (squid) and *polvo* (octopus). You can get good pork, fair but often tough beef, and first-rate chicken, rabbit, and ham. The small sidestreet cafes will provide you with good filling meals, including house wine (*vinho da casa*) for miniscule prices.

The country produces great wines, especially the many varieties of port. Not only do the natives and visitors enjoy the ports, but also Vinho Verde (''green'' wine, which happens not to be green), and the excellent brandies. The Portuguese today are the world's foremost wine-drinkers, and when you try their produce yourself, you'll know why.

Their tap water cannot be so highly recommended. Drinking it anywhere except for Lisbon and Oporto can cause diarrhea. Out in the sticks, stay with bottled water, beer or wine. Take some Lomotil with you if you have a sensitive stomach.

In Iceland, food, like everything else, is not inexpensive—but it is generally quite good and wholesome. It should come as no surprise to anyone that in this sea-surrounded country, fish is one of the ordinary items on the menu—nor that it is invariably excellent. The Icelanders have had centuries to learn how to catch fish efficiently, and how to cook them well. Haddock is probably the most popular fish dish to appear on the table. All of the dishes offered (lamb, mutton, whale, and *skyr* —the national dessert that seems to be a cross between cottage cheese and yogurt) seem fairly plain, at least by Continental standards, but they are good and nutritious, and Icelandic pastries are tops. Cold buffets are popular, and the selections offered would almost make a Swede envious. You won't starve in this volcanic little country, but you won't get by cheaply either. Nevertheless if you are here on Icelandair's stopover package, as many American tourists are, you'll get a pretty good discount on your meals.

In Italy, veal, ham, macaroni, chicken, and fish form the basis for the most popular dishes. Many tourists patronize the *trattoria,* which are restaurants that have somewhat lower prices than the full *ristorante.* There are also snack bars that have reasonably good food and budget prices. Dishes popular with Americans are *risotto, gnocchi,* and *lasagne.*

As mentioned earlier, Switzerland can seem like several countries, many of her customs and traditions reflecting German, French, and Italian influences. This is also true of Swiss food. Generally speaking, the food is good and somewhat expensive. Cheese dishes, particularly a variety of fondues, are quite popular everywhere. (A note of caution: a Swiss acquaintance told us that to put any sort of cold drink in your stomach while eating cheese fondue is to invite disaster.) The local wines are good and fairly inexpensive.

As in many other matters, Spain's food, meal hours, and restaurant service are a bit unusual. For one thing, lunch usually isn't served before what we think of as midafternoon, and dinner starts in mid- or late evening. The service is often less than top quality, and the food itself, which is generally cooked in olive oil, strikes many visitors as having, at best, an odd taste, and at worst, being inedible. All of these problems are most likely, of course, to be found in the budget-level establishments. If one can afford a better restaurant he can expect good food, good service, and, in comparison to comparable eateries in other countries, decent prices. The only alternative to the high-priced places is to pry out of a Spaniard a recommendation about small cafes that serve good food at low prices. Such places are available, and the natives know where they are. A final tip for Spain: try Sangria with one of your meals. It's an unusual fruit/wine drink that can be excellent.

There is one type of eating establishment to be found almost everywhere in Europe that we haven't mentioned: the Chinese restaurant. They serve much the same selections you would expect in such places in the States, although the dishes bear names derived from the local language (sometimes translated into English). They provide filling food that is not ordinarily expensive, and they seem to stay open on holidays, Sundays, and sometimes during hours when other restaurants may be closed.

Generally speaking, eating seems to mean more to Europeans than it does to North Americans. Their food is better prepared than ours, and they are in far less of a rush to devour it. There are more stand-up joints and sandwich and hamburger shops than there used to be, especially in the larger cities, but most of the restaurants are still traditionally European—clean, slow, and usually excellent. So while it is almost too obvious to say, one good idea for the budget tourist is to try to learn where "they" eat, and to eat there too. When you can find such a place, you'll find good food and good prices—but since it won't be designed for tourists, you'll probably have to deal with the most frightening invention of modern man: the European menu. We'll talk about that shortly.

When you have been lucky enough to discover such a place, don't forget that you represent all of us to the other diners, and remember that you are there to eat, to enjoy, and *to learn*—no matter how smart you are. It is extremely annoying to hear one of our countrymen yelling: "Why *can't* I get a rare porterhouse?" What would he think if he heard a European in *his* favorite bistro at home arguing loudly for *Entrecôte à la Provencale*? He'd say, "How come that dolt can't eat a good American hamburger like everyone else?" Anyway, our hypothetical Archie Bunker is not only impolite, but stupid. He can get a porterhouse anywhere at home; in the Hinterlands, he'd eat as the Hinterlanders do if he were smart. Learning how to eat is one of the lessons Europe has to teach us. Forget that it's a snail. Eat it. You won't be sorry.

This is eating out in its purest form.

Menu coping

There are many ways you can embarrass yourself in a European restaurant, even if you have the best of manners. One of the best known is the point-at-anything-on-the-menu-and-pray trick, in which case the waiters will eventually come out and carve up a live octopus in front of you and cook it while you (and it) squirm about. Almost as bad is the old will-you-please-help-me-order-and-teach-me-your-language-at-the-same-time stunt, a move which can be guaranteed not to make waiters love you. And they don't work for tips in Europe, because they usually aren't given them.

As usual we have a suggestion or two. One idea for avoiding any self-inflicted humiliations is to ask for the "menu" or *prix fixe* meal, which in Europe is the meal of the day. It is usually good, simple, and inexpensive. Some restaurants and cafes advertise in their windows with a sign that says "tourist menu" or *plat du jour*. This does not indicate, as you might guess, that some sort of royal rip-off awaits within; in fact, it is a sign to watch for if you are being careful of shekels. In Italy it's called the *Menu Turistico* or *Prezzo Fisso,* and in Denmark, *Dagens Ret.*

Cafeterias are always fine, too, for those who would like to see what they're getting, or at least be able to point at something that looks like it might not disagree with them. In Berne, for example, we discovered the Gfeller am Barenplatz (at 21 Barenplatz), which provides excellent food at low prices in a cafeteria on the second floor that works and looks as all of them should. Such a place removes all language problems, leaving you with nothing but calories to worry about. There are also excellent cafeterias everywhere in the Scandinavian countries.

But when you eat in places other than cafeterias you will often face having to order from a piece of paper that is covered with unrecognizable squiggles. This is not always the case; many of them have colored photographs of the various dishes offered. Occasionally they are printed in several languages, sometimes including English. We found one like that at Gisela's, a fine little cafe at Donkersteeg 11-13, in Ghent, and it made interesting reading. To give you an idea of what you may face and to show you that it's not going to be as bad as you may think, we'll quote a few items from both sides of their menu, which shows *their* translations:

Tussenrib op z'n Provençaals	*Entrecôte à la Provençale*	Ribsteak Provençal
Weiner Schnitsel	*Escalope Vienoise*	Weiner Schnitsel
½ *Kip aan't spit*	½ *Poulet à la broche*	½ Chicken (fried)
Hot dog	*Hot dog*	Hot dog
Krabsalade	*Salade de crabes*	Crab Salad
Toast mit Tartar	*Toast Cannibale*	Toast Cannibal*
Koffee tas	*Café tasse*	Coffee

*This is a raw meat sandwich — as is a *Broodje Tartare* or *Filet Americain.* We suggest avoiding all of these uncooked meats. They could give you health problems.

Note: perhaps the most interesting thing of all on this menu is the note at the bottom—"Service charge and VAT are included—no tips."

As this makes clear, many such words look or sound much alike, and some of them—weiner schnitzel, hot dog, spaghetti, steak—survive translation without significant change. But now we must prepare you for the day when it's all in another language. For such times we are going to give you a brief survival menu:

English	Dutch	French	German	Italian	Spanish
soup	soep	soupe	Suppe	suppa	sopa
eggs	eieren	oeufs*	Eier	uova	huevos
cheese	kaas	fromage	Käse	formaggio	queso
chicken	kip	poulet	Huhn	pollo	pollo
steak	biefstuk	biftec	Steak	bistecca	bistec
veal	kalfsvlees	veau	Kalbfleisch	vitello	ternera
fish	vis	poisson	Fisch	pesce	pescado
coffee	koffie	café	Kaffee	caffè	café
sugar	suiker	sucre	Zucker	zucchero	azucar
cream	room**	crème	Sahne	crema	crema
vegetables	groenten	légumes	Gemüse	legumi	verduras
salad	sla	salade	Salat	insalata	ensalada
dessert	dessert	dessert	Nachtisch	dessert	postre
check	rekening	l'addition	Zahlen	conto	cuenta

*Phonetically, one egg is une oeuf; two eggs, du zoo; some eggs, day zoo.
**Or for the kind of cream the Dutch really love, it's (believe it or not) slagroom (whipped cream).

Now you never need to starve in Europe. Here we are going to add a few more words in the same languages for those times when you get thirsty:

water	water	eau	Wasser	acqua	agua
milk	melk	lait	Milch	latte	leche
beer	bier	bière	Bier	birra	cerveya
wine	wijn	vin	Wein	vino	vino
whisky	whisky	whisky	Whiskey	whiskey	whisky

As you can see, everyone agrees on at least one thing, which is somewhat ironic because most Europeans usually don't even drink the stuff. Anyway, we think that if you keep things fairly simple it's not too difficult to order from a foreign menu. But there are a few things to bear in mind. For example, never order à la carte if you must conserve your funds. Don't forget, too, that excluding breakfasts, bread and butter are not served with European meals. They cost extra, and until you've had a waiter interrogate you about how many rolls or pieces of bread you ate (so he can charge you for each of them), you can count yourself both fortunate and poorly travelled. The same thing holds true for coffee or wine; if it's not included in the prix fixe meal price, it's on you. Here you must be careful: coffee is extremely expensive in Europe (from forty cents to two dollars a cup!) and any wine you order, outside of the house wine, can also bear an unpleasant charge.

It would be fine if you could temporarily forget your steak-and-baked-potato background and try the specialties available in each country (you don't want to be like the klutz who pretends that he's really in Peoria, do you?). The Europeans have a number of dishes which are world-renowned, not to mention odd and different ways of preparing their food, and you should try them (one that you may *not* wish to try is *steak cheval*—horsemeat). You should also make up your mind to have leisurely meals, at least when you dine in a restaurant or a hotel. Most Europeans consider it uncivilized to eat and run; indeed, many of them feel that a meal that lasts less than two hours and seven courses is a mere snack. Their way is worth trying, not to mention fattening. And one way to save money is to remember that it is sometimes possible to have a dish split between two people. The phrase for this in French is *pour partager.* While the idea is perfectly acceptable in France and parts of Belgium and Switzerland, it is not in Germany.

But to reverse ourselves for a moment, we would have to say that eating in a small cafe, an ice cream shop, tea shop, pub, or a snack bar can also be interesting and memorable in Europe. The cuisine will not be spectacular, but it can be very good, and what is done to it can be fascinating. And even there you will find that you are not pushed in any way to leave your seat, or to order anything that you don't really want. All of the larger cities have American-style hamburger joints these days. Like here, their food isn't very good, but sometimes they can give you a welcome change. They will also remind you how uninteresting our food is compared to Europe's.

In finding an inexpensive place to eat, not to mention in finding an inexpensive place to sleep, one must ordinarily get away from the tourist areas. This sounds pretty obvious, but European opportunists all over the Continent get rich simply because tourists refuse to leave the big, well-lighted streets to shop for rooms or meals in the nearby alleys. The grand deal is almost never on the grand via, the grand street, or the grand canal. If you can't find out where *they* eat or take rooms, just walk a little ways off the main thoroughfares—and generally you'll be in the right neighborhood. In most areas your only real worry in these sidestreet cafes will be whether or not you will face language problems.

But if the personnel speak English, whether in a restaurant, hotel, or boozery, you can probably expect to pay for it in the tab they'll eventually give you. That is a fairly sure indication that they are not in business to serve the natives; they're there to deal with unsuspecting tourists. This does not, of course, hold true in areas like Holland or Denmark, where practically everyone speaks English.

Prices for meals in the cities can be two to three times higher than in the little towns. As one example of this, a tourist menu that would cost ten or twelve guilders in Rotterdam or Amsterdam will cost six or seven guilders in smaller towns like Delft or Gouda. Indeed, as far as such things go in France, a European friend told us that he and his wife recently had an excellent meal in a Paris restaurant for something over one hundred francs each, and the following evening they had one that was just as good, for which they were charged fifteen francs, in a little French village. As in America and Canada, the prices in large cities are always high.

Grocery stores in Europe are important to anyone who wishes to travel on a low budget. Yogurt usually has a picture on top that shows the fruit that flavors it. Butter can sometimes be found in tiny little packages. Be sure that any meat you buy is precooked or smoked. If you have a 220-v immersion heater, you can get instant coffee, cans of thin soup (boullion), or tea. If you cannot consume a whole loaf of bread during your stay, you can get small packages of crackers.

In canned items, you can find lunch meats, sardines, baked beans, tuna and salmon, crab meat, and so on. Fresh fruits and vegetables are always available. Milk is often available in small bottles, and cereals and cookies to go with it are usually easy to find.

Liquid nourishment

Europeans do not drink as Americans do. They drink, sometimes quite a lot, but mostly beers, wines or their own strange liqueurs. They ordinarily do not have cocktail hours before their evening meals, and they are largely unfamiliar with our types of cocktails. Over there a martini is a glass of Mr. Martini's vermouth, and manhattans, old-fashioneds, and whiskey sours do not exist—except in the bars of American hotels, where they are expensive.

Because Europeans do not often drink iced drinks (except for Spain), ice cubes are also difficult to come by. "Ice" means "ice cream" there, and "ice cube" has no meaning at all. Not that you'll probably get any anyway, but the best phrase to try

The pub may be Britain's greatest social invention.   British Tourist Authority photo

is "ice blocks." (When we tried this terminology on one woman in a bar in Austria, she finally asked, "Do you mean frozen water?")

Unfrozen water is also hard to find in Europe. Several things can happen if you ask for water with a meal. You will be told that people shouldn't drink the stuff (the W.C. Fields argument), you'll get a carafe of it without accompanying glasses, or you'll be served bottled water and made to pay for it. It is a very difficult problem. One solution is to carry a small aspirin tin with you. Showing it to the waiter may get you some H_2O, although once when we tried this ploy the waiter just tapped his head and smiled sympathetically.

Although some travel books question whether or not it is safe to drink tap water there (especially in rural areas of Spain and southern Italy), we have never been bothered by it anywhere we went. Nevertheless, people who are inclined to have stomach problems might wish to follow such suggestions and stick to bottled water at least in Spain and Italy. We have reason to believe, however, that most of Europe's water is purer than ours in the States and in Canada, and most experienced travellers don't worry about the water or ice of northern Europe. Most of them don't get much of either for that matter.

There are opportunities for tourists to get free drinks in some of the large cities. They are provided by Europe's great breweries. These wonderful establishments seem delighted to have you stroll through, see how they do their thing, and end by having drinks and snacks on them. They are located in many of the larger towns and cities, and they will provide you not only with an interesting tour, but a free "meal" and drinks as well. In Amsterdam, Bols has a 300-year-old tavern that provides free drinks at the delightful drinking hour of 10:30 a.m. Carlsberg and Tuborg offer the same privileges every weekday in Copenhagen, and here the tours go on until 2:30 p.m.

Most of the Europeans seem to have little or no sympathy either for rumpots or teetotalers. They believe in what they think of as moderate drinking, which often means incalculable quantities of beer or wine. They are usually not hooked on, or cannot afford, what we think of as hard drinks. Nevertheless, you will frequently find whiskey sodas and gin-and-tonics on the menu, and they are usually pretty good. They are not uncommon in the low countries and in England.

If in the course of your trip you should suddenly find yourself very thirsty for that American-style cocktail you sometimes have at home, you may find it in a canned or bottled version in a liquor store. You will not see these pre-mixed martinis, manhattans, whiskey sours, etc., very frequently, and when you do they are expensive and not very good, but it's a tip worth remembering if you ever feel like you're beginning to experience withdrawal symptoms.

The drinking man's (or woman's) Spain is not bad. Ice (*hielo:* yale-o) is readily available, as are drinks of every sort, often not at out-of-sight prices. Spanish homegrown and brewed wines and cognac (which include brandies) are very reasonable (and sometimes pretty good), and they have their own whiskey, which we have not had the courage to try.

Every country seems to have its own specialties. Austrians make and enjoy a wide variety of beers and wines, as do the Germans, the Swiss, and the Spanish. The Italians make and drink excellent wines in a mind-boggling range of types and tastes. Among the Spanish wines are some excellent sherries and a number of different brandies, both types ranging from dry to sweet. The Dutch make and enjoy fine beers (*e.g.,* Heineken, Jupiler, and Amstel) and liqueurs (*e.g.,* Bols), one of which some Americans like: jonge (young) jenever, a gin that is taken straight, often with meals, and warm or cold. It will not make martinis. The Belgians make beers that are probably the most potent available anywhere. The popular drinks in Scandinavia are beers (*e.g.,* Carlsberg and Tuborg) and aquavit (or snaps). The British like beer and gin, and their beer (with the exception of lager) is often served at room temperature.

You can get an American martini in a British pub by ordering a gin and a dry martini. You will get two glasses containing equal amounts of both, which will allow you to mix your own drink (and probably throw out nine/tenths of the vermouth in the process). Another English drink that is often kind to the American or Canadian palate is "bitter." A pint of this wonderful fluid will do much to relieve tired feet and jaded sensibilities.

And this is as good a place as any to mention the insane closing hours of British pubs. By law, most of them are closed in the afternoons, and they usually throw everyone out and shut their doors at 10:30 p.m. It is an astonishment to hear them ring a little bell and yell "Last call" at 2215. But it happens, and none of the British are able to explain why. "We'll change that one of these days," they say sourly.

One sometimes finds that a given type of beer will have an "Export" or "Special Export" label; it is stronger than the ordinary beer of that brand. Even more difficult than knowing what beer to order, for most tourists, is to understand and cope with the fantastic selection of wines available wherever they go. You will occasionally run into wine peddlers in the street who will let you sample their wares from little plastic cups, which is an excellent way to learn which brands you like best. Without this help it is a bit difficult to know what to buy in wines because there are so many different brands, labels, and vintages. The only other thing you can do (outside of just choosing blindly) is to ask advice of the store proprietor or get brand names from Europeans you meet. It makes a good topic of conversation on the trains, and they usually seem quite willing to give such advice.

But even if you drink stronger drinks at home, don't be misled by these innocent-appearing wines. They can do something to you in a hurry, at least if they are not consumed in moderation. England, Belgium,* Holland, and the Scandinavian countries do not produce their own wines. But the other countries do, and ordering *vin ordinaire* or "house wine" in a liquor store or at the table will not only draw looks of approbation, but also very reasonable prices for excellent wine. If you are trying to keep within a budget, it is either this or local beers, most of which are also excellent.

---

* The Belgians do produce a low-quality white wine in small quantities.

General tips

One last possibility for saving money on the food and drink bills is to take demi- or full-pension arrangements with your lodgings. On a demi-pension plan you will be fed two meals a day, while a full-pension arrangement will provide you with all three meals. Sometimes such a plan is required to get lodgings at a particular place, and sometimes they won't give it to you unless you stay a certain length of time, but it is a good idea generally in that it is relatively inexpensive, and the food is usually quite good. And it is always possible when you can't get back for a particular meal to ask the hotel personnel beforehand to pack you a lunch to carry with you. We have taken such lunches when we were going to be out hiking, and they are ordinarily excellent. Don't be embarrassed about doing this; if you're on a pension plan, you've got it coming. You've paid for it. It would probably be well to ask, when you want such an arrangement, whether the hotel people would like you to order it the night before, or in the morning before you leave.

One warning: sometimes European food and drink can hit the traveller with various kinds of intestinal difficulties. Many Americans assume that this is bound to happen, but it isn't. Often such stomach upsets are the result of drinking too much wine or strong coffee, but sometimes they can result just from a change of diet. If such difficulties hit you, use the same remedies you would use here and hope that the problem doesn't last long. We are told that it usually doesn't.

A few unrelated but possibly useful tips: European veal is far better than ours, but their beef is not as good. When you buy meat in the grocery stores to eat in your room or on the train, be sure that it is precooked. Fruits and vegetables must always be washed, because, like us, the Europeans spray their crops. Hot chocolate is usually excellent over there, especially when you are tired of drinking so much coffee. Always add up the charges on your check; there are a few unscrupulous waiters in Europe. And lastly, a tip on tipping: this confusing nonsense is not practiced in most parts of Europe as it is in the States. Many Continental tabs you will receive have service and taxes included, and they will say so, in which case you are not expected to tip beyond the price. If you were really taken by the service (or the waitress), it is all right to leave two or three *small* coins—but not more. Over-tipping is considered gauche in Europe (except perhaps for France, where tipping is expected and widespread). In England, some restaurant bills include gratuities while others do not. Again the bill will tell you if fifteen percent has already been added in. In countries that have value-added taxes (VAT, TVA, or BTW) it is a good idea to look at the menu to see whether these taxes (and service) are extra or *compris.* Such extras can add as much as thirty percent to your bill.

Many Americans seem to lack the savoir-faire necessary to open up conversations with the natives or to put themselves into situations that engender the possibility of embarrassment. Often they do not realize that being outgoing provides the probability of great rewards, and they don't try. This is extremely unfortunate; ignoring the natives can prevent you from experiencing what we think is the best that Europe has to offer her visitors.

A case in point: On a recent trip to Greece we discovered a small restaurant in Athens, the Kri Kri at 30 Pendelis, just behind the Chandris Hotel, a deluxe hostelry located directly between Athens proper and the Athens airport. This little eatery is an undistinguished sort of place. It has no jukebox, no flashing lights, and no go-go dancers. Instead, we soon learned, this family-owned and operated business has superb food, low prices, and a friendly Grecian atmosphere.

If you look a bit bewildered when you stumble into such a place, as we apparently did here, you will be escorted into the small kitchen, as we were, to savor the sights and smells of fine cooking. You will be made welcome, as we were, even if you don't speak their language and they don't speak yours, and you will eat like royalty at paupers' prices.

We are not trying to give an unsolicited testimonial to a small restaurant in a city you may never visit at all. Instead we are trying to encourage you to be bold, to take small chances, and to let yourself go a little. If you visit a small cafe like the Kri Kri and you love the meal, as we did, go back and shake hands with the chef afterwards, as we did. If you do, he and all of his staff will remember you when and if you return.

Being this outgoing pays many rewards. The third evening we visited the Kri Kri we met a waiter who hadn't been there before, and he spoke English. He was the chef's son, and from him we learned a lot about the family, the business, Athens, and Greece. When this sort of thing happens (and it will, if you make *your* effort), you will find yourself *accepted*, almost *belonging* at that moment. You will have given yourself a brief chance to become a part of the European scene, a regular, or perhaps almost a celebrity.

This won't work everywhere, of course, but it pays off surprisingly often, particularly in places that are not tourist havens. It doesn't involve glad-handing, or back-slapping, or being loud; it is simply a matter of overcoming any natural shyness you may have, and perhaps showing your appreciation for good service or good food.

When you show the Europeans that you care about them and what they are doing, they will reciprocate by caring about you. Don't worry about misunderstandings or misadventures; worry about missed opportunities.

Show those Europeans how suave, understanding, and charming you are; they'll do the same for you in return.

All in all any idea that will keep your food budget down is worthwhile. The Europeans generally treat food and drink with respect, and yet they don't spend a lot of money on their stomachs. Eat where, what, and the way they eat, and you'll have a happy and modestly priced vacation.

Chapter Twelve
The Next Best Thing to Being Here

> *. . . it is silence which isolates.*
> —Thomas Mann

When travelling in other countries, most Americans who telephone home place the calls from their hotel rooms. That can be a very expensive mistake. Let's just suppose that Bill and Irma Morgan* call home from Italy to find out whether their children have burned down the house or driven their grandmother crazy yet, and to report that they themselves have sore feet, are nearly broke, and are having a marvelous time. They place the call from their room, and the hotel switchboard operator takes down all the information and tells them to be patient, that she will ring them when the call goes through. They wait, anticipating the chat with their dear ones, as they enjoy the stupendous dry wine they've just discovered that day.

Within a few minutes their phone buzzes. Bill picks it up and finds himself talking to his mother. Irma looks at her watch, noting the time, because they have agreed to try to hold the call to three minutes. Grandmother says the kids are fine, that one has lost a tooth, and that the other has said that she loves granny's cooking best of all. Irma, listening in, winces. Bill describes their stay in Rome, talks a little about the city, and gives the telephone to Irma. She asks a number of questions about the children, and listens intently to Mother Morgan's responses. She also talks to both of her daughters. Bill eventually gets back on the phone and winds up the conversation, sending all their love and remarking that they will call again in a few days.

---

*These characters, like the soon-to-appear George and Patty, are fictitious. None of them are intended to resemble any living human beings except in some of the mistakes they make here—which are truly representative of the kinds of blunders uninformed tourists make in Europe.

179

Irma looks at her watch. She has no idea how long they talked. "I lost track," she says. "But I'm sure it was more than three minutes. Six or seven, maybe."

"Not to worry," Bill says, grinning. "Whatever it cost, it was worth it."

Bill is wrong. When they check out of the hotel the next morning, they learn that the call cost them $156. In the ensuing argument, they discover that the call was placed person-to-person, and that it cost $39. They also learn that the hotel makes a three-hundred-percent surcharge, which has raised the price to $156. There is finally a good bit of yelling, but the hotel people won't back down. "Pay," they say, "or we call in the *polizia*." With the cost of the room, the total hotel bill is $176. "It's overhead," the hotelier says. "We have to pay English-speaking operators to run the switchboard."

"Three hundred percent overhead?" Bill yells.

"Well, it's not really three hundred percent overhead," the hotel official now lies. "Your call lasted a total of almost twenty minutes."

"Like hell it did! Let me see the charges from the phone company."

The proprietor refuses, telling them they couldn't understand a bill in Italian. After some more argument he again threatens to call the police, so Bill and Irma spend most of their remaining travellers' checks to pay the bill. They leave the hotel vowing never to return—to the hotel, to Rome, to Italy, or to Europe again.

On their way back to the States, they promise themselves that after they see the kids they will call up AT&T and raise nine kinds of hell.

What did they do wrong?

First, they called from their hotel, putting themselves at the less-than-tender mercies of its proprietor, who can add any surcharges to telephone calls that he wishes—as can nearly any hotel owner in nearly any country.

Second, they did not specify that their call be station-to-station. Had they done so, the basic price of their call would have been about twenty-eight dollars. If they had been on this rate and kept their call to three minutes, it would have cost only a little over seven dollars.

Third, they called during the "day" hours. If they had called after 10 p.m., on the "night" station rate, their call would have cost only about twenty-one dollars. Had they kept it down to their intended three minutes, it would have cost only about five dollars. In that case, even with the outrageous surcharge tacked on, they would have only had to pay about twenty dollars for "the next best thing to being there."

Our little horror story is fictional, but it represents the truth. This sort of rip-off happens to unwary American tourists in other countries every day. Even people who know better than to do what Bill and Irma did can have problems with the European phone systems. Let's look at one more hypothetical case, this one involving more experienced travellers than Bill and Irma. These people, whom we shall call unimaginatively George and Patty, know about night rates, hotel surcharges, and the sizeable differences between station-to-station and person-to-person charges. Nevertheless, even they run into unforeseen problems in calling home to talk to granny and the kids.

They leave their hotel room just before about 11 p.m. and walk to the nearby post office they had scouted out earlier in the day. They have figured the time difference and know that their children will be home and awake, because it will be mid-afternoon at home. They find a number of tourists in the post office call station, but they are served immediately by a pleasant young man. They tell him they want to place a station-to-station call, give him the area code and number, and say that they will pay him after the call is completed. The young man makes a suggestion to them. "Why use up your money here? I'll just have it put on your next phone bill at home."

They consider that a great idea, so they thank him and take a seat. Minutes later the young man waves them into a nearby telephone booth.

George picks up the receiver and finds his mother on the line. She sounds as if she's standing next to them. Patty looks at her watch, noting the time because they too have agreed to try to hold the conversation to three minutes. They don't manage to do so, of course, but they enjoy hearing from granny and the kids. "So maybe it cost ten bucks," George says as they leave the booth. "It was worth it."

Over the next three weeks they make four more calls home from different countries, always specifying that the charge be billed to them at home. When they get their next telephone bill, after returning home, the five calls are on it. Knowing that they talked more than three minutes every time, they had expected the total cost of the calls to be thirty to thirty-five dollars; instead the total charge is $103. There is nothing they can do but pay the bill and write AT&T a vituperative letter.

Where did this couple go wrong?

First, they said the call could be put on their bill at home, which the telephone clerks did in every case simply by reversing the charges—which automatically put the calls on a person-to-person rate. If they had been on the station rate, the five calls would have totalled only about fifty-five dollars.

Secondly, they always talked longer than they expected to, as most people do. Had they held each call to three minutes and been on the station rate, their total bill would have been only about twenty-six dollars for the five calls.

So there are a number of ways that a tourist in Europe can be ripped-off on making calls home. You can do it to yourself, through ignorance, or someone else can do it to you, if he is sufficiently unprincipled. The hotel surcharge is the biggest danger. These surcharges fluctuate not only from country to country, but vary widely from hotel to hotel, even within a given country. Therefore calling from a hotel for anyone who is trying to stay within a budget while travelling in another country is a pretty big gamble. The surcharge percentage can be almost anything. One returning traveller reported getting one that amounted to four hundred fifty percent from a Munich hotel. Another complained that he was overcharged eight hundred percent for two calls by a high-class hotel in Paris. Many ritzy hotels across Europe have been known to make surcharges ranging from one hundred to three hundred percent on their client's calls. Such charges can be forced on the hotel's guest even if he direct dials the call himself, if the call goes through the hotel switchboard. Though it is far less likely, big surcharges can be added by the hotels even for collect or credit card calls.

While there is probably little one can do but pay in the face of one of these robberies, there are two possibilities for on-the-spot recourse. One can ask for the hotel's complaint book, which might do something to change the result of the debate. In some countries, such as Spain, the government does check such books regularly and will not hesitate to fine or close down a hotel for substantial and serious charges made against it by its clients. If there is no complaint book, one could threaten to write the government about the whole situation, and ask the government officials to check their country's telephone records on the call in question.

The other possibility is to try to bring the whole matter before the country's tourist information officials. This might not help, but it is most certainly going to get some attention from a group of people who are more interested in promoting tourism than in seeing the hotels make excessive profits. And they really do; Ed Carr, AT&T's Director of the Long Lines Department, quotes one foreign hotel manager as admitting he made $35,000 *in one season* by raising his telephone surcharges.

According to AT&T officials, such problems are common. Many of the disputes between travellers and hoteliers get extremely ugly, they report. In one case, a U.S. government official was made to pay $686 by a Beirut hotel for calls that should have run $270. When the man objected, he was reminded that he had a Jewish name and his passport was still in the hotel safe.

"There is usually nothing we can do about these individual complaints," the AT&T men say. "We have no control over foreign telephone companies, either on their procedures or their rates. The relationship between the American and European companies is primarily one of cooperation. Each European country has its own independent telephone system, most of which are government-owned—and the rates for calls between the United States and any one of the countries is established by mutual agreements between AT&T and the countries' telephone administrations. As far as the hotel surcharges are concerned, we are pretty much helpless in the case of most of the countries. It concerns us a great deal."

AT&T is working on this surcharge problem, trying to find a way to protect American travellers from such odious practices. In 1976 they began a program called Teleplan, which sets maximum limits on hotel surcharges for calls to the United States. At this writing, the only countries which are participating in Teleplan are Ireland, Portugal, and Israel. Under this plan, credit card or collect calls to the U.S. from any hotel in any of the participating countries will be only about a dollar and a half. For calls charged on the hotel bill, the new surcharge will be a moderate percentage of the cost of the call, with a maximum of about ten dollars. Some hotel chains are participating in the plan: Hilton Hotels worldwide, Trust Houses Forte in the U.K., and Marriott and Golden Tulip Hotels in Holland.

Nederland Post Telefoon en Telegraaf photo

*Calling home
during the night-rate hours
saves money
and reaches your party
during their daytime hours.*

How Europe's telephones work

In order to avoid being clipped on calls home from Europe, it is helpful to have a small understanding of how the telephone systems there work. Although the equipment and rates for calls vary from country to country, the "pulse-metering" system is the basic means of levying charges. This technique is designed to keep track of pulses as you talk, and each pulse is charged at an established rate. You do not hear these pulses when making a call, of course, but they increase in speed proportionately with the distance of your call, and they must turn into a steady hum when a call is passing through one of those underwater cables to North America, or bouncing off a satellite.

Many European public telephones have a little button that makes the average American tourist think "coin return." It is not. This button must be depressed when you hear the other party's voice on the line. If it is not pushed, the other person won't be able to hear you and will hang up.

There are other surprises for visitors. Some telephones work with the insertion of the coin of the realm where they are located; others require special tokens that must be purchased at newsstands or tobacco shops. Some airline terminals and railroad stations have special telephone bureaus manned by multilingual personnel who will help the poor tourist understand the intricacies of their systems, and to place calls as well. In many countries there are call stations in the post office buildings. In Spain, on the other hand, where the government does not own the telephone system, there are separate public telephone offices that tourists can use. In some countries certain telephone booths are marked above the door with the colors of the countries of the European community. International calls can be placed from these booths, either collect or on a credit card.

Some of the European countries' telephone systems are better than others, but all of them are relatively good these days. Switzerland's is one of the best, not only in Europe, but in the world. Many of the countries' systems have special numbers for getting the time, the weather, and so on, but there are a plethora of these special numbers in Switzerland. By dialing the proper number there you can get sports results, the news, road conditions, a note to tune your musical instrument by, and, finally, some kind of answer to any question you can think up. This latter service is reached by dialing "111," which will put you into contact with an English-speaking genius who will tell you instantly what the weather conditions are anywhere in Europe, when the next express train leaves for Berlin, where you can find an English-speaking doctor, whether or not you should tip a theatre usher, or how cheese fondue is made properly. Because number 111 seems to be able to answer any question both instantly and accurately, one cannot help suspecting that the line goes directly to God. If so, He is actually a She. She provides an incredible service in Switzerland.

Even the British telephone system, as archaic and annoying as it is, is not difficult to use. When you pick up the receiver you should hear a dial tone. Dial your number, and you will hear a ringing that sounds a little like an American "busy signal." If and when someone answers, this signal will become shrill, which means that you should shove in a coin. For short calls, five pence will be enough; for calls that will last longer, use a ten-pence coin. Whatever you put in initially, if you keep talking the telephone will finally begin to shriek for another coin. If you don't press one in, the line will soon go dead.

As in other countries in Europe, numbers often have nine digits. The first two digits are prefixes for long distance; they may be ignored for a cross-town call. The long-distance prefix for London from another city is 01.

The following shows what coins to use for local calls in each of the countries:

Country	Coins Used (local calls)	Country	Coins Used (local calls)
Austria	*schilling*	Italy	*L50* — can use
Belgium	*5 Bfr*		*gettoni* (tokens)
Denmark	*1-Kr coin*	Liechtenstein	*20 centimes*
England	*5-p or 10-p coin*	Luxembourg	*3 Fr*
Finland	*50 pennia*	Monaco	*40 centimes*
France	*40 centimes* — can	Netherlands	*25 cents*
	use *jetons* (tokens)	Norway	*1-Kr coin*
Germany	two *10-pfennig* coins	Portugal	*1-escudo* coin
Greece	*Dr 1*	Spain	*3 ptas*
Iceland	*10 Kr*	Sweden	*25 öre*
Rep. of Ireland	10-p coin	Switzerland	*40 centimes*

You can get information about special numbers, how to use the phones, or what the pulse-metering rates are from the telephone bureaus or any telephone directory anywhere. You will find that you can get a lot of good information from one of these directories even if you aren't fluent in the language in which it's printed. As one example, you can learn the hours and costs of their night and weekend rates, a worthwhile thing to know if you are going to be calling home.

It is possible to make collect calls to the U.S. from every country in western Europe, and they are billed at the person rate for the first three minutes. After three minutes, the cost automatically drops to station rates.

As shown in Table One, the U.S. can be dialed directly from many of the central western European countries. To do so, one needs to dial the access code shown in the table for the country he is in, the country code (which is "1" for the U.S.), the routing code (the American area code) and the telephone number. So a call from Italy to New York City would be dialed 00-1-212- and the telephone number. If a country has special dial rates, they will apply only to station calls, and they will cost only about two-thirds as much as operator-assisted station calls. Bell System credit card calls are possible from all of these countries except Germany and Portugal, and they can be placed either at station or person rates.

TABLE ONE: CALLS FROM WESTERN EUROPE TO THE U.S.

Country	Direct Dial Possible	International Access Code	Country Code	Credit Cards Accepted	Special Dial Rates	Reduced Rates
Austria—Linz	yes	00	1	yes	yes	none
—Vienna	yes	900	1	yes	yes	none
Belgium	yes	00	1	yes	yes	*
Denmark	yes	009	1	yes	yes	*
Finland	no			yes	yes	*
France	yes	19	1	yes	yes	none
Germany, Fed. Rep. of	yes	00	1	no	yes	**
Greece	yes	00	1	yes	yes	none
Iceland	no			yes	no	none
Ireland	yes	16	1	yes	yes	*
Italy	yes	00	1	yes	yes	*
Liechtenstein	yes	00	1	yes	yes	none
Luxembourg	yes	00	1	yes	yes	***
Monaco	yes	19	1	yes	yes	none
Netherlands†	yes	09	1	yes	yes	*
Northern Ireland	yes	010	1	yes	yes	****
Norway	yes	095	1	yes	yes	*
Portugal	no			no	yes	*****
San Marino	yes	00	1	yes	yes	*
Spain†	yes	07	1	yes	yes	*
Sweden	yes	009	1	yes	yes	*
Switzerland	yes	00	1	yes	yes	none
United Kingdom	yes	010	1	yes	yes	******
Vatican City	yes	00	1	yes	yes	*

* Reduced rates are from 10 p.m. to 10 a.m. Monday through Saturday, and all day Sunday
** Every day, dialed calls only midnight to noon
*** Every day 9 p.m. to 9 a.m.
**** Dialed calls only, Monday through Friday 10 p.m. to 10 a.m., Saturday and Sunday all day
***** Monday through Saturday midnight to 10 a.m., Sunday all day
****** Dialed calls only, Monday through Friday 8 p.m. to 6 a.m.; Saturday and Sunday all day
† In dialing the U.S. one should wait after dialing the international access code
  for another dial tone before dialing the country code.

How to make inexpensive calls home.

There are a number of ways that one can keep down the cost of transatlantic calls from Europe. Since the biggest possible expense is the hotel surcharge, it is best either not to make calls from your hotel room, or to ask before calling if there is a surcharge levied, and, if so, how much it is. Many of the small budget hotels do not make surcharges. But it is wise to ask, because the hotelier can usually make any surcharge against calls he wishes. And there is nothing you can do but pay it, as AT&T's top operator once learned himself when he got hit for one to the tune of one hundred dollars in a European hotel.

AT&T officials suggest the following procedure if you should find yourself in a hotel where it is possible to direct dial calls internationally: dial your party in the U.S., quickly tell them where you are and give them your phone number there, ask them to call you back, and hang up. This will be a very inexpensive call, they point out, because European countries do not charge a three-minute minimum on direct-dialed calls. Then, they add, your friend will return your call on the lower U.S. rate structure.

Another possibility, one that holds promise of even less expensive calls because there can be no surcharge, is to call from a public telephone station. To keep costs at a minimum, here one should take advantage of night rates, specify a station-to-station call (if possible), and either pay for the call on the spot in local currency or charge it to a telephone credit card. Charging against a card has two big advantages: it will allow the tourist to conserve his supply of foreign currency because the call will be billed to him at home, and it will save him money because the call will be charged to him at U.S. rates—whether he calls station-to-station or person-to-person. As one example, a three-minute station "day" call from Holland to the U.S. is roughly $9.60; you could make the same call on your credit card and eventually be billed at home for only $5.75. This can be done from most of the European countries, either for station, person, or reduced rate time calls. It offers the traveller a possibility of making considerable savings everywhere on his calls except from the United Kingdom, where the special dial rates are even less expensive.

Credit card calls can be placed from public call stations or from hotel rooms, but there would still be nothing to prevent an unscrupulous hotelier from attaching a surcharge for the call. Such a rip-off is far from unlikely, in fact, in Italy or Germany, and not impossible in France. And some hotels will not allow credit card or collect calls, for reasons that are all too apparent. They can't stick you as hard in such cases.

When you are trying to save money by making credit card calls or station-to-station calls (or both simultaneously), write such instructions on the ticket you have to fill out in the call station. Doing so will give you an additional argument to make with Ma Bell when you return home if you are billed at the wrong rate—

although you will find that Ma will be pretty understanding if your bill shows the call as having been put through at a different class or type than you actually asked for. We have had this happen (a credit-card call put through at the person rate rather than the station rate we'd asked for), with the bill being charged at not only the highest rate, but at *their* rates rather than U.S. charges. The telephone people checked the number of minutes the foreign telephone administration had charged, multiplied that number by U.S. rates, and saw that we had been over-charged. In addition, they accepted our word that we had asked for a station rather than a person rate, and adjusted the bill to what it should have been. We never learned whether or not they subsequently fussed with the foreign telephone company. At any rate, it adds veracity to your story to be able to say truthfully that "we wrote it *this* way on the ticket."

Calling home from the public call stations with a Bell credit card is a simple matter. No money changes hands, no complicated communications are required, and there is ordinarily no long wait for the call to go through. You simply give your card to the person behind the window, say "station-to-station" (or "person rate" and give him the appropriate name if you are making that sort of call), and then spend the next ten or twenty or thirty minutes concluding the call you promised yourself wouldn't last more than three minutes. If you are not making a person-rate call, *do not* say the name of the person you hope to speak to. You must include the two-digit code used for international calls that is on the back of the card.

When you are finished, retrieve your credit card from the call station employee you dealt with and say "thanks" in whatever language you can manage at the moment.

By now you may be wondering why you can't just use anyone's phone to make direct calls, get time and charges immediately after your calls, and pay them on the spot. You can—if the owner of the phone agrees—from a restaurant, bar, or private home.

It is a simple process. The phone owner calls the operator first and asks for an overseas line, asking that the call be person-to-person or station-to-station (whichever you specify), gives the U.S. area code and telephone number, and asks that the operator call back afterwards to give the time and charges. Then you usually have a few minutes' wait until the connection is made and the operator calls back. When you have completed your call, the operator will ring once again and tell the phone's owner what it cost, and you pay him or her in the local gelt. This is a simple technique for making such calls, and it is relatively inexpensive— except again in the United Kingdom, where a self-dialed call is cheaper.

The tourist who wishes not to use up his foreign currency, or to take advantage of lower U.S. phone rates, could do this same thing but ask the phone owner to give the operator his telephone credit card number rather than paying in cash after completing the call.

The AT&T men and some experienced travellers suggest that one should always make calls from hotel rooms on a reverse-charge basis because most hotels will only levy a small charge, perhaps a dollar, for placing the call. In addition, they point out, the basic charge for the call will be billed later at home at U.S. rates. While there is something to this argument, such calls will usually be placed at the person-to-person rate for the first three minutes and will consequently be fairly expensive. But they will not, advocates of the idea argue, be anything like as high as the surcharges might be. Nevertheless, such a strategy is not economical for calls from a telephone that will involve little or no surcharge. One might also be worried that he could still get hit later with a big surcharge from the hotel.

To sum up, then, there are several things you can be sure of about making calls home from overseas. You should try to avoid excessive hotel surcharges by checking about the matter before touching the phone, or just calling from public telephone stations instead. If conserving your supply of foreign currency is important to you, call collect or on your credit card. If keeping down telephone costs matters to you, avoid collect and person-to-person calls, use your credit card, call on night or weekend rate-reduction hours, and attempt to keep your calls short. If you ever manage to keep one to less than three minutes, you can probably consider yourself the first person ever to do so. If you do talk quickly, remember that there is not a three-minute minimum on dialed calls.

It appears to us that using one's credit card for calls home from Europe is the best idea of all. It will save you money, allow you not to use up your European currency, and help you to avoid rip-offs in hotels. If you don't happen to have one, you can get it from Ma Bell without cost or difficulty.

Direct dial or credit card calls to Europe

Since you might wish to leave instructions with someone at home to call you in Europe at a specified place and time, we will have a brief look here at how one can make such calls on the station rate. The simplest way for your friend to do it, if he has the requisite codes and the number, is to dial the call. If he doesn't have the number, he should dial "0" and ask the operator for the overseas operator, and then give her the requisite information: type of call, country, city, and the telephone number. If he doesn't know the telephone number, he should give her the address of the residence he is calling, or the name and address if it is a hotel. She will then ask for directory assistance from the operator in the country he is calling and get the correct telephone number. There is no charge for this service.

At this point your friend has a choice. He can let her put through the call for him and assume that it will be billed on his next telephone company statement. He can also ask her to bill it to his (or your) telephone credit card. And lastly, he can hang up and direct-dial the call himself. As strange as it seems, the charge for the call will be the same no matter which of these three strategies he adopts.* The reason

---

*Except for the United Kingdom, which accepts direct-dialed calls at a lower rate than is charged for operator-assisted calls.

for this is that not all areas in the U.S. yet have the capability of dialing international calls directly, so all station calls, even when operator-assisted, are charged at the same rate. In the future there will be yet another rate, a less expensive one, for dialed calls. At that time, there will be three rates, with credit-card calls being charged at the intermediate one.

If your friend wants to direct-dial you (wherever you are), he can easily get the necessary codes from the operator, or from a Bell Systems booklet "International Dialing 011 and 01," or from a more detailed booklet, "The Fastest Most Direct Route—International Direct Distance Dialing." Either of these small publications will tell him how to direct dial such calls, listing for various countries the access, country, and routing codes, and indicating how many digits local numbers should have, as well as the various cost rates that pertain. Both of them provide city routing code numbers, but the latter booklet also describes the signals one will hear for "ringing," "busy," or "out of service," as well as tables of time differences.

To direct dial a station call one must dial the international access code (001), the country code (listed below), the routing code (depends upon the city called), and the telephone number. Most day-rate times are 5 a.m. to 5 p.m. For collect, person, or credit card calls, just dial "0".

Every country listed here but Iceland has special dial rates which generally run a little more than half the cost of station-to-station day calls, and less than a third the cost of person-to-person day calls. Where there are reduced rate times, calls made during these periods will run a quarter to a third less than regular hours calls. If you want specifics on these costs, ask your local operator before placing your overseas call, or call 800/874-4000 for cost information or dialing instructions.

Your friend should remember that the U.S. also has night and weekend rates (at least for some of the countries called), and the night rates generally apply from 5 p.m. to 5 a.m., and that such reduced rate times and charges are based on the country from which the call is being made—not the country called. So from the standpoint of the rates at which the call will be billed, he only has to think of U.S. charges; from the standpoint of whether you will be available and awake, he needs to consider time differences.

Note: if the local number he has is preceded by an "0" or "01" or "9," or, for France, a "15" or a "16," he should ignore these prefixes. They are used only for calls within Europe.

Person-rate calls to Europe are charged at the highest rate for the first three minutes; after that, they drop back to the station rate. At the moment, all other types of calls are charged at the station rate.

Table Two: Calls from the U.S. to Western Europe

Country	Country Code	Reduced Rates
Austria	43	none
Belgium	32	5 p.m. to 5 a.m. Monday through Saturday, and all day Sunday
Denmark	45	5 p.m. to 5 a.m. Monday through Saturday, and all day Sunday
Finland	358	5 p.m. to 5 a.m. Monday through Saturday, and all day Sunday
France	33	none
Germany, Fed. Rep. of	49	Daily—5 p.m. to 5 a.m.
Greece	30	none
Iceland*	*	none
Ireland	353	5 p.m. to 5 a.m. Monday through Saturday, and all day Sunday
Italy	39	5 p.m. to 5 a.m. Monday through Saturday, and all day Sunday
Liechtenstein	41	none
Luxembourg	352	5 p.m. to 5 a.m. Monday through Saturday, and all day Sunday
Monaco	33	none
Netherlands	31	5 p.m. to 5 a.m. Monday through Saturday, and all day Sunday
Northern Ireland	44	5 p.m. to 5 a.m. Monday through Saturday, and all day Sunday
Norway	47	5 p.m. to 5 a.m. Monday through Saturday, and all day Sunday
Portugal	351	5 p.m. to 5 a.m. Monday through Saturday, and all day Sunday
San Marino	39	5 p.m. to 5 a.m. Monday through Saturday, and all day Sunday
Spain	34	5 p.m. to 5 a.m. Monday through Saturday, and all day Sunday
Sweden	46	5 p.m. to 5 a.m. Monday through Saturday, and all day Sunday
Switzerland	41	none
United Kingdom	44	5 p.m. to 5 a.m. Monday through Saturday, and all day Sunday
Vatican City	39	5 p.m. to 5 a.m. Monday through Saturday, and all day Sunday

*Not possible to direct dial

Cables, letters, packages, and post cards

It is also possible to cable between the United States and Europe. There are day and night letters, the latter being delivered the day after they're sent, and running half the cost of day letters. For cables to Europe, you must have at least seven words in a day letter (including the address and your name), while the night letter requires a minimum of twenty-one words. Words can be run together: fifteen characters constitute a word in the address or message, while five are considered a word where numbers are used. To give you an idea of costs, at present the charge for a day cable from Chicago to Geneva is 26½ cents per word, but the Geneva-Chicago rate is 43 cents a word.

If anyone at home knew in what hotel or pension you'd be located on a given date, they could get a cable to you there on that date. You could also consider cabling from Europe to let someone know, for example, that you have decided to remain at a particular lodging for two or three days so they could cable or call you there if necessary.

In the States, Western Union will take such international messages on toll-free telephone lines from any place in the country. In Europe the cable companies are Western Union International, RCA, or ITT. With the help of a computer, Western Union will translate cables into any foreign language. They will also charge the costs to your telephone bill. Finally, it is also possible for your friends in the States to send you a ''reply paid'' message so you can respond without having to pay at your end.

Lastly we will point out that a night letter sent from Europe before midnight will be delivered the following day, while one sent *after* midnight will not arrive at its destination until the day after that. In other words, the reduced-rate night letter means that your message will not be delivered until one day after you send it.

And how do you get mail in Europe? It's not easy. The American Express offices used to hold it for travellers, but most of them have given up doing so. If you are interested in learning the location of the few that still give this service, call one of their offices and check with them. Many of the Thomas Cook agencies hold mail for their clients. But perhaps the most reliable of all is to have people address their letters to you in care of General Delivery (*Poste Restante*) at the post office in any large city you'll be visiting. They will, in theory at least, hold such letters for you until you pick them up. This has worked very nicely for us, but we might point out that you do need to show your passport in order to identify yourself.

Will you perhaps want to mail packages home, either to friends or to yourself? You can do so easily, but you are only allowed to send items worth 25 dollars or less without paying customs duty. You cannot send alcohol, perfume, tobacco, heroin, or pornography in this way, or, needless to say, any fruits or vegetables. The package should be marked plainly ''Gift—value under 25 dollars.'' Such packages will not affect your three-hundred dollar customs exemption when you return.

Phyllis has had one rather good idea associated with contacting people at home. She has asked friends and relatives to save any post cards we send them, and she now buys and mails cards from everywhere we go. It is a nice way to stay in touch with people, and ultimately you will end up with a bunch of pictures that are nicer than your over or underexposed photographs. We would suggest, though, that in any given country you mail your first card from a post office so you'll know from then on how much postage is required. If you don't, your friends may get your cards marked ''Postage Due'' and be dunned for a fairly stiff amount, because the Post Office is allowed to add on a service charge to the amount due.

Mail, including post cards, must bear the postage of the country from which it is mailed. One usually buys stamps in tobacco shops, but they can also be purchased in many hotels, or, of course, in any post office. Post cards are available everywhere—everywhere, including cathedrals, restaurants, and tourist information offices. With luck an airmail-stamped post card will get home in two or three days; on the other hand, it may never get there at all. In view of the way our postal system functions (and ''malfunctions'' is doubtlessly a better word), this may not be any reflection upon the Europeans at all. Airmail cards or letters should bear the words *Luftpost* or *Par Avion*. In Spanish, it's *Via Aerea*. Do not forget to include the words ''United States'' in the addresses on your mail. And if you have a tendency to be suspicious of people, you may wish to put your cards and letters into post boxes yourself (hoping that you will be able to distinguish them from garbage cans). One does hear stories about unscrupulous hotel personnel steaming the stamps off of their guests' mail and throwing the letters or cards away.

So that's about all we can think of to tell you about staying in touch with home base. All in all, the whole subject may again be an argument against the idea of travelling without a set itinerary, as free as a bird, because it certainly would be difficult for friends or relatives to get in touch with you—but we still think it's the way to go. So if you're worried about what might happen to your kids while you're out of touch, leave letters with several grown-ups you trust, giving them the unqualified right to make decisions related to the children's health and well being while you are gone. Then you can worry about what the adults are liable to do too.

Chapter Thirteen
Avoiding Tribulations

To fear the worst oft cures the worst.

—William Shakespeare

Recently we were standing in a large crowd outside of Buckingham Palace in London waiting to see the changing of the guard. When the guards came toward us up the street, resplendent in their red coats and tall black hats, a fairly nice-looking older man standing nearby said, "Excuse me, but it's going to be difficult to get good pictures from here." Waving his arm toward a deserted spot across the street, he said, "That's where you should be." Well, it didn't look like it because no one else was there, but we went over anyway.

So began a day with John Simpson, an elderly student of English history who is very knowledgeable about the city he loves. We stood where he suggested, and he was absolutely right. We got excellent pictures. He came across the street then and said, "One more suggestion, if you don't mind. If you'd like more photos, you should go to the end of the street, turn left, and go down to the first guard house. There you will see the guards really changing. You'd better hurry. I'll just walk down there with you so you won't get lost."

On the way to the spot he had recommended we asked him some questions about himself. He was a retired interior decorator, he said, adding, "I just like people. I know many tourists haven't much time to spend in London, and they don't really get to see much. So sometimes when I see them I just jump forward and offer a suggestion or two, as I did with you. Takes a bit of cheek, you know. But I do it anyway."

Well, as you would guess, he was right about the little guard house. We got exceptional pictures there, and as we left the area Mr. Simpson showed us an unmarked house where one of Henry the VIII's mistresses had lived many years before. All in all, he was a delightful and knowledgeable man, and we asked him to share a beer with us for his kindness. He agreed to a small one. He refused a refill, and declined our offer of lunch. He gave us some excellent advice and tips as we all sat there, and we were grateful to him—but beginning to be just a little suspicious at the same time. When it became clear he would continue on with us for a little while, we asked him what he wanted in return. He brushed the question aside: "Happy to do it. I'd like every visitor to London to really see something of it. After all, it *is* the greatest city in the world." He had a devilish smile.

It was a busy day. In the company of our newly found friend we visited Westminster Abbey, Whitehall, No. 10 Downing, St. Paul's Cathedral, Parliament, and, after a boat ride on the Thames, the Tower of London. (The Tower and the Crown Jewels which are kept there are well worth seeing.) John was fantastic. He always knew the right place to stand to get the best photos, he was full of enchanting stories about the places we saw and the history behind each of them, and he was always courteous and somewhat self-effacing. While we liked him and felt a little sorry for him, our suspicions of his motives kept growing. We attempted to talk to him again about why he was giving us his whole day, to which he responded, "I haven't anything else to do anymore."

At the end of the day we invited him to dinner with us, telling him how grateful we were for his kindness. He refused dinner, but said in a stumbling manner that he would be willing to accept "some small token of our gratitude."

"Like what?" Alan asked, suddenly feeling a little hostility toward the man.

"Twenty dollars."

After some moments of silence, Alan asked, "Why didn't you say this was business instead of pleasure when I asked you earlier in the day? Why weren't you honest with us?"

Mr. Simpson didn't have an answer for that. Then the argument proceeded to grow to such proportions between them that Phyllis excused herself and went into a nearby coffee shop. After a lengthy debate on the sidewalk Alan gave the man a few dollars, told him goodbye, and went into the cafe. Mr. Simpson came in moments later, sat down, and said, "I wanted to say goodbye and to thank you again. I'm sorry that you misunderstood. I have to do this; I have no other income."

How could you stay angry at a man like that? We couldn't, and we thanked the old swindler and told him we had enjoyed his company and his patter. Because of what had happened we were not feeling especially friendly toward him, but it was impossible to be really unhappy with the old guy. Finally he got up to leave. He said, "I hope you don't think badly toward me—or London. Thank you again, and goodbye."

In retrospect we don't feel badly toward him—or London. He made our day there. We saw and learned far more with than we would have without him. So we don't relate this incident either to complain or to prove how naive we are; we tell it because we learned subsequently that London is overrun by people like him who will try to separate you from a bit of cash to show you around. It is such a large problem that the British will warn you about it, saying that licensed guides have identification cards and lapel badges, and that you should not get involved with anyone who is not licensed. And from what we hear, many of the free-lancers are lousy *and* tricky, which would be annoying. In a case of that kind, we'd call a bobby into the negotiation. We hear they are not very sympathetic to these chaps.

So about all we can say on this matter is, okay, have your eyes open. Remember about our experience when someone tries to get that friendly with you. Remember that most strangers, even elderly Britons, are not likely to do you many favors for nothing.

And we also say, "Cheers to you, John Simpson, you old crook, wherever you are. And thanks again."

Various problems in various places

There are a number of problems worse than misunderstandings one can run into in Europe. Being swindled in the streets by nice old guys is only one of the unpleasant possibilities a person might experience. In this chapter we are going to discuss such eventualities, ranging from being robbed to being caught smuggling contraband through customs. We are including this not because it's fun stuff, but because you're going to be on your own, and it's going to be up to you to keep yourself out of trouble.

But before we make you too nervous, let us say that many Americans (including us) are envious when they see how free European countries seem to be of danger to one's person or property in the streets. Even young girls alone apparently feel safe walking anywhere at any time of the night, although a person would doubtlessly be looking for trouble if he or she strolled about in the dock areas of port cities in the wee hours.

So that adds up to a memorable truism: you are less safe strolling among the wharves than you are when walking around the downtown areas, and you will face more danger in the cities than in the villages. But people do take chances, as foolish as it sounds, trying to mingle with the interesting sailors from other lands, or with the drug addicts of the back streets of the big cities. To us it sounds not only adventurous, but a good way to avoid the discomforts of advancing years. Other places of danger of one sort or another are Europe's night spots. Many of the low-class places are the homes of B-girls, pimps, prostitutes, thieves, and muggers. They are also known for watered drinks and padded checks. Sounds like anywhere.

You will see numerous signs in Europe warning you to beware of pickpockets. We wondered if the pickpockets' guilds might have put them up, because they do make you feel your wallet, which tells every pickpocket within a mile where you keep it. Some European visitors like to have a money belt, key case, or small purse to carry extra money or travellers' checks. It is insurance against embarrassments at the cash register, as well as being difficult for pickpockets to get at.

The most valuable possession you will have with you on your trip will be your U.S. passport. They are worth at least a thousand dollars and maybe a lot more on the European black markets, so it is wise to take care of it. If it should be lost or stolen, run, don't walk, to the nearest American consulate or embassy.

In an earlier book we suggested that a person should carry his passport with him at all times, even when he took an evening stroll to see the lights and to window-shop. We now have some reservations about that idea. Many European countries have been bringing in common laborers from other countries over the last few years, with a resulting rise in crime statistics, particularly street robberies in the larger cities. If you were to get into trouble you should have the passport with you to identify yourself to the police; but if the most likely sort of trouble you might get into on an evening stroll is being robbed of your passport, perhaps it would be wise to leave it locked in your luggage or in the hotel safe.

In view of the foregoing arguments, it might also be wise to ask the people who run your hotel or pension if it is safe to take an evening stroll—at least in the larger population centers.

At the risk of offending the Italians, we would name Italy as the country that provides the biggest risk of one sort of rip-off or another. Why this is so we do not know. While most people there are doubtlessly as honest as people any-where else, they do seem to have the misfortune, especially in their larger cities, of having a good deal of crime. Most of the other European countries are relatively free of these problems, but Italy is considered a danger spot by most Europeans. They tell many stories about visitors having pockets picked, hand bags and cameras grabbed away from them, and belongings stolen from public lockers.

Of the many sad stories we'd heard about such problems, we will tell only two here. In late 1976 a young American girl of our acquaintance passing through Italy on a train dozed off for a few minutes just outside of Milan. When she awoke, all her luggage (which contained her money and her passport) had disappeared. Usually European travellers are extremely nonchalant about leaving their bags by their seat for long periods of time as they wander about the train. They aren't usually so care-less in Italy. There they keep a pretty close watch over their possessions, and you would be smart to do the same. In fact, we are told that whole bands of young thieves often sweep through Italian trains, robbing sleeping tourists or unattended luggage. This is said to be prevalent on night trains heading for Switzerland. As a consequence, tourists travelling by train on such runs (or perhaps anywhere in Italy) might be wise to ship their possessions through on the baggage car.

The other story is even worse. It was told to us recently by an American friend who lives in Rome. Not long ago, he said, a female tourist was walking along a street in Rome. It was daylight. She had apparently heard about the purse snatchers on motorscooters, because she was holding onto the strap of her shoulderbag with one hand. Well, a young ruffian on a scooter shot by and grabbed her purse. She wouldn't let go, and, as it turned out, he wouldn't either. He dragged her so far through the streets that she died of her injuries two days later.

Because of this common form of thievery in Rome, he told us, many tourists now walk closer to the buildings than the street, and carry purses and cameras on their shoulder that is away from the curb. Lastly he advised that when couples stroll through Italy's larger cities they should always have the man on the street side.

According to a UPI article that was published in February, 1978, these purse-snatchers strike every forty-five minutes in Italy. ''In Rome alone more than 3,600 purses will be snatched by the end of the year . . . nearly 1,200 of the victims will be Americans . . . .'' The article went on to say, ''They go after the people who are least likely to fight back. Once they pick a victim they don't care what they have to do to get the bag—break her leg, her hip, her collarbone, her arm, or dislocate her shoulder. That's how we hear about a lot of these cases—from the hospital.''

We fully agree with a British woman who was quoted in the UPI article: ''Maybe it's time tourists stopped coming to Rome for a while. Maybe if we all just stayed away they'd be concerned enough to clean these thieves out.''

We've already suggested that you might wish to avoid some of Europe's larger cities; now we've given you some good reasons to think very carefully about visiting Rome, at least until this sort of dangerous threat to person and possessions is eliminated. Rome is a beautiful city—but who would want to see it from a hospital window?

There are also Frenchmen who see tourists as ripe plums to be picked. To many European minds, France is second only to Italy in crime, and they tend to be rather careful when visiting there. Pickpockets abound in the larger cities, the low dives are very low and dangerous, money-changing at supposedly top rates in the streets is common (and invariably a swindle), and both men and women will sidle up to tourists with whispered offers of various kind of naughties (which, we hear, are generally not produced). It is also a country in which one would be wise to keep close tabs on his passport.

England also seems to provide its share of dangers for tourists—mainly in the metropolitan areas, especially London. We've seen a number of pickpocket warnings there too, and shortchanging tourists who don't understand the coin of the realm is also said to be a popular sport. We heard that the ''lost wallet'' and other schemes are commonly practiced in the streets, at least in London, as is the ''I'll-take-your-picture-for-money'' racket. We know an American high school girl who was approached by a creature shaped like King Kong who snapped two photos of her and then demanded the equivalent of five dollars. Frightened to death, she gave him the money and her address, but she was at least luckier than most. Eventually she received the two pictures, both of which were, of course, lousy. You may run into such "photographers" (often armed with Polaroid cameras) anywhere in Europe. Ignore them or give them a firm "NO!" That word is understood by everyone.

It pays to be cautious in all of the big cities. The Europeans are usually a bit wary in such places themselves. It is in the metropolitan areas that you will be accosted by beggars (often crooks, according to our European friends), people who come up to you and make sly remarks, and decrepit-looking types who sidle up and try to sell you "gold" rings, sunglasses, shawls, and "art" photographs. You may also be offered high-class Swiss watches at extremely low pirces, and if you'd enjoy owning a timepiece that looks like a Rolex but runs like a Timex, you should buy one. A visitor to Madrid or Barcelona will experience a good deal of this sort of thing, but a head shake is usually sufficient to get rid of such entrepreneurs.

Another thing you may be subjected to in the big cities is what we think of as "involuntary tipping." You buy, let's say, a beer. The waiter brings it to you, and he brings your change, usually in a little dish. If you don't pick it up right away, the waiter will sometimes grab it up, slip it in his pocket, and say "thanks." When that happens to you, get up shaking your head, which will make the waiter drag the money right back out of his pocket and hand it over. It is the sort of small ugly thing that doesn't occur in the small towns.

Police, security, and governmental officials
If you like uniforms, you'll love Spain. At times one has the impression that the various types of police and military men outnumber the civilians, and many of them carry small machine guns(!). Others carry automatic pistols, and all of them sport wicked-looking truncheons. European friends have advised us that these rough-looking fellows (especially the Guardia Civil in their patent-leather hats) are not people to mistake for bus drivers, to ask dumb questions, or to try to tell funny stories while slapping them on the back. Fortunately our only experience with any of them has involved asking directional questions of the traffic cops (who are comparatively innocuous-looking), and though we've never met one who could speak English, they point very well. If you have occasion to see how they direct cars around, you'll realize that they get a lot of practice in pointing.

You may find, in fact, that the police in the various European countries either look like they're made up for World War III or for a costume party. Some of them do wear strange-looking uniforms, and some of them look pretty tough, but we think that most of them are conscientious, underpaid civil servants—and as pleasant and helpful as anyone could be when asked for directions. The British bobbies, for example, are known for their pleasant manners. At the same time in most countries the police will react to wrong-doing swiftly and perhaps a bit roughly. The French, Spanish, and German police have such reputations. Their police forces in. the large cities will swoop in to quell some sort of disturbance very quickly, and they will do whatever is necessary to stop the trouble, including arresting everyone who appears to be involved. It is partly because of seeing such scenes that we make the following suggestion.

Occasionally in Europe you may witness what appears to be the beginning of an argument, a brawl, or even a riot. It is a good idea to stay out of such fracases. How are you, with your doubtlessly poor command of the language in question, going to intervene or referee such a squabble? If you try, you'll probably get arrested or punched in the face, and only learn subsequently that the whole thing was either a lover's tiff, or one more round of shoving that's been going on between these two or three old guys for the last thirty-five years.

We've witnessed a few such altercations in various places in Europe (always in the larger cities), and it has invariably happened that it stopped by itself, or the police finally hauled off everyone—absolutely everyone—who was involved. Europe generally is a pretty quiet, peaceful place by American standards, but at least in the large cities, where people are crowded together, little problems can crop up—and you'd be smart to be looking the other way when such things occur.

Perhaps it's shameful to advise people "not to get involved," but indeed most of us won't at home—so how much sense does it make to do so in a foreign country? The whole question, or possibility, if you will, may again constitute an argument for staying as much as possible in the smaller places. The little towns are pretty quiet.

Looks like a character right out of Dickens, doesn't he?

ILDY & SONS LᵀᴰDₜ

Law Booksellers
Publishers.
porters. Valuers

British Tourist Authority

Perhaps customs and security people are like the cops in the respect that many of them have a talent for looking at you in such a way that your knees turn to jelly. We've had a few problems of our own with them on our trips in the past. Nothing serious—just a time or two where we got a bit sweaty. (Is *that* the way those sharp-eyed guys catch you, by observing water dripping into your eyes as you approach?) Actually you can never predict how such things are going to go. We were subjected to a tough security check a couple of years ago at the Tower of London, where the Irish Republican Army had already set off one bomb and were threatening to deliver another. Of the two of us, Alan was the obvious target. He looked like a middle-aged James Bond with a camera case, film, notebooks, and a small bag (containing toilet supplies, maps, and other incidentals) hanging all over him. He went right through, while innocent-appearing Phyllis had her big purse upended and everything in it given a close scrutiny.

And again, on one of our most recent trips, we went through Chicago's O'Hare Airport on the way over with no security checks at all. We were really surprised; we expected it as anyone would. When we returned from Schiphol Airport in Amsterdam we *didn't* expect it, but for some reason we went through the most humiliating baggage and body search either of us had ever experienced. It happened exactly the other way around on the next trip: we were treated like Bonnie and Clyde at O'Hare, and completely disregarded at Schiphol.

At any rate, when we arrived at Chicago after that trip, the customs people were waiting for us, fangs gleaming. We must have the profiles of heroin smugglers; if they are spot-checking, they will always pick the two of us out of a crowd of five thousand. Were we worried? Yes, we were worried. We know, as all travellers do, that you must keep receipts for purchases made overseas, and we had—but we didn't know where they were. On top of that problem, we had an Indonesian knife, an African spear, six bottles of French perfume, a bit more high-class liquor than the permitted one quart per person, a box of tulip bulbs, and a few other questionable items. For no real reason, we were ill at ease—most people *are* in these situations. Maybe, like us, they just don't like seeing their dirty laundry thrown about in front of everyone.

The knife, the spear, the perfume, the liquor, and all the rest of our little purchases were handled, but not discussed. The tulip bulbs drew a crowd. They were the kind of bulbs that are guaranteed to be okay for exportation from Holland, and were so marked, but a little man still found it necessary to stick a knife into each one. Eventually we got our slashed bulbs and other meager possessions back, and departed with sighs of relief.

Seriously, though, the customs procedure usually isn't much of a problem. You should have all luggage unlocked, receipts for purchases made in Europe available, and be prepared to answer all of the inspector's questions. You never attempt to bribe or tip the inspectors. Ordinarily they will open only one bag, and then, if you're lucky, they won't really want to paw through your dirty laundry. Each person has a three-hundred-dollar exemption, which is based on retail value of the purchases. The officials will ordinarily try to figure everything in your favor, and they are generally pretty lenient unless you are trying to sneak something through that is against the majority's political and social views of decency, such as Cuban cigars or pornography. If you have something that requires the payment of duty, you'll probably be asked to pay up right on the spot.

One thing about customs searches that you should be aware of, though, is that most victims of a *real* going over have had their names called in by an anonymous do-gooder (or do-badder). If you steal towels from hotels, or otherwise displease some European, he can make your life uncomfortable at your next security or customs check—espeically if he has your passport number, which, of course, the hotel personnel will. All he has to do is make a telephone call and say he has reason to believe you're carrying a firearm or a few pounds of hash, and you're going to have an unpleasant time ahead.

U.S. Customs Service photo

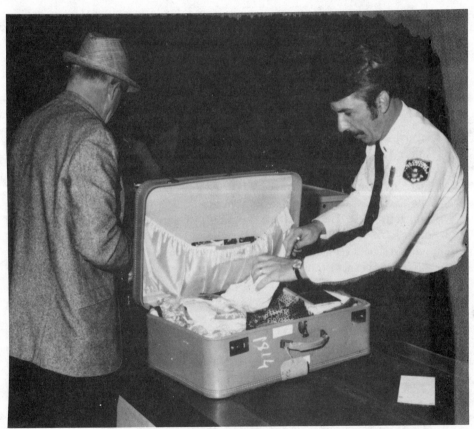

This strikes most people as an anticlimax to their trip.

A note on tax-free purchases, whether made on ships or aircraft over international waters, or in tax-free shops in airports: these purchases are only free of taxes of the country that provides the tax-free sales. They are always liable to U.S. customs taxes when you bring them home. It's sad, but true.

The three-hundred-dollar exemption for each person is based upon *fair retail value* with the following limitations:

1. articles left for alterations cannot come under exemption if shipped later.

2. you must be out of the country for at least forty-eight hours.

3. you have not used this exemption (or any part of it) within the preceding thirty days.

4. prohibited articles, *e.g.*, absinthe, narcotics, obscene publications, fireworks, switchblade knives.

5. limit of one hundred cigars; no Cuban tobacco; no limitation on cigarettes; one quart of liquor (if twenty-one or older).

Articles of foreign manufacture taken abroad should be registered before you go. Watches, cameras, binoculars, and jewelry are typical items that can cause you problems, and you could be charged duty on a Swiss watch you'd owned for years if it looked new, and was still a current model. It is a good idea to register such articles. The customs officials are generally kind, fair, and well-informed about prices and values—*but they can make no judgments about where and when* you bought a particular article unless you can offer proof.

You can send gifts home from overseas (not alcohol or tobacco) without incurring duty charges if you write on the package "Unsolicited Gift—Value Under $25." These need not be declared upon your return to the U.S.

The customs registration offices at airport embarkation points will furnish literature about duties, trademark restrictions, and items that can be imported into the U.S. without duty charges from ninety-eight countries and forty independent territories. The folder that describes the duty-free items and countries of origin is titled "GSP and the traveller."

If you should get into some sort of difficulty in Europe, you could visit the nearest American consulate (not Embassy, unless, of course, they are combined). We say *could* advisedly. You will read in other travel books that the Consulate officials can and will provide you all kinds of help—flying you home in an emergency, loaning you money, providing legal help, etc. Generally this is not true, and a Consulate official told us that nine out of ten Americans who get into trouble do not contact them. One of their "services," they told us, is to inform police officials back home about your difficulties "so you'll be in trouble there too"(!). It made us understand why people in trouble might want to keep the fact to themselves.

In response to our questions, consulate officials told us the following: they will *not* arrange to fly you home on the Military Air Transport Service if you miss your charter or have an emergency at home, as one travel book says they will. They will not loan money "officially," although they sometimes have small sums that wealthy Americans have donated that can be tapped "when all else fails." If a traveller is completely destitute, they can have him "repatriated," which they characterize as "the most expensive way to travel." When this happens, Uncle Sam takes your passport and keeps it until he forces you to pay in full for your repatriation. They will not provide you with legal aid, and they will not bail you out of jail. They would visit you there if you wished. Wow.

Gratuitously, they informed us that they would replace lost passports, adding that one would have to go through a good deal of questioning and trouble to get the replacement. They said that an American citizen should never give up his passport to anyone, that it is the property of the United States government.

Obviously we were not much impressed with the kind of "help" we heard described, and we concluded that it would be well not to get caught at anything in Europe. We do think that if someone got into some difficulty and was completely innocent of any crime himself, they might provide him with some kind of help.

Unfortunately, however, we didn't find out what it would be.

Final thoughts about avoiding troubles

Frankly there are not an extraordinary number of ways to get into trouble in Europe —or going or coming. All that is required is a little bit of care—and perhaps a certain amount of glibness. It would spoil your trip if you came to believe that everyone over there was out to take you—in fact, you will feel very safe and secure in most parts of Europe. And you will be, and that's the problem. You can sometimes feel *too* safe. Just don't forget these few simple-minded rules, especially when you are in cities with populations above fifty thousand.

Don't buy *anything* from anyone on streetcorners.

Don't give up your passport for any reason. Hotel personnel *do not* have a right to take it from you to keep overnight.

Don't get involved in other people's fights.

Be a little sceptical if you meet Mr. Simpson or one of his colleagues in London.

Don't change money with anyone but authorized money-changers.

Always look at and count your change, and don't let anyone pick what he wants from your hand.

Keep an eye on your possessions, particularly in Italy, France, and in any large city anywhere.

Before you pay the bill, even in nice restaurants, itemize it and check the arithmetic.

Don't ever listen to any garbage about holding watches or wallets as "security," and don't give any money to anyone to show your "good faith."

Don't let anyone lure you away from the well-lighted streets with promises of a "good time."

Don't buy or carry any drugs. The penalties for doing so are exceedingly high in many foreign countries. So just put the pen mechanism back in your ball-point before you go, leave the hollowed-out book behind, and don't take any chances. We don't know anything about European jails, but who wants to find out?

Don't take "souvenirs" from places where you stay; if the proprietors call the border officials, you won't get out of the country without a lot of problems.

Keep a record of your travellers' check numbers in two or three places, retain the receipt you got when you purchased them, and carry the addresses of the people who issued your credit cards.

If you should lose something in Europe through the negligence of transportation or baggage people, make them pay you then and there. If you should have something stolen, talk to the police and bring home copies of their report to present to your insurance company.

Keep receipts for everything you purchase. You may be required to show them at customs on your return, and you would need to show them to your insurance agent if your new possessions somehow got separated from you before your return.

Remember to register foreign-made items you are taking along with customs before you leave.

It might be wise to grant a power of attorney to a friend, relative, or lawyer before you leave home so they could act for you if your house burned down, was flooded, or burglarized.

Lastly, we'll say a word about the worst (or conceivably best) loss you could have: losing your travelling companion. If you and your partner were to get accidentally separated in Europe, you would not by any means have a Guinness "first"—it seems to occur frequently. But it would be a good idea for the two of you to agree before you leave home on what both of you will do if you should get separated. If it happens to you in a town where you do not have a room, you could have agreed that in such an eventuality you would meet in front of the train station (the one you came into when you arrived, just in case there is more than one where you are), or you might have specified the police station, or the post office. All you have to do in this case, obviously, is to have identical targets in mind if you lose each other.

What is more likely to happen is that one of you will make a train and the other won't. We've had this happen, and have known of it happening to other careless or clumsy people. Obviously it would be nice if you had agreed upon a procedure for such difficulties, and it really doesn't matter what the procedure is as long as you both understand it. Possibilities that occur to us are: 1) the one who made the train will get off at the next station and wait for the other one to come on the next train; 2) the one on the train will return, and the one left behind will wait where he or she is; or 3) the man will always come to the woman, whether she was left at the original departure point or has gone on and will, by this prior agreement, be getting off at the next station.

If you have such a prior arrangement but are thoroughly sick of each other when you do get separated, either of you can improvise and just go the other way.

Chapter Fourteen
Diverse and Sundry Entertainments

The use of travelling is to regulate imagination
by reality, and instead of thinking how things may be,
to see them as they are.

—Samuel Johnson

Perhaps at this stage you might well be wondering whether your vacation in Europe will consist of nothing more than getting from place to place and hunting for inexpensive lodgings. Well, in spite of having already confessed that these two activities can be time-consuming, we will now add that you will nevertheless have a lot of free time to explore and to have a good time. Distances are relatively short in Europe, so you really won't use all that much time getting from here to there. Your problem may be the reverse of what you are worrying about: you may find yourself with a lot of hours to fill and, if you are on a budget, very little money to spend on high-priced recreation.

Some of the best possibilities in Europe for pleasant and inexpensive entertainments have to do with the many festivals that are held everywhere throughout the year. It is easy to get listings of times, dates, and places of these events. Fodor's books contain a good deal of information about them, but much more complete listings can be obtained from the national tourist offices of each country.

Some of the possibilities among these special events and festivals include flower shows, Grand Prix road races, religious celebrations, special art shows, film festivals, ballets, operas, concerts, stage plays, historical celebrations, pilgrimages, carnivals, trade fairs, holiday observances and sporting events. These festivals and special events are so frequent and widespread that it would be wise to check the listings once your plans are fairly well fixed to see whether anything of particular interest to you might affect your own itinerary.

You will find when you are in Europe that many ideas for inexpensive entertainments will strike you. Indeed, one of the nicest things about Europe lies in the opportunities it presents for simple pleasures like walking or bicycling through the narrow, cobblestoned streets, looking at the homes, shops, and parks and gardens. To us this is a form of adventure that neither requires nor encourages speed. At its best, it is a leisurely kind of discovery trip which can provide new surprises around each corner.

Sundays are extremely quiet days in most parts of Europe. Knowing this, we once spent a Sunday in Bruges, Belgium, with the intention of taking a quiet stroll through the ancient part of the city without facing the distraction of hordes of shoppers, people going to work, and so on. As we expected, the first parts of the old city we walked through appeared totally deserted. It was enjoyable to stroll along the quiet cobblestoned streets listening to our own footsteps and the church bells. But finally we rounded a corner and saw a square that was jammed with people, flowers, children, dogs, and tourists. We never did learn what was going on, but we walked through and looked in the open shops and wondered why a traditionally quiet Sunday morning had been transformed into what looked like a weekday afternoon. After we got through this small area, we rediscovered ancient, silent, Sunday Bruges again. Europe is full of pleasant little surprises.

No matter what your religious attitudes are, the churches and cathedrals of Europe are always worth a look. Surprisingly, there is often a small charge to enter them, but some of them are free—and all of them are interesting. Such places of worship contain beautiful art, wood carvings, and stained glass, and many of them can provide you with an excellent aerial view of the city below from their towers or steeples. While climbing worn stone steps up to these lookoff points is a common practice in Europe, it is a far cry in effort, expense, or height from whizzing up in a fast elevator to the top of a skyscraper in an American city. For one thing, it requires more exertion, and for another, it can frighten you severely if heights bother you. If they do, you could be in for a variety of sensations when you indulge in this time-honored pastime. Sometimes even some of the steps are *outside,* where you are guarded from a fall only by a rickety iron railing that looks as if it's about to fall off because of its own weight, and all of the lookoffs are seemingly (but not actually) precarious.

Such views allow you to take great photographs, look at the lay of the land, and, if you are so inclined, to feel dizzy, sick, or frightened to death. It's a great, cheap sport, and if being off the ground by more than six feet frightens you, you'll hate it. If you do not have such acrophobia, these climbs are well worth the effort.

You may be lucky enough to find yourself at one of the free concerts Europeans seem to love. These may be anything from classical to jazz concerts, and they may include the "Sound and Light" (*Son et Lumière*) spectacles that are so popular on the Continent. We recently attended a marvelous concert in the town square of

Rothenburg, Germany, which was played by the School Band of America, a talented group of high school musicians who perform in Europe each summer under the auspices of the U.S. State Department. The crowd there loved it, and so did we.

There are other free musical entertainments in the form of street performances by young student minstrels. Europe is full of young people, many of whom carry all their possessions on their backs, and many of whom are Americans or Canadians. One often sees these youngsters entertaining crowds for donations by playing guitars, flutes, or violins. You will find that you'll often be touched by their efforts, and will flip a coin or two to them as you stroll on.

If you are in London you should find out what stage plays are on. London theatre is generally quite good, and, compared to Broadway prices, pleasantly inexpensive. You will also find that you will not be embarrassed if you didn't bring your evening clothes along.

London offers a number of attractions to visitors, the most popular of which is the Tower. It is a fascinating place, particularly the spot where so many royal heads were cut off in the past. England's crown jewels are also here, and they are compellingly beautiful. The Tower is open Mondays through Saturdays from 0930 to 1600, and from 1400 to 1700 on Sundays.

Visitors can get information about where to go, what to do, and hours that various London sights are open by telephoning 730-0791 between 9 a.m. and 6 p.m. every day. The Tourist Information Centres are also very helpful to travellers, and they provide still another number you can call for information: 629-9191. A recorded announcement of each day's principal events can be heard on 246-8041.

As an example of what the budgeteer can do if he's really determined, we had a great desire to swim in the Mediterranean Sea on a recent trip, but we were a bit cowed when we arrived in the millionaire country of Monaco, wondering if we'd have to lay out a small fortune to get an air-conditioned bathhouse with built-in hi-fi on the beach. When we finally went down there, carrying a small bag with towels and bathing suits, we went into the public toilets, changed, and ran down through the hordes of people and threw ourselves into the salty water. Eventually we went back and changed again in the same place. As we made the long, long climb back up the road, Phyllis said: "Do you realize that we really swam in the Mediterranean?"

Alan replied: "And do you realize that it didn't cost us a cent?" adding, "Did you see those women's suits?"

Priorities differ from person to person.

One fine form of entertainment is "Meet the ____" type of programs, which are available in many European countries. The tourist offices usually make such arrangements, which generally amount to meeting the natives who share your interests and who are in your age bracket. Sometimes the pairing up is arranged on the basis of mutual professional interests, but it will in any case give the tourist the chance to talk to Europeans, see their homes, and make new friendships. It's a super idea, and you might want to consider giving it a try.

All travellers enjoy looking at Europe's castles, and most of them find Germany's Neuschwanstein breathtaking.

Shopping sprees

Shopping, of course, is an interesting way to spend some of your free time. Not only are Europe's shops interesting, but their flea markets are even more fascinating. At one of them we once spotted an Indonesian knife that looked like a nice souvenir, and we decided to try to buy it. The owner, who appeared to be about fourteen years old, asked us twelve dollars for it. We strolled on, saw another one like it but in better condition for thirty dollars. We went back and offered the boy three dollars. A long bargaining session followed, which ended after a half hour with our buying the knife and an African spear for nine dollars total. It was a happy ending: we were pleased with our purchase, and the young entrepreneur looked as if he had just made the deal of the century. Perhaps he had.

Shopping in Europe is a rather strange and interesting adventure. The stores have merchandise that is often quite different from the comparable items we see in the States. Many luxury items have struck us as being both alien and beautiful, while more commonplace things like utensils didn't impress us very much. We observed on our most recent trip that prices there are very high now, and that it would require real taste and great care to buy nice gifts or souvenirs. We priced watches in Switzerland in 1980, and concluded that inflation rates have killed the bargain prices of old on their timepieces.

Many shops and business establishments in Europe close for lunch every day from 12 to 1400, although now some of them close from 1215 to 1330. Practically everything everywhere is closed on Sundays and Saturday afternoons, a matter to remember when planning your itinerary. As stated before, Spain's hours are even odder yet by our standards. Most businesses and stores are open mornings, closed from about 1330 to 1630, or even 1700 hours, and are open again until 2030 or 2100. Many of Italy's stores are also closed during the afternoon siesta hours, usually from 1300 to 1600 hours.

If you are going on a guided tour of Europe, you should realize that your guide will usually get a commission on what you buy—if you shop in the stores he recommends. In such a case, of course, you will pay his commission by paying a price that has been boosted to cover it.

We were recently in a small town where most of the shops stretched along the beach for about three city blocks. We noticed that the tour buses all parked in a square at one end of this line of stores. We wanted to buy one of the handmade wool sweaters that are sold in this area, and we priced a particular style in all of the shops. The sweater we wanted was approximately $30 in the shop that was closest to the square. The price dropped by about $2 in each shop as we went away from the square. We bought one in the last shop for $18.

It was clear that not many tourists were willing to walk three blocks from their bus, and indeed it is probable that few of them realized how profitable such a short stroll might be. But in addition, we learned that the guides on the buses were telling their passengers that the first shop was ''approved.''

With all that in mind, consider the fact that most people who take guided tours tip the guide at the end for being so nice to them.

Minitours

There are many other ways to spend time without spending money simultaneously. Many cities' tourist agencies give out maps with walking tours marked on them and historical points indicated and described. Some Spanish cities have a nice idea for sightseers that involves running a city bus around the city and coming back to the same point where one boarded it. It provides a good view of the city for just a few cents, and it can be helpful in getting oriented to a strange place. These autobusses are called *Circunvalacion* ("Sur-coon-vol-a-shon," roughly, or "Circular") and they are so marked.

Many industries and businesses are pleased to show tourists how they do their thing. In Chapter Eleven we mentioned touring the breweries to see how they make the stuff and to sample it as well. You can visit the china factory in Delft and see how the beautiful blue pottery is made, fired, painted, and finished. In other cities in the Netherlands you can visit chocolate and cheese-making plants. In Switzerland you can visit the many watch and clock museums, several of the best being in Le Locle, Neuchatel, and Geneva. In Germany and Italy and France you can visit the factories that make such vehicles as Mercedes-Benz, Porsche, Volkswagen, Fiat, Citroen, etc. Reservations must be made from three to six weeks ahead for these visits; further information about this can be obtained from the appropriate tourist information offices in the U.S.

In Holland or Belgium you can visit interesting diamond-cutting "factories." You will not see diamonds split, no matter what television commercials you have seen that suggest otherwise; no one sees *that* but the man who does it. You will be shown replicas of some of the more famous diamonds of history, and you will be given a chance to handle some smaller real ones yourself. You will learn how the stones are cut and polished. These tours are free, but the people who run the establishments are quite willing to sell you diamonds—and to try to convince you that you can save as much as fifty percent by buying from them rather than from a jeweler in the States. If you have such a purchase in mind, you should check with American Express for recommendations of reputable firms and any other advice and information you can get. At any rate, you will not be pressured to buy in most of these establishments. The people in them seem glad to have you visit, to look, and to learn (yearn?). Presumably they feel that if you don't buy on this visit, perhaps you will the next time you come to Europe.

For fairly small tariffs you can visit hundreds of museums and art galleries. Some of the most famous are the Van Gogh Museum and Rijksmuseum in Amsterdam; the British Museum; the Academy of Fine Arts in Venice; the Kröller-Müller van Gogh Museum near Arnhem; and so on. They are everywhere, and most of them have very reasonable entry fees or no fee at all. As mentioned earlier, it is also possible to view great works of art in many of Europe's cathedrals.

If you are near The Hague in Holland, you can see one of the most unusual paintings in the world: the Panorama Mesdag. You view it from its center, and you are completely surrounded by it and its 3D foreground of sandy beaches. Painted in the late eighteen hundreds by four artists, one of whom was named Mesdag, it is a picture of Scheveningen (a Hague suburb) as it was then. It is four hundred feet in circumference and covers more than seventeen thousand square feet of canvas. Although you will be only about 125 feet from it on any side, it is so realistic you will feel like you're seeing for miles. It is really a worthwhile and strange work of art to see. It is the largest painting in existence.

Belgium offers visitors a chance to take a stroll through another century in its Gardens and Castle of Annevoie in Dinant, a small town a short distance southeast of Brussels. It is extremely popular with tourists in the know, including some of our fellow-countrymen. It is necessary to use the word "incredible" to describe the gardens, which contain beautiful old trees, flowers of every color and type, waterfalls, and a fantastic variety of fountains—all of which have been operating for the last two hundred years without mechanical help, running only on natural water pressure and gravity. The gardens are especially interesting because the formal sections are balanced by natural areas, an arrangement that indicates the virtues of both ways of thinking.

The chateau is eighteenth century, and it is a beautiful place. If one could see only one castle in Europe, this wouldn't by any means be the worst choice. The people who live here, as well as the middle-aged son who resides in a smaller house on the grounds, work regularly with the gardeners to keep the place proper for its awed visitors. There is a good restaurant nearby for hungry travellers, and you are encouraged to bring your own picnic lunch if you prefer, which will allow you to eat at one of the tables provided (and have liquid refreshments from nearby, if you wish), in the sight of one of Europe's best panoramas. Day trips by train here from Brussels are possible, and if you do it that way, show your ticket to the garden gatekeeper for a fifty percent discount on the entry price—which is about two dollars per person for entry to the gardens, three dollars for walks through both the gardens and the castle (open only on weekends).

There are many zoos in Europe, some of which are reputed to be excellent, but on this we are a bit sceptical. Generally they are old, and because they were built before the modern thinking about keeping animals in the open became current, they are often marked by small dirty cages. The Antwerp Zoo, which is supposed to be one of the most modern in Europe, didn't really strike us as being all that up to date—but, by contrast, we found much to admire in the Parque Zoologico on the outskirts of Madrid. New, ultramodern, and very large, this zoo looks like a happy place for its residents and its patrons. You can get there by public transportation, but you have to do a *lot* of walking once you're there. It's a big, big place. One surprise: if you are wearing a camera you'll be charged a few cents extra when you enter the zoo. If your pictures usually turn out like ours do, they should really give you a discount.

There are also a number of open-air zoos in Europe in which the animals run loose and the people are in the "cages." Some of the best are in France and Germany. There is one at Givskud, Denmark, another at Hilvarenbeek in southern Holland, one close to Stockholm, and yet another at Arnhem, Holland. The latter, called the "Safaripark" (or "Wildsavanne"), is the home of about three hundred wild animals that live freely on fifty fenced-in wooded acres. People visit this transplant from Africa in automobiles or in the Safari Train, which is not a train, really, but a series of big glassed-in cages pulled by a truck. Before this train leaves to go behind the fences, the vehicle doors are all locked from the outside by an attendant. If you have your own (or a rented) car, you can drive in, provided that you obey the rules they give you, which are mostly related to keeping you from getting eaten.

You do have to be careful in this transplanted lion country. There has been one bad incident here in the past. A man who was taking photographs from an open car window was dragged out by a lion and ended up in a less-than-satisfactory condition moments later.

During this absolutely fascinating ride of about one hour's duration, you will see a variety of other animals—giraffes, rhinos, emus, wildebeestes, zebras, etc.—living in their natural habitat. But the lion plateau (*simba steppe*) is most incredible to see, and if you are fortunate, you will see a specially equipped park-official-driven Land Rover which the lions will follow, and indeed climb upon because the brave driver feeds them by throwing raw meat out of his windows. The animals do not usually climb up on the other cars, but this is not unknown, so be careful! You are absolutely safe in the "train," because you couldn't get out for a stroll even if you were crazy enough to do so.

The entrance fee to the Arnhem Burgers' Zoo (about $1.50 U.S.) entitles you to ride the train behind the fences, and we recommend the trip highly. It's quite a sensation to see a hungry lion staring at you from inches away. It makes you understand how a lamb chop must feel, at least while it's still attached to the lamb.

Germany has some excellent safari parks. Towns that boast of them are Schlitz, Gmeinweiler, Stukenbrock, Selfkant, and Hodenhagen. The one at Selfkant-Tuddern is especially easy to get to, being located near the southern border of Holland and the eastern border of Belgium. It is not necessary to have a car to go through this one. Safari-buses are available to take you through in safety and comfort.

Denmark's Givskud Safariland, which covers two hundred acres, is a home for elephants, lions, camels, llamas, ostriches, zebras, antelope, water buffalo, zebu cattle, wild pigs, and reindeer. The officials here are also very strict about safety precautions for guests. It is open to the public from Easter through the end of October. You must have a car to go through this one.

Near Rødby, Denmark, one of the main landings for ferries from Germany, is the town of Bandholm, where there is yet another wild animal park. This one is called Knuthenborg Safari Park, and you must have a car to drive through if you visit here.

Sweden's Kolmården Safari and Animal Park is about two hours southwest of Stockholm. It boasts of many exotic birds and a number of animals, including giraffes, elephants, rhinos, zebra, antelope, and tigers, all living on this ingeniously constructed nature reserve of more than five hundred acres. You can drive through this one, or view it from three hundred feet up from a gondola of Kolmarden's three-kilometer-long aerial cableway. The park is open from 10 a.m. to 6 p.m. from early June through the end of August. During other parts of the year the hours vary, so a visitor would be wise to check with the tourist information office.

Not only can you see how wild animals live in Europe, but you can also take a look at how people live under a form of society that is very different from ours. Denmark is perhaps the world's most highly socialized country, which may be a reason for many people who have strong feelings one way or the other about socialism to want to pay a visit. We can't anticipate, of course, how you'll react to it, but we will pass along the following information to help you decide whether or not you'd like to have a look at it yourself. In the first place, the Danes pay very high taxes; one small businessman told us that he pays the government over sixty percent of his income each year. These taxes seem to have put many of the country's pensions and small hotels out of business, and driven many people who rent rooms in their homes to hide the fact so they can hide the income—which makes them difficult or impossible to locate. On the other hand, no one here starves, or wants for health care, or has to do without an education simply because he cannot afford it.

Denmark does an excellent job of taking care of its old, sick, tired, and poor. All elderly people get a pension from the government, and those who cannot take care of themselves are put into nice little apartments where doctors, nurses, and other specialists are available. Medical care is free to the Danes, including stays in hospitals, doctor's services, operations, and so on. We were told in Copenhagen that if a tourist is hurt or becomes ill there, the government will see that he gets what he needs. After he is well they do try to recoup from his insurance company, but if he has no insurance and he is poor, any charges against him will, in effect, be paid by the Danish taxpayers.

If this sort of society interests you and you are going to be in Copenhagen, there is a tour called the "World of Tomorrow" that will introduce you to these interesting social institutions and benefits. And, indeed, if you make one of the quick jumps from Denmark to Sweden, the Swedes will be happy to show you some examples of their thinking and activities along these same lines.

Miscellaneous cheap entertainments

It is always a good idea to ask the national tourist offices in the U.S. about special passes or discount arrangements they may have for visiting museums, art galleries, and historic places in their countries. You can, for example, get an "Open to View Ticket" from a BritRail Travel International office that will give you entrance to more than four hundred of Britain's top tourist spots. As another example, Alitalia Airlines offices sell a special pass that will admit you to many of Italy's major art galleries and museums.

You may find that you are attracted to the many famous "homes" of Europe, the former residences of such people as Mozart, Michelangelo, Beethoven, Shakespeare, Brahms, Goethe, Nietzsche, Ann Frank, the great Flemish painters, and so on. If such giants of the past interest you, you would probably enjoy seeing how and where they lived.

You can visit "The world's smallest city," Madurodam in The Hague in Holland. An exact one twenty-fifth size, this little city covers about four acres. Complete with canals and moving ships, this little village is lighted by forty-six thousand lights. It has castles, cathedrals, homes, gardens, an airport, and—you name it and it's probably there. It is open from April 1 through the first Sunday in October. The Dutch claim that twenty-two million people have visited it since it opened in 1952, and we believe it—there were at least five million people there on the day we visited it recently. There is another of these teeny towns at Middelburg, Holland. Either of them is worth seeing once, we think, although we're not really sure of that. We leave it to you to decide whether or not you have a childlike mind, or want to find out what it feels like to be a giant.

One of Europe's most interesting and picturesque caves is the grotto at Han-sur-Lesse (near Rochefort in Belgium's Ardennes Region). This is also the home of a relatively tame open-air zoo, not a very important one, but the grotto is well

The Bard lived here four hundred years ago.

The authors' photo, England

worth seeing. The Lesse River runs through these caverns, its level at the moment depending upon recent rains and melting snows, and you will exit from the caverns on an electric boat on this underground river. Near the end of this guided tour you will see two spectacular sights: the main room, which contains in its enormity a snack bar and countless tables and chairs for hungry, thirsty tourists, and a display of incredible footwork down the rocks to you by a torch-carrying athlete who gives you a visual idea of the tremendous heights of some of these subterranean rooms by his flight from above.

Other economical entertainment possibilities: Many European theatres show current American movies with the language of the country printed at the bottom in subtitles. So if you see a movie that interests you, just ask at the box-office if it's English-language. Another entertainment anyone might enjoy is riding the glass-topped tour boats in the cities which have canals. They are always informative, and occasionally the people who give the spiels are amusing as well. It's a nice way to see a city, and we would particularly recommend taking one in Amsterdam or Bruges if you are there anyway.

Many tourists who like "sights" are attracted to the cable cars, cog railways, ski lifts, funiculars, etc. in the mountains of Europe. These strange forms of transportation do carry people up to the great views, and they all share one characteristic: none of them look especially thrilling when being viewed from the bottom end. Some of them look a little different from the top, or from half-way up. These conveyances *can* be pretty sensational, especially when you see that there is nothing between you and the ground but a thin piece of sheet metal or a tiny seat. Fear does strange things to people. We once saw a tourist jump from the seat of a ski lift over an unpleasantly deep ravine, and we have seen another person take the whole ride in a cable car huddled on the floor, crying. We would be especially nervous for anyone who is afraid of heights riding the ski-lift chairs. The cable cars or gondolas aren't all that bad, at least in the respect that they are all sealed up (you *can't* jump).

Other available sights include the enterprises in many of the larger European cities that are invariably called Sex Shops. These stores sell various items, magazines, and books that are related to sex (surprise!). Alan was looking in the window of one in Copenhagen (where there are many of them) at a magazine cover that portrayed a pleasant-looking but immodestly dressed female who was fastened to a wall with what appeared to be fifty pounds of log chains. At his side, Phyllis said, "I think they're chain stores."

Alan looked at her, uncertain about whether to laugh or not.

"They've all got the same name," she said innocently.

You will see such establishments throughout Europe, especially in the large cities. In Vienna, in fact, one of the attractions for visitors listed on a big sign in the center of the city—along with Schonbrunn Palace, Belvedere Castle, and a variety of churches and cathedrals—is a sex shop.

Well, anyway, we thought we'd mention these places so you could be sure to avoid them. We've heard that American women often enter these shops, saying embarrassedly, ''I thought I'd get something for my sister.'' We hope you don't have any sisters like that, or at least that you won't admit it while you're in Europe.

Europe also offers another, related free entertainment. Many visitors walk through the red-light districts where they get a view of the world's oldest profession in open operation. The two most famous of these areas are the Reeperbahn in Hamburg and Oude Zijds Voorburgwal in Amsterdam. In either area one can see a genuine sociological phenomenon in the form of a real, honest-to-badness red-light district, replete with generally unattractive females and their ages-old symbol, a burning red candle or red light bulb. Some of these ladies stand outside their places of pleasure, and others sit inside (often rather carelessly, one might say) looking out at the crowds of passers-by and potential customers. When a man does go into one of these little establishments, the woman will pull the curtain in the faces of the people on the walk, many of whom will continue to stand there until she reopens it.

Should one anticipate the possibility of danger in ''nightseeing'' in these areas? We've heard it both ways. We've read that you could get rapped over the head, and also that both areas are watched carefully by the police to keep the tourists from hurting each other. We have only walked through the one in Amsterdam, having heard that it *is* a safe area, while the Hamburg street is reputedly full of crummy night clubs and creepy characters.

We strolled through Oude Zijds Vooburgwal at a fairly early hour one evening, and found it to be a quiet-looking residential area. However, some, and perhaps most of the people around seemed to have some alcohol in their systems, so we wouldn't have wanted to start any arguments with anyone—but then we never do. It was well-lighted (pun intended) and open, and we were not made nervous by it. But whether the operation would disgust or bemuse you, it is a free sight you won't see in many other places.

Another fascinating and free experience in the sort of strange happenings Europe offers its guests from abroad is to be found at the Speakers' Corner in London's Hyde Park. Characterized in a British Tourist Authority publication as a place ''where soap-box orators address stray dogs and huge crowds with equal enthusiasm'' it is also a forum where members of the crowd often respond to the speakers with some enthusiasm of their own. Here you will hear pitches for or against religion, communism, capitalism, democracy, abortion, and almost any other subject you can imagine. It is a personification of free speech, free thinking, wild debate, and an occasional touch of fine madness. There are usually a number of London's finest, marked by blue helmets and stern visages, milling through the crowds, which may be the reason everyone seems to keep his temper slightly below the boil-over point.

Londoners think that the best performances in these minor theatricals occur on Saturday and Sunday afternoons and evenings.

How would you like to take on an enraged fighting bull weighing more than a ton with your bare hands? If you wouldn't care to try it for yourself, perhaps you'd like to see someone else do it. To see that you have to go to Portugal, where such daredevil wrestling is an old-time and popular sport.

Like their Mexican and Spanish brethren, the Portuguese love bullfights—but bullfights with a difference. There the bulls are not killed—at least not in the ring. Another difference is that most of the fighting between man and beast is done on horseback. And for the biggest difference of all, part of the show consists of pitting unarmed, unprotected men in combat with this animal that has been bred and trained to be fiery, to attack, and to show the greatest courage.

During the first part of the ceremony all the gaily dressed cavaliers, matadors, and forcados (the men who wrestle the bull) are introduced in the ring. The cavaliers are astride beautiful horses, which, you will learn when the fighting begins, are able to dance, run backwards and sideways, and stop and turn on a dime.

After the bull is let in the matadors (or capas) go to work with their capes, an exercise that shows the cavaliero which way the bull will toss his head when he charges. The matadors soon leave the ring to the cavaliero and his horse—and, of course, the now-enraged bull. This bullfighter then proceeds to make various sorts of passes at the bull, during which he imbeds darts in the animal's shoulders. The horsemanship is absolutely breathtaking, mostly because the bull and horse are so close together so often—and so dangerously.

When the cavaliero has placed all of the darts, he rides out of the ring, and the forcados appear. There are eight of them. They face the bull in a straight line, and the first man advances on it, taunting it as he comes. Being in no mood to accept this cocky behavior, the bull charges. The lead forcado throws himself between the horns and grabs the loose skin on the bull's chest. The second man throws himself onto the first man and holds him down between the bull's horns. The other men grab the animal wherever they can, and the last man grabs its tail. At this point they have immobilized it, and everyone lets go but the man at the tail. Oftentimes the bull will then drag him around the ring trying to shake him off, a great crowd-pleaser.

That is the way this part of the sport is supposed to work, and the way it often does. But not always. Sometimes the bull hooks in an unexpected way when it charges the first man, and if he doesn't get onto its head everybody goes down like dominos. Any or all of the forcados are liable to be hurt when this happens, not only by being knocked down by the bull's charge, but also by what happens next. The enraged animal usually tries to run over them again, doing a clumsy tap dance on anyone who is still on the ground. In fact, the men with capes often have to rush in to get the animal away from mauling the forcados.

When the whole thing goes sour in this way, the forcados sometimes get up and limp, hobble, or run to the surrounding fence and crawl over it to safety. Sometimes one or two or even all of them will get themselves straightened out and come back in the ring to tackle the bull again. This show of bravery always delights the crowd, but it often turns out even worse than the first try for the forcados. It is a marvel that any of them live through these encounters, and don't get hurt worse than they usually do.

Finally the time comes to get the bull from the ring so the next fight can start. This is accomplished by herding a bunch of cows in, apparently to get the bull's mind onto sports other than fighting. It often doesn't work that way; the bull is so worked up that he'll often try to hook the cows. Eventually, however, he calms down a bit and follows the cows out of the ring. A short time later he is slaughtered, simply because he cannot be allowed to fight again. The bull learns quite a bit in his first and only fight, and the cavaliers and matadors know that if he were given a second chance, it is likely that he would be able to kill someone or one of the horses (moral: it doesn't pay to become too smart if you're a bull).

The Portuguese bullfight is a splendid sight to see. The pageantry, the uniforms, the horsemanship, and the courage of both the men and the animals is unforgettable. It's a super-high-class rodeo, with overtones of life and death. If and when you're in Portugal, be sure to go see one. Perhaps Wide World of Sports will even bring this spectacle into our living rooms one of these days. We've suggested it to them, and we hope they put it on. It's something that everyone should see at least once.

A visitor to Europe does not have to be bored simply because his rating in Dun and Bradstreet is poor (or missing altogether). He does have to keep his eyes open, and to have some awareness of what is going on. But even if he is a careless sort who hasn't done his homework, he can find something that is new and different and interesting to experience wherever he goes. Indeed, as we have said before, for the want of anything better to do, it is always nice to take a walk in quiet streets that are like nothing you will ever see or experience in Denver, Columbus, Peoria, or anywhere else in the United States or Canada.

In the next chapter, we will try to tell you how to see—and understand— some of the most fascinating aspects of Europe—not its art or its festivals— but the things that really make it *Europe*.

Chapter Fifteen
Seeing Beneath the Surface

*Genius, in truth, means little more than
the faculty of perceiving in an unhabitual way.*

—William James

One well-travelled American has said this: "Most people who visit Europe, at
least on their first trip, are like children who are suddenly getting a chance to view
the adult world for the first time. They have little sense of the world's history,
they don't understand what is being said, and they consequently just LOOK. Stare.
Gawk. Shoot pictures. They are curious, but their curiosity rarely manages to help
them to understand what they're experiencing. They don't know how to turn their
curiosity into an asset, and it often just remains an unscratched tickle." We
agree, and this chapter is about seeing, and understanding what you see. It is also
about some of the differences in thinking and perspectives between Europeans
and North Americans, differences that are fascinating to try to understand.

There are two parts to this question of what you may see and understand in
Europe, one having to do with *things,* and the other with *people.*

In dealing with *things,* we are considering aspects of technology, human ingenuity, and various efforts to preserve the past and to create the future. Although Europe's technological achievements differ from our own in many ways,
they are similar in one major respect: like our Golden Gate Bridge or our great sky-
scrapers, they are specific answers to particular needs. Like us, the Europeans
have a high-level technology, but because their problems and aspirations are
different from ours, their solutions and their techniques are also different.

In thinking about how one might try to gain some understanding of the *people*
of the various European countries, we will be considering such factors as their

attitudes, motivations, histories, and even geographical locations. The kinds of questions one might consider on this subject include these:

What has happened to ''British reserve''? Did it ever exist, or was it a fable?

Why are the Danes so friendly to outsiders?

What has fighting the sea (and sometimes losing) over thousands of years done to the collective or individual Dutch mentality? Why didn't they ever conclude that it would be easier and less expensive to take land from their neighbors rather than from the North Sea?

What social and historical events have served to make the Spaniards so different from other Europeans?

Why haven't the Belgians, who, like the Dutch, live in a low country and face extreme population pressures, tried to expand into the sea as their next-door neighbor has?

Why are the French so devoted to the culinary arts?

These are difficult questions. We have no definite answers to any of them, but we have some theories, and you will also if you think about and discuss such matters as you travel through Europe. If you do, rather than simply looking at what is merely obvious, you'll increase the pleasure of your trip enormously and educate yourself simultaneously.

In the same sense that one need not be an art critic to enjoy painting or a psychologist to be interested in people, you do not have to be an engineer or specialist of any kind to appreciate some of the aspects of humanity and human ingenuity you will see in Europe. But just as some viewers get more enjoyment from a work of art by reflecting about why it was done in the way it was or why certain colors were used, or even by doing some background study about the painting or the artist, it is possible to increase your appreciation of what you see by indulging in some self-directed questions.

Here are some of the kinds of questions that intellectually curious travellers like to consider when they are looking at old buildings, castles, or unusual architectural or engineering accomplishments:

Why was it built here?

Why was it built the way it was?

What sort of equipment would they have had in those days to make the work possible?

What could it have meant to the builders (why did they build it)?

What does it mean now to the people who maintain (or are restoring) it?

If they cannot answer some of their own questions, experienced travellers often look for literature which does provide answers, and such descriptive write-ups are ordinarily made available to visitors at major tourist attractions or in the museums. It is also often helpful to ask questions of the people who operate the outstanding dams, exhibits, and castles, or the personnel in the nearest tourist information offices.

From here on in this chapter we will make little effort to separate the ''things'' from the ''people.'' There is always a close interconnection between human beings and what they create, and it is often difficult to distinguish between the two. The whole idea is to exercise your curiosity, to keep your eyes and your mind open for anything on any subject that is unusual, and to try to understand what it means, how it occurred, or even why it is strange and alien to you.

Many cities in Europe offer walking tours, either for free or for a tiny fee, that can serve as an excellent introduction to wherever you find yourself. Very often they are run by volunteer guides whose only reward for their service is the pleasure of introducing visitors to the city they love. Some of these guides are so good that you will feel that they could easily hold their own on a TV talk show, while others, doubtlessly doing the best they can, are not all that interesting. But both sorts of people, perhaps surprisingly, need the sort of intelligent questions you could ask in order to perform to the best of their capabilities. It is to their advantage, as well as yours, for you to ask searching questions.

Guides, information office personnel, and people in the streets are used to hearing such questions as: ''Where is the cathedral?'' or ''Could you tell me where I could find a good restaurant?'' As you can imagine, any of them find it much more interesting to be asked such questions as these:

What is its place in history?

Are there any legends associated with it?

What are its unusual architectural features?

Why is it important?

What (more) can you tell me about it?

If they only tell you how old it is, as they sometimes do, you might say, ''I'm impressed by its age, but why is it important?'' Unless they are totally incompetent or ignorant, they will enjoy hearing such questions, and they will do their utmost to answer them.

From *your* standpoint as a person who is not being led about Europe by a professional guide, such answers are the difference between ignorance and understanding. To look at the Minster Cathedral in York, England, for example, from the standpoint of complete ignorance is to see it as a huge, photogenic building with some probable significance. To learn that it is known to have been a little wooden church in the early part of the seventh century, converted into a stone church after 627 A.D., rebuilt late in that century, destroyed by fire during the Norman conquest, replaced by a Norman cathedral in the late eleventh century, rebuilt in the twelfth, transformed into a Gothic cathedral and subsequently altered during the thirteenth, enlarged in the early part of the fourteenth and again several times in the fifteenth, burned twice in the nineteenth, and had its highest tower and its foundations reinforced in the twentieth century because it was about to fall down—work which resulted in discovering that the structure was built over a second-century Roman legionary fortress, which has now been made open to visitors—adds considerably to its interest to the modern-day viewer's eyes. Having such historical perspective makes it more than just a beautiful building to walk through and to photograph.

Any inhabitant of York would doubtlessly be pleased to talk about this interesting history if asked, but none would ever approach a visitor and volunteer such information. You have to ask questions of the sort indicated above if you are to understand the real significance of what you are seeing. And the first time you do this and are rewarded with information that increases its interest twentyfold, you'll have discovered how to get other people to help you see beneath the surface.

The point is that even when you walk through a street and find it interesting, you are doubtlessly missing countless details that could make it far more meaningful to you if you only knew about them. (One tip: don't forget to look *up* on such walks. Many of the most interesting details of Europe's buildings are located high off the streets.) If you see a dam or a bridge and can only conclude that it's large, impressive, or pretty, you've probably missed its essence. If you finally leave a charming little village with no thought in your head except a question about whether or not all your photographs will come out, you may as well also realize that you don't know the first thing about what you've just seen.

If you do ask questions, you will often meet people who can make the sounds, sights, and smells of the past come alive for you, showing you what the place was like centuries ago, giving you a far better appreciation of why it is like it is now. Even if what they tell you seems insignificant when you first hear it ("These wood carvings are so old that their surface has begun to turn to stone"), you will often find that possessing the knowledge of such seeming trivialities will give you an entirely new way of looking at what is in front of you.

Most cities' guide books are helpful in providing this sort of information; the people in the tourist information offices, at least if asked the right kinds of questions, can enlarge on such matters; and the Michelin Green Guides are a good source of information. But perhaps most important of all is for you to ask your own intelligent questions in the hope of getting intelligent answers. One of the reasons this is so is that there are sights in Europe, both large and small, that you could stare at forever without having any real comprehension of what they mean.

This sobering thought applies to questions about people as well as their creations. In such cases, you simply have to forget about your natural modesty and reserve, and ask someone—even an innocent bystander—whatever it is you want to know.

For example, you might try asking a Frenchman, "Why is food so important to you?" or "Why don't you care much for people of other nationalities?"

Ask a Spaniard, "Why do you think the French care so much about food and drink?" or "Why do you admire the French so much?"

Ask an Italian, "Why do you think you have more crime than other European countries?"

Ask a Swiss or a Swede such a question as this: "After having stayed out of wars

The authors' photo. England

York's Minster was a little wooden church twelve hundred years ago.

for so long, why is your country so heavily armed today? Is it to keep you out of future wars, or do you think you'll be right in the middle of the next one?''

We have asked such questions and have received a whole spectrum of answers.

You will also find that asking such questions will often motivate the person you're talking with to ask you some questions back. Favorite examples from our own experience are, ''What do you think of President Reagan?'' and ''What did you think about Nixon and Watergate?'' and ''Why are you Americans always in such a hurry?'' Answering the questions you get back is always more difficult than asking your own—but it is still rewarding. It's enlightening to discover for the first time what you're willing to admit to someone else about your opinions of current or recent leaders, or about other controversial questions. This kind of give and take helps you to learn something of the world that reaches beyond your everyday life.

Perhaps a single example of the sort of interesting conversation a simple question may elicit in Europe will encourage you to give it a try yourself. We were in Denmark not long ago, shopping in a small store, when we noticed that the pro-prietor looked rather bored. We introduced ourselves and asked if we might put a question to him that had nothing to do with his store or his merchandise.

''Oh yes indeed,'' he answered in flawless English and with a charming smile. ''Always happy to talk to Americans. What is your question?''

''We have the impression,'' Phyllis said, ''that you Danes feel some bitterness about your high taxes. Are we correct?''

''We have very high taxes,'' he answered. ''But we are not really bitter about them. We like to complain—who doesn't? I pay sixty-five percent of my income to the government.''

''Pretty bad,'' Alan replied, unable to think of anything more sensible to say.

''Yes,'' the shopkeeper said. ''But let's make this comparison between us and you. When I go to a doctor, for something small or something big, I don't pay. My taxes pay. The same is true for prescription medicine, for the dentist, for my retire-ment. No one wants or starves here. When my children go to school, even upper-level school, I don't have the—the tuition and bills you have. The taxes pay it.''

''You get bombs and bombers,'' he said, a little smugly. ''I get—and my family gets—what we need to live and to be happy and healthy. From my reading, I know you don't get any of that, and maybe you are the people who should complain.''

''Perhaps so,'' one of us said. ''We are certainly nothing like as socialized as Danish society.''

The shopkeeper (whose name we didn't know and never learned) smiled and gave us the coup de grâce: ''*Your* problem is that you pay all sorts of *hidden* taxes—which we don't—so I suspect that you pay as much as I do. And for what?''

Well, depending on which side of the socio-economic-political spectrum you find yourself, you can agree or disagree with this man as much as you like. But the whole conversation could be characterized as interesting, could it not? Different? Thought provoking?

It's an alien viewpoint, from a man who lives in a different sort of society from ours.

It doesn't matter whether you believe—or agree with—such a person and his viewpoint, or whether you don't. What matters is to hear it, and to think about it. It's educational to do so. It stretches your mind.

A love for the ancient

Another example of the sort of question that could hit your mind, if you allow it enought latitude, has to do with the ancient buildings and old-town areas you see all over Europe. Everywhere you will see old walls, buildings, churches, and castles that have either somehow managed to survive the ravages of time and the elements or which have been lovingly restored. This is intriguing to many of us from the United States, who continuously see our older buildings torn down and replaced by something new. In the name of progress we demolish, rebuild, and modernize to such an extent that we have very few monuments or reminders of the past. It makes you wonder: "Why do *they* spend so much money and talent on trying to save the out-of-date? Why are they different from us in this respect?"

We're not sure of the answer, but we do know that Europeans are not nearly so taken by the concept of "progress" as Americans are. They have polluted air and water as we do, particularly in their larger cities, but they also have their old fountains, monuments, and buildings—and they love these reminders of earlier times. Many Europeans dislike or even hate the more modern parts of their cities, while they all seem to hold a high regard for the old sections, and although

The authors' photo

Much love and money is required to keep a building old-fashioned but new for centuries

we have often heard them complain about their overall tax rates, they seem to be entirely complacent about the huge sums the governments spend to refurbish and restore old buildings. Tiny Holland, for example, has over forty thousand protected buildings and historical artifacts. The work does cost a lot of money and it requires the attention of many kinds of skilled craftsmen, some of whom have to learn how to do things exactly as they were done centuries ago.

Not only is the preservation of historic buildings a big thing in Europe, but even the protection of certain ''views'' is a part of the work. Hundreds of thousands of structures and views are under the protection of the law across Europe. The whole business of restoration is very complicated. There is no desire to create museums or places that are just for show; the intent is to make the buildings, no matter what their age, entirely habitable in the twentieth century. But the outside appearance is another story, which partly accounts for the fact that power and telephone lines are often buried rather than being allowed to show. In addition, complex decisions have to be made, as one friend told us, ''about what point in a building's life its restoration should reflect. If it was built in the 1500's, had a wing added in 1650, was partially destroyed by fire in 1700, and 'modernized' in 1850 or 1900, to what stage does one restore it?'' And indeed, he went on to explain, the restorers often have to look for the thin line between purity, keeping things inside as they were in the past —and common sense, allowing the changes needed for modern living.

One of the most famous walled cities, Rothenburg in Germany, is kept in its original Middle Ages condition by the people who inhabit it. The city administration has decreed that each householder shall spend a certain amount of money each year to keep his property in its original condition, and no modernization or adding on is allowed. The town consequently looks as healthy and medieval today as it must have looked a thousand years ago, and visitors who have imaginations can hear in their minds the sound of horses' hooves ringing on the cobblestones, the sentries' cries from the parapets, and the sound of invaders trying to scale the thick gray walls.

Other famous walled cities are Spain's Avila, Mérida, and Toledo, England's Chester, and France's Carcassone. Germany boasts of many such cities, some of the best, as mentioned before, lying along the Romantische Strasse. There are numerous others, one of the nicest being Nüremberg. Sweden's (and possibly Europe's) finest is Visby, located on an island in the Baltic Sea. In fact, many European towns which look ultramodern around the railroad stations have carefully maintained old walled-in areas some distance away. People who are interested in antiquity would be wise to search out such places and find lodgings in them. In Rothenburg, for example, there are a number of beautiful old homes inside the walls which provide rooms to tourists at very reasonable rates.

Almost all visitors to Europe are fascinated by the old castles, palaces, and fortresses that are seen everywhere. Among the most famous are those at Fussen and Heidelberg, Germany; Salzburg, Austria; Ranier's Palace in Monaco; Buckingham Palace in London; and the Alcazars of Segovia and Seville, Spain. Such lovely buildings are not only monuments to their creator's abilities, but also to those who have served as their guardians in more recent years.

Europeans not only work hard at maintaining and restoring the treasures from the past, but they spend a great deal of time and money in locating and digging up such relics. Not only Italy, but most of Europe is covered with remainders of the Roman Empire. Most of these treasures are carefully protected, although ironically many of the recent modern buildings in Rome have covered or destroyed many of the Roman artifacts, and the French have done the same thing in various parts of their country.

One of these old Roman villages was discovered not long ago in Santiponce, Spain, a small village just outside of Seville. The Spanish government has named the site Italica, and has sponsored its uncovering and restoration. The original village was begun in 206 B.C. There is a large coliseum that you can walk through, as well as crawl around in its underseat labyrinth of musty tunnels. You can stroll along other paths which will take you past beautiful mosaic floors, still-standing columns, and parts of buildings and walkways that have been excavated. There is also a small museum that houses some of the best finds (although many of them are now in Seville's Palacio de Lebrija and its Archeological Museum in Maria Luisa Park). Entry to the ruins costs about seventy-five cents, and the Seville-Santiponce bus ends its run right at the Italica gate. We would not recommend the site as something one should cross Europe to see, but anyone who is nearby might consider a visit.

Spain has another Roman treasure that did not have to be unearthed. In fact, it is so big it can be seen from a long ways away. It is the incredible Aquaduct in Segovia, a monument to the past that we would rank with such man-made wonders as Boulder Dam, the Golden Gate bridge, Holland's Delta Works dams, and the pyramids. Nearly one hundred feet high, it has more than one hundred arches, and appears to be in perfect condition in spite of its imposing age (about nineteen centuries!). It is colossal, it is magnificent, and it is an imposing tribute to the engineering abilities of the Romans, not to mention the taste and restraint of the people who followed them—who didn't knock it down or deface it. It is a sight that takes one's breath away. It almost *is* worth a trip across the Continent.

Segovia is a nice town that lies about two hours northwest of Madrid. Not to give away all of its secrets, it also has old walls, a marvelous late-Gothic sixteenth century cathedal, and the Alcazar, a fortress-castle that nearly but not quite rivals in appearance some of Mad Ludwig's creations in Germany. This elegant former home of kings and queens is still furnished as it was in earlier days, and it is also very much worth seeing as another view of olden times.

Unsual museums

Among Europe's most interesting sights one must include the numerous open-air museums which are also indicative of the Europeans' devotion to the past. These unusual culture centers contain houses, farm buildings, workshops, mills, and

Segovia's ancient aquaduct

The authors' photo. Spain

chapels from olden times. Such buildings are dismantled and taken from their original sites to an open-air museum, where they are reassembled with loving care and with the same techniques and fasteners that were used originally. Most of them are staffed, at least during the high season, by people in period costumes who are living and working in the manner of their forebears of generations ago. They are found all over Europe, and many of them have "free" days, often on Saturday or Sunday. Any or all of them are worth visiting; they will make you a quasi-expert in European history—and teach you a good deal about seeing beneath the surface.

Belgium's open-air museum is at Bokrijk, which is east of Brussels near the border of Holland. With a grand total of 1350 acres, it is Europe's largest museum of this sort. It requires a lot of walking to see it all, but it is a stroll through time with many surprises. One can come here by early-morning train from Brussels and return that evening on a reduced-fare ticket, or stay in nearby Hasselt, rent a bike, and use it to cover the intervening four miles to this huge glimpse of the past.

Holland's Openluchtmuseum at Arnhem, which occupies about eighty acres of ground, contains more than 125 structures from Holland's past. Most of the buildings have a lived-in look, and indeed you will see people demonstrating the old-style techniques of making paper, draining water from land, farming, and so on, as well as beautiful furniture and costumes from Holland's past. The ever-thoughtful Dutch have designed walking tours of one, two, and four hours, although we have to say that if you are as healthy and as intellectually curious as we hope you are, you would be foolish to schedule anything less than a day for this marvel. Sadly, it is not open year round. But you can visit it between April 1 (or, if Easter falls before then, from the Thursday before Easter) to November 1. It is right next door to another attraction, a fine zoo and safaripark.

Denmark has several of these museums. Copenhagen's Frilandsmuseet, located just out of town by Lyngby, is an eighty-nine-acre park that is open year around, but only on Sundays from November through March. Near Skive (NW Jutland), there is an unusual one called Hjerl Hede, where townspeople in old costumes show how people in the past made a living on the heath. The Old Village contains forty re-erected buildings and Denmark's oldest farm. There is also a Stone-Age settlement which is inhabited and in full operation during July. Another open-air museum is at Aarhus, Denmark's second city. It contains fifty-five old buildings from the seventeenth, eighteenth, and nineteenth centuries in the center of the old town area. Still another one, a reconstructed town of twenty buildings called Funen Village, is located in Odense. Also in Odense is the Montergarden, a museum of cultural history that has sixteenth- and seventeenth-century town buildings.

Sweden's Skansen Open-Air Museum in Stockholm boasts of 150 old buildings. Here are whole farms, complete with animals, not to mention a zoo, art galleries, and an amusement park. Also in this area is the famous Wasa Museum. The Wasa, a mighty Swedish warship, ignominiously sank in the harbor on her maiden voyage in 1628. In 1961 she was raised and today she can be seen in all of her earlier near-glory, being sprayed constantly with liquid plastic and boric acid so that her timbers, unused to open air as they are, will not dry out.

Norway also has several of these tributes to her past. Oslo's Folkemuseum contains 150 buildings from all over Norway. It is located in the same area as the Norwegian Maritime Museum, the Kon Tiki Museum, and the Fram Museum, which contains the ship that has visited both Arctica and Antarctica. The most outstanding building in the open-air musem is a carefully preserved twelfth-century stave church. The Folkemuseum is open year round. There is another one on the outskirts of Bergen. Called Old Bergen, it is open for visits year around, but the old wooden buildings themselves are open only from May 10th through September 15th. It is a miniature nineteenth-century village, complete with old houses, workshops, and a marketplace. One hundred and twenty miles north of Oslo lies Lillehammer, the home of yet another open-air museum. Maihaugen contains one hundred old wooden buildings, all furnished with antiques representative of the buildings' original uses. The best sights are the nine-hundred-year-old stave church and the old Bjornstad Farmstead.

Still another of these reconstructed villages lies in Germany in a suburb of Kiel, a town named Rammsee. It contains fifty-four old reconstructed buildings. In Bavaria, in a small town named Tittling (not far from Regensburg), is the

Open-air museums indicate a difference in thinking about time and tradition between Europeans and Americans.

Museumdorf Bayerischer Wald, which contains old buildings brought in from the surrounding area of Bavaria.

Even more than Europe's countless old-town areas, open-air museums provide the possibility of seeing and gaining a real understanding of how our forebears lived in the dim past. They are extremely popular with Europeans, and any American should find them no less fascinating, especially in view of the fact that many of their buildings are much older than our country—and because many of our ancestors came from just such places.

Other well-known museums related to the preservation of the past include the Viking Ship Museums at Copenhagen and Oslo, the Renault Automobile Museum in Paris, and Porsche and Mercedes-Benz Museums in Stuttgart, the various national and ethnological museums found in the larger cities, and the small, sometimes highly specialized exhibits found even in the smaller towns, or in the castles. A cynic might well think that these thousands of displays of various sizes and forms across the Continent are probably just schemes to separate tourists from their money, but we don't think so. We've seen too many of them that charged either nothing or a mere pittance for entry. We think that their existence is somehow related to the Old World love of the really old world.

There are also many museums in Europe that are dedicated to the present and the future. One of these is the Danish Tekniske Museum in Helsingør, Denmark, which presents a history of science and technology, as well as a countless array of examples of how technology works today. Another is the Deutsches Museum in Munich. It has been called the most exciting technological museum in the world; whether it is or not we can't say, not having seen all of them, but it is certainly one of the biggest. It has over nine miles of aisles and exhibits.

Millions of people have visited this museum since it was built in 1925. It has a hands-on sort of character; you are encouraged to push buttons and to make things work for yourself. Some of its interesting exhibits include the plane-tarium; the aircraft section, filled with weird-looking old airplanes and gliders; the ship section, crowded with fine models and even a full-size nineteenth-century sailing ship; the ''Man and Space'' display; and the automobile collection.

If you have any interest in how our world works, you would find this museum an inspiring and fascinating place to visit. You could see other remnants of history such as a fifteenth-century printing shop and a medieval alchemist's study. But the museum is by no means dedicated just to the history of science and technology. Here you can also see the latest developments and discoveries of physics, chemistry, and engineering. If it is the sort of thing that interests you, you could spend a lot of time in this huge showplace.

There is another outstanding museum dedicated to essentially the same subject matter, but with a far different appearance and approach, at Eindhoven, Holland. It is called the Evoluon (pronounced more-or-less like a-vool-u-own), a marvelous non-flying saucer that is 103 feet high and 252 feet across (or in diameter). It looks like two shallow dishes with one sitting atop the other so their rims touch. The lower of the two is supported on columns by hinges, which allow for expansion and contraction due to temperature changes. The two saucers are squeezed together at the rim by 105 miles of heavy steel cables that surround them.

The inside of the structure is no less twenty-first century. It contains more than 65,000 square feet of floor area, on various levels, that are filled with the most imaginative displays you'll ever see on this planet. Your senses are barraged by lights, sounds, and movement. It is what anyone who has seen the movie *2001* expects an apartment house on the moon in 2050 to resemble. The exhibits are excellently done, and all captions and explanations are given in English. They are designed to show you not only what man's ingenuity has done *for* you, but also what it is doing *to* you. You can rent a cassette player that will explain in much more detail what you are seeing. The subjects covered in the museum include presentations of world population growth, scientific research, technology (sound, light, color, machines, nuclear physics, communications techniques, and computers), and industrial techniques. Unlike other science museums, it presents you with a philosophy, a not-altogether optimistic view of the future. Because of this it is more of an *experience* than a museum. You are invited to get involved: many of the displays require you to push buttons, turn cranks, and operate things to make it all work. It would be fascinating even to someone who didn't know a particle accelerator from a washing machine.

One expects to see little green men pouring out of Evoluon.

Netherlands National Tourist Office photo

Evoluon was opened in 1966 by Holland's big electronics company, Phillips. They sell themselves a bit in the museum, but not annoyingly so. The museum contains a nice cafeteria, a souvenir shop (the souvenirs are strange, and you'll probably buy something), and it costs about two dollars per person to enter. Open year-round (except for New Year's and Christmas), its hours are 9 a.m. to 5:30 p.m. weekdays, 10 a.m. to 5 p.m. Saturdays, and noon to 5 p.m. Sundays. It is possible to buy inexpensive Day Rover train tickets from almost any place in Holland to this understanding of the present and glimpse of the future.

Ingenuity applied to current problems

Now let's have a brief look at some of the ways Europeans are using scientific and engineering techniques to solve present-day problems. These again might be matters that would appeal to the intellectually curious tourist.

Everything in this subsection will be about the Netherlands, because this small country is unique in that so much of it lies below sea level, and much of its present land area has been taken from the water. There is no room for this heavily populated country to grow but into the North Sea. The Dutch have been fighting back the ocean for twenty-five centuries, with the result that they have become the best hydraulic/ocean/fluid-flow engineers on earth. The visible results of this expertise constitute some of the most unusual sights a visitor could hope to see anywhere.

When the Romans invaded the Netherlands just before the birth of Christ, they found the inhabitants living behind crude dikes. It is now known that people had been living in this area for thousands of years before that time. It is believed that these early inhabitants lived on the higher parts of the land and well back from the North Sea's occasional floods. Then, perhaps in the fifth century B.C., they began to build huge dikes against the ocean. These early walls were crude earthen structures that were washed out by the tides or eaten away by mollusks for centuries until the Dutch began to build their dikes with stone and concrete. There is also evidence that they were stealing land from the sea at least twelve centuries ago. History records the time when even the Amsterdam area was under water.

Today the Netherlands is much larger and shaped differently than it was centuries ago, thanks to the perseverance of the Dutch. They have stolen much of their land from the sea, protected it behind great walls, drained it, and made the resulting land arable and the captured water fresh. They refer to this work as ''shortenening the coastline,'' which seems to us to be a modest way to describe it.

Holland's symbol is the windmill, and the country still has about a thousand of them, but most of the larger mills are no longer used to drain the land. Their function has been taken over by huge pumps, which are far more reliable and effective, even if not as attractive. Today the windmills are used in several ways: as family dwellings, as museums, or just as tourist attractions, in which case the sails are often allowed to turn in the breeze. Most of them are kept in good repair, partly because the Dutch think of them as back-ups to the electromechanical pumps if things should ever really go against them again in their battle with the sea.

One of their earliest modern efforts to defeat the North Sea was to try to shut off the 3,000-square-mile Zuider Zee and turn most of it into a fresh-water reservoir and some of it into new farmland. The Zuider Zee project was started in 1919. The dam was built out from the land in both directions with stones and clay from the bottom of the Zuider Zee. As the last opening got smaller and smaller, the North Sea tides sent huge walls of water crashing through, washing out the bottom and carrying away materials as fast as they were dumped in. Finally on May 28, 1932, the Dutch built an underwater wall by the opening to calm the incoming tides and managed to close the dam. They subsequently pumped out over 500 million tons(!) of water, and worked hard to eliminate the salt that remained behind in the ground so it would grow crops. They have been successful, and today crops from these new territories (some of which are more than twenty feet below sea level) support a large part of Holland's population.

The dam, the Afsluitdijk, 22 miles long, 330 feet wide, and 22 feet high with a highway across the top, lies just north of Amsterdam. If you wish to see it, you have to take a bus to get there, and if you take one from Amsterdam, you will be put off the bus part way and told to cross the road and stand by a bus stop sign to catch another bus coming in another direction. This is the regular transfer point to go to the dam, because the first bus doesn't go there. The second bus comes along within a few minutes. Except for this transfer in the middle of nowhere it is a nice ride.

The new lake behind the dam is called the IJsselmeer.* Crossing the dam to reach the ''new territories,'' the polders on the other side, is an experience. Out on the wide dam you look off one way at the cold, bleak, grey North Sea; when you turn around you see the cold, bleak, grey IJsselmeer—and if the tide isn't strong in the North Sea it's hard to tell the one from the other. You can leave the bus at the Monument, the place where the dike was finally closed. It is a good place to get a bite to eat, to look at souvenirs, and to stand for a time and reflect upon the

*Names can give you problems in Europe. It helps (but not much) to remember that *they* would have trouble with Schenectady or Chickamauga.

mightiness of man at his best. It's an inspiring place. The next bus across will pick you up, either to take you back toward the Amsterdam area, or toward the polder area on the far side.

If you make this trip, on the far side of the dam you could head south down the side of the IJsselmeer and visit the land freshly stolen from the sea—the polders. We have always had an interest in how the Dutch turn this "new" land into liveable areas—how they drain off the water, how they build buildings on this initially muddy land, and how they lay out the villages and attract people to come and live in them. The difficulty of the job is shown by the fact that when the land is first drained it is so muddy and soft that a man can't walk on it. The Dutch use huge machines that have sufficient surface area to allow them to ride atop this ooze to trench out and drain the land. They have nicknamed such machines "ladies with big feet." But let's look at still another problem, which has to do with the first inhabitants of these new lands. The story suggests how unusual this country is.

When the land is first drained, various birds are the first creatures to try to move in, but, of course, there is absolutely nothing there for them to perch on or build nests in. They are followed by small mammals such as rabbits and mice. The mice are a particular threat because of the damage they do to new crops and because they multiply so rapidly. So one of the first jobs the engineers do is to build nests for falcons and put up shelters for owls, which are thus attracted to the area. They keep down the mouse population to limits that prevent them from completely taking over the new land. The whole thing is refreshing to those of us who have grown up in a culture that believes in sprays and poisons, and often forgets about the unpleasant side-effects on other flora and fauna (including ourselves).

A final remark about the new lands themselves. In the IJsselmeer, the Noordoostpolder (Northeast polder—see how easy Dutch is?) was built first, and it had a great error built into its design. Unlike the newer polder (you'll see it just to the southwest in the lake on our little map), it had no stretch of water left between it and the old mainland, and because it is lower than the original land, the water now drains from that area into the polder—a fact that in no way pleases the resident farmers.

There is another interesting difference between the Northeast and the Southwest polders. When the government began to build villages in the Noordoostpolder, they laid out small little towns at short and regular distances from each other. It was a logical, engineer's concept—but these little villages have never developed socially because of their size and placement. There is very little for the inhabitants to do in their off-hours. This error is not being repeated in the newer polder. The new one looks a lot less like a chessboard then the older one, not being laid out in such an artificial pattern. It has also struck us as interesting that the Dutch claim that when their government puts up such a brand new village, it first builds three schools and three churches, and the homes and shops all come along later. The polder that is now being built, just northeast of Amsterdam, is shown on our map by dotted lines.

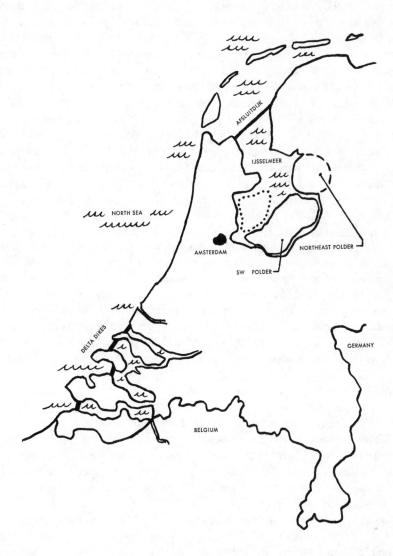

We have to confess that the polders are not scenic. Any traveller who could not appreciate the fact that they were recently under water might find them boring. They are absolutely flat, divided at close intervals by canals and drainage ditches, and frequently under cultivation. They look, of course, unnatural—and *that* in itself might serve to capture the interest of intellectually curious visitors.

That is by no means the end of the story of Holland's dramatic fight with the sea. The next portion has to do with a terrible flood that hit the southwest part of the country in 1953, a disaster that killed 1,835 people and covered vast areas of land with water. Right afterwards, while they were still repairing the damage, the Dutch made a national commitment to prevent such a thing from ever occurring again. They decided to dam off their southwestern islands from the sea, drain some of the water from the enclosed areas, and convert the remaining captured seawater into fresh water. They began work on the dams immediately, with one of them, the dam across the Haringvliet, being designed to have sluice gates to hold out the North Sea, and, when necessary, to release fresh water (and, in the winter, ice) from the inside into the sea. This required seventeen huge doors in each side of the dam. To start with, they dropped 93,000 concrete blocks weighing two and one-half tons apiece into the Haringvliet channel. They built an artificial island in the middle of this underwater footing, and built the first sluices on it as the tides flowed around each side. When they were done they opened the big doors so that the force of the tides would go through their gates, which allowed them to complete the dam out from the artificial island to the land on either side. These huge doors, slightly larger on the land side (420 tons each) and those on the North Sea side (400 tons each), were lifted into place by a 275-ton-capacity crane, a feat that was made possible by building each door in two sections. When the job was complete, there were seventeen inside and seventeen outside doors that could be lifted or lowered at the touch of a button to keep out the sea and to control the level of the water inside. They're big: when worked together, they can let out 26,000 tons of water a second!

When we visited the Delta Works recently we had the good fortune to meet one of the engineers who works in the control room controlling the big doors. He was a nice chap who spoke good English. Unable to think of anything else to say, we asked, ''Well, is it designed to keep out any storm the North Sea might ever put up?''

''No,'' he said, grinning. ''Do you understand 'the point of no return' in engineering design?''

''Yes,'' Alan the science writer said. ''I understand it.''

''We've designed the dam to withstand *almost* any storm the North Sea could give us in the next thousand years,'' the engineer said. ''But we couldn't spend the money required to withstand the *one* really big one that the computers told us could hit within that time-span. When and if we get *that one,* the water will come over the dam.''

''Good,'' Alan said. ''We should be okay. We're leaving in the morning.''

''Ah,'' the engineer said. ''But perhaps *tonight's the night!*''

The Dutch are sanguine and humorous folks.

When you visit the Delta Works today you see a long, long dam with a highway across the top of it and big doors in its sides. In the Delta Expo Building you will be shown a model and a nice film presentation that explains exactly how it was done, and you will be taken inside the dam to see the huge gates and their adjusting mechanisms. You may be surprised to learn that the complicated model of the whole thing in the Exhibition Hall took about as long to build as the real thing—which was fifteen long years. It is a marvel of hydraulic engineering, the only dam like it in the world, and if you come to see it, you will be glad you did. It is open for inspection from late March through the middle of October.

The fable about the boy sticking his finger into the dike is, of course, completely false. But the Dutch are a unique people living in a unique circumstance, and it should strike any American visitor that they seem so generally friendly, convivial, and at ease in view of their absolute vulnerability to the forces of nature or of anyone who might attack them. "We couldn't last twenty minutes against a real on-slaught by the sea or from any other country," they say. "Not twenty minutes."

And then they smile.

Final thoughts about European ingenuity

We have touched briefly upon some of the fairly obvious ways that Europeans differ from Americans in their devotion to the past and their development of technologies to answer needs related to the unusual geographic and topological features of their countries. Other examples of the latter would include the geothermal heating systems of Iceland; tunneling expertise in the mountain areas; Switzerland's unique defense system, *e.g.*, hidden tank traps in their roads; the French solar furnace in the Pyrenees; Sweden's underground submarine bases and air-fields; the carefully planned houses and apartments for old people in various countries; and, certainly not least, their efficient mass-transportation systems.

As stated elsewhere, the European train system is generally extremely different from ours. It is largely electrified, the rails are usually welded (which prevents the "clickety-clack" we are so familiar with), and the cars are ordinarily well designed for every human comfort. The engineering accomplishments shown in many of the mountain tunnels and bridges are spectacular, and we would like to describe one of them here.

Near Interlaken, Switzerland, there are two small villages, Grindelwald and Lauterbrunnen. From either town one can take a cog train to Klein Scheidegg, and from there catch another cog train to the highest railway station in Europe, the Jungfraujoch at 11,339 feet. Four and one-half miles of this trip are made *inside* the mountain, and the train stops at two places where huge windows have been cut through the mountainside to allow passengers to see the view. This engineering marvel took sixteen years to build.

From the Jungfraujoch station it is possible to go up further in an elevator to an area containing a restaurant, a post office, a weather station, and an ice palace. From there you can see an incredible panorama of mountains and glaciers, and you can return to Interlaken via whichever village you didn't start from. It is one of the great sights of Europe.

Another example of an engineering triumph in Europe that is considerably different from anything one might expect to see in the United States is the "sloping lock" at Ronquieres, Belgium, just thirty minutes by train south of Brussels. It has more to do with transporting goods than people, but it is fascinating nonetheless. For centuries freight has been hauled in Europe on waterways, both natural and artificial, and of course much of it is still moved this way. One hundred and fifty years ago work was started on a canal between Charleroi and Brussels, a route that had been dreamed of for nearly two hundred years previously. It was a difficult job because of the varying heights of land between the two cities, and when it was finished it had thirty-eight locks and one tunnel, all built to overcome the different ground levels encountered.

A lock, of course, consists of a portion of a canal in which water levels can be controlled by means of gates to allow ships to reach higher or lower levels on their journeys. That is their purpose and their disadvantage: they cost the passing ship or barge a great deal of time. It is not possible to pass through locks quickly.

After World War II the Belgians began to extend the canal on up to Antwerp, and to cut the travel time on the Charleroi-Brussels portion by installing a "sloping lock," which in reality is not a miraculous way of making water lie at an angle, but instead a system of huge railway tank cars that hold water and ships-in-transit, and haul them up or down a rise of 68 meters over a distance of 430 meters. These huge tank cars, which weigh about 5,000 tons when fully loaded, are level on top but slanted on the bottom at the same angle as the incline of the tracks over which they move. Because the boats carried displace their own weight in the water, the tank cars can carry vessels as heavy as 1350 tons, although instead they often carry four 300-ton barges.

The sloping lock was begun fifteen years ago, and over the succeeding years it has moved thousands of ships at relatively high speed from one level to the other. This stunning engineering achievement is a sight well worth seeing. It is open to the public only in May, June, July, and August.

One sees evidences of the Europeans' concern for moving goods and people in efficient ways. You are faced with a fantastic array of buses, trams, streetcars, subways, boats, and even horse-drawn conveyances all over Europe, and you can get anywhere you wish to go without a car. The intellectually curious traveller can't help observing the ingenuity involved in dovetailing all of these mass-transit systems together in such effective ways. It is a good example of both "people" and "things." Europeans obviously have a cultural and social attitude toward mass transportation that differs greatly from ours, and, as one consequence, have developed the requisite technology to get people from place to place rapidly, safely, and inexpensively.

Such things as efficient transportation facilities or the splendid condition of so many old buildings can be taken for granted and given little or no thought at all if one fails to realize that they are not just "foreign"—but are instead the results of basic attitudes and priorities, and represent a general philosophy and cultural background that is quite different from our own. As such they deserve more than the casual inattention they often get. If one understands, for example, that the great European cathedrals were not built to be places of worship, but instead as offerings to God, he will not be so confused by their size, ornateness, and lack of amenities for human comfort. Why include central heating, comfortable seats, and so on, for a congregation that was never envisioned as belonging there?

It would be a good idea to try to remember, when admiring the old buildings, that they aren't the way they are simply because they were so well built hundreds of years ago. It adds something to understand how much love and money has been spent by generations of people to keep them that way. Having such realizations will help you understand something about the real meanings and uniqueness of the countries you see all too briefly. Indeed, if keeping your mind and eyes open just causes you to spot something strange, *e.g.,* an odd decoration on a building, you will find that even if you can't discover what it means or symbolizes, it will have special meaning for you *simply because you found it.*

The main argument, then, is that even if your time in Europe is limited, you still don't have to see it superficially—and you won't if you develop the ability to look for meanings rather than just for sights, or can just see what's there to be seen and run the input through that magnificent computer you're carrying on your shoulders.

If you do gain such understandings on your trip, you'll learn something not only about Europe and Europeans, but also about your own country and yourself.

Chapter Sixteen
Four- and Five-Star Spots

*. . . no visitor can ever be adequately prepared to judge
a foreign city, let alone an entire nation;
the best he can do is to observe with sympathy.*

—James Michener

We agree fully with Mr. Michener: one *should* observe with sympathy. We have tried to be sympathetic with the countries we are about to discuss, but we are convinced that a useful travel book should not slide over a place's disadvantages in the name of sympathy. To do so would be unfair to you, so we will continue in this chapter to disclose negative as well as positive aspects of the places discussed, at least as they strike us. We do not intend to be unsympathetic, but neither do we wish to hide facts that we consider important and of possible use to you.

Some of the cities, towns, and areas we will discuss in this chapter are familiar to everyone, and some are not. We have omitted discussion of the various capitals and larger cities, with a couple of exceptions, mostly because information about them is readily available elsewhere. Indeed, many travel books imply that the most important town to see in any country is its capital, an opinion we find a little difficult to comprehend. We do not believe that once you've seen Paris you know France, or that Amsterdam teaches you everything about the Netherlands, any more than we believe that New York City is representative of the United States. We have also largely avoided talking about the tiny little villages because of the difficulty of imagining exactly what you would like to see—and because you can get tips about such places from the Europeans you meet. So most of the material to follow has to do with fairly intermediate-sized towns, some of which are on the tour routes and some of which aren't. We have avoided some rather well-known towns, like Heidelberg and Innsbruck, because they are fully described in other travel books. At any rate, we have tried to consider those we introduce from the standpoint of the liberated traveller.

One final disclaimer: while we have found reason to enjoy all of the places about to be discussed, we realize that you might not like some of them at all. We are not describing them in order to convince you that you should visit them; we are only trying to suggest possibilities, not so much in terms of *where* to go, but *how* to see the places you do visit. We are well aware, as you should be, that the weather, whom you happen to meet, and how you feel can color your opinions of the places you visit almost completely. But if any of these towns or areas interest you, you may wish to turn to other references for more exact details about what is there, what to look for, and so on.

Austria

Nothing will ever shake our conviction that the train ride through the Austrian Alps between Innsbruck and Salzburg (the route through Kitzbühel) provides one of the most stunning bits of scenery one could ever see. To ride along in perfect comfort watching the snowy, majestic Alps, the little villages nestled far down in the valleys, and the lovely Bavarian farms is by itself worth your visit to Europe.

□

For a thousand years Feldkirch has stood among the mountains on the banks of the Ill River, welcoming and sometimes fighting off visitors, many of whom were worse than modern-day tourists. It is close to the Liechtenstein border, which means it's quite close to Switzerland, relatively close to Germany, and not too far from Italy. It could consequently offer you a good location to settle down in for a few days and from which to make day trips in every direction.

The town itself is worth seeing. The church at Cathedral Square (1287) is nice, the little streets and shops are pleasant, and the old castle/fort that overlooks the town has a wonderful restaurant. It has a lot of entertainments for a small place: swimming, dancing, fishing, shooting, mini-golf, riding, tennis, camping, walking to and through a nearby game park, and mountain hiking with or without a guide. If you stay here for three days or more, the local tourist office will arrange for you to get a 10% discount on everything.

Other travel writers tell you to stay in Innsbruck; we suggest staying instead in Feldkirch, which is only 2½-3 hours away by car or train. If you do, and commute between them, you'll save money, you won't get lost, and you'll see better scenery.

□

Would you like to learn to hang-glide in the Alps from Heinz Dorler, the European champion of the sport? Such lessons are offered in Kirchberg am Tirol—a stupendously charming little village centered between Innsbruck and Salzburg, not far south of Munich, and about two hours north of the Italian border. As this makes obvious, like Feldkirch, it too would be a good center for outward day trips—and it would certainly be a nice place to come home to each night.

□

Kirchberg and the area surrounding it should not only fit anyone's mental picture of a Tyrolean village—but even improve upon it. We would challenge anyone to find a prettier place to visit. The town offers such activities as hiking on a fantastic array of well-kept and -marked trails, tennis (indoor and out), swimming, fishing, and skiing—which is excellent all around the village in winter, and possible year-around on a nearby glacier. It is just next door to Kitzbühel, the even more famous ski-resort, but its prices are generally lower and it is not so crowded with tourists.

□

If flowers, nature, and hiking sound like vacation components to you, you might wish to consider Wagrain, a quiet little village a little south of Salzburg that is known as Austria's most beflowered spot. Living there runs about one-third the cost of The Sound of Music town, which is only an hour away. The town's high season is the dead of winter, when skiers come from everywhere to speed down the slopes, but in spring, summer, and fall—when the snow's white is replaced by nature's brightest colors, Wagrain takes on a new life. She lowers her prices, and she then beckons to the nature-lover. The best flower months are July, August, and September, and the best hiking on the surrounding 40 kilometers of well-marked trails and mountain paths is available during the latter two months.

The town is not on the train line, so visitors in the know either drive in or catch postal buses from the nearby villages where the trains do stop. If you come here via rail, check connections with postal buses before you leave, and be sure you know where you will leave the train.

Accommodations range from posh to low-cost, and many farms in the surrounding heights offer low-priced rooms. Painters, bird- and animal-watchers, nature-lovers, and fitness-freaks could have the week of their lives in this overlooked Eden.

□

Austria has a fine open-air museum at Stübing, a small village minutes away from Graz, the country's second city. It is farm and farm-building oriented, and it is constructed as a mini-Austria, with buildings from the eastern part of the country being at the beginning of your stroll through the past, and buildings from the west (Voralberg) being at the end. Here you find homes, mills, barns, forges, kilns, a bakery, sawmills, religious shrines, a school, an aviary, and other buildings that were once dedicated to farm life. Most of the homesteads include the original furnishings and utensils, and it is extremely interesting to learn how walls were fitted together at the corners during various periods and in different places.

Graz is as yet still unknown to the wider world of tourism, at least in the sense that Innsbruck, Salzburg and Vienna are reputed to constitute all of Austria. As a consequence, it is still inexpensive and unexploited, and it provides its occasional visitor with some unspoiled sights and experiences. You can eat in the castle above the city (the outdoor tables offer exceptional views); you can visit a church/cathedral that is drab outside and splendid inwardly; and you can visit an armory/arsenal that has the capability of arming 16,000 soldiers with body-armour, chain-link underwear, shields, enormous swords, and rifles so large and heavy that an average man would be ruptured trying to lift them. There is a crazy and fascinating clock-tower above the city, and a wide variety of only slightly less interesting buildings and façades to see.

The local tourist office will give you a visitor's pass booklet if and when you drop in, a little document that will give you chits for free coffee here, a free glass of wine there, free tours of the city and the castle, and great discounts on other sights and experiences.

Belgium

Belgium is small, crowded, and fascinating. Bruges and Ghent are both marvelous examples of low-country antiquity, and they invite quiet strolls through their "old town" sections. Top sights in Bruges are the Belfry and Halles, a thirteenth-to fifteenth-century monument whose tower contains an eleven-thousand-plus-pound bell (!); the Church of Our Lady, which contains a statue by Michelangelo; St. Savior's Church, which is famous for its stained-glass windows; and the Episcopal Palace. There are also numerous museums, and a stroll through the cobblestoned streets of the older sections is a fascinating experience.

Ghent also has a fine old-town section (a short tram ride from the train station). Sights worth seeing in this area include St. Bavo's Cathedral, which contains van Eyck's wonderful *The Adoration of the Mystic Lamb;* St. Nicholas' Church; St. Michael's Church; a collection of old homes and guild houses; and the ancient (1180 A.D.) Castle of the Counts of Flanders. The tourist information bureau, which is directly across a small park from the train station, has a small folder that describes these and other points of interest, and provides an excellent walking tour of Ghent.

The first-time visitor to Ghent should not miss the pleasant little show in the Town Hall. With the help of a huge model, and cleverly used spotlights, recorded seventeen-minute presentations in English and three other languages tell the visitor all about the city's history—and a fascinating history it is.

□

Two Belgian towns of historical interest that are visited by many Americans and Canadians are Waterloo and Bastogne. Waterloo, just a short distance south of Brussels, is the site of Napoleon's defeat in 1815. Today Waterloo is a pleasant little town. The site of the big battle is dominated by a huge mound of earth topped by an enormous bronze lion that was erected by the Dutch government. It is one of the sites of human history and madness, and the resting place of fifty thousand men.

Bastogne, located southeast of Brussels near the border of the Duchy of Luxembourg, is the home of one of the great battles of World War II. Occupied by the American 101st Airborne Division, it was surrounded in December, 1944, by the Germans. The Americans held out day after day until the twenty-ninth of the month, when General Patton's tanks pushed through the lines and saved the city

A glimpse of why Bruges is a favorite town of American and Canadian visitors.

and the 101st. The major sights today at Bastogne are the placid fields that were areas of death and destruction thirty-odd years ago, the immense American memorial that is shaped like a star, a museum that displays the equipment and uniforms of the men of both sides who fought here, and a sound and light show-of-sorts that describes what happened here in 1944.

□

Ypres is another charming old city that could provide a tourist with a pleasant base of operations. With its many guild houses, churches, and its inspiring cathedral, it is a nice place to see in itself. The visitor can walk atop its ancient walls on two sides of the city.

□

Kortrijk is a nice small town that is not tourist-infested, although it would be if it were better known. It is located on the river Lys just a few miles from the French border, making it ideal for forays into the countrysides of both France and Belgium. Generally its hotels will charge in the range of twelve dollars to fourteen dollars for a bathless double, and there is a pleasant hostel there that serves clients of all ages. It can provide single or double rooms for just a few dollars a night for bed and breakfast. But it is necessary to add that not all of Belgium's hostels can accommodate people other than students. The tourist information offices can provide further details.

□

Brussels is a nice town, it is expensive, and it has a lovely square called the Grand'Place, a twelfth-century marketplace of ornate gold and gray buildings that takes one's breath away—especially when it is lighted at night. It is a square where one can stand, facing first one way and then the other, looking up at façades with his mouth open without feeling the least embarrassment. Everyone there, including Belgians who have lived in Brussels all of their lives, will be standing around doing the same thing. It is, incidentally, lighted in many different ways, one after the other, on weekend evenings between 9:30 and 11 p.m. There are also sound and light shows there on some weekend evenings, with commentaries in various languages (including English) about Brussels. There are also free concerts of various kinds in the Grand'Place in the summer. Times and dates can be obtained from the information office near the square.

Even if your plans only call for passing through Brussels you might consider making a brief stop between trains at Central Station and walking over three blocks to see this old square. It is an incredible sight, and we've never heard anyone who has seen it say otherwise.

Denmark
There is much to be said for southern Denmark, the area pretty much directly north of Hamburg. The village of Kolding is a picture post-card place. It is the home of a disintegrating seven-hundred-year-old castle, a lovely twenty-acre garden containing more than two thousand different plants and flowers, and many fascinating buildings in the downtown area. Be sure to examine the Tourist Information Office of Kolding with care. The building is ancient, and it's a beauty.

☐

And not far north of Kolding is a safari-park, much like Arnhem's, at Givskud. A nearby village, Rodekro, is tiny, charming, and very friendly, and, as we said a few chapters earlier, it would be a nice place to stay for a time and to use as a base for bike trips through the Danish countryside. Both of these villages, in fact, are on a bicycle route to Germany, which is not far away. The route is an old army road.

Also nearby is the six- to seven-hundred-year-old-village of Åbenrå, a place that is popular with tourists in the know. The whole area is beautiful, the sort of place that makes you better understand what you can remember of Hans Christian Andersen's fairy tales.

☐

Just southwest of Kolding, over on the western seacoast, is Ribe, the oldest town in Denmark. In addition to its lovely old homes, you can see there what is left of a twelfth-century palace/castle, and a very fine twelfth-century cathedral. If you were to enter or leave Denmark by this route along the coast, you would see many picturesque little towns and villages.

☐

Odense is also an interesting place to visit. It is the home of Hans Christian Andersen, and it is possible there to see where he lived and to learn about his life in this ancient town. We were impressed with the thirteenth-century cathedral there, a Gothic structure that makes your shutter-release finger twitch.

England
Bath advertises itself as "an architectural masterpiece among world cities," and it is, and one presumes from its fascinating Roman baths that it has been so for a very long time. Its Abbey, narrow streets, river, unusual gardens, and surrounding tree- and home-studded hills combine to give it the appearance of everyone's imaginings of what a charming English village should look like. Actually, there are eighty-five thousand people living in Bath, but it doesn't seem nearly that large. It has a surprising number of museums for its small size, including the Roman Baths and Museum in the center of town—a remarkable preservation of a two-thousand-year-old spa; the Museum of Costume—claimed to be the largest display of clothing to be found anywhere, including even an Underwear Room; and museums concerned with art, geology, bookbinding, carriages, toys, and, surprisingly, American history. It is an entertaining and edifying place to visit.

Free walking tours through the city are offered twice a day with guides who both love and know their ancient little town. It is one of those rare places that is not only a nice place to visit, but would be a marvelous place to live as well.

☐

Another popular spot with American tourists, second only to London, is Stratford-upon-Avon. With its half-timbered houses the town is worth seeing in itself, but of course most people go there to see Shakespeare's birthplace, Anne Hathaway's Cottage, and the Memorial Theatre (which struck us as being marvelously ugly). But the church where the Bard is buried, with the gardens and tree-lined

In the land of double-deck buses, Chester is a town of double-deck sidewalks.

entrance in front, is beautiful. Whether you'll love or hate the place we can't guess, but you may find it a bit too commercial to suit you, with Will Shakespeare's name on everything you see. There are tours from London to this old town, and it is always tourist-infested.

□

Located near the Welsh border halfway up to Scotland, (three hours from London), Chester is located in a most agreeable part of England. Surrounded by rolling meadows, stately old farmhouses, and four old castles, Chester is the only town in England which still has a completely walled-in section. The Romans started building it nine hundred years ago, and today you can walk along its top all the way around. If you do, you will see Roman soldiers' barracks, as well as the remains of the even-earlier Britons, being dug out, tremendous views of the Saxon-Norman-English town inside, and panoramas outside of the English countryside and even, on clear days, of nearby Wales. Guided walking tours on the walls and through the city leave the tourist information office in the city center twice a day.

Although part of it is walled in, Chester has a different character from such walled cities as Rothenburg in Germany. Here the walls cannot be seen from many parts of town, and there are many modern buildings inside the walls. But while it is not as pure in its antiquity as some walled cities, it is still fascinating.

Chester is famous for its "rows," a series of shops built one above the other with the top ones having enclosed walks above the street level that look almost like long balconies from the ground. There are many old half-timbered buildings, pleasant little pubs, and a cathedral dating from the tenth century. It was in this building that Handel completed *The Messiah*. There is also a six-hundred-acre zoo which has animals kept in open enclosures amidst beautiful gardens. You can travel from one part of the zoo to another by boat, a delightful way to do it.

One nice trip from Chester is a visit to the towns along the Welsh northern coast. It can be made in a day, or, for anyone who is really short of time, within a half a day by road or by rail. The first few towns are a disappointment. They are crowded with amusement parks, bingo parlors, and a half-million caravans (trailers) which are rented to people who spend some time there. If you come here by train, in about one hour you will arrive in Llandudno Junction, where you can get off and catch a bus at the curb in front of the station for about a mile in the direction from which you just came, where you will find Conway Castle. It is impressive, both in size and grandeur, and it is fun to explore. The whole trip can be made in three hours if time is important, and it is only one example of the many possibilities Wales offers to people who are visiting the western side of England.

□

Not having seen every city in England, we are unable to say categorically that York is the most appealing town to visit in the United Kingdom—so we will simply say that we, other Americans we've met, and countless Britons consider it to be an absolutely outstanding place to see.

York is located directly north of London on the major rail line to Edinburgh.

To get there takes approximately two and one-half to three hours by fast train. It is not overrun by tourists, at least not in the sense that Stratford *is*, and it is not overly large in size. Part of it is enclosed in medieval walls which do not quite cover the whole perimeter, but nevertheless provide a nice high two and one-half-mile-long walkway from which you can see the city from many different viewpoints.

York offers something to everyone, regardless of their range of individual interests. There is a large railway museum which contains an incredible assortment of locomotive and railway cars from England's past. There is an awe-inspiring cathedral called the Minster (described more fully in Chapter Fifteen),

The Shambles is one of the best-preserved (and best-named) medieval streets in Europe.

The authors' photo. England.

and a number of interesting and photogenic churches. There are excavations of both Roman and Viking structures to be seen, and museum displays of the artifacts that have been found in these digs. The Castle Museum, so named because it is located on the site of York Castle, is a huge exhibit of all sorts of remains from England's past, carriages, instruments of war, and re-creations of old streets, shops, rooms from private homes, and original old prison cells. There are other museums, an art gallery, a gallery of photography, botanical gardens, and many old buildings of historical significance that are open to the public.

Many of the city's streets are narrow, cobbled, and picturesque, with ancient buildings leaning toward each other, even across the streets in some instances. It is delightful to walk through these streets and to visit some of the little shops and pubs. There are excellent guided walking tours of the city, one of which is called "Haunted and Historic York"—an evening walk which is great fun that can be arranged through the local tourist information office. There are also bus tours into the surrounding countryside which are inexpensive, fun, and educational. They will show you English moors, dales (valleys), the coast, and quaint little villages. One such run takes you to Haworth, the home of the Brontë sisters, a touristy but nevertheless interesting little town.

For the liberated traveller, York is a Mecca. It's beautiful, it's relaxing, it's easy on the purse, and it offers something to everyone. It is a mixture of modern life combined with medieval England, the ancient Roman empire, and occasional influences brought here by the Saxons, the Normans, and the Vikings. It has always been cosmopolitan, in the nicest sense, and it still is today.

☐

Approximately an hour's train ride north of York is the beautiful city of Durham, built on seven hills (shades of Rome, Edinburgh, etc.). If you come into the station at night, you will see a particularly breathtaking sight, the great Norman Cathedral and immense castle that stand brilliantly lighted on one of the hills. Surprisingly, the cathedral is bathed in whitish-blue light while the castle is illuminated with amber tones, but it is aesthetically outstanding.

But Durham's beauty is also there during the daytime. The river Wear winds around the city and you can walk beside it in a wooded gorge and look at these two magnificent structures and also the rest of this interesting town. The city planners have done an excellent job of supervising modern building plans so the results blend into the medieval architecture. There are two museums of interest, the Durham Light Infantry Museum which traces the history of the County's own regiment and also features constantly changing art displays, and the Gulbenkian Museum which is devoted to oriental art and treasures. It is a city of immense beauty, but take your time walking around it. Once you go down a hill, you can be sure around the next corner you will be going steeply up. Durham is two and a half hours south of Edinburgh on the main train line from London, so it is a convenient stop for a few hours, a day, or a number of days.

□

Less than two and a half hours from London by train from King's Cross station lies the beautiful Roman city of Lincoln. Its outstanding architectural structure is its beautiful cathedral, The Minster. It was originally built in 1092, shattered by an earthquake, rebuilt in the 12th century, and added onto in almost every succeeding century. It boasts one of the four remaining original copies of the Magna Carta. It commands the hill overlooking most of the city of Lincoln. Particularly at night the floodlit cathedral seems to guard and protect all those below.

Equally protective of Lincoln, but in a military way, is the nearby Norman Castle. Incidentally it is a steep walk up to the Minster and the Castle, but it is a walk worth the effort. We suggest you take it slowly, stop often and look about you, but do avoid going up the street called Steep Hill. Save that one for coming down. You will be rewarded by not only the Minster and the Castle but by other fine examples of building styles including the twelfth-century Jew's House. There are fourteenth- and sixteenth-century half-timbered medieval houses in Lincoln with names like Green Dragon, the Harlequin, Cardinal's Hat, and White Friars House.

But you can do many things besides oohing and aahing and snapping pictures of buildings in Lincoln. There is a theatre open 52 weeks a year which boasts top performers producing pre-West End shows and number one national tour productions. In addition, there are two movie houses. There is opportunity to indulge in every sport possible from indoor swimming to boating, bowling to tennis, golf to football—or you can be a mere spectator. There are three major museums: The City and County Museum, depicting archaeological and natural history of Lincolnshire; The Museum of Lincolnshire Life, depicting history of the area from the 17th Century to the present; and the Usher Gallery, an art gallery which includes collections of Peter de Wint's famous watercolors, Tennyson manuscripts, watches, coins, etc. From Lincoln you can easily go to Boston where the Pilgrims originally planned their trip to the New World, Nottingham of Robin Hood fame, and the bracing North Sea coast.

Lincoln is not just a city on the route between Edinburgh and London. It is a treasure.

France

Despite our general aversion to large cities, we always remember Paris with fascination, because it is as different from other metropolises as San Francisco is (used to be?) from any other American city. Paris reeks of charm, generally (although in spots it just plain reeks). Top sights, of course, include the Louvre, the Eiffel Tower, Versailles, Napoleon's Tomb, the Arc de Triomphe, Notre Dame, Sainte Chapelle, and the Luxembourg Gardens. But beyond those tourist attractions, we have found Paris a fascinating place just *to be*—to walk about, to observe from sidewalk cafes, to compare what we saw with what we had read about it. The people, the traffic, the old buildings, the cobbled and bricked streets— *Comme c'est beau!*

One of the reasons we have included this mention of Paris (in addition to the mere fact of its elegance) is that we have found that one can get by inexpensively there if he must watch his budget. It is possible to find relatively inexpensive lodgings and meals if one has the time and inclination to do the necessary research and hunting around. A still better idea is to stay in a little village outside of Paris. Senlis, which is about a half-hour northeast, would be an excellent choice. It is quiet, inexpensive, and has a fine Gothic cathedral and some Roman ruins to see.

□

One of the cities that stays in our memories, primarily in terms of narrow streets, half-timbered houses, storks, and a fantastic red-colored cathedral—is Strasbourg, a truly great town in anyone's judgment. It is located at France's western edge, right on the German border.

□

Another French city that is well worth seeing is Rouen, a short distance northwest of Paris. It is on the route one would take if he were crossing the Channel for Le Havre. Not only is it a picturesque place to visit, but history buffs might want to see where Joan of Arc was held and interrogated before being burned in 1431. Also not to be missed is the incredible Notre Dame Cathedral.

□

Whether you visit France during the high- or the off-season, it would be nice if possible to pass through the French Alps. They are impressive, and many of them are furnished with cog-trains or cable lifts for visitors whose mountain-climbing skills are limited. Anyone with a car might wish to drive through the tunnel under Mont Blanc, entering on the French side and emerging in Italy.

Germany

A favorite route of travellers in Germany is along the Rhine River, a trip that can be made by boat or train (the tracks parallel the river), or, indeed, by automobile. The river banks consist of steep hillsides, many of which are guarded by ancient castles. The most scenic portion of the river lies between Koblenz and Mainz, a short boat trip, but many travellers take the boats from Cologne to Mainz, a cruise that takes a day. Such boat rides are free to holders of the Eurailpass.

□

It strikes us as difficult or impossible to do justice to Germany's Romantische Strasse (Romantic Road) with mere prose—or at least with *our* mere prose. It begins (at its northern extreme) at Würzburg and stretches down across Bavaria to Fussen or to Munich, depending upon which route you take from Augsburg. All of the medieval villages along the road are fascinating, but none are more interesting than Rothenburg ob der Tauber and its sister city Dinkelsbühl. The bus that runs along the Romantic Road makes lengthy stops in both of these walled villages. This bus run is free to Eurailpass-holders.

Both towns have modern areas, but what you want to see lies behind the gray walls that surround the old town areas. The oldest portion of Rothenburg was founded about the middle of the tenth century, and today it is a living museum. Its inhabitants live in homes that are centuries old but kept in perfect condition. A stroll along, or atop, the high walls is surely one of the most interesting walks anyone could take anywhere on the planet. Literature is available at the square where the buses park (and there are always many of them there from all over the Continent), information which will tell you what is where, including the churches, the main market place, the old torture chambers, and so on. There is a nice swimming pool just outside of Rothenburg's walls, which is complete with changing booths and rental lockers (small refundable deposit for padlock and key).

As we mentioned previously, Rothenburg is a nice place to stay over for a day or two, not only because of what it *is*, but also because a majority of its visitors *don't*. It primarily attracts day-trippers.

Further south on the road, Nordlingen and Augsburg are also living cities from the past, and Fussen is the home of two of Mad Ludwig's most beautiful castles, Neuschwanstein and Hohenschwangau. You will hear many tales there about Ludwig, his interest in ''modern'' devices, his extravagances, and his mysterious death—described to us by one local as resulting from ''trying to swim in shallow water with a large and unfriendly burgher sitting on his head.''

Neuschwanstein, with its artificial cave, fantastic throne-room, and Ludwig's incredible bedroom (be sure to look out of its window!) is the ultimate castle. As you will see from the decorations in the castle, Ludwig was a great admirer of Wagner, whom he knew well. It is not a sight to be missed, and it is open all year around. For a really fantastic view, stroll up to and across the nearby bridge. Take your camera!

□

Freiburg, a fairly sizeable city, is located in southern Germany quite near the French border. The capital of the Black Forest, it is a university town which is marked by a beautiful early Gothic cathedral with an incredible lacy 370-foot steeple. It is a building that took centuries to build, and of course it reflects the many architectural styles it grew up through. It is beautiful inside and out, and if you are lucky, as we were, you may be there when someone is playing the huge organ. The town itself is very attractive and not very commercialized, but the cathedral is outstanding. If you are ever there in the evening, you will find the lighted spire an unforgettable sight.

□

Eastern Bavaria is Germany's least expensive corner, all in all, and in our opinion its friendliest area. It contains many beautiful reminders of the past, sights to gladden the eye and brighten the camera lens of the beholder.

Regensburg makes a superlative argument for this point of view. It can document an 1800-year history, beginning with a Roman camp built in 179 A.D. It escaped bombing in W.W. II, so it now considers itself the best-preserved Italian-looking city in Germany. Its cathedral, which shows its age in many ways, was started in limestone, completed with green sandstone (which does not weather well) and has a lot to say to the observant. For example, look for the Devil on one side of the huge front doors (now sealed) and the Devil's Grandmother on the other side. No one now knows why they were carved there. Other strange sights to view include two carved pigs in one wall, and the rather Mona Lisa-like "Smiling Angel," the most pixiish-looking angel anyone has ever seen.

The City Hall is another fascinating building, where in the lower levels you can see the actual torture instruments that were once applied to local ne'er-do-wells. It is a sobering but interesting experience that gives you back a little of the respect for modern justice that you might have lost recently.

Being on the Danube, Regensburg provides its guests with the opportunity for sightseeing boat rides, the shortest of which is less than an hour, and the best of which is probably to Valhalla, a Grecian shrine that was built by one of Mad King Ludwig's forebears. This is a three-hour trip, and a memorable one.

Other nearby sights and experiences include crossing the Stone Bridge over the Danube to find the really inexpensive rooms, meals, and beergardens; visiting the Monastery Cloister Weltenburg about 14 km. out of town, where you can drink strange dark beer made by the monks on the premises and look into one of the most inspiring churches you will see anywhere; and looking in on the nearby Befrei-unghalle, a strange and not very attractive (on the outside) building dedicated to past German wars, battles, and generals, which is most pleasant to see (on the inside) and which is situated in a spot that provides an unforgettable view of the Danube.

In our judgment, Regensburg is worth ten Munichs, twenty-five Frankfurts, and fifty Hamburgs.

□

Nürnburg seems much smaller than its 500,000-person size, at least to a visitor who stays in its walled-in Old Town. One need not be here for more than an hour before he understands the city's long-standing fame for charm and beauty. The old-town area is filled with wide pedestrian malls, some fantastic fountains (one of which has a number of stone women whose breasts spout streams of water), classy shops and aged but new-looking buildings. There are nice churches, all of which are worth seeing for their stained-glass windows and priceless works of art. The basement of the Town Hall contains a labyrinth of dungeons for sightseers with curiosity about such matters, and there is a splendid castle to see and about three miles of old walls to explore. There are also many nice museums here, including an unusual museum of toys.

Nürnberg was about 85% destroyed during the war, but today it has been rebuilt pretty much as it was before the forties. The old town area is beautifully lighted at night, giving it a rather fairytale appearance. It's in a good location for day-trips to such tourist attractions as Rothenburg, Regensburg, Bamberg, Frankonian Switzerland, Bayruth, Frankfurt, Wurtzburg, etc.

It is not an expensive place, with rooms costing from about ten dollars a night up, and the local tourist office offers a one- to three-day package deal that includes bed and breakfast, admissions to all museums, entrance to the castle, the zoo, and the dolphinarium, free city sightseeing tour, a light meal of local food and drink, and so on for quite reasonable fees. Should you write to the local tourist office to inquire about this package (''Weekend Funnel'') and mention that you read about it in this book, you will get a 10% to 20% discount off the price charged for the same package by travel agents.

Nürnberg is a nice place to visit, and if a tourist could only see one German city, it would by no means be a poor choice.

Passau, which lies just on the German side of the Austrian border, is a pleasant 2,000-year-old city that enjoys the joining of three rivers—one of which is the not-so-blue Danube. It has a great cathedral, some narrow old streets, an over-1200-year-old castle to be explored (and you can get food up there), and a nearby animal park to walk through. We hope you see more animals there than we did; they were a bit shy when we were there. But the park is a beautiful place, and it is very popular with Europeans. It is called the Nationalpark Bayerischer Wald.

From Passau, you can take 3½- to 5-hour sightseeing trips down the Danube, or you can take Russian boats clear to the Black Sea. The ports of call on these trips are wowsers: Vienna, Budapest, Istanbul, Yalta, Belgrade, etc. There are American agents for these trips: Alumni Holidays, Inc., 11 E. Adams, Chicago 60603; and INTRAV, 120 South Central Avenue, St Louis 63105.

Passau is a nice place to see for itself, its prices are generally low for Germany, and it would make a good base camp for day-trips to Munich, Yugoslavia, Austria (especially Salzburg), Regensburg, and so on.

□

Lindau is a fairy-tale town that resides on an island in Lake Constance, right near the Austrian border. Replete with colorful, twisted, upward-reaching spires, cobblestoned narrow streets, and beautiful old buildings, Lindau is a place to walk around, for listening to church bells, and for thinking deep thoughts. To anyone who has a fix on antiquity, Lindau is nostalgia personified with ancient German sights, sounds, and odors attached. An off-season visit there offers a possibility for a sojourn in the past; a visit during the summer months means having to share the place with a million other gawkers.

Greece

As you no doubt know, the Parthenon in Athens is one of the world's great wonders. What you don't know, if you haven't seen it, is how incredibly beautiful and awe-inspiring it is. It is no longer possible to go inside the building, and some of it has been destroyed (by explosives stored in it by invading Turks, many years ago), but it is marvelous to look at from every angle. When you see it, be sure to look down its horizontal planes to see how much they are curved. The Parthenon's builders knew that straight lines do not look straight from a distance, so they didn't use them—but you may be surprised at the extent of the curvature.

The Parthenon is certainly one of the world's greatest treasures.

□

Delphi is located in a beautiful high spot in the mountains on Greece's mainland, about four hours from Athens. It is the legendary home of the oracles, who turn out to be ill-educated females whose words were considered sacred truth for many centuries. In actuality, their words were interpreted to clients by priests who were masters of meaninglessness—e.g., "Know thyself!"

The oracle sat in the Temple of Apollo, the remains of which you can see at Delphi today. There are also ruins of a Greek treasure house, a Castilian fountain, and a stadium where chariot races were run. These magnificent leavings seem to strike some visitors as "a pile of rocks," but they are actually quite interesting, and the setting is incredibly beautiful (the floor of the ravine in front is about 2,000 feet below). At the same time, it has become a terribly touristy place.

We wouldn't rate the town itself as good or bad. It's touristy, being composed of a number of hotels and souvenir shops, and yet not uninteresting in itself. It would also make a good base for day trips to the surrounding area, which includes Arakhova, just a few kilometers away, where you can buy (or see being made) woolen handbags, rugs, bedspreads, etc. It is an interesting little village, and public buses run regularly between it and Delphi.

Another interesting town is Itea, a port town on the Corinthian Gulf at the base of the mountains. About 30 minutes from Delphi by public bus, it has its points of interest, especially if you care about waterfronts and all that they entail.

In the opposite direction (up rather than down), you can reach the ski center on Mt. Parnassos, which is crowded with people in December, January, and February. There isn't much to see or do there in the rest of the year, but you can indeed look down over the rest of the world where people have the misfortune to live at lower altitudes.

Delphi can be reached in a number of ways. You can just go there, which strikes us as best of all. You can visit it through a one-day tour from Athens. You can see it (last) on the "Four-day Classical Tour" of Greece, a pre-arranged tour of such places as Corinth, Mycenae, Olympia, Epidaurus, Nafplion, and, finally, Delphi.

□

The 14,000-seat limestone theatre at Epidaurus should be counted as one of the world's marvels. Still used for performances, it was created in the 4th Century. It has the most incredible acoustics, allowing one to hear whispers on the stage from the top row. You will observe and hear demonstrations of this marvel from the guides of the tourist groups that are always there.

If it were unique in no other way, the theatre is surprising in that it hasn't been battered to bits by nature or unfriendly visitors over the centuries.

The ruins of the citadel at Mycenae are pretty incredible. This walled city flourished between 1600 and 1100 B.C., and when you see it you wonder how the huge rocks were cut and placed by puny humans; later people wondered this same question and surmised that the giant Cyclops had built the place.

If you visit this spot (which is still being excavated 100 years after the work began), you'll want to photograph the famous Lion Gate and think about the techniques your ancestors might have used to put it up.

☐

Nafplion sort of fits the picture in your mind of a Greek village. It's picturesque, and it would be a nice place to spend a few days. It has a pleasant stretch of waterfront lined with outdoor cafes, a fortress on an island in the harbor, and a huge fortress high above the town. It's only three hours from Athens by bus or car.

This pleasant little spot has a number of hotels, good restaurants, and a youth hostel (beds for about two dollars a night). The action on the waterfront at night is worth seeing, and becoming involved in if you can.

☐

People who care about athletics, archaeology, sculpture, and natural beauty should enjoy Olympia, the site of the first Olympic games almost 800 years before Christ was born. Much of the site has now been excavated (from as much as 15 feet underground), and most of it is pretty well broken up. But enough of it is standing to show you what was where, especially with a good guide and some imagination. You can then see the floor of the original gymnasium, and you can see in exact detail how it all looked nearly 1800 years ago from a model in the nearby museum. The Museum is a treasure trove, and its greatest piece is the famous statue of Hermes.

The site is enormously interesting; the town itself is not.

If you are not with a tour group, you might stand near one and hear the tales of what happened to women who tried to attend the games, what penalty was levied on unscrupulous athletes, and how Nero won his events. Many could be disappointed in the stadium itself. It is simply a level ground of stone with start and finish lines. There are no seats for spectators, because there weren't any then, though there were (and are) seats for judges. These grounds are considered sacred by the Greeks, so don't make the mistake of running in the stadium. It is a no-no, even if you're fast.

Finally, if you tire of ancient ruins, look around yourself. The Olympic site is situated in a magnificent location featuring tall majestic trees, and a view of hills and valleys that is quite beautiful.

Do be careful where you wander here; the grounds are home for snakes. When you see the spaces between and under the many rocks, you will understand why.

☐

Hydra, a pretty little town on a pretty little island in the Aegean Sea, looks about what you might expect a Greek village to look like. For a variety of reasons, the temperature not being the least of them, we would not recommend coming here in July or August. It was mid-October when we first saw the town, and it was packed with tourists then—and it was warm, almost hot out.

Old cannons greet you when you arrive in the harbor that is ringed by steep hills.

White houses, separated by narrow, winding streets, cover these slopes. Donkeys are used to carry the goods that arrive by ship up these grades, and they are very photogenic indeed. The whole scene is pretty sensational, and consequently, as you would imagine, touristy.

Hydra would be a nice place to spend a few days, especially early or late in the year, before the hordes of barbarians have arrived or after they have gone.

□

There are more tours of varying durations being run to more places by more organizations from Athens than one would believe possible. Some of the more notable ones are city tours of Athens proper (which includes a visit to the Acropolis); a half-day tour to Cape Sounion, where the remains of a temple to Poseidon is visited (a tour we found not to be worth its price of about $12 a person), a one-day boat tour to the islands of Aegina, Poros, and Hydra (cost about $25 per person, and worth it—especially Hydra). You may find it a long boat ride; but the boats are nice, providing good food and drink, as well as multilingual descriptions and histories of the places you visit. Landlubbers will find them exhilarating.

Ireland

Ireland has many villages and towns that attract foreign visitors, but perhaps none of them is more popular than Killarney. This attractive little town, about 200 miles from Dublin and 80 from Shannon Airport, is located in the southern mountains near other tourist attractions such as Limerick, Cork, and the beautiful and numerous peninsulas that make up the country's southwest coastline.

Killarney is charming. The city center consists of shops, delicatessens, hotels, B and B's, and a plethora of pubs. The latter are lively at night, many of them featuring the singing of old Irish ballads (and if you don't try the beloved dark Guinness ale, you will have missed one of the world's great taste treats).

The surrounding area is fantastic. The scenery, as the old postcard saying goes, is great: mountains, waterfalls, castles, flora and fauna, pretty winding roads, the countless walking paths into the forests. A favorite day-trip from Killarney is the "Ring of Kerry," a 109-mile trip that can be made by tour bus until October 1st, and by car year around. The nearby village of Kenmare is a cute little place. The whole area is covered with farmhouses that provide visitors with rooms, meals, and, in many cases, free fishing. In 1981 they cost about $12 for a single room and breakfast, in the range of $11 each for dinner, and many of them would rent the accommodations alone for $6.50 per person. Prices are about the same in downtown B and B's and guest houses in Killarney.

Although we have resisted naming specific lodgings in most places, we are going to make an exception here for a guesthouse we have visited in Killarney, simply because we liked it so much. Called Linden House, it is an exceptional place to stay. The food is superb, all double rooms have bath or shower and toilet, and the charge for a double room (including breakfast) in 1981 was $13.00 per person, with singles running $16.50. The owners and members of the staff couldn't be nicer. Home was never so comfortable and pleasant as the Linden in downtown Killarney.

Holland

Delft is a marvelous old city interlaced with canals which are overhung by beautiful trees. The local tourist bureau, which is located on the Marketplace (three canals, or four to five blocks, from the station) has a fine little booklet that tells what's where, and we will quote a few words of it here: "It is a true open air museum of old Dutch architecture through all its periods, full of bourgeois splendor and etched with history." We couldn't have said it better.

The New Church (which, being of the fourteenth century, is not very new) stands at one end of the Marketplace near the V.V.V. (the tourist office). It is the resting place of some of Holland's Royal Family. At the opposite end of the market square is the Town Hall, another interesting edifice that is dated as seventeenth century, with the tower from the fourteenth century (how they managed that we don't know). Other places to visit include several museums, the Old Church (thirteenth century), the Royal Delftware factory, and the East Gate (fourteenth century), and the Prinsenhof Museum, a furnished castle-of-sorts that is fun to explore. In the summer it is possible to take boat rides on the canals, although the locals have expressed the view to us that the ride is not worth its price, so we haven't done it.

Delft's other great virtue, at least to us, is that it is surrounded by some of the prettiest bicycling country we've ever seen. Marvelous little bike paths, some of them atop the dikes, run in every direction to surrounding villages, and the countryside is pure Dutch—ducks, flowers, greenhouses, and canals.

□

Maastricht, the oldest and southernmost town of any size in Holland, was a part of the Roman Imperium in the dim past. Maastricht was left to its own doings when the Roman legionnaires went back to Rome in the fourth century to try to fight off the barbarians. Maastricht people then spent a lot of time fighting Napoleon's troops, and, incidentally, losing, and later trying to decide whether to belong to Belgium or the Netherlands.

Today most of the walls around the city are gone, but some of the gates remain, and there is one nice section of the old wall that has a pleasant walkway along the top. Maastricht's architecture doesn't look Dutch, having more of a French or Italian appearance. There are, of course, nice old churches there to visit and photograph—one was started in the sixth century (and completed six hundred years later!), and another was built in the 1200's. The town's streets are narrow, cobbled, and winding; without (or with) a map you can be lost in seconds. Markt Street, for example, winds around an old square, and building numbers seem to start with "1" at every corner.

One of the area's main attractions is the nearby (fifteen kilometers) town of Valkenburg, a popular resort for Dutch travellers. It boasts of old Roman ruins, plus many other attractions, including—hold your breath—hills, including Holland's only lift! But perhaps the area's biggest attraction is Mount St. Peter, a hill just south of Maastricht that was formed eighty million years ago of a soft kind of sandstone that hardens in the open air, making it quite suitable for building construction. It has been mined for a long time; the Roman historian Pliny described the man-made caves formed by this digging in 50 A.D. Today the tunnels number more than twenty-two thousand, stretching more than two hundred and fifty kilometers in all, clear into Belgium in one direction. It is always fifty degrees Fahrenheit in the tunnels, and their walls are covered by visitors' names, by sculptures, and by old charcoal drawings—including a large copy of Rembrandt's *Nightwatch*.

You can visit these caves, but only with a guide (who will charge a toll of about one dollar per person). He is worth it; people have gone in on their own in the past, become lost, and died. The local V.V.V. office, which is an excellent one, can make arrangements for you.

□

For someone coming into Holland from France or Belgium, Middelburg (on Walcheren Island) would be a marvellous place to make a first stop. This fifteenth/sixteenth-century town is famous for its national monuments; every other building in town is considered to be one. It has been under restoration for many years, having been badly bombed and burned during World War II, as well as flooded when bombs breached the dikes of Walcheren Island. It has a charming old medieval abbey, a nice museum, a town hall considered to be one of the most beautiful in Europe, many nice hotels and pensions, which are largely within the strictures of a budget-traveller's pocketbook, typically pleasant Dutch shops and stores, and another miniature town like the one at The Hague, this one a one-twentieth-life-size model of Walcheren Island that shows such landmarks as Middelburg's Abbey. All this beauty and charm is located in a village populated by only thirty-six thousand inhabitants, a number that is swelled enormously in the summer because of the area's popularity with European tourists.

Middelburg would make an excellent base for bicycle or bus trips to other lovely villages just a few kilometers away. One of these, Veere, a tiny, tiny little hamlet, is world-renowned for its years and its authentic charm, including its fantastic Town Hall (1474) and a beautiful church dating from 1384. There you can see some of the town's original fortifications, including old cannons, and, we must warn you, you will think are seeing every other tourist in the world if you try to fight your way through its streets during the heights of the high season.

□

Near the center of Holland, just a pleasant bike or bus ride of about fifteen miles from Amersfoort, is the ancient village of Naarden, which may have the strangest shape of any town in the world. Naarden is a well-fortified little town on an artificial island created by the moats which surround it. The land inside the water is roughly circular, its perimeter having six arrowhead-shaped peninsulas jutting out into the inside moat. The water between these "arrowheads" contains small artificial islands, and all this is surrounded by a wall and yet another moat. It was designed to let the town's defenders of old fire at attackers from every direction, and you will see the gun ports and some of the cannons they used. It apparently worked; we were told that the town was never taken over the centuries. It is possible to walk around the city on top of the wall, and indeed you can even go into it to view such attractions as the town museum built into one of its cellars.

Naarden itself is a wonderful place to walk about and see the sights, one of the best of which is the elderly City Hall, which contains some beautiful furnishings and a three-dimensional model that shows exactly what the places looks like to a high-flying bird. And it looks very strange indeed, a true relic of the dim past.

□

Finally, we shall mention one last ancient Dutch village that is the sort of place independent travellers like to discover for themselves before the new barbarians, the tourists, take them over. And not many tourists have been here yet. Heusden is surrounded by a wall, outside of which is a series of moats, outside of which are other defense walls. There are three old (but operating) windmills sitting on the walls, and the buildings in the little town are old, old, old. Indeed, time and the destruction of various invaders have taken their toll, but the Heusdeners have been busily restoring the entire place to what it used to be, and in 1980 the work was nearly complete.

Heusden can be reached by bus (line ALAD BV, bus number one) from the city of Den Bosch. That ride will take the visitor southwest for thirty minutes—and back in time a thousand years.

Iceland

At first glance, Iceland is a bleak, barren, volcanic sort of lunar surface. It shows you what the earth looked like when it was young. Located about two hundred miles below the Arctic Circle, it is the fifteenth largest island on earth. There are few trees here; they were turned into buildings long ago, but today the Icelanders are planting new trees for the future. The country is largely devoid of people as well. Its forty thousand square miles contain only a quarter of a million people, ninety thousand of whom live in Reykjavik (Rayk-ya-veck), the capital city.

One's second impression of the country is somewhat different. The rocky, twisted landscape doesn't change, of course, but a closer look at the place shows the visitor brightly colored buildings and a style of architecture that is strange— even alien—but nonetheless interesting. It looks like a cross between some of Russia's more utilitarian buildings and those of the old Incan Empire. There are many sorts of woolen articles of apparel for sale, not to mention the simple and beautiful items of Scandinavian design that are sold everywhere. The Icelanders believe in keeping up with, or ahead of, their neighbors, and their prices are out of sight. But their country is incredible, and every traveller with explorer's blood in his veins should see it at least once.

Iceland's inhabitants, descendants of the Vikings, all seem to speak English, and they are a pleasant people. It is a land of fishing, statues, concrete buildings, scenic geysers, active volcanoes, sheep, and Icelandic ponies (and they look like what you would get if you sent to Hong Kong for a horse—small, fuzzy, short-legged, they seem often to be running like mad and getting nowhere.) It is an unpolluted land, clean and rather virginal in character, and it is a place where people can swim year-round in the thermally heated swimming pools. It is different, and it offers a fine bonus to a trip to Europe.

Italy

Venice is more beautiful and interesting than its photographs. When and if you visit Venice, you will want to tour its canals, walk its narrow streets, and cross its countless bridges. You will certainly want to visit the Piazza San Marco (Saint Mark's), where you will see the magnificent Basilica and the Doges' Palace. Looking in any direction from the center of this square will make anyone's heart pound. It is one of the world's great sights. There are many islands to be explored across the lagoon, where one can view Italian skills in making lace and beautiful glass figurines. Very few cities in this world have a character that is entirely their own, but Venice certainly does.

Those famous gondoliers, it turns out, can sing—and they are quite willing to make their passengers pay outrageous prices to enjoy the sights of Venice while being serenaded. Maybe it's worth doing once, but you can see the same sights (without the musical accompaniment) for pennies on the *vaporettos* or *motorscafi* (boatbuses). And if you do take a gondola ride, make an agreement about the price *before you go*—and then *stick with it,* no matter what develops. Venice, being the tourist haven that it is, is pretty expensive all the way around. The best time to visit is in September or early October. The weather is still nice, and the tourists are mostly gone. It will consequently be a little less expensive then.

In spite of our personal aversion to such travel techniques, we have to point out that one could go to Venice from Innsbruck and back again within twenty-four hours. The whole trip takes about six hours, which would permit the traveller to see the Italian countryside during one leg of the trip, get a few hours' glimpse of Venice, and get some sleep on the other leg. So if you felt that in spite of Italy's strikes and other problems, and Venice's high prices, that you would like to have at least a few hours there, this is one way you could do it. We have known of people who have done this, leaving most of their valuables stashed in a safe spot in Austria. If you do stay overnight in Venice, you can avoid the city's high hotel tariffs by staying in Mestre, a little village just a few minutes by bus (about five miles) from the center of Venice.

□

Verona, which is a stop for trains between Venice and points north, has a Roman coliseum that is better preserved than Rome's (which is now closed to the public anyway). It is consequently worth consideration for at least a short stop-over for travellers who are passing through the area.

□

Lovers of art have always considered Florence their Mecca. It is full of beautiful buildings, and many of them are filled with stupendous works of art. The highlights of the city are the colorful cathedral, the Campanile, countless museums, churches, and palaces, the Baptistery of San Giovanni, and a wealth of shops selling paintings, jewelry, ceramics, leather goods, antiques, and fine clothes. Florence is an Italian center of culture, and if you should have problems finding a room at an acceptable price, try the little villages outside of town. They are all connected to Florence by tram lines.

Liechtenstein

Does the idea of visiting a pint-sized country appeal to you? Like a fine jewel Liechtenstein (LICK-ten-stine) can dazzle—especially when you get behind the surface (Vaduz, the capital, which is the arrival point for nearly all visitors) to the mountains and small villages which are only minutes away. These beautiful spots are easy to visit via the little country's excellent bus system, or, if you have a car, the fine highway system.

Liechtenstein is a miniature Switzerland. The coin of the realm is the Swiss franc, although the language, perhaps oddly, is German. You can get to Vaduz by car or Swiss postal bus from Buchs or Sargans in minutes. The Eurailpass or Swiss Holiday train pass are both accepted for this short ride. You then face 61 square miles of hiking, skiing, concerts, theatre performances, fishing, riding, swimming, mountaineering, tennis, bowling, hang gliding, or just looking at some of the most sensational scenery in the world. Don't try to come by train (there is no station in Vaduz) or by plane (there is no airport).

This small country offers a big seven-day discount package that allows the visitor to stay in any of more than 40 hotels, guest houses, or private pensions across the country, admissions to all museums, wine-tasting in the Prince's vineyard, a ride in a chairlift, walking tours, maps, passes to swimming pools, and, in some cases, a main daily meal in addition to breakfast. Prices range from less than $100 to a bit over $200, depending upon the kind of accommodations you want. If the idea interests you, write the Liechtenstein National Tourist Office, 9490 Vaduz, Liechtenstein for information or bookings, or write any of the Swiss National Tourist offices.

Luxembourg

Formerly called the Gilbralter of the North, Luxembourg City possesses many reminders of the past—and for those who haven't the time or inclination to visit any of the rest of the little Duchy, many of these sights can be seen right in the capital city. There is a bus tour for slightly over five dollars that leaves from outside the railroad station, and, better yet, there is a walking tour of about two hours' duration that includes the most interesting sights. This hike doesn't cover everything, of course, but it is possible to walk for many miles past, on, and through the old fortified walls. The tourist information office will provide you with a description of the walking tours.

The huge ravine through the center of town adds a great deal to the attractiveness of Luxembourg City.

A bit before 1000 A.D. a castle was built here, and later, walls were built from it around the town to defend it from marauding neighbors. It was nevertheless captured many times, and its various temporary owners added to the fortifications while they were in residence. At its peak, there were three fortified girdles around the city, twenty-four forts, sixteen more heavily armed defense areas, and a sixteen-mile-long network of casemates that housed workshops, kitchens, sleeping areas, and thousands of horses and soldiers. Between 1867 and 1883 much of this huge fortress was dismantled because Luxembourg had become a neutral country, but because almost thirteen miles of the tunnels remain, there is still a lot to see today. In fact, it is so big and complex that new discoveries about it are still being made. Only a few years ago important remains of the old original castle were located. The walls and fortifications provide a grand sight in June, July, and August, when they are beautifully lighted in the evening.

Another place that many Americans visit is the American Military Cemetery where General George Patton and five thousand of his men are buried. It is one of the major stops on the city bus-tour route.

□

One of the best ways to save money and to get to know something about the Grand Duchy of Luxembourg is to settle down in some small town outside of Luxembourg City. Echternach is an ancient town, going back to the time of Christ, and is consequently full of photogenic old buildings and views, including medieval walls. It is a short distance northeast of Luxembourg City, and there are buses between the two towns.

□

Vianden is another attractive town. It boasts an enormous castle, walks through and views of nearby picture post-card scenes, incredible old ramparts, and a charm that has hypnotized many travellers in the past. It is north of the capital on the Luxembourg-German border.

□

Clervaux lies in the northern part of the country, toward the south of Holland and the edge of Belgium. It is medieval in character, with a fine abbey, a beautiful church, a chapel, and many agreeable sights on the slopes around it. Like many Luxembourg villages, it also has a youth hostel and a first-class campground.

Portugal

Many tourists fly into Lisbon and then head directly south to the Algarve, Portugal's lovely southern coast. It is always crowded with sun-worshippers, and people swim there in the Atlantic pretty much year round.

If you are going to make this trip by car you should have no problems except for the occasional bad stretches of road. If you are going down by train, your journey faces an unusual beginning: you cannot board a train for the Algarve in Lisbon. Because the bridges across the river to the south do not carry trains, it is necessary to begin your trip by taking a ferry boat across the huge Tejo river, a small voyage that will land you in the train station at Barreiro, where you can catch your train on southward. (A word of warning: if you wish to get there within a week, get a direct or rapid train—avoid the locals, which are often passed by donkey carts.)

There are many nice places on the Algarve coastline to be visited, but our favorite place is Albufeira, partly because of its location in the center of the coast, and partly because it is a charming place in itself. The Atlantic pounds it on one side, while its other flanks are guarded by steep rocky cliffs. It's a lovely place.

From Albufeira it is possible to make visits up and down the coast by bus, train, or car. High points include Portimao, a pleasant fishing village; Lagos, a former Moorish town that has remains of 8th-century walls (and five miles west is Ponta

Piedadi, where you'll find a lighthouse and breathtaking views of rocky arches in the sea); and Sagres, another pretty fishing village.

□

The Algarve is nice, but there is more to Portugal. Just north of Lisbon, for example, is an old walled city called Obidos. It is a quiet place (maybe a bit dull for some people), but it is a great find for those who care about the past. It has two fine places to sleep, a pousada inside the walls, and an estalagem outside.

Still further north is Nazaré, a coastal fishing village that might have been created by a European calendar designer. With its sandy beaches, high rocky cliffs, cable railway from the low part of town to the high, its fishing fleet (made up of the strangest, most colorful little boats found anywhere), Nazaré is a find. Although small, it has a number of fine restaurants and hotels, little shops (most of which are pretty tourist-oriented), and some picturesque streets. About two hours north of Lisbon, the town is not on a train line. Rail passengers have to get off at nearby Valado and take a bus or a taxi to this lovely little place.

Still further north is Coimbra. While its narrow winding streets and many levels up and down the slopes make it an easy place to get lost, it provides some fine buildings to see, including a palace, castle museum, cathedral, churches, and attractive shops. It also has a medieval university, the second oldest in the world. Perhaps its most intriguing sight is an excavation of a walled Roman city at Conimbriga, which is about ten miles away. Coimbra buses run to a spot about a mile from these ruins, which requires one to get a taxi for the remaining distance, or to have a pleasant walk.

Way north in the country, in the wine region, you discover Braga, a 2000-year-old town that shows its heritage in Roman, Visigoth, Romanesque, Gothic, Manueline, Baroque, and Neo-Classical architectural styles. It is a fascinating menage of buildings, old streets, tiled walls, and surprises around every corner. Its fine Church of Bom Jesus, which should not be missed, offers a superb view of this old city. The bus to this religious shrine leaves every few minutes from the corner opposite the tourist office in the center of town.

□

To the east of Lisbon one finds Evora, a charming town that has a lovely pousada, a five-star estalagem, and a few nice pensions. There is a relic of an 1800-year-old Roman temple, 14th- and 17th-century walls, two palaces, a cathedral, an ancient university, and a number of interesting and not-so-interesting churches, some of which suggest to the uninitiated eye a total lack of uniformity in style and character.

Evora is a worthwhile stop for a day or two. Nearby points of interest include Estremoz and Vila Viçosa, towns of considerable historical importance to Portugal. The latter was the home of royalty during the Middle Ages and the Renaissance, and consequently contains a castle, two palaces, a fortress, and a number of old churches.

Portugal has much to see, and there *are* three directions to go from Lisbon.

Scotland

Although we have usually ignored Europe's capitals because they are so big, so costly and frequently so unrepresentative of the country, as with Brussels and Paris, we are making an exception here. And Edinburgh is indeed exceptional. It is cosmopolitan but friendly, small but filled with things to do, an exciting town that is known for its steep hills, antique shops, marvelous pubs, and fine stores. It is also famous for its "Royal Mile," a street that runs between a castle and a palace that is occasionally occupied by Britain's royal family.

Among its other virtues for tourists, Edinburgh has one of the finest tourist offices in Europe. It is next door to the railway station in the center of town, and it will provide you with information about Edinburgh itself or the whole country. It offers a "Book a Bed Ahead" service, and it has a computer-booking system. This not only provides you with instantaneous information about room prices, availability, and facilities, but keeps you from having to stand in the long lines that this function ordinarily requires in tourist offices.

Accommodations are not expensive here. The city is covered with B and B's, guest houses, small hotels, and deluxe emporia. The University of Edinburgh rents rooms in its residence halls during the summer months.

The city offers many possibilities for recreation. It has more than 30 golf courses, a fantastic park in the city that offers views from on high, many museums, photogenic old churches, an outstanding botanical garden, and a huge, 80-acre zoo. This institution is open every day of the year, and at 3:30 every afternoon provides a sight you can see nowhere else in the world: a walk around one end of the place by a huge group of penguins apparently headed for afternoon tea. These strolls have taken place for the last forty years.

Two more of Edinburgh's interesting sights, not far out of the city, are bridges. The Forth Road Bridge, a modern suspension bridge, opened in 1964 and made the ferries that had long crossed the River Firth obsolete. The other bridge, which is not far from the first one, is the Forth Rail Bridge. Carrying only trains, it was opened in 1890 and immediately recognized as one of the engineering wonders of the world. It still is; you could look at it forever and never understand how it could have been built nearly a hundred years ago.

The area surrounding Edinburgh is unbelievably beautiful. There is a white sand beach at Gullane. There are lochs (lakes), of which two, Loch Lomon and Loch Katrine, are well-known to travellers. Callander, a charming small village only 40 minutes out of the capital, has dozens of rooms to rent. Finally, out of the immediate area one can consider such tempting places as Loch Ness (as monstrous as that sounds), Dundee, Aberdeen, the Isle of Skye, and, of course, the Scottish Highlands. There are many interesting day trips from Edinburgh that can be made on tours, by taking a train, by coach, or in a rental car.

Edinburgh is rare among Europe's capitals in that it won't bore you, break you, or burden you with difficulties or problems. The Edinburghers speak English (with a wee burr), they like people, and they are kind and generous. The old saw that the

Scot is stingy and a little aloof is entirely wrong. And the ancient rumor that Edinburgh is pronounced as if it were spelled "Edinboro" is entirely correct.

Spain

On Spain's northern seacoast lies a city that strongly resembles Monaco, with large white buildings serving as a backdrop to a long, sunny, golden beach. But it is not, at least altogether, a rich man's town. As a world-famous resort area, San Sebastián draws its share of dukes and princes and wealthy industrialists, and overall it seems a bit on the high side for Spain—but it is a fun place even for us less-fortunates—it does not seem to put you down merely because you are on foot rather than behind the wheel of a big Mercedes.

The town offers a variety of entertainments, ranging from swimming in the surf to climbing on the incredibly craggy rocks that reach into the sea. It does not, as far as we could see, have much to boast about in the way of old or exceptional buildings. It has been a sort of playground for a long time, and it is crowded with fun-seekers during the summer (when it is also the temporary home of the Spanish government because of Madrid's heat). So even though it is not as hot as southern Spain, summer is still not a good time to visit. Prices are high, the town is packed with tourists from everywhere, and it can be pretty warm. There are many hotels, pensions, hostels, and even apartments available for rent year around, and most of them will force you to take at least a demi-pension eating arrangement, which, as elsewhere, is a good deal if the place has a good cook.

All in all, then, San Sebastián might be a good place for a liberated traveller during off-season. It is even closer to France than Barcelona (and a better place to visit, in our opinion), so it offers a tourist who is close by a chance to learn quickly whether he might wish to explore Spain further or to turn around and go the other way.

One possibility for peseta-squeezers would be to stay in a nearby small village on the sea named Fuenterrabia. It is a lovely little town, only a few minutes and a few cents by bus from San Sebastián, and it is possible to get a single room there for under five dollars. However, anyone who has a hankering to sleep in a castle could also try that in Fuenterrabia. There is a *paradore,* a government-owned hotel, high above the town and the water, that was a castle in the days (as they say) of yore. This absolutely incredible "hotel" is three-star, and it has only sixteen rooms (all with baths). A double room lets for about $10.00 a day, a bargain if one wants to sleep with the ghosts of knights. Many people do, so it is necessary to have advance reservations for this one. The town itself is almost on the Spanish-French border.

□

Seville was the city immortalized by Bizet in *Carmen,* and anyone fortunate enough to visit it will understand why: it is surely one of the most lovely, romantic cities anywhere. It is particularly unusual because of its Moorish architecture. It is a long way from the center of things, being six hours by rail south of Madrid (which itself is about a day southwest of Paris) but one could certainly argue that any visitor to Spain who missed it could consider himself unfortunate.

Seville's skyline is marked by towers and steeples, the most notable of which is the Gold Tower, which has occupied the left bank of the River Guadalquivir since 1220 A.D. The main tower of the Giralda, the third-largest cathedral in Christiandom and one of the last to be built in the Gothic style, was begun in the twelfth century. It is the resting place of several members of Spanish royalty, as well as Christopher Columbus.

The city abounds in parks, ancient buildings, gardens, museums, and old quarters with twisting narrow streets and handsome courtyards. It is an attractive, quiet place to spend a few days, and for anyone who likes to take photographs, it is almost worth going there for that alone—especially to try to capture on film the Gold Tower, the Cathedral, and the imposing, unbelievable structures covering an immense half-circle at the Plaza de España.

□

The Spanish Island of Mallorca (May-or-ka) is a tropical paradise in the Mediterranean Sea. The distance of 132 miles from Barcelona can be covered by boat in eight hours, and the least-expensive fare (which buys you only a place to sit down) is about seven dollars one way. Palma, the capital city, is a lush green, palm-studded home for about 250,000 people, and often about that many more tourists. The average temperature year around is sixty-one degrees Fahrenheit, a fact that is reflected in the countless beaches.

On the whole island there are about one and one-half thousand hotels, hostels, and pensions, which provides some indication of the touristy nature of the place. These lodgings range from budget to ultra-deluxe, but it is possible to rent a bed for as little as three dollars a night. Many of the little villages are fantastic to see, and Palma itself provides such sights as a fourteenth-century castle, an incredible thirteenth-century cathedral with many flying buttresses, remains of old walls from the sixteenth century, the Almudaina Palace (originally the home of Moorish kings), and the Spanish Village (Pueblo Español), which provides the visitor with a potpourri of different types of Spanish architecture down through the ages along its narrow streets and in its squares and courtyards.

Switzerland

God must have been in an artistic mood when he created Switzerland, and the Swiss have responded in kind by building a neat little society that fits the landscape perfectly. Nowhere is this more evident than at the eastern end of Lake Lucerne, where one finds Brunnen, an incredibly pretty little town settled between towering mountains and the serene blue lake.

If we had only one more week of our lives to spend in Switzerland, we'd forego the cosmopolitan pleasures of Geneva or Zurich or Lucerne and opt for Brunnen. What more could one ask of a town: boat trips, mountain hikes, bicycling, reasonable prices, a centralized location in the country, yodeling, Alpine horn blowing, dances, concerts, cable cars, good food, and a name you can't mispronounce. We shouldn't have told you about it; if all of you go there it will be ruined.

Even ignoring the town's idyllic setting, Brunnen has a nice central location. It is easy to make day trips from there to Lucerne (by rail, car, or boat), Zurich, Locarno, Lugano, or even Italy. A variety of boat trips to interesting places can be made on the lake, and about any spot in eastern Switzerland is readily available from this location.

Thanks to the imagination of its tourist office director, Brunnen offers its visitors some intriguing possibilities of its own. As do other areas of Switzerland, it provides the "Wanderpass," which will give you the opportunity to see the area by foot, bus, boat, or train at unbelievable prices (the transportation is free, whatever option you choose). You get bed and breakfast, choice of a huge variety of hotels, and all the guidance you might need for under $20 a day! These programs cover 2, 4, or 7 days, and they constitute one of the world's great travel bargains.

To bring this hymn of praise for Brunnen to an end, we will mention the town's "Special Offers." There are one- and two-week special programs for senior citizens, guided walking tours, nostalgia trips, sailing excursions, art and history tours, and "economical weeks." These offerings are a nice compromise between ordinary overly regimented tours and going your own solitary way. They provide advice and guidance, two meals a day, accommodations, a guide, rides on cable cars, boat trips, overland trips to spots of interest, visits to museums, etc., all for a cost of about $30 a day. And nicest of all, these "special offers" are not guided tours in the worst sense—you have time for yourself in these programs to do what you wish.

If any of these possibilities interest you—or if you just find Brunnen intriguing —talk to your travel agent, or to the Swiss National tourist office, or to Swissair. If you book any of the "Special Offers" tours with the Brunnen tourist office directly, you'll get an additional 10% discount if you mention that you read about it in this book. If you wish to write to Brunnen, the address is: Tourist Office, C.H.- 6440 Brunnen.

□

With the dollar being in ill health, Switzerland cannot be considered an inexpensive place to visit—unless you're careful with your funds. If you are, which amounts to shopping for the best-priced accommodations, not staying in the larger cities, and avoiding multi-star or -fork restaurants, you can see this lovely country at reasonably low cost.

On a recent visit to Switzerland, we looked hard at the current price of single bathless rooms in the eastern part of the country. We avoided taking rooms in large cities, and we learned that Switzerland offers over 100,000 single-room accommodations for $18 a night or less. As an example, we visited Zurich but stayed in Baden, a charming small town just a few minutes northeast. The lowest-cost single we found there was $12 a night, with doubles running about twice that. It would be difficult if not impossible to find a room at that price in Zurich.

In Schaffhausen, located on the Rhine near Europe's largest water cascade, we found nice, clean singles for $12 a night, including breakfast, at the Hotel Baren near the train station. In fact, we found singles for as low as seven dollars a night in private home pensions, and they were invariably clean and comfortable. Switzerland is still affordable, if you will just take the trouble to find the bargain-priced accommodations that exist everywhere.

And Switzerland is even more affordable off-season (but remember that winter is *high* high season in the big ski resort areas). But many of the country's villages of lesser renown, most of which do offer winter cross-country and downhill skiing, have a lot of empty restaurants and hotel rooms during the winter months. This offers one the opportunity to see the country when prices are low, the crowds of tourists are elsewhere, and when it is at its most beautiful. Skiing is often just as good at the unfamous places, the prices are far less, and you don't have to wait in long lines for the lifts. You could spend a week in Appenzell, for example, seeing the country as God probably really intended for it to be seen, riding in horse-drawn sleighs, sitting in front of roaring fireplaces, and having a great time at bargain prices.

□

The town of Schaffhausen and the area surrounding it, just north of Zurich on the Rhine River, is a pleasant place to visit. It's not an ancient town, but its buildings go back as far as 400 years, and many of them are extremely ornate. There are countless fancy oriel windows, muraled walls, and richly carved samples of wood-work. All this is overseen by an old castle/fort and bounded by the Rhine. Many tourists boat from here down to Constance.

Just a couple of miles south is Neuhausen am Rhine, the site of Europe's largest water cascade. It is impressive. The train from Zurich stops there, or you can reach it from Schaffhausen by train, trambus (about $1.20), or foot. It is a pleasant little walk from S., but to really see the rapids once you're there you have to climb down (and back up) about 3,000 steps. It's worth it. And if you like getting a little damp you can take a boat from one side that will deposit you on a big rock in the middle from which you can see the torrents in every direction.

□

St. Gallen is a town that too many visitors miss. It shows its age in a nice way. It was "invented," as the Swiss like to put it, in the early part of the 7th century, and weaving has been important there for over 800 years. Today the town is world renowned for its textiles and embroidery work, and tourists who know what they're doing can make good buys.

St. Gallen is well-known for its oriel windows, painted façades, and its absolutely fantastic baroque cathedral. In addition to all this, it offers some nice rooms at very reasonable prices.

Not far away, a bit south, one finds Appenzell, a remarkable little village in the foothills that is watched over by some sizeable mountains. This popular spot offers such attractions as these (depending, obviously, on the season of year): ski slopes, indoor swimming, a number of small handwork craft industries, hiking routes, outdoor swimming, trout fishing, several museums, a strange nine-pin European version of bowling, a cinema, cross-country skiing, and mountaineering. Many of the buildings have beautifully colored and decorated fronts, and there is a small old-and-new cathedral that shows both gothic and baroque designs, plus a nave that is oddly twisted out of kilter.

It's a rather quiet place, and an awfully nice spot to visit.

□

Chur (Koor) is not a name that springs to most tourists' minds when they think about Switzerland, but if the idea of a 5,000-year-old city appeals to you, Chur fits the bill. It is the oldest town in Switzerland. The Romans were late-comers here. It is located in the eastern end of the country, not far from Austria or Italy, and it is the gateway to Arosa and St. Moritz, the renowned skiing resorts. It has a large old-town section, replete with ornate walls and windows, interesting old churches, and a museum of artifacts from the town's long history which is interesting even to people (like us) who are somewhat tired of museums.

If you were looking for an inexpensive base to use in exploring Switzerland, Chur would be a good choice, both because it's a nice place to be and because it offers visitors a 7-day "Holiday Scheme" that is a money-saver. In 1979 this little pass covered seven nights in a hotel (including breakfasts, service, and taxes), and seven meal vouchers worth about $10 each, all for as low as $150. You can arrange the same thing for three nights if you wish. In addition, you can get a free "Bonus Pass" that will give you entrance to all museums, swimming pools, plus use of bowling alleys and a cable car ride up a nearby mountain, a guided tour of the city, etc. You can get these bonanzas through the Chur tourist office, one of the Swiss offices in your own country, or your travel agent.

If you want to see Switzerland at its very lowest cost, go in the summer, stay in small villages, and get a hefty discount by staying in one place for more than three days. A room taken in summer can cost as little as 50% of the winter rate, and a room in a small village will run only about 35% of the cost of a comparable room in Geneva, Zurich, or Lucerne. In other words, an overnight stay in a well-known city in winter could cost you $50; the same class of room at the same time of year in a village might run $17; and you could find the same rooms in the summer, respectively, for $25 a night and $8 to $10 a night.

□

We will devote our last remarks about this country of ups and downs to an area touched upon in the last chapter, which is called the Jungfrau Region or the Bernese Oberland. The Jungfrau, or "young woman," is a startling mountain that looks down over the villages of Grindelwald, Interlaken, Lauterbrunnen, Mürren, Wengen, and Wilderswil. While we confess that many of Switzerland's towns and villages have their charms, this Jungfrau Region seems to us to be an outstanding place for people who love the open air, hiking, and unforgettable scenery. Unsurprisingly, the whole area is a skier's paradise (and perhaps Waterloo), but it is also a come-to-life version of everyone's view of high-altitude Swiss life, cow-bells, flowers, and healthy-looking mountain people included.

It is an area of extreme heights, geographically speaking. You will see narrow-gauge cog railways, ski lifts, and cable cars on every side, and you will also be privi-leged to see fantastic waterfalls. If unsupervised touring is your thing, you will love walking up or down between any of these lovely little towns, and you will not take long to understand the querulous, immodest, and apparently sincere ques-tion of every Swiss citizen: "Wouldn't *everyone* want to live here if he could?" Well, it is immodest, but you may soon understand why they feel that way.

Lauterbrunnen, with its magnificently high waterfall; Wengen, with its picturebook views of waterfalls and mountains and its fine ski runs; and Grindelwald, with its Alpine atmosphere, fine skiing facilities, and nearby glaciers, are all wonderful bases for long walks and day-long searches for new sights and sensations. And as we mentioned in the last chapter, these towns offer the possi-bility of an incredible ride to a train station/lookoff that is located in the stratosphere. Nearby Gstaad is no less attractive, and it is an equally fine base camp for walks into Switzerland's beautiful panoramas. Everything about this area will leave one absolutely breathless—including, for budgeteers, the prices.

Perhaps the best-known town in this region is Interlaken, which seems to us to be overrated. With its many hotels (perhaps nearly one hundred) it is considerably more touristy and expensive than the little villages in the mountains above it. Nevertheless it is a lovely place that deserves to be seen if you are in the area; but we would suggest that you go on up the slopes to find a place to sleep.

□

We are compelled to mention Berne here. It is small for a nation's capital, medi-eval, and utterly charming. To us it is a far better place to visit than Switzerland's other principal cities, such as Geneva or Zurich. If you're at all like us you'll like Berne but you'll wonder why the resident are so crazy about their bears. But you'll see many of the locals around the pits, and you'll probably be there too. And after-wards we suspect you'll wonder why. It is somehow not one of Europe's out-standing sights. But the city itself is well worth your time—perhaps a couple of days of it.

□

Switzerland is covered by charming Alpine villages, many of them far off the main routes, and they are generally less expensive and more truly Swiss than the big places with the big names. Like Holland and Austria, Switzerland strikes us as a country about which any really bright visitor would ignore approximately ninety-nine percent of what travel agents and travel brochures say, and indeed avoid altogether the towns that all inexperienced tourists rate as "musts," *e.g.,* Geneva, Lucerne, Zurich, and so on.

An itinerary planner
Now that we've provided you with some facts and a good deal of opinion about

Europe and the Europeans, you may feel more confused than ever about where to go and what to see during your visit over there. One way to think logically about such questions is to make a planner—a listing of the factors that matter to you, and to try decide which countries will seem to fit them best. Even this exercise is not easy, but it is an improvement over not thinking at all.

We have created a planner of our own here to give you an example of how it works. We have filled it with some interest factors that would be important to us, ten countries, and votes based upon our own experiences and prejudices. The numerical votes cover a range from five for "superior" down to one for "poor."

Interest Factors

	Austria	Belgium	Britain	Denmark	France	Germany	Holland	Italy	Spain	Switzerland
Things to see and do										
castles, old buildings and cities	4	3	4	3	5	5	3	4	5	4
bicycling	3	4	5	5	4	4	5	3	1	3
art exhibits and galleries	3	5	4	3	5	5	5	5	4	3
historical places	3	5	5	3	5	5	4	5	5	2
cathedrals and churches	4	4	5	3	5	5	3	5	5	3
have conversations with people	4	5	5	5	2	3	5	3	1	3
Country Characteristics										
friendliness of people	4	4	4	5	2	2	4	4	2	2
safety of person and possessions	3	4	3	5	2	3	4	1	3	5
inexpensive rooms available	5	3	5	2	3	4	4	4	4	2
quality of food	3	5	2	3	5	3	3	2	2	4
easy on the budget	4	2	4	2	3	2	3	4	4	2
beautiful country	5	4	4	4	4	5	4	4	5	5
liberated travel easy	4	4	5	5	2	3	5	2	1	5
percentage of people who speak English	4	5	5	5	2	3	5	3	1	4
Totals	53	57	60	53	49	52	57	49	43	47

Superior = 5   Above average = 4   Average = 3   Below average = 2   Poor = 1

Now you might wish to try filling in your own interest factors, choice of countries, and votes in the blank matrix below. There are, of course, many other interest factors you might consider: number and quality of museums, musical entertainments, sporting events, festivals during the time you plan to be there, time and distance to get there from your arrival point in Europe, ancient ruins, possibilities for camping, etc.

Interest Factors

Things to see and do

Country Characteristics

Totals

Superior = 5	Above average = 4	Average = 3	Below average = 2	Poor = 1

When you have filled in this little matrix you'll find that you've given yourself some guidance about your own overall feelings towards the countries listed. When you add up your votes for each country, the ones with the highest totals will be the ones which fit your preferences best. But while this is one way to get the number of countries you will visit down to a reasonable total, you still have to remember that not only are these just guesses that you've made, but also that your results are just numbers. As plain cold numbers they do not reflect any "howevers." To illustrate, we suspect that we might not rank Britain quite so high if her prices weren't so favorable and the common tongue were not English. We know we'd rate Denmark higher if her prices weren't so astronomical. And we would raise Spain from last position if we spoke good Spanish, or if English were commonly used there, or if liberated travelling weren't so difficult in that beautiful country. You will have to examine such qualifiers when you have your own totals. If you care about skiing, you'll doubtlessly give some extra weight to France, Switzerland, Germany, or Austria: if you speak German, you'll probably take that into consideration when thinking about Germany and Austria; if you're not going to have much time to spend in Europe, you have to think about the geographical locations of some of these countries.

The whole exercise is pretty subjective. We were unable to agree on some of the numbers we put in ours, so we made some compromises. You may have to do the same thing with your travelling companion. But even so, we think the planner will be of help to you.

If you feel that you haven't enough experience or information to rank your interest factors numerically against the countries you've put down, try just putting in check marks where you feel that a given interest can be well satisfied by a particular country. Even the total number of checks for a country will give you some better understanding of your own desires and anticipations.

We hope you'll fill in the blank matrix. It will help your thinking even just to put down your own interest factors, and you may find your numerical totals a bit surprising.

□

We have wondered if we have made Europe sound as if it is totally comprised of charming old villages, magnificent scenery, and outstanding places to visit. All of the statements like "This is a super place" and "Here you will find low prices and high adventure" suggest that it's just not possible to go wrong in Europe. Of course that's not true; Europe has more than its share of spots that are dull, dull, dull. We've been in places that we could not enjoy, either locations that abounded in miniature golf offerings and other such "entertainments," or, at the opposite end, towns or areas where there seemed to be absolutely nothing to do or to see. We think it pointless to name these places; were we to do so, we'd give you a directory rather than a readable book.

Perhaps a certain degree of the "buyer beware" attitude should operate on such choices. Don't find it too easy to believe the national tourist offices, travel books (including this one), travel magazines, or comments your friends make on the subject of where the best places are. After all, the conventional wisdom is that the largest cities are the top places to visit; we may be wrong from *your* standpoint, but we find it impossible to agree with that idea. A few hours here and a few hours there is the strategy most tour groups tell you is ideal, an idea that we find beyond understanding. *You* must decide what is best for *you*, and it's not easy to do.

Here are a few thoughts on the matter. First, ask your travel agent or the appropriate national tourist office for explicit information about a place that you think might interest you. Relate your questions to your own interests, and don't settle for answers that are composed largely of adjectives.

If you have some possible places in mind, get a Michelin guide that covers them, read it carefully, and try to decide which descriptions fit your interests.

Go to the library and look up the town name in the encyclopedia and the Readers' Guide to Periodical Literature. You'll probably learn something about it that way.

Lastly, and particularly if you plan to settle down in this place for a time and make it a base, visit it when you get to Europe. Stay overnight. If it looks better and better to you as a little time goes on, it's your place. If not, move on.

Most of Europe is interesting in one way or another to outsiders, but some places are a lot more interesting than others. Think about what it is you want to see— art, old ruins, special scenery, history, etc.—and be sure that your selected place fits at least part of the bill.

When you find one that fits all of your interests, then you've found a place that you could live in the rest of your life, let alone just a few days or weeks.

It is a matter that obviously needs to be considered carefully.

A royal palace,
the Mediterranean,
and a tropical climate —
c'est beau!

Chapter Seventeen
A Light View of Packing
—and Red Tape

*The only pleasure I've gotten from carrying these #†!! bags
around Europe was in noticing how many
other tourists make the same mistake. And that wasn't much!*

—an American tourist in Denmark

Should you carry fourteen changes of underwear for your two-week trip? Are four pairs of shoes apiece enough? Should you carry formal, quasi-formal, and informal clothes? Is it essential to bring sulfa drugs, splints, and water purification tablets? There are two answers to these questions:

1. You are not considering a trip to the North Pole; and

2. If you can't carry it yourself for considerable distances, don't take it.

History has not recorded the name of the traveller who reputedly brought back less from Europe than he took over there, but there is a rumor that it happened once twenty years ago or so. People usually have all sorts of packages and plastic bags with them when they return, ordinarily filled with souvenirs and things they bought before departing from the European airport's duty-free area.

All of this constitutes one argument for taking only one bag with you. Not only is this nice when you are *going,* having one hand free for showing your passport or adjusting your glasses, but it reserves one hand for carrying all those trinkets *on your return.* You can count on looking pretty much like a pack horse when you come back; and you'll *really* look like one if you start off that way.

281

But having one hand free for your trip over and back is not the main argument. The main argument is this: you need that hand free for the whole trip. You really can't travel in the liberated way if you have too much luggage. Even two bags per person will force you to take taxis, hire porters, be on a continual lookout for luggage lockers, face all sorts of problems in the trains and on the buses or trams, and, finally, to spend extra time going through customs inspection procedures. You won't have to carry the bags across Austria, of course, but you will probably have to lug them between train stations and your lodgings once or twice every day, or perhaps every two or three days—and that's liable to be a goodly distance. Taking too much luggage with you is one of the worst mistakes you can make. It may be hard for you to imagine now, but you can get by nicely with one small bag, even for three or four weeks—and if you do so, you'll find no reason to regret it over there.

Everyone carries too much with them to Europe. We only carry one bag apiece, and we usually find that we've taken several things along that we wish we'd left at home. It's so easy (and stupid) to think, "Oh, I just might need this shirt" or "Perhaps I'll need another pair of slacks." For years we have been trying to learn to think, "I probably won't need *that,* but if it turns out that I *do,* I'll buy one in Europe." Try hard to think that way. Even if you can do so, you'll still take too much. You'll find out by about the third day of your trip—or even earlier. You may know it before you even get to the airport—because of your aching arms.

Here are a few suggestions—ranging from the pertinent to the impertinent— for packing lightly. Some of them have been offered before in other travel books, but in total they are considerably different from some lists we've seen (" . . . a man should be able to get by with three suits, one topcoat, an informal jacket . . . ") Good Lord! Why don't they remind you to bring a wheelbarrow as well? You'd need it.

These are our rather modest suggestions:

1. Buy nylon underthings (both male and female) and take only two or three of each item. You can wash them out easily, and they will dry overnight. While it's true that such things only weigh ounces, every ounce and every item matters— for reasons which we will explain shortly.

2. Take light plastic rain jackets with hoods. The kind that fold down to practically nothing are best because there will be threatening days when you'll have to carry them in your pocket or purse for the day.

3. Consider carrying a light, water-resistant backpack in one of your bags— remembering that you are hoping to carry only one small bag apiece. It can be useful for mountain hiking, or as an emergency bag when you've hit that once-in-a-lifetime deal on good wine or inexpensive antiques or a purchase that you just haven't yet been able to mail home.

4. Shoes: It would be wise to pick your shoes carefully, to wear them for a couple of weeks before you go, and to practice wearing them while you are carrying your luggage. If you don't your feet are liable to swell during the first day of your trip—

It's easier to hold hands when you're leaving ...

... than it is when you are coming back.

and then you are in trouble. The wrong shoes can ruin your holiday, especially when you walk for miles every day. And if you follow our thinking, you will. You will probably only be able to take the shoes you wear, so choose carefully.

On one of our trips, Phyllis took two pairs of shoes—that is, she wore one and carried a pair for dress. The latter were sandals that packed down very flat, but because she didn't pick the other pair wisely she eventually had to wear the sandals all the time—even, believe it or not, when we were climbing and hiking in the Swiss Alps. She is now convinced that the next time we go, she will chooose two pairs of shoes with much care and not worry about appearance so much. She now thinks that one pair will be hiking boots.

But if you are cramped for room, *one* pair, comfortable but adequate in appearance for anything, is enough. If you can manage that, it will mean a lot of cubic inches in your bag for more important items. Incidentally, if you are going off-season when you may encounter moisture on the ground, comfortable leather walking boots are excellent. You will see many people wearing them in Europe. They are "in."

5. Clothes for all occasions: Europeans do not seem to be so conscious these days as they used to be of ties, coats, dresses, etc., for concerts, dinners, and such occasions. We have taken lightweight matching windbreakers, both for chilly evenings and for appearance, and turtleneck shirts—which seemed to be acceptable for anything, no matter how formal.

You cannot, of course, overlook the important factor of *when* you will travel, and *where* you plan to go. If you make your trip in early spring or late fall, you could experience some cool weather, especially in the northern areas. In any case, a sweater that doesn't take too much room in your bag is nice to have along. If you are going to countries with coastlines, swim suits are worth considering. If you are going to Spain, you can take your walking shorts, whether you are male or female, although you should be warned if you are female that rather than the looks of disgust you will get elsewhere in Europe, in Spain your exposed legs will generate male remarks, automobile horn honks, ogling, and occasional pinches or pats on the derrière (which you may get anyway if you are nice looking). Shorts are not, at least on grown women, welcome in most of Europe. And they are *really* welcomed in Spain.

6. Medical supplies: the possibilities here include an anti-diarrhetic, bandaids, aspirins, and perhaps a good, all-purpose antibiotic salve or ointment. Women might think of another item or two they'd wish to take for an extended trip, although tampons and sanitary napkins are readily available in Europe. Sunburn prevention cream is also worth considering. Tablets for upset stomachs are probably worth taking. Think twice before taking any spray cans of anything. If the tops come off and the buttons get pushed over in your luggage, you'll have a mess. If you are on a prescription drug, take an adequate supply and an extra prescription or two—and they should be typed, not written in that upside-down Swahili that MDs love.

7. Miscellaneous: Film (it's expensive in Europe, and the price often includes processing, which is not useful to you); a small supply of Kleenex is worth considering for a variety of reasons; an adjustable strap or two (to put around your bag if and when it breaks, or to fasten things onto the bicycles you rent); a sewing kit; a few plastic bags (for your dirty laundry, or for grocery stores—where there is usually a charge for bags—or for pinning onto the bottom of wet clothes from your nightly washing to keep them from dripping on the floor); wash cloths; several packets of cold-water detergent; a travel lock; a short length of chain and a padlock for "closet" doors with handles in the center; two spoons for eating or making coffee in your room; a short length of light line and a few paper clips or spring-clip clothes pins for your evening washing routine; and perhaps a folding umbrella. A small battery-powered or wind-up alarm clock may be worth taking; some pensions and budget hotels will not provide wake-up services.

As you think hard about your European plans and your packing, you may, depending upon your habits and intentions, think of other small things you'll want to take. A corkscrew for opening wine bottles is one example. Another item is a small plastic flask or bottle for carrying water on long train rides. A small flashlight is useful to have for lodgings that do not provide the lighting that you might expect between your room and the toilet. A little soap is worth taking too—because it's not furnished in most hotels or tourist rooms.

Although it appears to us that there has been some improvement in toilet tissue in some of the countries over the last few years, much of it still resembles wrapping paper or thin wood veneer. If you have the room, you might consider smashing a roll flat and putting it in your bag. Of course the only problem is that when you need it it's always in your suitcase, unless you can remember always to carry a bit in your pocket or purse.

The current in the walls across most of Europe is 220 volts, or thereabouts, an amount of juice that will put your electric razor on the ceiling in seconds, turn it into a smoking hulk, and drop it on your head moments later. Within the countries of Belgium, France, Italy, and Spain the voltage level even varies from one area to another. In addition, the prongs on plugs are generally round and, in some places, short and fat, and in others, long and skinny. So if you must take electric appliances from this country, they should be switchable from 110 to 220, or you will have to take a step-down transformer as well as an assortment of conversion plugs for their outlets. You can buy such kits, but to us it sounds like a lot of extra weight, money, and trouble. If you have to shave, how about a safety razor?

An item you can buy in Europe is a 220-volt immersion heater. It will allow you to make coffee or hot chocolate in your room, and will pay for itself in two or three days because of the high restaurant prices for such drinks. Tip: if you buy one of these, you should also buy an adapter plug that will allow you to use it anywhere. If the heater you buy has long, thin prongs, get an adapter that will take them on the female side and have short, fat prongs on the other side; or vice versa. You'll need yet another style in the U.K.

We are aware that most females love clothes, and usually want to take too many of them on their trips. Phyllis is no exception; she always begins packing by trying to get a ridiculous amount of clothing into one small shoulder bag—and she knows better. It usually takes her a couple of days and a lot of agonizing to make the necessary choices to get the pile small enough to fit in little bag, and then invariably she realizes early in the trip that she still took too much. She puts it this way: "What I have finally realized is that you don't need all the latest fashions. You don't see the same people day after day when you're travelling. Those you do see won't know if your outfit is one of a dozen or one of two, and in any case you are too busy seeing Europe to worry about your appearance. I have found that by switching tops with two different pairs of slacks, I am able to look more-or-less presentable. Although we are not night clubbers and we never expect to be invited to have tea with Princess Grace or to have an audience with the Pope, I still always begin packing with those 'What if I need . . . ?' thoughts. I once took along a rather nice dress, which I never found an occasion to wear in all those weeks we were gone, so I just had to carry it all over Europe. Now I don't even think about bringing a dress—or walking shorts. Now I think about how heavy that bag can get and how my arms can hurt—and I've almost learned what I hope *you* know: that everyone does take too much with them, and it's a terrible mistake."

We have no desire or reason to wish to insult the average American woman or man (we're not even sure that such people exist). Nevertheless, we confess to a belief that most Americans, male or female, often seem overly concerned with their own comfort. The woman particularly will more often than not carry too many possessions to Europe with her, including such items as electric hair dryers—which won't work on Europe's current anyway.

She is such an important part of this hypothetical couple we have discussed. First of all, her response to the idea of travelling independently in Europe may simply be: "No, I couldn't enjoy that. If we were to go over, I'd want to stay in *nice* places." If she feels that way, or if she does agree to give it a try—and then wants to bring along 150 pounds of belongings—she's destroyed any possiblity that it could have been the trip of a lifetime for herself and her partner. We hope that we haven't made liberated travelling sound like a two-week fishing trip in the boonies to such a person. Instead we hope we've given her reason to believe that living a little differently for a short time, sleeping in places that are not related to well-known chain hotels, and sharing absolutely everything—the joys and the frustrations and even the occasional lack of American-style comfort—with her companion on a day-in-and-day-out basis—could be one of the best experiences of her life.

Most of all, we hope that we've convinced her that she shouldn't carry everything she possesses—or even one-tenth of it—to Europe. There's very little comfort involved in *that*, we can say for sure—and the one of us who knows that best, Phyllis, has already said so.

One of our friends suggested to his wife that for their first trip over they should pack one small bag apiece, put on the shoes they intend to wear, and take a long walk before they go, to see if they can carry what they packed for a good distance. It sounds like an excellent idea to us. It would have been a good idea for a couple we met not too long ago in the Innsbruck train station. They had three large bags, a medium-sized one, and a small one—not to mention her purse and two cameras! They admitted they were spending a lot of money on taxis, and a lot of time trying to find little carts in the train stations to use in wheeling all of these possessions around. We felt sorry for them. They did too.

When we began to needle the man gently, he said, "It's crazy all right. And the really funny thing is that this big one is nearly empty. We got so tired of lugging all that weight around we mailed a lot of things home—but we still have the (unprintable) suitcase."

One item of luggage that you should think carefully about (if you will travel as a couple) is the woman's purse. Phyllis thinks it best to carry a shoulderbag. But the size of the bag is important if you both plan to use it as the repository for passports, travellers' checks, train tickets or passes, and other incidentals such as extra film, cash, maps, notebooks, phrase books, flash bulbs, aspirins, Kleenex, toothbrushes, credit cards, and some of the coin of the realm. It is nice to have one large enough to be used as a catch-all, because it can always go with you if you, say, decide on impulse to visit the dining car on the train. If you *do* use it to carry most of your valuables, it would be helpful if it had a lock on it. But some experienced travellers consider it foolish to carry your passports and money in such a bag, particularly in Italy or France. It is a thought worth considering. At any rate, the choice of such a catch-all bag may prove to be one of the most important decisions you'll make, so think rather carefully about it.

Your aircraft free baggage weight limit for tourist class is forty-four pounds (twenty kilos), incidentally, and it costs a great deal to exceed that limit. You are not, of course, charged for the weight of items you carry in your hands or pockets, but forget that because you shouldn't carry nearly that much junk with you anyway.

And that's about it. You are not planning a safari. It's going to be a civilized trip through one of the most civilized parts of the planet. As we know well, it's not easy to keep yourself down to one small bag each for the two, three, or four weeks, but it can be done. A husband and wife can help each other with such comments as "No, you certainly won't need *that*," and "Look, I gave up taking my camera tripod, so you can leave out that damned negligee." This form of intercooperation will not only help to lighten your loads, but will dissipate a lot of hostilities *before* the trip begins. It's an improvement over arguing through a half-dozen countries.

Nonessentials

For some people (including us, we have to admit) travelling pretty much by the seat of the pants adds to the fun—and, of course, it also causes one to be lost more often and to have more problems. For those who do not have this sense of derring-do, we would suggest taking Michelin Guides to the countries to be visited. As we indicated in Chapter Three, they are doubtlessly the most thorough and complete guides available. Full of invaluable tips, they each cover a separate country, and each of them costs from three to eight dollars, depending on their size. They do not include the sort of philosophical advice we are offering in this book, but they do go into great detail, providing ideas about what to see and when to see it.

We are not talking here about the Red Guides, which rate hotels and restaurants, but instead the Green Guides, which describe the towns and cities and give capsule histories and background information. They may often tell you even more than you want to know about a given country, town, or cathedral, but one might argue that that is a great deal better than standing there looking at something wondering what it is, how old it is, and whether it's a grain elevator or something that really matters.

The main disadvantage of carrying these books is that one of them will displace, say, a pair of socks, a knit shirt, and two rolls of film in your luggage (they are about 5 x 10 x ½ inches). And that, for you, like us, might not be a price you're willing to pay for a little good advice. And then too, as with us, maybe finding out about things for yourself is worth all the difficulties it causes.

It is always useful to have a camera hanging around your neck in Europe; otherwise people might not recognize you as a tourist. Some people not only wear them as an identification device, but actually try to use them from time to time. In case this describes you, remember this: camera malfunction is one of the most common maladies to strike unsuspecting tourists who are thousands of miles from home. Have a good camera mechanic lubricate it and look it over before you leave home.

And if it really did happen that she wouldn't let you take the camera tripod because you wouldn't let her take her negligee, carry a six-foot piece of furnace chain. It will easily go in your pocket (or your bag). For slow-shutter-speed work in museums and cathedrals, you can attach one end to your camera, stand on the other end, and pull it tight—which will overcome your heartbeat and respiratory motions. For this kind of shooting you should also, of course, have a cable release for the shutter. And you might want to look into the new 400 a.s.a. color film which, along with the chain or a tripod, should allow you to shoot about anything anywhere without flash.

Anyone who knows anything about photography is always surprised to see people blazing away with flash units at subjects that are fifty feet to a hundred yards away. The little inexpensive flashes (e.g., flashcubes) are good for only a few feet, and only the best electronic flashes can adequately light a subject twenty feet away.

Another camera suggestion: if you do not have a single-lens reflex camera (which will *not* let you shoot with the lens cap on, because you look *through* the lens to frame your picture), get a haze filter and leave it over the lens instead of using a lens cap. It will give you better photos outside, protect your lens, and never give you prints or slides that are totally black.

Actually there are a number of good arguments for not taking a camera to Europe at all. Unless it is small enough to go into a pocket, it does mark you as a tourist everywhere you go. It and your film will take up valuable luggage space. The cost of the film and for developing it can be considerable, and it might be less expensive to buy ready-made slides and pictures for later memory sessions. And finally, some people who only see the sights through a camera viewfinder never really see anything at all. So it might be wise, when deciding what to take with you, to consider not including a camera, or just taking one of the little pocket cameras that are so popular now. The cheaper ones take poor-quality pictures, but they do not have some of the disadvantages of the bigger cameras.

If you are going to carry film with you, you may wish to carry it separately from your other possessions and have it hand-searched rather than X-rayed at the airport. They say those machines won't damage your film, but we know professional photographers who would never allow their film to be "photographed" that way. It is a matter you can decide for yourself. If it turns out in

Cobblestones call for good shoes, strong legs, and a healthy sense of balance.

Spanish National Tourist Office photo

Europe that you didn't bring enough with you, buy Kodak-brand film even if its price does include processing charges—Kodak will develop and print the film in the U.S. without further charge to you.

At any rate, the main message here is to pack light. It's an important principle: you will eventually come to regret bringing even small, light items that you don't need. A thirty-pound bag, as a rule of thumb, will seem to weigh fifty pounds after one hundred yards, seventy-five pounds after a block, and at least one hundred by the third country you reach. But the argument for carrying as little as possible goes beyond the weight problems. You're going to be living out of that bag, and you're going to have to handle and paw through everything you've got with you about forty-nine thousand times. Every item that is there but isn't needed is always going to be between you and what you really want.

What to wear

Which clothes you wear on your trip clearly depends a great deal on where and when you're going. European temperatures are pretty much like ours, generally speaking, all around the year, and maybe just a bit warmer—but it is always either cool or cold in the mountains. But you should not be fooled by generalities, either theirs or ours: Switzerland by our standards is a very small country, but with all its geographical ups and downs it has temperatures varying wildly all across the country throughout the year. It can be freezing in the mountains, and hot as Hades in the valley a few miles away. It can be like that even where the ground is relatively flat. The Swiss claim a temperature range in the Geneva region during September of from 40° to 73°. You could be fairly cool or fairly warm, depending upon the time of day and your luck.

Incidentally, temperatures in Europe are always given in degrees Centigrade. An easy mental conversion from Centigrade to Fahrenheit is to double the degrees Centigrade, substract ten percent from the result, and add thirty-two to get the degrees Fahrenheit. In other words, $20°C.x2 = 40$; $40-4 = 36$; $36+32 = 68°F$. Any temperature that you run into that is between 8 and 25°C will be pretty comfortable. Some people can make good estimates of C to F conversions by remembering three Centigrade temperatures: 0, the freezing point of water; 21, comfortable room temperature (about 70°F.); and 37, normal body temperature. And if you want to impress your friends or win a TV contest, you might point out that you know that both scales come together at one point—they are equal at -40°.

We suppose that the sensible thing is to be prepared for any possibility—cold, rain, snow (at least in the mountains, whenever you're there), and heat. We always dress pretty casually for the trip across. Alan ordinarily wears a nylon sport shirt which is convertible to tie wear, a pair of workman's trousers which would hold a press through a typhoon, comfortable, waterproofed shoes, and a light, washable, wrinkle-proof windbreaker. Phyllis usually wears a sleeveless shell or blouse, slacks, leather walking shoes, and a jacket. If the weather is cool when we leave, we both wear lightweight turtleneck shirts instead, which look reasonably good, are easy to wash out, and can keep one fairly warm. In fact, we've learned that some couples who are not too far apart in girth buy and take several of them in the same size but in different colors so they can share them during the trip!

Women are foolish to carry or to wear jewels on European junkets. They might get robbed, for one thing, but even if they don't they'll look show-offish to the natives.

If you stay in pensions or budget hotels, you will not run into any situations in them that will require evening dresses or tuxedos. But if you should decide, even on the spur of the moment, to go to an opera or to a four-star restaurant, you would probably like to have the clothes to suit the occasion. So you have to decide for yourself whether you wish to carry dress-up clothes for the possible occasion where you'll need them—an occasion that may never arrive. We think the turtle-necks, while borderline in appearance, are the best answers to such possibilities.

One last comment: if you do take too much junk with you, which you probably will, get a box in Europe and ship what you don't need back home.

Generally, then, we recommend that in choosing your clothes, as in your packing, you should try to be prepared for any eventuality ranging from a blizzard to a visit to an opera, you should consider comfort before appearance, and you should remember that they do have clothes (and shoes) for sale in Europe.

If this doesn't seem sensible to you, take everything you can think of, and be sure not to forget to bring along a burro as well.

Unwrapping red tape

Our servants in Washington are not unaware of our occasional desires to travel. They have shown their cognizance of such matters by legislating an absurd three-dollar airport departure tax and by making passports available to us at only several times what they should cost. In addition, they have set aside tax monies to protect us from ourselves by establishing a tough customs service (service?) that prevents us from bringing into the mother country such dangerous items as Cuban cigars or pornographic publications. Not only do these safeguards make us all feel more secure, but we also have to pay for them and, indeed, endure them when we travel. This is about how to endure them, live with them, and pay for them.

Although making your travel arrangements is not as much fun as looking forward to or actually making the trip, getting your passport, reserving trans-portation across the Atlantic, and so on, it is not nearly as bad as, say, going to boot camp. But such arrangements do, as you will soon see, require a little head-scratching. However, getting a passport is an easy matter. It costs a bit of money and takes a little time, but all in all it's a fairly easy procedure. And if you like the idea of giving the government some money so it will give you a document to prove that you are who you told it you are, you'll find the whole thing positively enjoyable.

Anyone who is thirteen or older must have his or her own passport. Children under 13 can be included in the passport of a parent. Joint passports between husbands and wives are no longer available, though a couple holding a still-valid joint passport can travel on it until it expires. Actually, we'd counsel getting rid of your joint passport and obtaining new, separate passports. They will give you more potential freedom, especially if you come to face unforeseen separations because of illness, missing a train, or simply because you decide you'd like to spend a day or two apart from each other in the course of your trip.

In fact, if you are taking a child with you, we'd suggest getting him or her a separate passport too. How can you anticipate who might get sick, or have to come home early, so that you know which passport to include the child on in advance?

You can get further information on passports from a travel agent or from any postoffice designated to handle the paperwork.

Thinking of you as one-half of a pair, we would like to say a word or two about how two people travelling together might best survive and even enjoy a European adventure. No matter how congenial the two of you are, there are those times during a long, drawn-out exploration of foreign lands that can try men's and women's souls. If such problems occur, they usually crop up during the latter stages of the trip. Until then everything has been new and interesting, and sharing has been easy and fun. Then it happens. He (she) wants to go to a bullfight, or a grand prix, or an opera, and she (he) becomes adamant: "I do not want to see men destroy an animal (or each other, or peoples' eardrums)." It can be a tense time. If and when it happens, we can't predict how you'll finally compromise and/or resolve the question, but we can tell you one thing: you are really fortunate to have each other over there, wherever and whoever you are. We have both travelled solo quite a bit, and doing so, in spite of the disagreements that can occur between a pair, is a very, very long second to doing it together.

Think about that when disagreements occur. Ask yourself: "What would it be like for me if he (she), as wretched as he (she) is, weren't alongside?" Such a question at those bad times may snap you back to reality, and make you realize that as unpleasant, disagreeable, and stupid as your partner/friend/travelling companion can be, he or she is probably the only person in all of Europe who really loves you.

While it is very pleasant to travel with someone who cares about you, partly for the sharing of experiences and partly for the fact that problems seem smaller when looked at by two people, either person may reach a point where they would just like to be alone, even if only for a few minutes. After a few days of twenty-four-hours-a-day togetherness, you may have an impulse to get away from him or her, perhaps just for a short time, or maybe for an hour or two—or maybe even for several days. If you do, and you follow your instinct, you'll probably find it an interesting experience. For that period neither of you will be relying on the other as you have been before, and you'll find out how different it is just to deal with your own sensory inputs and reactions without hearing about his or hers.

If you ever do try one of these solo trips, you'll find that it's easier and more interesting to meet the natives than it is when you're hanging on to your spouse.

And with those rather simple thoughts in mind, we'd counsel any pair to think hard before agreeing to go with another couple. Doing so could make any of the problems that we've just discussed many, many times potentially worse, and we'd guess that any pent-up frustration or unhappiness in such a situation would eventually result in big problems. After all, the four of you could be fairly well locked into being together the whole time, and it would be rather unpleasant if you became sick of each other. You might be wise to think hard before agreeing to such an arrangement.

You also have to decide about shots before you leave, and it is a simple decision for most people these days. You will not be required to have any shots at all—not even smallpox—to visit any of the western European countries. This could change if there were an outbreak of something over there, so it is always wise to ask your travel agent or someone with your airline just to be sure. But today the western European countries are at least as disease-free as the United States. If you don't believe it, have a look at recent statistics that rank the U.S. against those countries on longevity, infant mortality, etc.

However, if you do have some sort of physical problem it might be well to have a chat with your M.D. before you embark. There are lists of English-speaking doctors around the world available, the best known being available from Intermedic, 777 Third Avenue, New York City, 10017. For five dollars (or ten dollars for a family) they will provide a listing of good physicians around the world. A similar organization is the International Association for Medical Assistance to Travellers, Inc., which can be reached at 350 Fifth Avenue, Suite 5620, New York City, 10001. It might also be worthwhile to let your dentist have a look in your mouth before you leave; we have heard that Europe has excellent dentists, but fortunately we haven't ever had to do any research on the matter.

Many people believe that only their own country has any sort of acceptable medical system, and have great concerns about the care they might receive in any other part of the world. We do not. We have learned that medical science has no national boundaries. We have had a few small physical problems in Europe, and always located excellent treatment and very small charges for the service.

Perhaps a single small example will prove our point. One night in 1979 we were in a small village in Portugal. Phyllis became sick—very sick—and lost consciousness. As a small place in a poor country, it was hardly an ideal spot to have such a problem, and even the timing was poor: it happened late at night. Alan commandeered a taxi, and spent the time during the short ride to the local clinic alternating between panic and thoughts about confronting a veterinarian who had spent most of his day working with sheep and goats in a filthy manger.

As it turned out, we found a clean, well-lighted medical facility, a young doctor who spoke English, and a solution to our problem that proved to be perfect. It cost us the equivalent of $3.50 U.S., and gave us a real understanding of and respect for emergency medicine, even in out-of-the-way places in Europe. We hope it also alleviates any fears you might have on this subject.

It would be wise to check with your insurance company before you go to find out whether your homeowner's policy covers theft of personal belongings you are carrying while you are away from home. If it doesn't, you might wish to have the coverage extended; if it does, ask how you can register expensive items by serial number, a formality that could prevent a lot of arguments if you should lose something overseas. Having registered the item with U.S. Customs, as suggested in Chapter Thirteen, will also serve as evidence with the insurance people that you *did* have it when you left.

Reflecting on the word "lose," you should be aware that items which are lost —even by railroads, airlines, or baggage handlers—may not be covered by theft insurance. If someone loses one of your bags in Europe, you'd better fight it out there, rather than waiting until you return home to do battle with your insurance company.

Finally, we'd like to mention the Educational Cooperative, 176 West Adams, Chicago, 60603, (telephone 312-726-0042). This organization offers educational, informational, and travel services to students, young people, schools, and members of the academic community. The people here can provide you with flights, ground tours, expeditions, and all sorts of helpful advice. Twice yearly they publish *Taking Off,* a well-written, large-format publication that provides information about transatlantic flight possibilties, travel on six continents, ground transportation bargains, and so on.

Chapter Eighteen
Off We Go Into the
Wildly-Priced Blue Yonder

I think it's outrageous what you have to pay to fly.
—Sir Freddie Laker

As we said in an earlier book, "the transatlantic flight picture may be the most occult of the manmade mysteries." But at that time it was as stable as a bicycle with trainer wheels compared to what it is today. Now it's a unicycle. As fuel costs go up, the Civil Aeronautics Board brings out new regulations, the competitive picture between the charters and the scheduled lines continues to evolve, and the whole industry gravitates toward more freedom of competition, everything changes constantly.

Thus the problems created for you—and for us, in trying to make sense of the matter—are formidable. It isn't much of an exaggeration to say that anything we put down that was true when we wrote it may no longer be true now—as you read it. We are consequently going to simplify the whole picture as much as possible, hoping to give you a general overview that will help you in making good decisions about getting there and back. We shall try to avoid giving specific details about fares, departure points, destinations, or future plans of the air carriers. If we didn't, we'd be giving you out-of-date information.

We are assuming that you're going to fly. Given the relatively short lengths of time they have to vacation, most people do. Well, there are a lot of ways to fly, and prices depend not only on your trip's distance, the season, the day you leave, your age, how long you will stay in Europe, and where you sit on the plane, but also on which of the many kinds of plans you choose. Consequently, these prices vary all over the place, and they change with great frequency as currencies fluctuate in

295

value, fuel prices increase, and so on. Depending upon where and when you wish to go, you should shop for prices before you leave—and you must give yourself some time on this: many of the fares require advance booking, some as much as a month ahead.

The whole thing is mind-boggling. The scheduled airlines even list seasons differently depending upon whether you're heading east or west. They also have all sorts of affinity, non-affinity, group, and incentive group fare schedules, not to mention inclusive tours, which include ground transportation charges. Indeed, they also have various surcharges, one of which is for flying on a weekend (but not for every fare). This added charge may be disappearing; a number of lines have already dropped it. Some lines have three classes of seats: first, businessmen, and economy. In first class, some carriers have reintroduced the Sleeperette seat, which, because of the huge space between seats, will allow one to stretch out nearly flat.

Air fares vary by seasons, which may also change from year to year. You should ask about this matter before buying a ticket, because you'll save money if you can avoid flying during the high (peak) season period. In fact, you can get the low-season fare *both ways* if you depart any time before the high season begins or after it ends. The date of the departure determines the cost both ways on scheduled flights.

There are also Youth Fares available, as well as children's and infant's discounts. The latter vary in cost for different types of fares, so it is a matter that has to be discussed with a travel agent if you are taking small ones with you.

In addition to their other fares, many of the scheduled carriers are currently offering budget and stand-by flights. Another idea, a fairly recent one, is "bulk fares." Under this plan a tour operator will buy a block of seats from a scheduled airline and sell them at discount prices to individuals. It's worth inquiring about.

It's quite a range, isn't it? Now if we achieve a little understanding of the associated rules, regulations, and limitations, we'll have taken a step toward learning how to ask the right questions of the travel agent or airlines ticket seller. It is an area in which it is wise to be your own "expert" for at least two reasons: the modern transatlantic flight picture is so complicated that even many travel agents don't understand it fully (many of them are oriented more to domestic than international flights), and every travel agent knows one thing for sure—the more expensive the fare he sells you, the more money he makes. Most of them are both fair and service-oriented, but in view of their commission arrangement with the airlines, they could hardly be expected to argue with a customer, who, through ignorance, asks them for a seat with a stiff price attached. It is to your advantage to have a good idea of what is possible, and to be able to ask the right questions.

Many airlines have close relationships with auto-rental companies, and some of them can help you to book accommodations in Europe. Once you have done your research and picked the best deal, you can buy your tickets directly from the airline if you wish. To do this, all you have to do is call their toll-free number, order your tickets, and give them your interbank or American Express credit card number. They will send you the tickets by mail.

Because of the current disparity between American and Canadian dollars, and the low prices of the Canadian lines, some Americans who live near the border now find it financially advantageous to go into Canada and fly from there. Your choice of your departure point is always significant, unless you live quite close to a European gateway. If you live squarely between Los Angeles and San Francisco, Detroit and Chicago, or Boston and New York, you have a decision to make that can affect your choice of carrier, your departure date, and even your fare.

If you take the trouble to think about all of these matters, gather some information and make some comparisons, and finally make an intelligent decision, you can save yourself a good deal of money. Getting there is *not* half the fun, as someone has advertised, but if arranged properly it can be half the cost that you might have paid.

Typical scheduled air carriers

As far as we know, all the scheduled air lines are pretty good these days—but some of them have their own particular merits, some of which we will discuss here. They are listed in no particular priority, and they are all lines which we have experienced for yourselves.

Icelandair can be credited with originating the idea of bargain fare transatlantic flights. They offer budget flights from Chicago and New York to Luxembourg. Their on-board service is excellent, and they kid no one when they say that Luxembourg is central to all Europe. They are able and willing to provide help and advice about car rentals, tours, hotels, and stopovers. All seats are tourist class, but there is nothing second-class about the service.

Lufthansa, in conjunction with Europacar Tours, offers a program called *Europe Your Way*. As the name suggests, it is designed to let you do your own thing in Europe, whether that involves going on your own with a car or camper, or by train, or on a fully escorted tour. Rooms can be booked before you go, or as you travel. It's an interesting plan all around. This German line is well known for its impressive safety record and its excellent service.

TWA offers every sort of fare, ranging down through budget and standby tickets. They specialize in fly-drive programs called Getaway Europe, which will provide you with rooms, cars, rail passes, etc. TWA offers a nice service for standby passengers headed for London from Kennedy Airport. Once they have their ticket, passengers can get a guaranteed booking in one of the Grand Metropolitan's 26 hotels in the central London area.

Pan Am will not only fly you to nearly any spot in the world, but will take care of you while you're there if you wish. The company operates tours around the world, and it has a worldwide rent-a-car network. They are interested in independent and budget travellers as well, offering fares in the budget and standby categories. The company deserves its excellent reputation.

Many experienced travellers consider KLM to be one of the world's great airlines, and their excellent literature (and our experience) would suggest that this is a valid opinion. Ask them for *KLM's Budget Travel Tips* or the booklets they can provide about Holland's museums, shopping in the Netherlands, Amsterdam, or their European motoring guide. The Dutch are nice people, and they have some of the nicest on their aircraft.

Air Canada, which has the reputation of providing first-rate service on their flights, has another advantage: they sell charter class fares, which are bargain-priced. They also, in concert with the Arthur Frommer organization, provide "Dollar-Stretcher Holidays," still another money saver. For someone who can fly from Canada, their Super Saver fare is worth examining. It's a fine deal. A.C., at this writing, still has a perfect safety record.

Olympic Airways, Greece's official airline, has a tradition of providing good food and excellent service. There is frequently at least one traditional Greek dish included such as vine leaves stuffed with meat or tomatoes filled with rice, and the meals generally are as good as or better than any we've ever had over the Atlantic.

There is an advantage to flying Olympic to Athens if you plan to catch a connecting flight to someplace else in Greece. Olympic uses the west portion of the Athens terminal, while all other lines dock in the eastern section. If you are making a connection to outlying Greece, arrival with Olympic at the west terminal will mean that you face no ground transportation problems in getting to your next place.

The largest privately owned airline in the world is British Caledonian. Their gateways to London include Houston, Dallas/Fort Worth, Denver, St. Louis, and Atlanta. In London they have facilities at Victoria Station and Gatwick Airport. Their inflight service, seating, food and entertainment are all first rate.

Aer Lingus is a first-class airline that not only provides transatlantic flights, but connecting runs from Shannon and Dublin to many European cities. They also offer a low-cost add-on fare to other points in Europe, fly-drive fares, and vouchers for visits to Irish castles, shows, and medieval banquets.

Iberia is Europe's second-largest airline, and certainly one of the world's best. The service, food, and in-flight amenities are top-class, and Iberia can provide you with a great deal of good information about ground travel, accommodations, and itineraries within Spain. They provide great connections into Africa.

Laker Airways offers low-cost, no-frills flights on their big DC-10s to London. If you are unable to get on one of their flights, they can sell you a ticket for the following day's flights. You can check seat availability by telephone at any of their departure points. Unless you work for (or own) an airline, this is doubtlessly the least expensive ride you can get across the Atlantic.

There are many other international air carriers, of course, and we think most of them are pretty good, and getting better. A few years ago you could hardly tell one from the other. Prices were fixed by IATA, and with some lines there seemed to be little or no interest in serving good meals or providing good service. Today there is more competition between the carriers, and one sees indications that no one wants you to end your flight muttering to yourself, "I'll never fly with them again."

They all want your patronage, and they realize that their business is getting more competitive all the time.

Recently there has been a good deal of grouchy mud-slinging in the press about how uncomfortable the transatlantic carriers have become. One hears tales of filthy or unworkable toilets, crummy meals, surly stewardesses (and stewards), takeoff delays, and so on. We will not deny that these problems occur, but we do not think they happen all that frequently. It's true that most seats are too small and placed so close to each other front to back that one has to sit in a fetal position, and that one can occasionally find a messy toilet. But one thing you have to remember is that while the staff on the aircraft spend most of their time acting as janitors or waitresses or waiters, they are really there for your safety. That is what they are trained for, so perhaps we shouldn't be surprised that they aren't always perfect hosts, hostesses, or bartenders.

Recent studies have shown that your chances of being killed in an air crash have become smaller and smaller over the years. In the late fifties the odds were about one in a million; today the odds are better than one in two-and-a-half million. Flying is the safest form of transportation there is, and that is an important part of what you pay for when you buy a ticket.

As far as on-board amenities are concerned, there isn't much you can do about the food (which usually *isn't* top class) except to spend the money for seats in first- or business-class (where it is a lot better). There are possibilities of doing something about the seating when you check in at the airport. If you are long-legged or disabled, try to obtain seats that face a bulkhead. These seats offer tremendous legroom, and there will be no passenger in front of you who will recline his seat into your lap. We might also note that people with wide shoulders will have a bit more room if they take an aisle seat.

We are really not certain why people care so much about this matter of on-board comfort (perhaps the Europeans are correct when they say that North Americans are too comfort-conscious). You are only on the plane for six or seven hours; why worry about trivialities? We feel that a person should spend those hours looking forward to the adventures ahead rather than wondering why the drinks aren't bigger, or why the food isn't hotter, or why the toilet is so far away. Who cares if the movie is lousy?

In spite of rising fuel costs air travel to Europe is still a bargain. It costs less now than it did just a few years ago. And that matter, incidentally, is what you should worry about. The dinner, good or bad, is a three- or four-dollar problem. The ticket is a five- or six-*hundred*-dollar expense (if not more), and you should be fairly relaxed on the plane if you know you did the requisite homework before you bought your ticket—and can feel pleased that you're sitting in the least expensive seat anyone could have gotten.

Such knowledge can allow you to ignore any little problems of the moment, and let you relax, thinking about the most important thing of all, that great adventure you will face as soon as the aircraft is on the ground. If you run into a really serious problem on the aircraft, talk to the stewardess about it. If she can't or won't help, write to the airline's Consumer Action Department when you get home. Include the date, flight number, and details about your complaint in your letter. If the airline itself doesn't give you satisfaction, write to the Civil Aeronautics Board.

Charter fares and regulations

Although many people still believe that you must belong to some affinity group for six months in order to get on a charter flight, this is no longer true. Not long ago the CAB ruled that anyone should have the right to travel at low charter rates without having to belong to a charter-sponsoring group, and this has been true in Canada for the last few years. In fact, there is reason to believe that affinity charters will eventually be phased out because of the existence of the new low-priced non-affinity charters.

Charter flights today come in a variety of forms, and while some of them require advanced bookings, not all do. Ticket prices are fixed once they are sold, but they can vary from tour operator to tour operator. The new charters no longer require advance purchase of tickets, they can be sold as one-way or round-trip, cancellations of flights are more carefully controlled, and ground packages may or may not be included.

The conditions and limits of charters vary from tour operator to tour operator, so a careful understanding of the contract is essential in buying such tickets. The basic regulations, which are designed to protect you, are set by the CAB— but many variations are possible. Depending upon the individual arrangements and contract between the airline and the tour operator, there will be penalties for cancelling flights, and these will vary, so again careful reading of the pertinent literature is important. It would be advisable to consider buying cancellation insurance if it is not included in the overall price.

Not only can you buy insurance against being killed on the trip, but also insurance against having your bags stolen, and even insurance against illness. The latter, which is commonly purchased these days, protects you against losing your money on prepaid fares where illness or something else forces you to cancel or change your plans. It can also protect your return charter flights, which is important because ordinarily if you get sick, hurt, or just miss the plane in Europe for any reason, that expensive seat flies home empty and you then have to stay in Europe for the rest of your life, or purchase another ticket on a regularly scheduled carrier. Such insurance is readily available, and not terribly expensive either— although some airline officials privately consider it to be too costly, and expect competition to drive its price down in the future. This insurance is also available for those scheduled fares that have fixed group returns or cancellation penalties.

People who fear charter flights today have unfounded worries. They are like people who refuse to ride buses because of a bad experience they had on a bus twenty years ago, or folks who are uneasy about riding European trains because of what they see of railroads in this country. Today charter organizations ordinarily use first-class, well-maintained aircraft, and their service on board is often better than anyone might expect. And yet one occasionally hears tales of charters being cancelled, poor refund practices, and so on. Like most everything else, it is a ''buyer beware'' market, and we shall try here to give some ideas of what one should be wary about—and anticipate.

It is important to read and understand charter flight contracts before you sign them. Doing so will tell you whether or not the charter group will let you off the hook if you die (most will) or get sick (few will) before they depart. If the worst should happen in Europe and you find yourself unable to take the return seat you've already paid for (and you don't have insurance to cover it), your first move should be to go to the airline that is flying the charter, present your case, and pray.

One last tip about charter organizations: any such outfit that you deal with has to be bonded under CAB regulations, but it would still be advisable to be sure the the money you pay them goes into an escrow account in a reputable, sizeable bank (rather than directly to the company). If it is put into escrow, it will be returned to you if the flight is called off. You should make your check out to the escrow account at the bank, not to the charter organization, to be fully protected. It is also wise to write the name and number of your flight and its departure date on the check.

Other money-savers

Stopovers, not in terms of prepaid hotel, meal, and sightseeing possibilities, but just as free stops, are always worth considering. You should inquire about the number of stopovers you could make if you are purchasing a seat on a regularly scheduled flight. They cannot be made on charter flights or APEX fares. Many routings allow stops at intermediate points between the flight origin and destination, some of them not even on a straight-line course between these two points. If any of these stops interest you, you could visit them without spending a cent extra for your transportation costs.

As one example, Icelandair offers an unusual stopover possibility. You will probably not be surprised to learn that their stopover point is Iceland. Some of their European flights stop there, and they suggest that you might like to stay for one, two, or three days to see Reykjavik and the countryside.

If you buy one of these stopover packages, you will be put up in one of the two first-rate hotels (and if you like to walk, we'd suggest that you try to get into the Loftleidir, which is just on the outskirts of Reykjavik). You will also get discount coupons for two meals a day, transportation between the airport and the capital, and bus tours (there are no trains in Iceland). The one-day deal provides a two-hour guided tour of Reykjavik. The second day puts you on a four-hour tour through the mountains, across the lava fields, and into the little village of Hveragerdi, where super-heated water bubbles and shoots up through the ground and is used to grow tropical plants (including bananas!) and to help supply the heating needs of homes and buildings in Reykjavik. This second-day tour is the low-season offering; during the high season (May 1 through September 30), one is also taken to see the waterfall at Gullfoss and the beautiful national park at Thingvellir. For the third day of such stopovers, either season, one is left completely to his own imagination—although he still has discount coupons for meals and accommodations.

The option of purchasing excursion air tickets that will allow you to fly into one city and eventually depart from another can also be a great advantage. (This arrangement is referred to by travel people as "open jaw," as ugly a term as has ever offended our ears.) Depending upon the cities picked, this can affect the fare slightly, but if you would like to start your trip in Paris and plan to visit Rome, you can avoid backtracking to Paris for your return flight. You can arrange to fly home from Rome instead. This possibility, like planned stopovers, might be worth discussing with a travel agent.

Incidentally, most of the airlines and charter organizations have toll-free telephone numbers. If you wish to deal with them directly, or to countercheck your travel agent's opinons, give them a call. If you can't find the appropriate number, look under "Air Line Companies" in the yellow pages or call 1-800-555-1212 and ask for it.

If you have to go some distance from your home to the departure point of your trip to Europe, look into the possibility of buying an excursion air fare from home to there (and return). Such a ticket will save you money compared to a regular economy seat, and if you should miss the scheduled domestic return booking because your transatlantic return is delayed in landing, have an official of the overseas carrier write you a note explaining what occurred. This little memo should be sufficient evidence to make the excursion carrier honor your return to home base without a fare penalty. When you book your ticket, tell the agent you are connecting with an international flight. If you connect within six hours on departure or return you can save the domestic eight-percent air tax. You will have to show your international ticket to get this discount.

There are other ways to keep down the cost of your air fare. One is to buy your tickets as far ahead of your flight date as possible. Most airlines will honor your ticket without adding on surcharges even if prices have gone up since you bought it.

Try to arrange to go during the low or shoulder seasons. You'll get a lower fare if you do.

Investigate bargain possibilities. Check with Icelandair, Laker, Capitol, and any line that is opening up a new destination. If you are a senior citizen, ask whether you are entitled to any special discounts.

Wherever you are going, there are so many possibilities that you should do plenty of shopping, and make careful comparisons. Perhaps the key word in this whole situation is "foresight" or "research." After you tell your travel agent or airline what your circumstances are, where you want to *go*, how long you can stay, and when you wish to leave, perhaps the best question to ask is this: "What is the best and least expensive way to get there?"

That has been and always will be the most sensible question to ask when you are going *that* far on an airplane. Today it is really important: with all the budget, stand-by, Super Saver, and APEX fares, not to mention the public charters, you are in a buyer's market. All you have to do to take advantage of this situation is know what you're doing, or ask the right questions and get some appropriate answers. If you do, you could cut the cost of your trip tremendously.

How to get and keep the seat you pay for

If you are on a regularly scheduled flight, you have to face the possibility that you could be "bumped" even though you have a reservation. One of the really charming aspects of current federal flight regulations is that they allow and almost encourage airlines to overbook, presumably to cover themselves against "no-shows." This obviously presents the possibility that you might be left standing on the ground, watching your plane leave without you. More than 150,000 passengers with reservations were bumped off of scheduled flights with U.S. lines last year. We learned about one flight in 1977 that had *fifty* more seats booked than were available. We were even more surprised to learn that everyone who showed up got on. There were more than fifty no-shows! That gives you some idea of why the airlines overbook.

Before you get too worried, let us tell you that being bumped is not nearly as likely a possibility for transatlantic flights as it is for domestic trips. Nevertheless it can happen, so you might wish to read on. Being bumped off of an overseas flight could certainly be unpleasant if you had confirmed hotel reservations or a tour departure booked at the other end.

If you should get bumped, and the airline that ticketed you can't get you to your destination within four hours of your expected time of arrival overseas, the airline has to refund the price of your ticket to you, if you wish, and to pay you compensation of as much as two hundred dollars. If you keep the ticket rather than taking a refund on it, you can use it at any time in the future.

However, no matter how your negotiations with the airline might come out, it still wouldn't be any fun to be bumped and left at the gate. There are things you can do to minimize the possibility.

Don't wait until you get to the airport to get your tickets. Pay for them and pick them up before the date of the flight.

To be able to prove you had a reservation, have the name of the person or agency who made it for you.

Check in at the airport well ahead of your flight time, perhaps even earlier than you are instructed to do so.

Be early at the gate for the final check-in.

If reconfirmation has been suggested to you, do it. It would be well to ask if you need to do this if no one brings up the subject to you.

If all these strategies fail (*i.e.*, you are still bumped), be prepared to give all kinds of reasons why you *must* make the flight, how much it will cost you if you don't, and to show why you would have grounds to sue the airline. (If you are serious about suing, don't sign the check they will give you. If you sign it, they are relieved of all obligation.)

If you arranged your ticket through a good travel agent, give him a call. If he books a number of flights with your airline, he should have enough clout with them to make them reconsider your case.

Demand a copy of the regulations that deal with bumping. If you have attended to all of the details listed above, mention that fact as you glance through the regulations. The chances will be excellent that the airline will decide to try to bump someone else.

Even the charter organizations overbook occasionally. If you should be bumped from a charter, demand your refund and compensatory payment or insist that they buy you a seat on a scheduled flight.

"Voluntary bumping" (as opposed to "involuntary") is now possible. If the aircraft is overbooked, the airline may ask who would be willing to give up their seat for a cash payment (the amount is not specified; you can negotiate it up as high as you can get it). But before making such an arrangement, you should ask a few questions:

When *can* you go? Make them give a confirmed booking on another flight rather than a standby possibility.

Will they also pay expenses you incur in waiting for another flight? Possibilities are cab fares, hotel rooms, meals, telephone calls home, etc.

Can or will they get you a seat with another line?

You can raise similar questions when faced with delayed or cancelled flights. If you are faced with a substantial delay in your flight, you should ask if the airline will pay for a meal, for a hotel room, for cab fares, and for telephoning people who will be meeting you at the other end.

If you are not on a charter flight, reconfirm your return flight to the U.S. from one of your airline's ticket offices at least seventy-two hours before your departure date, and then get to the airport well before the flight leaves.

Facts about flying

Aircraft wings do not push the vehicle over a cushion of air below the wings. The top of the wing is designed in such a way that a partial vacuum is created above the wing—so the plane is pulled upward by the low air pressure created there.

The international language of the air is English. All radio communications from aircraft to aircraft or airplane to ground is in English—even with the air carriers of countries where English is not the first language.

Aircraft make much better time flying from the U.S. to Europe than they do on the return because the high-speed high-altitude winds blow in an easterly direction.

The big jets have three onboard computers that do most of the navigation and flying. Those good-looking, well-paid pilots tend to be very modest. They make such remarks as this: "Most of the time I just sit here and read the gauges. Once in a great while—maybe once a year—something will come up that these marvelous computers can't handle. That's when I earn my salary.''

During the high season in the late seventies over 550 aircraft crossed the Atlantic each day. This was true until mid-1980, when rising fuel and fare costs cut into the number of people who were flying, which caused airlines to begin reducing the number of flights.

People with handicaps or unusual physical conditions can fly just like anyone else. The airlines have special wheelchairs that will fit through the cabin aisles, they will provide special seating, and they can furnish special meals upon request. People who are disabled or blind will usually be seated before other passengers are. With advance notice even oxygen can be supplied, and the big airlines have medical personnel who will provide special help and advice. Women in their ninth month of pregnancy are ordinarily not taken aboard unless they have a certificate from a doctor (signed within 72 hours of takeoff time) specifying that she can fly (*i.e.*, is not likely to give birth during the flight). Blind peoples' guide dogs can accompany their owners on board at no charge, and every effort is made to supply the person seating that will allow the dog to stay by their feet.

People with bad colds or blockage of sinus or ear passages should get medical advice before flying. People who are recovering from major surgery are frequently advised to avoid flying for at least 10 days.

The inertial navigation systems the planes carry are so good that an aircraft's position is always known to within three miles. Airplanes flying parallel tracks are required to stay 120 miles apart, and each has a corridor 2,000 feet high to maintain. Position reports to the ground are made every 40 to 45 minutes.

Traffic control for the North Atlantic is provided by Canada, the United Kingdom, Portugal, Iceland, and the U.S. The centers that provide the control are located at Gander, Newfoundland; Prestwick, Scotland; Santa Maria Island in the Azores; Reykjavik, Iceland; and New York.

Final thoughts

The spectre of jet lag deserves a word here. It results, of course, from flying across time zones. When you arrive at your destination, your bodily rhythms are at variance with local clocks by some hours: the air terminal employees think it is breakfast time, and your body thinks it is midnight. It is not terribly bad for some people, particularly experienced travellers, but it is grim for others, often those who are flying a long distance for the first time.

Here are a few tips for combatting jet lag:

1. If you can, have a short nap on the day of your flight, which will more than likely depart during the evening hours.

2. If you are on a night flight, forget about the movie (it probably won't be first-run anyway). Sleep as much as you can.

3. Hold down your alcohol intake. At high altitudes it can do you even more damage than usual.

4. Don't eat too much before or on the flight.

5. Drink as much water as you can. The pressurized oxygen systems tend to dehydrate your body, which adds to the jet lag problem.

6. Don't be impatient to get out there and see the sights or do business right after you land. If you will instead get a room and go to bed, even for just an hour or two, you will feel pretty good when you arise.

7. For the first day or two, ignore the clock. Eat when you're hungry, sleep when you're tired, and go sightseeing only when you feel good.

Here are a few other health tips for your transatlantic flight, courtesy of Air France.

If you have a cold or an ear problem, take a good decongestant with you on the flight.

If you've had a recent eye or ear operation, consult your physician before travelling.

If you wear a hearing aid, remove it before you get to the airport. Amplified jet noises can cause inner ear problems.

On the flight, loosen tight clothing and remove your shoes.

Remove contact lenses, particularly soft ones—dry air may cause them to harden.

Take vitamin C tablets if you are a smoker.

You would also be wise to consider the fact that airports everywhere have shady characters standing around thinking about the jewels, cameras, cash and travellers' checks you and other tourists are carrying. The rules for keeping these lowly types from getting any of your worldly goods are fairly simple:

1. Watch purses, cameras, and carry-on luggage with the greatest care.

2. Lock the luggage you are shipping, and do not put *any* valuables in it. In fact, if you have a choice between taking a new leather bag or an old, ratty, plastic one, you'd be smart to take the least-tempting-looking one. Not only do people steal bags at the luggage-retrieval area, but baggage handlers often open them for a look— and such people often have the keys and know-how for doing so.

3. Do not leave any possessions unguarded at your seat while you run off for a cup of coffee or to visit the toilet. Don't ask the stranger in the next seat to watch it for you while you're gone either; he or she might be stranger than you imagine.

4. Do not tempt pickpockets by carrying passports or wallets in easily accessible pockets or purses.

5. Be especially watchful in dense crowds or long lines.

6. And here, lastly, is a hard one to decide. Some travellers will not put their name and address on the outside of their bags, particularly on checked luggage. They know that there have been instances where someone at the airport would read that information and go rob the house during the next few days.

It does pay to be careful in air terminals.

And finally, although you may think it unnecessary to be reminded of this, *don't forget to take your passport.* You won't get off the ground without it, let alone see Europe. We mention the matter here because airline officials say they meet a surprising number of travellers at the airport check-in areas who have either left the document at home—or who didn't bother to apply for it at all. Also, the name on your passport must be identical to the name under which you booked your seat. Many a bride has not been able to depart and has had a honeymoon spoiled because the name on the manifest and on her passport did not correspond.

Once you get your ticket and your passport, you'll be facing a wonderful prospect. It will probably be something like this: lunch at home, dinner over the Atlantic, jet lag and breakfast in Europe, and your luggage in South Africa.

Really, the airlines do not lose checked luggage nearly as frequently as the many jokes on the subject might suggest. If they do lose or smash up a bag, they'll pay for it—up to $750. If that amount doesn't strike your fancy, you can buy additional coverage at the check-in desk. That costs about 10¢ for each additional $100 of coverage.

If your bags don't show up when you do, fill out the appropriate forms, keep a copy and ask for whatever you need to keep you going until it arrives (razor, cash, etc.).

Actually, the odds are that only one person on a 747 will have his or her luggage lost. It happens to only one in 400 passengers.

Do you have the sort of luck that tells you that you'll be *the one?*

Afterword

Well, after all that we hope that you now have a little better picture of Europe in your mind—and that you see yourself in the middle of it. If you have previously worried that you couldn't afford such a trip, or cope with language difficulties, or whatever, we hope we've given you a new perspective on the whole subject. Let us briefly reiterate the major points for keeping the whole thing enjoyable, educational, and inexpensive.

1. Shop hard to find the best possible, least expensive, way to Europe. At least use some foresight and purchase an APEX fare, get yourself on a charter flight, or consider the budget and stand-by tickets.

2. Pack light. Take nothing that is inessential. Keep your load to one small bag per person.

3. Go off-season if you can. At least try to avoid being there in July or August. If you are going on a scheduled flight, you'll save money if you book a spring departure date of no later than the last day of the low season, or a fall departure date of no earlier than the day after the last day of the high season.

4. If you're going to travel by train, remember that you must purchase your Eurailpass, BritRail Pass, or some of the countries' own rail passes before you leave home.

5. Wear comfortable shoes that will let you walk for hours without pain. Toughen up you legs by doing a lot of walking or biking before you leave.

6. Learn all you can about the countries you intend to visit before you go. Read. Talk to people who've done it. Badger the tourist agencies for information.

7. Study and practice at least a little bit of the languages that will be used where you go. Get records from the public library and listen to the pronunciation. Buy and study phrase books.

8. Make up your mind that you'll stop here and there, realizing that you can't learn anything about a place in a few short hours, and that you can save your money

money and your health by not being on the run constantly. Don't get Eurail-pathology. Try to keep your planned itinerary restricted to a SMALL number of countries.

9. Remember that if you patronize nightclubs, drink American-style drinks, and eat gourmet meals you are going to spend a lot of money—and that you'll be doing something you could do at home for less money.

10. Don't think of any country's currency as suitable only for use in a game of Monopoly. Remember that it *is* money (even if it doesn't look quite like it to you), and treat it with respect. If you learn early-on what it means in terms of the cash you're used to, you won't throw it around inadvertently.

11. Be prepared to ask for single rooms in hotels whenever you can't find an inexpensive tourist or pension room for the two of you.

12. Have your mind geared to the idea that some of your meals will come from grocery stores, and that some of them will be "tourist menu" offerings.

13. If you don't know how, teach yourself to haggle. It's not hard. Sometimes all you have to say is: "Sorry, but we can't afford that." Really good hagglers are always polite. Try it.

14. Try to learn to "see," to look beneath the surface of things, while you are there. Doing so will vastly increase your pleasure, it will expand your mind, and it won't cost you a sou.

15. Don't forget that you want to meet, talk to, and learn what you can from the Europeans. Make up your mind to be open and friendly, and not to be worried about starting conversations with, or asking questions of strangers.

16. Convince yourself that you will take neither yourself, your partner, nor the trip too terribly seriously. If you can't do that, don't go. Or at least take a guided tour.

And with that, dear friends, let us say that we hope we see you over there soon. We can imagine it. The four of us will be staggering toward each other over wet cobblestones, somewhere in a small town, in a driving rain, late at night. You will greet us first, perhaps, muttering something in very bad French or German, and we'll respond in equally poor French or German. Then we will suddenly all recognize each other as North Americans, and someone will ask, "Having any luck finding a room?," and someone else will answer, "No, but we've only been looking for a couple of hours."

"Us too," still another voice will groan, and one of you will say, "We decided to travel this way—our first trip over—because of a book we read called . . . ."

"We never read travel books," one of us will interrupt quickly. "We've found out that you can't believe anything any of them say."

And you know, friends, you can't. Europe is too big and too complicated to be summed up in a small book. But it does rain there, that's for sure.

So take your raincoats. And your independence. And your imagination.

Good luck and bon voyage. You're going at it in the right way.